Teaching Secondary and Middle School Mathematics

Teaching Secondary and Middle School Mathematics

DANIEL J. BRAHIER

Bowling Green State University

Allyn and Bacon
Boston ■ London ■ Toronto ■ Sydney ■ Tokyo ■ Singapore

Vice President, Editor in Chief, Education: Paul A. Smith
Editorial Assistant: Bridget Keane
Marketing Manager: Brad Parkins
Editorial-Production Administrator: Annette Joseph
Editorial-Production Coordinator: Holly Crawford
Editorial-Production Service: Omegatype Typography, Inc.
Text Designer: Carol Somberg/Omegatype Typography, Inc.
Composition Buyer: Linda Cox
Electronic Composition and Art: Omegatype Typography, Inc.
Photo Researcher: Susan Duane
Manufacturing Buyer: Suzanne Lareau
Cover Designer: Jenny Hart

Library of Congress Cataloging-in-Publication Data

Brahier, Daniel J.
    Teaching secondary and middle school mathematics / Daniel J. Brahier.
        p.   cm.
    Includes bibliographical references and index.
    ISBN 0-205-28614-3
    1. Mathematics—Study and teaching (Middle school)
    2. Mathematics—Study and teaching (Secondary)   I. Title.
QA11.B6999   2000
510′.71′2—dc21

                                                    99-32768
                                                    CIP

Printed in the United States of America
10 9 8 7 6 5 4 3   04 03

Photo credits and permission acknowledgments appear on page 407, which constitutes a continuation of the copyright page.

This book is dedicated to my father, Frank,
who has taught me the values of patience and persistence,
and to the memory of my mother, Joyce,
who was the author of the first book in the Brahier family
and a source of support and love beyond imagination . . .
"the finest of teachers I've ever known."

Contents

Preface

Teaching secondary and middle school mathematics has never been more exciting than it is today. The release of national Standards documents between 1989 and 1998 by the National Council of Teachers of Mathematics (NCTM) challenged educators and the general public to rethink the content, teaching strategies, and assessment practices of school mathematics. Meanwhile, the Third International Mathematics and Science Study resulted in the most comprehensive international comparison of mathematics education that has ever been conducted. The third millennium will begin with the release of a new NCTM Standards document—*Principles and Standards for School Mathematics*—which promotes a comprehensive mathematics curriculum for all students, rooted in significant research on how students learn mathematics and the role of technology in the teaching and learning process.

In the midst of all of the reform efforts that are put in motion, it is critical that both preservice and inservice teachers investigate the nature of the mathematics curriculum and reflect on research-based "best practices" as they define and sharpen their own personal styles. The format of *Teaching Secondary and Middle School Mathematics* is designed to provide the reader with the total picture of the multifaceted art of teaching. The book is divided into five units:

I. What Does It Mean to "Do," "Teach," and "Learn" Mathematics?

II. The Mathematics Curriculum

III. Teaching Mathematics

IV. Assessment in Mathematics

V. The Teaching Profession and Appendices

Unit I consists of two chapters that prompt the reader to think about the nature of mathematics and the psychology of student learning. Chapter 1 introduces the reader to the notion of mathematics as a process—a verb. Contemporary research on how students learn mathematics and develop dispositions toward the content area is presented through numerous classroom examples in Chapter 2. The two chapters comprising Unit II deal with the mathematics curriculum. Chapter 3 provides descriptions of current curricular issues, such as advantages and drawbacks to a school offering a "traditional" curriculum of Algebra, Geometry, and Algebra II, versus an integrated sequence of courses. The issue of promoting a core curriculum for *all* students is also discussed in Chapter 3, and Chapter 4 describes the nature of a local course of study and how to write and classify objectives. The reader is also exposed to the philosophy of several reform curriculum projects funded by the National Science Foundation.

The three chapters in Unit III illustrate in detail the teacher's role in planning and teaching mathematics. Chapter 5 outlines the unit and lesson planning process; Chapter 6 examines the role of the teacher in the effective implementation of a lesson plan, including the use of various tools for the promotion of classroom discourse. Chapter 7 explores the uses of technology in the teaching of mathematics, from graphing calculators to laser-disk programs and computers. Unit IV turns the reader's attention to the assessment process and begins in Chapter 8 with a detailed discussion on how to write a mathematics test, then expands the role of assessment to include alternative strategies that are available to teachers. Chapter 9 addresses the NCTM Assessment Standards and the promotion of equity through assessment, as well as discussing practical matters such as assigning and checking homework and determining final grades in a course. The final unit is a combination of one chapter and a set of appendices. Chapter 10 discusses the role of the teacher in the school community and how the mathematics teacher interacts with students, parents, and administrators in a lifelong cycle of personal and professional development.

The six appendices present a wealth of readings and information for a more in-depth study of mathematics education. Appendix A features complete reprints of two of the NCTM curriculum Standards from the working draft of *Principles and Standards for School Mathematics* (1998) as well as the reprint of a content strand from a state mathematics model curriculum. Appendix B provides complete reprints of an NCTM professional teaching Standard from the 1991 *Professional Standards for Teaching Mathematics* and one of the Guiding Principles from *Principles and Standards for School Mathematics*. Appendix C includes a complete reprint of an NCTM assessment Standard from 1995. Instructors in recent years have increasingly recognized the value of examining case studies in methods courses; therefore, Appendix D contains two cases for reading and discussing. The first case deals with teaching algebra; the other is an example of a probability lesson. Appendix E contains a topically organized list of over 100 Internet websites that cover a spectrum of topics, from professional organizations to lesson plans, exciting classroom problems, and on-line mathematics materials catalogs. Each site is presented with its title, Internet address, and a short description of what can be found at the location. The last appendix contains lesson plans and activity ideas for the classroom as a sampler to help preservice and inservice teachers think about the nature of a mathematics lesson. Organized into four sections—Algebra, Geometry, Statistics and Probability, and Discrete Mathematics—Appendix F features a complete lesson plan and ten classroom-tested activity ideas under each content area.

The book was written with both the instructor and the undergraduate or graduate methods student in mind. Given that some colleges and universities are on a quarter system, while others are on semesters, it is important to have a book that is realistic in terms of the number of chapters it contains. Therefore, the reading of approximately one chapter per week will enable a class to progress at a reasonable pace, because the chapters, by design, are relatively equivalent in length. The instructor may choose to follow the sequence of the book, which resulted from field-testing several alternatives. However, a class may have initial field experiences that require students to be writing lesson plans early in the course, so an instructor may choose to visit Unit III immediately after Chapter 1, which serves as an introduction to Chapters 5 through 7 on lesson planning, teaching, and utilizing technology in the classroom. Later, a class may return to the psychological and curricular issues explored in Chapters 2 through 4. However, regardless of how Chapters 2 through 8 are sequenced, a class should generally begin with Chapter 1, which explores the nature of mathematics education, and finish with Chapter 10, which encourages the reader to view the process of professional development as a lifelong endeavor.

General topics, such as effectively using manipulatives and technology, addressing the needs of all students (including those with learning disabilities), and utilizing classroom management techniques, are included in discussions throughout the book where the topics arise naturally in context. Each chapter begins with a list of anticipated outcomes and ends with a Conclusion section that summarizes the chapter and sets up the reader for the next. Each chapter also includes a glossary of terms, a set of approximately ten discussion questions that provide the instructor with ideas for activities and classroom interaction points, and an extensive bibliography with additional resources for the reader and the instructor to pursue for further information on the topics. The additional resources include books, journal articles, websites, and other resource materials.

The author's unique background as a secondary mathematics and science teacher, a middle school mathematics teacher, a guidance counselor, a high school principal, and a K–12 district curriculum consultant is evident as he explores the issues facing teachers of mathematics from many angles. The author is currently an assistant professor of mathematics education at the university level on a full-time basis but also teaches one section of an eighth grade Advanced Mathematics course in a local school every day. Consequently, the examples used throughout the book are "real" and carefully described, based on nearly twenty years of classroom teaching experience. Students in the author's mathematics methods courses have used drafts of the book for over two years and have provided detailed feedback to help in refining the book to its final form—one that is readable and interesting to a methods student. *Teaching Secondary and Middle School Mathematics* features a mixture of research-based theory, vignettes, and discussions of very practical issues of teaching mathematics at the secondary and middle school levels. As such, the book can be used at both the undergraduate and graduate levels for mathematics methods courses.

■ ACKNOWLEDGMENTS

First and foremost, I want to thank my family—my wife, Anne, our sons, John, Mark, and Luke, and my second set of parents, James and Loretta Kelley—for their support and patience throughout the writing process. I am fortunate to be married to Anne, an outstanding high school mathematics teacher, who read every word of the manuscript and gave me detailed feedback and suggestions for making it user-friendly and accurate. I am grateful to Jim Heddens (Professor Emeritus from Kent State University, Ohio) and Bill Speer (University of Nevada–Las Vegas) for their inspiration, wisdom, and advice in getting this project off the ground. Likewise, I very much appreciate the support of John and Susan Ward, who shared their insights as authors. A special thanks goes to Tom Bassarear, Keene State College, New Hampshire; Gerald R. Fast,

University of Wisconsin Oshkosh; Dana Johnson, The College of William and Mary; Anthula Natsoulas, University of Toledo; and Don Ploger, Florida Atlantic University, who reviewed the manuscript at various stages and provided me with a wealth of feedback and ideas. Thanks also to Frances Helland and Bridget Keane at Allyn & Bacon for their patience and advice. I am sincerely grateful for the diligent and meticulous work of my graduate assistant, Christine Lieb, who spent countless hours researching resource materials and websites, as well as developing items for the Test Bank in the Instructor's Manual. I wish to thank my students at St. Rose School in Perrysburg, who provided me with their reflections on many of the activities and teaching strategies described in the book and my EDCI 374 methods students at BGSU over the past two years, who used this book in several draft formats and gave me extremely helpful input on how to improve each chapter.

Teaching Secondary and Middle School Mathematics

What Does It Mean to "Do," "Teach," and "Learn" Mathematics?

The process of teaching mathematics to secondary and middle school students is very complex. Not only is the content often inherently difficult, but also differences in the learning styles of students make the selection of teaching methods challenging. Before examining the details of effective teaching, we must first consider what it means to "do," to "teach," and to "learn" mathematics. Although some view mathematics as a body of knowledge—content—others see mathematics as a verb—something one "does." Still others consider mathematics to be the interplay of content and thinking processes. In Unit I, we examine current thinking about what it means to do, teach, and learn mathematics. Chapter 1 discusses the processes involved in mathematical thinking, and Chapter 2 focuses on the psychology of mathematics education, including theories about how students learn and how they are motivated in the classroom.

Mathematics as a Process

After reading Chapter 1, you should be able to answer the following questions:

- What do the results of recent national and international mathematics examinations tell us about current practices in mathematics education?

- What are the five process skills often associated with doing mathematics? How are they developed in the secondary and middle school mathematics programs?

- What should be the role of problem solving in the mathematics classroom?

- Can you list and illustrate several problem-solving strategies that can be promoted in the secondary and middle school mathematics classroom?

- What does it mean to "do," to "teach," and to "learn" mathematics?

For a project in a Year I Integrated Mathematics class, Mr. James asked his students to think of an authentic example of a linear function that they have encountered in their lives. He asked his students to describe the function in words, to determine the independent and dependent variables, to generate a table of values, to write an equation based on the table, and to create a graph of the function. Finally, students were asked to present their functions to the class and were graded on their written papers and on the quality of their presentations. Mr. James listened to the presentations and read the papers enthusiastically, because he was able to see his students applying their understanding of functions to their lives. However, the projects submitted by Francis and Joyce were different from those of the others in the class, and Mr. James immediately faced a decision about how to handle their examples. Francis's function was worded as follows:

> The monthly fee for phone calls at my house is $10, which includes the first four outgoing calls. After that, every additional outgoing call costs another 50¢. The total cost for a month is a function of the number of outgoing calls.

Joyce's function problem was the following:

> My family belongs to a fitness club. The club has a flat rate of $55.00 a month, but in order to reserve a racquetball court you have to pay an additional $8.00

per hour. If you want a court for a fraction of an hour, it always rounds up to the nearest hour (1.25 or 1.50 hours = 2 hours = $16). The total cost of membership for a month is a function of the number of hours of court time reserved.

When Mr. James read these papers, he recognized a "teachable moment"—an opportunity to use the two examples generated by the students as tools to get the class to consider functions that appeared to be simple and linear on the surface but were actually much more complex. So, the following day, he handed out a sheet with the two problems retyped and asked teams of four students to carefully draw a graph of the functions and to think of other functions they have encountered that had the same characteristics or behavior.

On careful inspection, students realized that the shape of Francis's graph depended on whether the number of outgoing calls was less than or greater than four. They modeled the problem by drawing the graph in Figure 1–1:

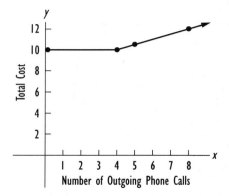

Figure 1–1 Graph of Francis's Function of Phone Service Costs

As students in the class presented their solutions, they shared similar examples, such as the cost of an on-line Internet service provider with a monthly access fee that includes a certain number of on-line hours, coupled with per-hour line charges after the number of free hours is exceeded. Mr. James recognized that, technically, the graph of Francis's function was not continuous; therefore, the individual points should not be connected to form a segment and a ray. He mentioned this point in passing but decided to save the discussion of "continuous" versus "discrete" for another day. More important, the students had discovered their first piecewise function with the rule:

$$\begin{cases} y = 10 \text{ if } x \leq 4 \\ y = 0.5x + 10 \text{ if } x > 4 \end{cases}$$

While exploring Joyce's function, students noticed that the monthly cost would be the same whether, for example, they reserved 2.25, 2.50, 2.75, or 3.0 hours of court time in a month. After some class discussion, they came up with the graph presented in Figure 1–2:

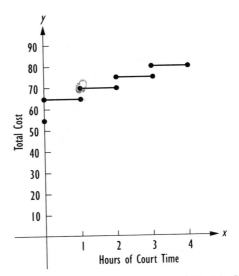

Figure 1–2 Graph of Joyce's Function of Health Club Costs

Toni then raised her hand and said, "That's not exactly right. If you rent the court for one hour, you pay a total of $63, but the graph has a point above both $63 and $71. Only one of those points can actually be there, or it doesn't make any sense." Mr. James validated Toni's statement by showing the class how an "open point" can be placed at the left end of each segment to avoid the confusion. He went on to define Joyce's example as a *step function* because of its unique nature. Meanwhile, the class offered additional examples of step functions, such as postage cost that remains the same until a weight limit is reached, and the price then "steps up" to the next level.

Mr. James's classroom is not unusual; almost every day students raise important issues and ask questions that a teacher can use as a springboard for further discussion. In this sense, the students have the potential to steer the class and not to simply be passive "sponges" that attempt to absorb mathematical content. Mr. James values the exploration of student ideas and entered the teaching profession not only because he enjoyed mathematics but also because he was excited about having the chance to work with adolescents at a critical time in their development as students and young adults.

There are a variety of reasons why people choose careers in mathematics education. In many cases, they have experienced effective teaching in their own school endeavors and want to pass that same level of enthusiasm on to the next generation. Others were simply good at math in school and, as a result to their interest in the subject area, have decided to try their hand at teaching young adolescents. Still others have had unfortunate experiences with teachers of mathematics in school and want to try to improve the situation for future students. It is important for educators to reflect on the reasons for making a career choice and to discern whether their primary interest was mathematics, working with young adolescents, or a combination of both. Although there is no formula for being an effective mathematics teacher, successful teaching requires a caring individual who is interested in both the field of mathematics and the development of young adolescents. This chapter introduces the discussion of mathematics teaching as a profession by examining the effectiveness of mathematics education over the past decade or so and evaluating various national and international assessments of student achievement.

■ NATIONAL AND INTERNATIONAL ASSESSMENT DATA

Beginning in 1996, results were reported from the most comprehensive international comparison of mathematics education in history. The Third International Mathematics and Science Study (TIMSS) report compared achievement, curriculum, and teaching practices in more than 50 countries around the world at the fourth, eighth, and twelfth grade levels. One of the questions asked of seventh and eighth grade students was:

If $3(x + 5) = 30$, then $x =$

A. 2
B. 5
C. 10
D. 95

This equation, most would agree, should be fairly simple for a 14-year-old to answer. In fact, by placing a thumb over the $(x + 5)$ expression, even a fourth or fifth grader should be able to reason that 3 must be multiplied by 10 to get a result of 30. So, in the parentheses, x would have to be equal to 5. However, in the United States, only 63 percent of seventh graders and less than 75 percent of eighth graders were able to answer this question correctly. In Japan and Korea, over 90 percent of the eighth graders obtained a correct answer.

On another item, students were given the sequence of triangles shown in Figure 1–3:

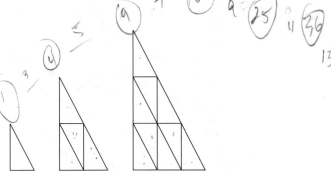

Figure 1–3 Sequence of Triangles in TIMSS Test Item
(Beaton et al., 1996. Reprinted with permission.)

The problem stated: "The sequence of similar triangles is extended to the eighth Figure. How many small triangles would be needed for Figure 8?" An examination of the sequence reveals that the number of triangles required is always equal to the square of the figure number. Therefore, Figure 8 should need 64 (8^2) triangles. On this item, only 18 percent of the seventh graders and 25 percent of the eighth graders in the United States were able to answer it correctly. In Japan, the results were 43 percent and 52 percent, respectively.

On a geometry item for seventh and eighth graders, students were shown the diagram in Figure 1–4:

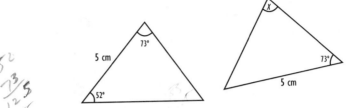

Figure I–4 Congruent Triangles in a TIMSS Test Item
(Beaton et al., 1996. Reprinted with permission.)

The question read as follows: "These triangles are congruent. The measures of some of the sides and angles of the triangles are shown. What is the value of *x*?"

A. 52
B. 55
C. 65
D. 73
E. 75

Fifteen percent of the seventh and 17 percent of the eighth graders in the United States answered this item correctly. In Japan, 40 percent of the seventh and 69 percent of the eighth graders found the correct answer. In fact, students in 25 out of 26 countries outscored the United States on this geometry question that involves fairly typical middle school mathematical content.

The results of the TIMSS achievement test not only placed eighth graders in the United States well below the international average, but the TIMSS study showed that the U.S. middle school and secondary curricula were less rigorous than in most other countries, with an overemphasis on number skills and a deficiency in algebra and geometry. Reports from the study described the mathematics curriculum in the United States as "an inch deep and a mile wide," meaning that U.S. schools tend to address a great deal of content at a surface level that does not promote understanding of the underlying mathematics.

Similarly, on the 1992 National Assessment of Educational Progress (NAEP)—often called the nation's report card—students at all levels demonstrated a lack of fundamental mathematical understanding. The following item, titled "Treena's Budget," was asked of eighth graders (Dossey, Mullis, & Jones, 1993, p. 116):

This question requires you to show your work and explain your reasoning. You may use drawings, words, and numbers in your explanation. Your answer should be clear enough so that another person could read it and understand your thinking. It is important that you show all your work.

> *Treena won a 7-day scholarship worth $1,000 to the Pro Shot Basketball Camp. Round-trip travel expenses to the camp are $335 by air or $125 by train. At the camp she must choose between a week of individual instruction at $60 per day or a week of group instruction at $40 per day. Treena's food and other expenses are fixed at $45 per day. If she does not plan to spend any money other than the scholarship, what are* all *the choices of travel and instruction plans that she could afford to make? Explain your reasoning.*

Take a moment to sketch out your solution to this problem and then read on. Consider the diagram (Figure 1–5) of the problem solution:

	Individual	Group
Air	$335 $420 $315	$335 $280 $315
	$1,070	$930
Train	$125 $420 $315	$125 $280 $315
	$860	$720

Figure 1–5 Matrix Showing Treena's Options

The matrix shows that Treena has four choices: (1) air travel with individual instruction, (2) air travel with group instruction, (3) train travel with individual instruction, and (4) train travel with group instruction. Of these four options, one of them exceeds $1,000, but all of the others would be within her budget. Eighth graders responding to this open-ended or free-response question were expected to arrive at the same conclusion.

This item was scored on a **rubric,** a grading scale on which a student can score a 0 (No Response), a 1 (Incorrect but something has been written down on the paper), a 2 (Minimal), a 3 (Partial), a 4 (Satisfactory), or a 5 (Extended Response). A 4 or a 5 on the rubric is considered an acceptable answer. Only 4 percent of the eighth graders tested in this national sample were able to perform at the 4 or 5 level. In fact, 59 percent of the students either left the item blank or wrote something totally off task and irrelevant on their papers, scoring a 0 or a 1 on the rubric. The writers of the NAEP report pointed out that the item was intended to be fairly simple, as it had a real-life context and allowed the use of a calculator. However, students were confused by the problem, had difficulty sorting out what was important, and were not able to explain their thinking. Moreover, although 18 percent of White students left the item blank, 30 percent of Black students and 36 percent of Hispanic students did not respond. Ten percent of "advantaged" urban students left the item blank, but 42 percent of "disadvantaged" (from low-income families) urban students left it blank. So, we perceive not only a lack of mathematical understanding but also a wide gap between the performances of various socioeconomic groups—a trend that was evident throughout the NAEP documents. Such data prompted the National Council of Teachers of Mathematics (NCTM) to assert, "It is essential that expectations be raised for all students, especially for students in demographic groups that have in the past been underserved by school mathematics education" (1998, p. 25).

Neither a simple algebraic equation, a visual pattern, an angle measurement question, nor an applied arithmetic problem should be unreasonably difficult for an eighth grader, yet these items were answered incorrectly by a large number of U.S. students who took these national and international exams. Why? What is it about the system that has made mathematics so inaccessible to so many students over the years? Mathematics anxiety and a general fear of mathematics are quite common, but how did these fears evolve, and how are they perpetuated?

Perhaps one of the greatest myths about mathematics is that "some people are natural math people, and some are not." A common misconception is that mathematical ability is inherited or predetermined. On the contrary, research does not support this idea of innate mathematical ability. Consequently, with the possible exception of severely disabled individuals, every student can become mathematically literate. Whether students will understand the content may depend not so much on the material itself but on the way in which teachers present it. Although a certain percentage of students will understand a mathematical concept despite a poor teacher, most students will only develop in an atmosphere created by caring, knowledgeable teachers.

■ THE NEED FOR REFORM

In the 1960s, students and their teachers experienced a mathematics reform movement known as the New Math, which was sparked by the launching of *Sputnik* satellites by the USSR in 1957 and 1958. The success of the *Sputnik* program fueled a national fear of falling behind the rest of the world and motivated U.S. educators to reconsider the topics explored in the curriculum. In her book *A Parent's Guide to the New Mathematics* (1964), Evelyn Sharp discussed the need for an updated mathematics curriculum, noting that a seventeenth-century teacher could readily walk into a 1960s classroom and teach mathematics because "the content of the courses hadn't changed in 300 years" (p. 11). Recognizing the need for mathematicians and scientists to be able to compete on a global level, the New Math exposed high school students to topics such as set theory and non-Euclidean geometry, which had not historically been explored until the college level. Sharp noted that the New Math moved mathematical topics down to lower grade levels to ensure that "all students" visited content that required much more rigor than had previously been the case. In his famous book, *Why Johnny Can't Add* (1973), Morris Kline assailed the New Math, stating that

The new mathematics is taught to elementary and high school students who will ultimately enter into the full variety of professions, businesses, technical jobs, and trades or become primarily wives and mothers [sic]. Of the elementary school children, not one in a thousand will be a mathematician; and of the academic high school students, not one in a hundred will be a mathematician. Clearly then, a curriculum that might be ideal for the training of mathematicians would still not be right for these levels of education. (pp. 21–22)

In its attempt to expose all students to higher mathematics, the New Math movement catered more to the top students than the marginal or average students of mathematics. Furthermore, the public was confused about its intent, and the movement eventually fell to the wayside, only to be replaced by a "back to basics" movement in the 1970s.

The mathematics reform effort that began in the 1980s, however, was very different. In 1980, the National Council of Teachers of Mathematics countered the "back-to-basics" movement in the famous book *An Agenda for Action* (1980) by suggesting that problem solving should be the focal point of the curriculum. The NCTM then released a series of three Standards documents in 1989 (*Curriculum and Evaluation Standards for School Mathematics*), 1991 (*Professional Standards for Teaching Mathematics*), and 1995 (*Assessment Standards for School Mathematics*). The contents of these documents were then updated and refined into one volume, *Principles and Standards for School Mathematics,* to set the tone for mathematics education in the third millennium. A **standard** is a benchmark that can be used by a school, a district, a state, or a country to determine the degree to which the educational program meets a list of recommendations. The Standards documents from the NCTM emphasized that mathematics should be for *all* students—regardless of gender, race, socioeconomic status, or any other factor that may have caused inequities in the past. This way of thinking was an invitation to stronger and weaker students alike to develop their mathematical abilities and a challenge for teachers to discern how to make the teaching and learning of mathematics accessible to all.

As we think of mathematics for all students, we will need to turn our attention to research on effective teaching practices. Within that body of research lies a great deal of evidence as to how to structure classrooms, how to pose meaningful, motivational problems, and how to use technology and teaching strategies such as cooperative learning to appeal to the vastly different learning styles and confidence levels of students in the classroom. We now assume, as a premise, that all of the students in our secondary and middle school classes are capable of learning mathematics, and we can begin to decide how to structure learning experiences for students that will appeal to their curiosity and intellect simultaneously. If students can be actively engaged in "doing" mathematics, they may be motivated enough to perform their best in the classroom and on assignments. Let's explore what it means to "do" mathematics.

■ "DOING" MATHEMATICS

Problem Solving

Suppose that you were asked to find the circumference of a circle with a radius of 5 centimeters. Easy, right? Sure, you simply double the radius and multiply it by π to get an answer of about 31.4 centimeters. But what if you didn't already know that the circumference of a circle can be found by multiplying $2\pi r$ or πd? You might have to resort to drawing a sketch of the circle, laying a piece of string on the sketch, and stretching it out along a meter stick to estimate the length. Can you think of another way to determine the circumference without knowing the formula? Here is another option: Draw a line segment with a ruler on a piece of paper, cut out the circle, roll it along the segment until the circle has completed one revolution, and then measure the length of the path. Finding a circumference is a routine task—an **exercise**—if you already know a formula and have encountered that type of question before. However, if the situation is new to you and you have no such formula, the question becomes a problem to be solved. A **problem,** then, can be defined as a task for which there is no immediate solution. The situation is generally unfamiliar to the person attempting to find the answer. When confronted with a problem, we have no choice but to dig deeply into a bag of tricks—a list of strategies—to attempt to solve it. It is important to distinguish between routine exercises that students do for practice and problem solving in the classroom. Also, keep in mind that an exercise for one student may be a problem for another. For example, the circumference question may be a problem for a sixth grader but an exercise for a high school sophomore.

Problem solving can be defined as the process by which an individual attempts to find a solution to a nonroutine mathematical question. Probably the most famous book on this topic was published in 1945 by George Polya, then at Stanford. In his book, Polya described problem solving as a four-step process: (1) understanding the problem, (2) devising a plan for finding a solution, (3) implementing the plan, and (4) looking back at the answer to ensure that it makes sense and to determine if another plan might have been more effective (Polya, 1945). Although much additional research and writing on problem solving have been conducted since his book appeared, most still cite Polya's four steps as being fundamental in solving problems and in teaching problem-solving skills in the classroom. In 1980, the NCTM document *An Agenda for Action* called for the 1980s to be a problem-solving decade. The NCTM *Curriculum and Evaluation Standards* (1989) listed problem solving as the first Standard at all grade levels, K–12, and *Principles and Standards for School Mathematics* also lists problem solving as the sixth Standard at all grade levels. But the vision of problem solving embodied in these documents goes beyond simple, routine tasks. Instead, they suggest rich, meaningful experiences through which students develop and refine strategies that can be used to solve other problems.

Consider the following problem:

> *A certain farmer in Florida has an orange grove. In his grove are 120 trees. Each tree ordinarily produces 650 oranges. He is interested in raising his orange production and knows that because of lost space and sunlight, every additional tree that he plants will cause a reduction of 5 oranges from each tree. What is the maximum number of oranges that he will be able to produce in his grove, and how many trees will he need to reach this maximum?*

It is unlikely that you have ever thought about this situation, and the problem does not have an obvious answer; therefore, it is probable that the statement constitutes a problem for you. How would you begin to solve it? Generally, people reach back and try to apply a strategy that they have used for similar problems in the past.

Take a minute with a piece of paper, and think about how *you* would solve it. Let's look at three ways the problem can be approached.

A middle school child might analyze the problem by *guessing-and-checking* in some orderly fashion. If 120 trees produce 650 oranges per tree, the current production must be 78,000 oranges. However, an increase of 1 tree will result in 121 trees but only 645 oranges per tree for a total of 78,045 oranges, an increase of 45 oranges altogether. Similar calculations can be organized into a *table* such as:

Table 1–1 Orange-Grove Problem Data

Total Trees	Oranges per Tree	Total Oranges
120	650	78,000
121	645	78,045
122	640	78,080
123	635	78,105
124	630	78,120
125	625	78,125
126	620	78,120
127	615	78,105
128	610	78,080
129	605	78,045
130	600	78,000

From Table 1–1 it is apparent that the maximum orange production occurs at 125 trees—the addition of 5 trees to the orange grove. However, students may notice some other things as well. For example, some may recognize that the orange production increases by 45 with the addition of one tree, 35 with the next tree, then 25, 15, and 5, decreasing beyond that point. The identification of this type of *pattern* can eliminate the need to generate the entire table, either by hand or on a computer spreadsheet. A seventh grader began by "guessing" what would happen if 10 trees were planted. When she realized orange production was the same as the original amount, she immediately yelled out, "I think it goes up and back down, so if it's back to normal at 10, then it must reach its maximum with five new trees planted!" Because of a clever first guess (some might call it lucky) and a careful analysis of its result, she solved the problem before most of the others in the class could even write it down.

Suppose that the same problem was raised in a first-year algebra course in which students had been exposed to the use of variables for problem solving. In this case, a student might *write a variable expression* $(650 - 5x)(120 + x)$, where x stands for the number of trees added, to find the total production. The first product determines the number of oranges per tree, and the second product represents the total number of trees in the grove. At this point, the student can *graph* the function $y = (650 - 5x)(120 + x)$ on a graphing calculator (see Figure 1–6) and TRACE (TRACE is a common command on a graphing calculator) the curve to its vertex, finding that the parabola peaks at $x = 5$.

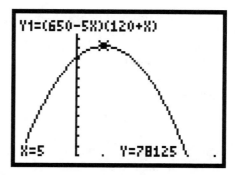

Figure I–6 Orange Grove Parabolic Curve on a Graphing Calculator

The student might also choose to solve the quadratic equation $(650 - 5x)(120 + x) = 0$ by setting the two factors equal to zero and find that the solutions are $x = 0$ or $x = 10$; therefore, the maximum must be the x-value halfway between the x-intercepts, or when $x = 5$.

Finally, a student with calculus background might choose to solve the problem by taking a first derivative to determine the maximum:

$$y = (650 - 5x)(120 + x)$$
$$y = 78,000 + 50x - 5x^2$$
$$y' = 50 - 10x$$

Setting the first derivative equal to 0, → *Slope of the tangent line is zero at the peak of the parabola*

$$0 = 50 - 10x, \text{ therefore}$$
$$x = 5$$

The orange-grove problem is said to be rich in that it is nonroutine and can be solved in a variety of ways. Depending on the grade level and experiences of the student, several problem-solving strategies can be applied, such as guess-and-check, make a table, look for a pattern, write a variable expression or equation, or draw a graph. Once students have effectively used a problem-solving strategy, they can apply the same technique to future problems as well. Ideally, a teacher would assign a problem such as this one, allow students to solve it individually or in small groups, and encourage students to share solutions and strategies so that students can reflect on their approaches when compared to strategies used by others. Then, if some students use a guess-and-check strategy but observe others writing an equation, they may choose to use an equation the next time a problem of this kind is posed.

A variety of resource books and materials provide students with examples of problems that use different strategies. Some of these resources are listed at the end of this chapter, and others are cited throughout the text. Some of the other common problem-solving strategies developed in the secondary and middle school mathematics classroom are:

- Act out the problem
- Make a drawing or diagram

- Construct a physical model
- Restate the problem in other words
- Identify and verbalize the given, needed, and extraneous information
- List all possibilities
- Solve a simpler or similar problem
- Work backwards

Any single strategy or combination of these may be used for solving problems, and they constitute the "tool kit" that a student carries to a problem situation. Research has shown that in order for students to be effective problem solvers, they must have plenty of tools in their kits so that if one method is not working, they can move on to another one. There is an old joke that mathematicians tell:

Q. How do you kill a blue elephant?
A. With a blue elephant gun.
Q. How do you kill a white elephant?
A. With a white elephant gun?
No, you strangle it until it turns blue and then use the gun you already have!

Often, solving a problem boils down to nothing more than forcing it to look like a problem you've previously solved and using the same tools to find its solution.

In *Principles and Standards for School Mathematics* (1998), the NCTM states that problem solving should allow all students to

- build new mathematical knowledge through their work with problems;
- develop a disposition to formulate, represent, abstract, and generalize in situations within and outside mathematics;
- apply a wide variety of strategies to solve problems and adapt the strategies to new situations;
- monitor and reflect on their mathematical thinking in solving problems (p. 49).

Similarly, in *Curriculum and Evaluation Standards for School Mathematics* (1989) the NCTM stated the following Standard for grades 5–8:

In grades 5–8, the mathematics curriculum should include numerous and varied experiences with problem solving as a method of inquiry and application so that students can

- use problem-solving approaches to investigate and understand mathematical content;
- formulate problems from situations within and outside mathematics;
- develop and apply a variety of strategies to solve problems, with emphasis on multistep and nonroutine problems;
- verify and interpret results with respect to the original problem situation;
- generalize solutions and strategies to new problem situations;
- acquire confidence in using mathematics meaningfully (p. 75).

Standard 1 for grades 9–12 reads:

> In grades 9–12, the mathematics curriculum should include the refinement and extension of methods of mathematical problem solving so that all students can
>
> - use, with increasing confidence, problem-solving approaches to investigate and understand mathematical content;
> - apply integrated mathematical problem-solving strategies to solve problems from within and outside mathematics;
> - recognize and formulate problems from situations within and outside mathematics;
> - apply the process of mathematical modeling to real-world problem situations (NCTM, 1989, p. 137).

Clearly, the emphasis of the standards has been, and continues to be, on using problem solving both to develop strategies for solving future problems and as a context in which to learn or practice skills. Ideally, in the contemporary view of mathematics, every lesson should include some opportunity for students to refine their problem-solving skills. In addition, students should be required to reason mathematically—to think—in every lesson.

Reasoning

Try this trick on a friend: Write down the number of the month in which you were born (e.g., if you were born in October, write down a 10). Double this number. Add 6. Multiply this new number by 50. Then, add on the day of your birth (e.g., if you were born on October 20, add 20). Finally, subtract 365. Now, ask your friend to give you the final number. On a calculator, secretly add 65 to that number. The result will tell you the day and month of your friend's birthday. This "trick" is particularly effective if you have several people do the calculation at once and ask for their answers, quickly telling each person the correct birthdate. But why does it work? Is it magic? No, it's mathematics.

Let m stand for the month in which the person is born and d for the day of the month. The steps of the problem for a person whose birthday is on October 20 are as follows, for that specific date and in general:

Instruction	Specific	General
Write down the month.	10	m
Double the number.	20	$2m$
Add 6.	26	$2m + 6$
Multiply by 50.	1300	$50(2m + 6) = 100m + 300$
Add the day of birth.	1320	$100m + 300 + d$
Subtract 365.	955	$100m - 65 + d$
Secretly add 65.	1020	$100m + d$

The answer 1020 represents the 10th month and 20th day, or October 20. Similarly, the final variable expression takes the birth month and moves it over two places to the left by multiplying by 100. When the day of birth is added, the result is a number from which the birthdate can be determined. With the power of algebra, this puzzle or trick can readily be analyzed.

In a mathematical situation, any time our students ask, "Why?," "How do we know that?," "What would happen if . . . ?," "Would it ever be true that . . . ?," they are asking questions that involve reasoning skills. In the orange grove problem, for example, the student might not be satisfied with seeing the production peak at five trees and might ask why this occurs. This can ignite a class discussion about how adding new trees may remove enough nutrients from the ground and shade enough sunlight from other trees so that eventually additional trees do more harm than good. Puzzles and other problems are generally only worth exploring if they engender discussions or discourse about why the problem works the way that it does. The pursuit of the question "why" in the mathematics classroom is critical. Students want to know, for example, why fractions are divided by inverting the last fraction and multiplying, why the formula for area of a circle is $A = \pi r^2$, why the value of the constant e is irrational, and why the first derivative of the sine function is the cosine function. As they study mathematics, students should become inquisitive and inclined to seek proof and verification of conjectures raised in the classroom. And this is most likely to occur in classrooms in which mathematical reasoning is valued.

Principles and Standards for School Mathematics (NCTM, 1998) lists reasoning and proof as Standard 7 and states that through emphasis on reasoning and proof in the classroom, all students will

- recognize reasoning and proof as essential and powerful parts of mathematics;
- make and investigate mathematical conjectures;
- develop and evaluate mathematical arguments and proofs;
- select and use various types of reasoning and methods of proof as appropriate (p. 49).

Standard 3 from the NCTM *Curriculum and Evaluation Standards for School Mathematics* (1989) for grades 5–8 states:

In grades 5–8, reasoning shall permeate the mathematics curriculum so that students can

- recognize and apply deductive and inductive reasoning;
- understand and apply reasoning processes, with special attention to spatial reasoning and reasoning with proportions or graphs;
- make and evaluate mathematical conjectures or arguments;
- validate their own thinking;
- appreciate the pervasive use of reasoning as a part of mathematics (p. 81).

Similarly, Standard 3 for grades 9–12 in the 1989 NCTM *Standards* reads:

In grades 9–12, the mathematics curriculum should include numerous and varied experiences that reinforce and extend logical reasoning skills so that all students can

- make and test conjectures;
- formulate counterexamples;

- follow logical arguments;
- judge the validity of arguments;
- construct simple valid arguments;

and so that, in addition, college-intending students can—

- construct proofs for mathematical assertions, including indirect proofs and proofs by mathematical induction (p. 143).

The *Curriculum and Evaluation Standards* (1989) uses the word *permeate* with regard to mathematical reasoning in the classroom. Every day that a child is in school, the student should be encouraged to reason mathematically by being challenged with "why" and "how" questions. In this way, students begin to recognize that it is not enough to be *able to* solve a problem; they must reason out the underlying mathematics, make conjectures or hypotheses, and communicate solutions and strategies to others.

Communication

Mrs. King teaches an Honors Geometry course in a small high school. In the spring, she divides her students into learning teams and assigns a famous mathematician to each team such as Gauss, Newton, Pythagoras, Descartes, and Euclid. Each team is asked to research the life and contributions of its assigned mathematician. Then, each student writes a term paper about the person, and the team creates a short skit about their mathematician that is presented to the class. The grade that students receive on the project is determined by a combination of individual written papers, self-assessments of how well the teams worked together, and the quality of their classroom presentations.

Students make presentations to the class and are assessed on their ability to communicate mathematically.

Mr. Shirley teaches in a middle school and requires his students to keep a mathematics journal. Students are regularly provided with prompts for their journal entries. Prompts include statements such as, "Identify the most difficult problem we solved this week and explain what made it difficult for you" and "Write a letter to a friend, explaining how to add numbers containing decimals. Be sure to include a diagram." By collecting the journals every two weeks, Mr. Shirley learns much more about how his students are thinking than he can gather during class time. Also, as students write responses to the prompts, they are pushed to clarify their thinking and to explain it to another person. Often, it is not until we are asked to explain something to someone else that we realize there are gaps in our own understanding.

How often have you heard someone say, "Well, I know how to do it, but I can't really explain it?" Or they simply say, "I just did it." Learning mathematics effectively should exceed the ability to demonstrate skills; students should be able to explain, describe, and clearly communicate solutions and strategies that lead to the answers. The ability to communicate mathematically is a major goal of current reform efforts. In order to validate our thinking or to convince another person that our thinking is accurate, we need to communicate verbally and in writing. Consequently, when we think of "doing" mathematics, we should include the process of communicating with others as a critical component. Projects, written papers, presentations, and journals are classroom strategies that promote mathematical communication.

In *Principles and Standards for School Mathematics* (1998), the authors point out in Standard 8 that communication should be stressed so that students

- organize and consolidate their mathematical thinking to communicate with others;
- express mathematical ideas coherently and clearly to peers, teachers, and others;
- extend their mathematical knowledge by considering the thinking and strategies of others;
- use the language of mathematics as a precise means of mathematical expression (p. 49).

Standard 2 from the NCTM *Standards* (1989) for grades 5–8 reads:

In grades 5–8, the study of mathematics should include opportunities to communicate so that students can

- model situations using oral, written, concrete, pictorial, graphical, and algebraic methods;
- reflect on and clarify their own thinking about mathematical ideas and situations;
- develop common understandings of mathematical ideas, including the role of definitions;
- use the skills of reading, listening, and viewing to interpret and evaluate mathematical ideas;
- discuss mathematical ideas and make conjectures and convincing arguments
- appreciate the value of mathematical notation and its role in the development of mathematical ideas (p. 78).

Curriculum Standard 2 in the 1989 NCTM *Standards* for grades 9–12 states:

> In grades 9–12, the mathematics curriculum should include the continued development of language and symbolism to communicate mathematical ideas so that all students can
>
> - reflect upon and clarify their thinking about mathematical ideas and relationships;
> - formulate mathematical definitions and express generalizations discovered through investigations;
> - express mathematical ideas orally and in writing;
> - read written presentations of mathematics with understanding;
> - ask clarifying and extending questions related to mathematics they have read or heard about;
> - appreciate the economy, power, and elegance of mathematical notation and its role in the development of mathematical ideas (p. 140).

Since the release of the Standards documents, we have seen considerably more emphasis on communication in the classroom. For example, many teachers have begun to use cooperative learning teams in which students have specific roles and depend on the input of others. We will discuss cooperative learning strategies in some depth in Chapter 6. Also, teachers who consider communication an important goal will frequently ask open-ended questions such as the example of Treena's Budget in which the student is required to show work and to explain the thinking process in words or with diagrams. When a student provides a "correct answer" in the classroom, logical follow-up questions are, "How do you know?" and "Tell me what you were thinking." Whenever a teacher pushes students to explain their reasoning, the level of questioning is enhanced, and students are challenged to communicate mathematically.

Connections

Consider the following problem, drawn from the Addenda series to the 1989 NCTM *Standards*. The student is provided with the diagram shown in Figure 1–7:

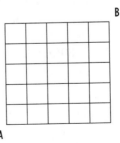

Figure I–7 Counting Paths from Oz
(Phillips et al., 1991. Reprinted with permission.)

The problem states that the city of Oz is located at point A and that a person wants to travel to point B, moving only right along horizontal lines or up along vertical lines. The question is to determine how many paths there are to move from point A to point B. Before reading on, take a few minutes with a piece of paper and pencil, and think about how you would proceed to find a solution.

Often, students approach this problem by tracing possible routes on the grid while searching for a rule or pattern that can be generalized. They will think about decisions that need to be made any time the pencil reaches an intersection point at which the "traveler" has a choice of directions to pursue. It is not unusual for students to struggle with solutions such as 5! or raising 2 to some power. These solutions, although incorrect, can help the students to refine their thinking and lead them to a different way of viewing the problem. Often, a useful problem-solving strategy is to *solve a simpler problem* and then *look for a pattern,* and the teacher may choose to lead them in this direction. In Figure 1–8, there are three smaller grids that students might consider.

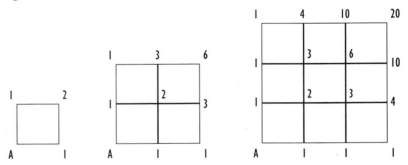

Figure 1–8 Simpler Problems Used to Solve the Oz Paths Problem

If the size of the map is 1 × 1, then there is exactly one way for the traveler to reach the vertices directly to the right and above A, the starting point. Consequently, there are two ways to reach the final destination. Using the same logic, students can construct a 2 × 2 grid and build on the previous map to find a total of six ways to get to the city. Can you trace all six possible paths in the second picture? Extending the idea to a 3 × 3 diagram, there are 20 paths that lead to the destination point. At this point, students might recognize the pattern and continue the process to find that there are 252 possible paths to get from point A to point B in the original problem. (Did you find this?) Turning the paper so that point A is at the top of the page, if we look only at the numbers, we might recognize a familiar pattern:

Figure 1–9 Pascal's Triangle

The numbers generated in this problem are located in Pascal's Triangle, as illustrated in Figure 1–9. Most students associate the Triangle with the binomial theorem or with the determination of probabilities, so the connection to this path-counting problem may not be intuitively "obvious." However, it is important for students to make this type of connection across topics in mathematics. It may also be difficult to categorize this problem, because it falls into content topics such as coordinate graphing, patterning, and discrete mathematics while making important connections to the study of advanced algebra and probability.

In other words, this problem unites several mathematical concepts within a single investigation. It emphasizes the mathematical **connections** between a variety of topics. In the classroom, students should be encouraged to think of mathematics as the connected whole that it is rather than see a course as a chapter of this and a chapter of that. As such, even the idea that one can take an algebra class one year and a geometry class the following year as if they are not inherently connected can be very misleading to the young learner. Recent reform efforts have called for teachers to use activities and examples that help students to see how the various areas of mathematics are related.

Principles and Standards for School Mathematics (1998) states in Standard 9 that connections should be made in the mathematics classroom to help students

- recognize and use connections among different mathematical ideas;
- understand how mathematical ideas build on one another to produce a coherent whole;
- recognize, use, and learn about mathematics in contexts outside of mathematics (p. 50).

Curriculum Standard 4 from the 1989 NCTM document for grades 5–8 reads:

In grades 5–8, the mathematics curriculum should include the investigation of mathematical connections so that students can

- see mathematics as an integrated whole;
- explore problems and describe results using graphical, numerical, physical, algebraic, and verbal mathematical models or representations;
- use a mathematical idea to further their understanding of other mathematical ideas;
- apply mathematical thinking and modeling to solve problems that arise in other disciplines, such as art, music, psychology, science, and business;
- value the role of mathematics in our culture and society (p. 84).

Furthermore, in the 1989 *Standards* document, NCTM Standard 4 for grades 9–12 states:

The mathematics curriculum should include investigation of the connections and interplay among various mathematical topics and their applications so that all students can

- recognize equivalent representations of the same concept;
- relate procedures in one representation to procedures in an equivalent representation;

- use and value the connections among mathematical topics;
- use and value the connections between mathematics and other disciplines (p. 146).

In the Standards documents, the idea of connecting mathematical topics to one another is joined with the notion of helping students to see applications of mathematics in other subject areas so that they come to an appreciation of the utility of mathematics across the curriculum. When studying genetics in a biology course, for example, the student can explore some practical implications of probability theory. Matrices can be used to model production costs and profits for a business, and a discussion of symmetry or ratio and proportion can be rooted in the analysis of a piece of art. Again, the very fact that students take an Algebra II class during first period and a Chemistry class during sixth period almost suggests that there is a wall between these courses, but, actually, each subject depends on the other, and unless teachers help students to make these connections by virtue of the problems posed, many of the applications are lost. Recent trends in the development of the middle school concept have addressed the issue of connections by providing teachers with common planning time, during which they can discuss and arrange for experiences that help students to make connections across the disciplines.

Representation

The *Curriculum and Evaluation Standards for School Mathematics* (1989) presented four mathematical processes—problem solving, reasoning, communication, and connections—and *Principles and Standards for School Mathematics* (1998) described a fifth process—representation. The mathematics classroom frequently involves students attempting to represent problem situations in a variety of ways, deciding which representation is the most helpful and appropriate in a given situation. For example, if you wanted to explore the orange grove problem in some depth, you might want to use an equation, as it is helpful in finding y-intercepts and calculating function values. On the other hand, it might be more useful to view a graph so that a comparison could be made to related real-world phenomena.

Similarly, the following three equations describe the same function:

(a) $y = x^2 + 2x - 15$
(b) $y = (x - 3)(x + 5)$
(c) $y + 16 = (x + 1)^2$

Although the first version is in Standard Form, equation (b) is factored to make it much easier to determine that the parabola intersects the x-axis at the points $(3, 0)$ and $(-5, 0)$. And while (b) is useful for finding the roots of the function, equation (c) may be much more helpful if one needs to know that the vertex is at the point $(-1, -16)$ and that the minimum y-value is at -16. Equation (c) masks the coordinates of the x-intercepts, while making it easy to determine the vertex. So, although all three of these equations are acceptable and reasonable, we choose a particular representation of the function depending on the context of the problem and what information we need. Likewise, while the fraction $\frac{3}{5}$ is considered "simplified" and, therefore, a desirable way to express a quantity, we may choose to represent it as $\frac{12}{20}$ if we have been asked to add $\frac{3}{5} + \frac{1}{4}$ or as 0.6 if the object is to find $\frac{3}{5}$ of 75.

Specifically, *Principles and Standards for School Mathematics* (1998) stated that

Mathematics instructional programs should emphasize mathematical representations to foster understanding of mathematics so that all students

- create and use representations to organize, record, and communicate mathematical ideas;
- develop a repertoire of mathematical representations that can be used purposefully, flexibly, and appropriately;
- use representations to model and interpret physical, social, and mathematical phenomena (p. 94).

Representation is an important part of the process of doing, teaching, and learning mathematics, because students often find themselves trying to determine the best and most appropriate way to model a problem situation.

■ CONCLUSION ■

Think back to Mr. James's classroom as described in this chapter. His students were asked to select a real-life problem and find a function that modeled it. We can analyze the class project and student responses through the lens of the five mathematical processes described in this chapter. First, students selected a function and were faced with the problem of expressing it in a variety of ways and determining how the function behaved so that they could explain it to others. As they explored the ways to write the function in a sentence, in a table, with an equation, and as a graph, they were faced with the task of representing their functions in a variety of ways and determining the strengths and weaknesses of each method of representation. When students made presentations to the class and submitted written papers about their functions, they were communicating the mathematics in written and oral form to their peers and teacher. Mr. James asked students to analyze two of the problems posed by others in the project; thus, he was promoting reasoning skills as students explored the question of "what about these functions makes them different?" Finally, the students were making connections among various representations of their functions as well as connecting algebra

concepts to real-world phenomena in their daily lives.

Books have been written on the nature of mathematics and what it means to do mathematics. Although many people think of mathematics as a content area—algebra, geometry, number theory, and so on—the purpose of this chapter is to remind us that mathematics is also a process, something that one "does." NCTM has defined five mathematical processes that should permeate every lesson every day in the classroom—problem solving, reasoning (and proof), communication, connections, and representation. They are often referred to as the *umbrella standards* because they constitute what students should be doing as they learn about specific content issues such as algebra or probability.

When a lesson is planned, mathematics teachers often consider the five umbrella standards and how they can be incorporated into the class period. The main intent of the class may be to learn to sketch a sine and cosine curve, but in the process, students are presented with problems and questions that develop their problem solving, reasoning, communication, connections, and representation skills along the way. As Mark Twain said, "Education is what's left over when you forget all the facts that your teachers made you memorize when you were in school." Students may forget how to factor a perfect cube six months after the method was taught, but if the lesson was effective, they will have learned to apply mathematical processes that will be useful long after the formulas have been forgotten. In addition, they should be able to reconstruct the method for themselves.

Recent surveys from industry consistently indicate that employers are looking for a workforce that has problem-solving and communication skills (see, for example, the *SCANS* [Secretary's Commission on Achieving Necessary Skills] *Report,* 1991). Businesses claim that they will undertake the necessary on-the-job training, but they need employees as their raw material who can think and work with others. Mathematics teachers can help produce reflective problem solvers by focusing lessons and activities on the mathematical processes. In the next chapter, we will turn our attention to how students learn and what the teacher can do to foster positive attitudes and dispositions toward mathematics in their students.

■ GLOSSARY ■

Communication: Communication is the mathematical process by which students express their mathematical thinking to others in oral or written form. Students are encouraged to go beyond "being able to do" the mathematics and to communicate their thinking to others.

Connections: Making mathematical connections is the process by which students connect the mathematics they are studying to (a) other areas of the mathematics curriculum (such as knowing how Pascal's Triangle applies to the binomial theorem in algebra while also being useful in determining sample spaces in the study of probability) and (b) to other areas of the curriculum such as science or social studies.

Exercise: An exercise is a task with which a person is already familiar, and doing an exercise is considered routine practice of a skill. This differs from a problem, in which there is no immediate solution.

Mathematical Processes: The National Council of Teachers of Mathematics has identified five processes that underlie the teaching and learning of mathematics. These *umbrella* processes include problem solving, reasoning, communication, connections, and representation.

Problem: A problem is a task that has no immediate solution, and the person solving it has to begin by defining the problem and identifying a strategy. This differs from an exercise, in which a person is already familiar with the task and merely needs to practice a skill.

Problem Solving: Problem solving is a mathematical process by which students attempt to identify what is needed, to set up a plan, to implement the plan, and to check the reasonableness of their answer (see George Polya's 1945 book). As students engage in problem solving, they develop a set of problem-solving strategies that can be applied in other situations. Some of these strategies include writing an equation, making a physical model, working backward, drawing a graph, making a table, and using guess-and-check.

Reasoning: Reasoning is the mathematical process by which students seek to explain "why" something happens the way it does or "what would happen if . . . " something were different in a problem. Mathematical reasoning deals with constructing proof (either formally or informally) that conjectures are true or false.

Representation: Representation is the mathematical process by which students take a given problem situation and attempt to model it in a useful way that will enable them to solve the problem. Different representations of problems are appropriate at different times, depending on the context.

Rubric: A rubric is a grading scale that is often used for scoring open-ended questions, essays, presentations, and projects within and outside of mathematics. Generally, each scale number in a rubric is attached to a description of student performance that is required to reach that particular level.

Standards: A standard is a benchmark that can be used by a school, a district, a state, or a country to determine the degree to which the educational program "measures up" to what is expected. The National Council of Teachers of Mathematics released three Standards documents in the 1980s and 1990s and another comprehensive document entitled *Principles and Standards for School Mathematics* in 1998. The intent of these documents was to provide a direction and set of goals for those involved in planning mathematics curriculum, instruction, and assessment.

■ DISCUSSION QUESTIONS ■

1. Why did you choose to enter the teaching profession and teach mathematics to adolescents? In what ways might your reasons for becoming a mathematics teacher influence your beliefs about education?

2. Take some time to explore either or both of the TIMSS websites listed at the end of Chapter 1. What are the implications of the results of TIMSS? What do the data tell us about mathematics education in the United States, including its apparent strengths and weaknesses?

3. Obtain the *Curriculum and Evaluation Standards for School Mathematics* (1989) and *Principles and Standards for School Mathematics* (1998) in hard copy or by visiting <http://www.enc.org> and <http://www.nctm.org>. Compare the philosophy and contents of these two Standards documents. How has the philosophy of mathematics education changed over the 10 years between these documents, and what appears to have remained the same?

4. Observe a secondary or middle school mathematics lesson (or view one on a videotape) and outline what the teacher does in the lesson to promote any or all of the five mathematical processes of problem solving, reasoning and proof, communication, connections, and representation.

5. What does it mean if someone suggests that you "place problem solving at the focal point" of your mathematics classroom? How is this different from what we have traditionally experienced in the teaching and learning of mathematics?

6. Identify a rich problem in a resource book, a textbook, or on the World Wide Web and explain how it can be used to promote and develop a number of different problem-solving strategies.

7. Identify a routine algorithm such as "adding up the total number of decimal places and counting that many to the left" when you multiply decimals, "inverting the second fraction and multiplying" when you divide fractions, or "adding the opposite" when you subtract integers. Then think about and discuss how one might teach a class how to use the algorithm while you are promoting the five mathematical processes in a lesson.

8. Discuss the degree to which Chapter 1 changed your thinking on what it means to "do," to "teach," and to "learn" mathematics.

■ BIBLIOGRAPHIC REFERENCES AND RESOURCES ■

Beaton, A. E., Mullis, I. V., Martin, M. O., Gonzalez, E. J., Kelly, D. L., & Smith, T. A. (1996). *TIMSS: Mathematics achievement in the middle school years.* Chestnut Hill, MA: Center for the Study of Testing, Evaluation, and Educational Policy.

Boston College. (1999). Center for the Study of Testing, Evaluation, and Educational Policy. Retrieved August 20, 1999 from the World Wide Web: <http://www.csteep.bc.edu/timss>

Charles, R. I., & Barnett, C. S. (1992). *Problem-solving experiences in pre-algebra.* Menlo Park, CA: Addison-Wesley.

Dolan, D. T., & Williamson, J. (1983). *Teaching problem-solving strategies.* Menlo Park, CA: Addison-Wesley.

Dossey, J. A., Mullis, I. V., & Jones, C. O. (1993). *Can students do mathematical problem solving?* Washington, DC: U.S. Department of Education.

Elliot, P. C. (Ed.). (1996). *1996 Yearbook of the NCTM: Communication in mathematics and beyond.* Reston, VA: National Council of Teachers of Mathematics.

House, P. A. (Ed.) (1995). *1995 Yearbook of the NCTM: Connecting mathematics across the curriculum.* Reston, VA: National Council of Teachers of Mathematics.

Illingworth, M. (1996). *Real-life math problem solving.* New York, NY: Scholastic.

Kenney, P. A., & Silver, E. A. (Eds.). (1997). *Results from the sixth mathematics assessment of the national assessment of educational progress.* Reston, VA: National Council of Teachers of Mathematics.

Kline, M. (1973). *Why Johnny can't add.* New York, NY: St. Martin's.

Krulik, S. (Ed.) (1980). *1980 Yearbook of the NCTM: Problem solving in school mathematics.* Reston, VA: National Council of Teachers of Mathematics.

Leitzel, James R. C. (Ed.). (1991). *A call for change: Recommendations for the mathematical preparation of teachers of mathematics.* Washington, DC: Mathematical Association of America.

Michigan State University. (1999). Research Center for the International Mathematics and Science Study. Retrieved August 20, 1999 from the World Wide Web: <http://ustimss.msu.edu>

National Council of Teachers of Mathematics. (1998). *Principles and standards for School Mathematics* (working draft). Reston, VA: National Council of Teachers of Mathematics.

National Council of Teachers of Mathematics. (1995). *Assessment standards for school mathematics.* Reston, VA: National Council of Teachers of Mathematics.

National Council of Teachers of Mathematics. (1991). *Professional standards for teaching mathematics.* Reston, VA: National Council of Teachers of Mathematics.

National Council of Teachers of Mathematics. (1989). *Curriculum and evaluation standards for school mathematics.* Reston, VA: National Council of Teachers of Mathematics.

National Council of Teachers of Mathematics. (1987). *The developments in school mathematics education around the world: Applications-oriented curricula and technology-supported learning for all students.* Reston, VA: National Council of Teachers of Mathematics.

National Council of Teachers of Mathematics. (1980). *An agenda for action: Recommendations for school mathematics of the 1980s.* Reston, VA: National Council of Teachers of Mathematics.

National Research Council. (1989). *Everybody counts: A report to the nation on the future of mathematics education.* Washington, DC: National Academy.

Ohio Department of Education. (1980). *Becoming a better problem solver: Book 1.* Columbus, OH: Ohio Department of Education.

Ohio Department of Education. (1980). *A resource for problem solving: Book 2.* Columbus, OH: Ohio Department of Education.

Phillips, E., Gardella, T., Kelly, C., & Stewart, J. (1991). *NCTM 5–8 addenda series: Patterns and functions.* Reston, VA: National Council of Teachers of Mathematics.

Polya, G. (1945). *How to solve it.* Princeton, NJ: Princeton.

Schmidt, W. H., McKnight, C. C., Valverde, G. A., Houang, R. T., & Wiley, D. E. (1997). *Many visions, many aims: Volume 1.* The Netherlands: Kluwer Academic.

Schoenfeld, A. H. (1985). *Mathematical problem solving.* Orlando, FL: Academic.

Schoenfeld, A. H. (Ed.). (1994). *Mathematical thinking and problem solving.* Hillsdale, NJ: Erlbaum.

Schoenfeld, A. H. (1983). *Problem solving in the mathematics curriculum: A report, recommendations, and an annotated bibliography.* Washington, DC: Mathematical Association of America.

Secretary's Commission on Achieving Necessary Skills. (1991). *What work requires of schools: A SCANS report for America 2000.* Washington, DC: U.S. Department of Labor.

Sharp, E. (1964). *A parent's guide to the new mathematics.* New York, NY: E. P. Dutton.

Shufelt, G. (Ed.). (1983). *1983 Yearbook of the NCTM: The agenda in action.* Reston, VA: The National Council of Teachers of Mathematics.

Learning Theories and Psychology in Mathematics Education

After reading Chapter 2, you should be able to answer the following questions:

■ How is research conducted in mathematics education, and how does it impact trends in curriculum, teaching, and assessment?

■ What are the key components of learning theories, such as those of Bruner and the van Hieles? What are the principles underlying the constructivist model of teaching and learning?

■ How do the use of inquiry and an inductive approach to teaching differ from the traditional model that emphasizes deductive methods? Explain why there has been a shift toward this inquiry-based approach.

■ What is motivation, and what can teachers do to help "motivate" students?

■ What does it mean to develop a positive mathematical disposition? Describe some strategies that might be used to promote positive dispositions and to counter math anxiety in students.

Chelsea is a sophomore student in Mr. Metzger's third-period Geometry class. On standardized tests, she has demonstrated the potential to be a high-achieving student. Mr. Metzger knows her and is aware that she is an intelligent girl with a promising future, but she is failing his class. At the beginning of the school year, when many of the problems used equation solving from algebra and simple formulas from middle school, Chelsea performed quite well. However, as the year progressed and the class started to work with increasingly more difficult definitions and theorems and to write two-column proofs, she began to struggle and eventually gave up. She rarely does her homework and finds her mind drifting off during class, unable to focus on the problems and proofs being demonstrated by the teacher at the board. After class one day, Chelsea apologized to Mr. Metzger and said, "I really want to do well in your class, but I don't understand it. I'm just not as interested in this class as I have been with other math classes in the past." She urged him not to take it personally, but as he watched her walk out the door, he knew that it couldn't be entirely her fault.

Perhaps you have known a Chelsea in your mathematics career (or maybe you *were* a Chelsea at some point). Every class includes students who have the potential to be successful but are struggling nonetheless. A common reaction is to dismiss Chelsea's problem as a personal issue that only she can fix. After all, if she is not consistently paying attention in class and doing her homework, how can you expect her to achieve acceptably in the course? However, the classroom is a two-way street that involves both the teacher *and* the learner, and there are ways a classroom teacher can help a student like Chelsea. First of all, if she has been having problems with two-column proofs all year long and is one of the smartest students in the class, her peers are probably struggling as well. It is entirely possible that the content is too difficult for many students in the class—developmentally beyond what they are ready to handle at this point. Second, Mr. Metzger should examine how he spends his class time and what he expects his students to be able to do. Chapter 1 discussed the importance of including problem solving, reasoning, communication, connections, and representation in every lesson. It may be that his chalkboard-based teaching style is simply not interesting to his students and that they need the sort of problems and activities that evoke curiosity and, therefore, motivate the class to want to do the work. When it comes to the personality and family concerns of the student, much is beyond the realm of what a teacher can do. But after close examination and reflection, every teacher should be able to identify areas for improvement in the way that a class is run that may, in turn, assist students like Chelsea to get back on track.

This chapter turns to the psychological concerns in the teaching and learning of mathematics. Because theories of educational psychology result from years of research in the classroom, the role of mathematics educational research will be explored before some current theories about how students learn are discussed. Then, a definition of motivation will be discussed, as well as what the teacher can do to help motivate students to learn. Finally, the chapter discusses what the National Council of Teachers of Mathematics calls mathematical **disposition**—the attitudinal side of teaching mathematics—and how it develops over time.

■ RESEARCH IN MATHEMATICS EDUCATION

The announcer of a nationally televised professional football game recently stated that quarterbacks aged twenty-five and under have a 35 percent winning percentage whereas quarterbacks over age thirty-three win 74 percent of their games. He used the data to argue that older players are better at what they do and that teams often "recycle" quarterbacks because their performances tend to improve significantly as they gain experience. What he failed to realize—or at least he never mentioned it—was that only the best quarterbacks in professional football are still playing when they are more than thirty-three years old. As a result, the data should be no surprise to the viewer—we would expect that the *reason* a quarterback would still be playing beyond age thirty-three is that he has been very successful and has a high winning percentage. Less-successful quarterbacks have already left the game by the time they are thirty years old and are no longer included in the data. In short, the statistics were mathematically accurate, but conclusions drawn from the data were questionable.

Similarly, a newspaper recently reported that "90 percent of all divorced adults blame the break-up on the other person," and another headline stated that at a famous university, 94 percent of the faculty considered themselves "above average" instructors. Not only do headlines such as these sometimes make us chuckle—after all, shouldn't 50 percent of the teachers be at or above average and 50 percent be at or below average?—but they inevitably make us ask questions such as, "How do they know that? Who did they ask? Are these statistics reasonable for the whole population? Does the conclusion make sense?" Research is the process of gathering and analyzing data so that the results can be used to inform decision-makers. For example, if a state raises its maximum driving speed from 65 to 75 miles per hour, and research data show a significant increase in highway fatalities during the following year, the legislature may use the research to argue that the speed limit should be lowered again. Decisions are based on mathematical information every day in our world.

However, we must use caution because some data and, therefore, the results of some research reports are flawed. Let's suppose you ask five of your best friends whether they generally vote Democrat or Republican, and four out of the five say that they are Democrats. Is it logical to assume that 80 percent of all adults are Democrats? Of course not! The sample size you chose was too small to generalize from, and you selected a unique part of the population—college-educated and, perhaps, all of the same gender and living in similar situations. If you really wanted to know what percentage of the population belonged to each party, you would need to take a large national survey that included a reasonable mix of geographic regions, socioeconomic groups, genders, and so forth. In addition, you might want to compare your results to the data from similar studies that have been conducted to look for patterns, similarities, and inconsistencies. You hope that you would never have to make a significant life decision based on one, potentially flawed, study.

Just as the legislature makes speed limit decisions based, in part, on fatality-rate research, educators should ideally write curricula and select teaching and assessment methods with current research in mind. Chapter 1 looked at the results of the TIMSS and NAEP tests. Once you are aware that fewer than one in twenty eighth graders could respond acceptably to the Treena's Budget problem, you may begin to ask more questions that require reading, analysis, and a clearly-communicated response in your classes in order to give students more experience with this type of problem. In fact, a school district may use research such as the TIMSS or NAEP reports to influence the topics taught in school and the type of expectations established for student progress.

In general, two major types of research in education guide our decision-making—quantitative research and qualitative research. **Quantitative research** deals with gathering numerical data and analyzing it. For example, Slavin et al. (1990) described a quantitative study in which some high school students were placed in heterogeneous (mixed-ability) classes, and others were placed in homogeneous (ability-grouped) classes. At the end of a school year, the students in mixed classes significantly outperformed their peers. In short, they scored higher on achievement tests when they were members of heterogeneous classes. Similarly, a study conducted with junior high school students in Israel showed that although high achievers performed about the same in heterogeneous and homogeneous groupings, students at average or low-average levels achieved significantly higher while participating in heterogeneous groupings (Linchevski & Kutscher, 1998). In this article, the authors argued against ability grouping and tracking practices. On the other hand, quantitative research can also argue in favor of ability grouping. For example, a study by Rogers (1998) suggests that all students benefit from homogeneous grouping, particularly those who are gifted. Therefore, decision-makers need to thoroughly explore a large base of research before reaching any conclusions and acting upon the data.

Historically, educators first used quantitative methods. If we wanted to know, for example, whether calculators improve the learning of a particular concept, we could pretest two classes to establish that they are similar in background and proceed to teach them—one with calculators and one without. Then, by comparing scores on a posttest, we could determine whether the calculator-based class actually outperformed the other and report those results to the education community. Recently, however, there has been a trend toward more qualitative research in education as researchers have become skeptical about the degree to which we can describe student performance based solely upon numerical data. We have seen a similar trend in the assessment of students in mathematics classes as is discussed in Chapters 8 and 9.

Qualitative research involves the collection and analysis of nonnumerical data such as videotapes of classroom episodes, scripts of student-teacher conversations, audio recordings of interviews, or written summaries of student journal entries. For example, a qualitative study involving first- and second-year algebra classes showed that teachers who prompted their students to write a five-minute response to a problem or question at the beginning of class several days per week tended to adjust their lesson plan accordingly, gaining more insight into student understanding than they would have without the prompts (Miller, 1992). The data for this study consisted of written student responses, written teacher reactions, and notes from meetings and interviews with participating teachers. Although it is possible to attach numbers to the qualitative raw data (e.g., one can count how many times students responded in a particular way), the research is primarily involved with "words" taken from observations and interviews, rather than "numbers" from tests.

Some research in mathematics education is an attempt to prove that one teaching or assessment method is better than another, as was just described in the calculator example, and is referred to as **experimental research.** This type of research has its roots in agriculture: A farmer would apply a particular brand of fertilizer to one field and not to another to see if the field with the treatment produced a heartier crop. In a study conducted by Whitman (1976), she found that students who learned to use the "cover-up" method of solving equations—as described in the TIMSS example for solving the equation $3(x + 5) = 30$ in Chapter 1—along with traditional symbol manipulation outperformed their peers who were only taught to manipulate the symbols with pencil and paper. A teacher can translate such a study into practice when deciding how to approach equation solving in a middle school classroom or in an algebra course.

In making educational decisions, it is often helpful to simply have a base of information. A study that is undertaken for the purpose of generating statistics and information for discussion, but not necessarily for comparison, is **descriptive research.** The following are some examples of the results of descriptive studies: The National Research Council (1989) reported that 75 percent of all jobs require a basic knowledge of algebra and geometry. Stiggins (1988) found that teachers spend 20 percent to 30 percent of their work time designing and implementing assessments of student progress. One of the TIMSS reports showed that 83 percent of the eighth graders in the United States were in classes of between 1 and 30 students, whereas 93 percent of the students in Korea were enrolled in classes with 41 or more students (Beaton et al., 1997). It is interesting, however, to note that Korean eighth graders significantly outscored U.S. eighth graders on the TIMSS achievement tests. The information presented in this paragraph is not intended as a foundation for arguing one position over another; it is purely a description of what is going on in the schools. Descriptive research frequently results from surveys or interviews and serves to inform the education community about the status of some program or situation.

Table 2–1 is a generalized summary of the types of research that can be conducted in education and illustrates the way in which research can take on several different formats, depending upon the intent of the researchers.

Table 2–1 Comparison of Research Methods

	Experimental	Descriptive
Quantitative	Experimental study conducted by comparing quantitative data	Descriptive study containing quantitative data
Qualitative	Experimental study conducted by comparing qualitative data	Descriptive study containing qualitative data

Most experimental studies are quantitative, and much of the descriptive research in mathematics education is qualitative. However, any study can, of course, contain both quantitative and qualitative elements. In fact, some of the most powerful research conclusions can be drawn when, for example, test results of student performance can be extended through a series of open-ended interviews with students. Interviews often allow researchers to probe the students' thinking more deeply than a written test, and they can quote student comments in the research results.

Research in mathematics education serves either as a catalyst for change or as an affirmation of current practices. After several studies have been conducted and patterns about teaching and learning begin to emerge, an educational theory is often formulated. We now explore some of the theories on teaching and learning that have evolved over many years of educational research and address the question of how a student actually learns mathematics.

■ LEARNING THEORIES IN MATHEMATICS

Think back to some of the teachers you have had in your educational career. Were any of them extremely knowledgeable in the area of mathematics but ineffective in the classroom, leaving you or others in the class confused? Perhaps you spent the semester or the year feeling as though the teacher was teaching mathematics but not teaching the students. Clearly, there is a difference! It has been said that the best mathematics teachers are those who not only have an understanding of the content but also have a firm grasp on how mathematics is learned—teachers who are knowledgeable about theories of child development and can appreciate how students come to know and be able to do mathematics. Richard Skemp, who wrote a popular book entitled *The Psychology of Learning Mathematics* (1971), stated that "problems of learning and teaching are psychological problems, and before we can make much improvement in the teaching of mathematics we need to know more about how it is learned" (p. 14). His comments are backed by research that suggests that teaching teachers to reflect on how their students think can have a significant effect on student achievement (see, for example, the discussion on Cognitively Guided Instruction by Fennema and Franke, 1992).

Skemp also stated that "the learning of mathematics (is) . . . very dependent on good teaching. Now, to know mathematics is one thing, and to be able to teach it—to communicate it to those at a lower conceptual level is quite another" (Skemp, p. 36). A study conducted by Ball (1990), for example, described the difficulty that elementary and secondary preservice teachers had in representing the problem $1\frac{3}{4} \div \frac{1}{2}$ in a form that promoted understanding of the process. Although the undergraduates could "do" the problem, only about half of the secondary mathematics majors (and none of the elementary preservice teachers) could put the problem into a form that helped students understand what they were doing. So, as we think about teaching secondary and middle school students, it is important to focus on how they think and develop as learners of mathematics. Let's look at some of the current theories on teaching and learning that are influencing reform in mathematics education.

Bruner's Stages of Representation

One of the cognitive theories of learning was formulated by Jerome Bruner. Bruner, who was born in 1915 and received his doctorate in 1941 from Harvard, theorized that learning passes through three stages of representation—enactive, iconic, and symbolic. His theory has led to the extensive use of hands-on materials—**manipulatives**—in mathematics classrooms. We can illustrate these three stages of cognitive development with an example of combining similar terms in algebra.

In the primary grades, children often use a manipulative known as **base ten blocks** for exploring basic operations and place value. A set of base ten blocks (see Figure 2–1) is made up of cubes that measure 1 cm on a side; rods, often called *longs,* that are 10 cm × 1 cm × 1 cm; and *flats,* which are 10 cm × 10 cm squares with a depth of 1 cm. Each unit cube can represent a "1," while the long is a "10," and the flat is a "100."

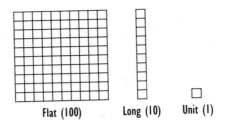

Figure 2–1 Base Ten Block Representations of Whole Numbers

When children are asked to add 124 + 235, they can represent the numbers with base ten blocks, as shown in Figure 2–2:

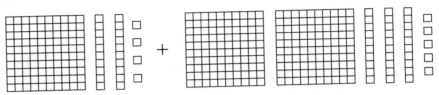

Figure 2–2 Representation of 124 + 235 with Base Ten Blocks

The child can readily see that there are 3 flats, 5 longs, and 9 unit cubes, so the sum of 124 and 235 must be 359. No pencil-and-paper computation is needed to do the problem (remember that this is still a problem for early elementary children, not an exercise!), and the design of the blocks makes it intuitively obvious to children which digits to add, as they simply combine the blocks that have the same shape and size.

Similarly, this notion can be extended to the teaching of algebra in the secondary or middle grades. The manipulatives often used are referred to as **algebra tiles.** A standard set of algebra tiles as shown in Figure 2–3 includes three shapes—a square that is 1 cm on a side, a long that is 1 cm wide and several cm long, and a flat that is a square whose sides are the length of a long.

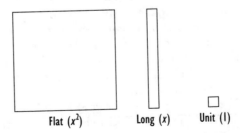

Figure 2–3 Algebra Tiles

Algebra tiles are based on an area model, so we assume that the small square is 1 cm × 1 cm, representing 1 square unit of area. The rectangular long is 1 cm × x, so it stands for x. The flat is $x \times x$, so it represents an x^2. So, let's say that a student was trying to simplify the expression: $2x^2 + 3x + 5 + x^2 + 6x + 7$. A representation of the problem with algebra tiles would resemble Figure 2–4:

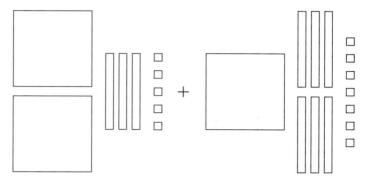

Figure 2–4 Representation of $2x^2 + 3x + 5 + x^2 + 6x + 7$ with Algebra Tiles

A student can fairly easily recognize that there are 3 flats, 9 longs, and 12 units, so the expression must simplify to $3x^2 + 9x + 12$. This process and the meaning behind it can be taught without the use of pencil and paper and without any discussion of what constitutes similar terms. Again, the notion that the terms are *similar* is logical because the tiles that are combined have the same shape and size. The seasoned mathematics teacher knows that a typical mistake made by students is to take $3x + 6x$ and get $9x^2$, but with the use of algebra tiles, students will rarely make this error because they have a visual image to rely upon. If the primary grade teachers have skillfully and meaningfully used base ten blocks, the transition is even easier because students make connections between adding digits with the same place value and combining similar terms. Algebra tiles can model other concepts as well. For example, most commercially available sets are made of flat pieces of plastic with different colors on each side, allowing one side to represent a positive term and the other side to represent a negative term. Students can then deal with polynomials having positive and negative coefficients. The subject of algebra tiles and their uses will be revisited in Chapter 6.

Bruner's theory postulates that learning begins with an action—touching, feeling, and manipulating. It is difficult, if not impossible, to have a conversation about apples if one has never actually held an apple. This first stage is the *enactive* or concrete stage. Students are operating in the enactive stage when they learn to count, add, and subtract using base ten blocks in the first grade. They are also in the enactive stage of learning about similar terms when they manipulate algebra tiles on their desks to "feel" what it means to combine the terms.

The second stage of learning, according to Bruner, is the *iconic* or pictorial phase. This stage depends upon visuals, such as pictures, to summarize and represent concrete situations. For the elementary student, this may mean that the child puts away the base ten blocks, is given a piece of paper, and is asked to draw a picture of what it means to add $243 + 335$. By analyzing the picture, the teacher can determine the degree to which a child is able to visualize number operations. Essentially, the students are drawing on paper what they already know how to do with the concrete manipulatives, but, again, it is virtually impossible to draw a picture of an apple if we don't hold a real one in our hands first. So, the enactive phase is followed by an iconic phase in which the picture represents a physical object and serves as a further abstraction.

Bruner's third stage of learning is the *symbolic* or abstract phase. It is called symbolic because the words and symbols representing information do not actually have any inherent connection to the information. The numeral 3 has no meaning in and of itself and only takes on meaning if we have first held 3 of something in our hands and worked with pictures of things arranged in groups of three. Similarly, asking students to visualize an angle with a 45° measure assumes that they have had experience with drawing angles and measuring the angles with a protractor. Of course, the word *apple* has no meaning either unless we have touched apples and can recognize them in a picture. The use of symbols allows a student to organize information in the mind by relating concepts together.

It is critical, according to Bruner's recommendations for sequencing teaching episodes, that learners progress through all three stages. If a student, a month or more down the road, makes the mistake of thinking that $3x + 6x$ is $9x^2$, it is easy for the teacher to take the class back to the concrete or pictorial stage of representation for intervention. However, if the teacher did not follow Bruner's stages and started by teaching the topic with the symbolic manipulation, the student has no model upon which to fall back. It is also important that the teacher allow students to progress gradually from one stage to the next, which is not as easy as it may seem. If students are ready to move on to the next level but are continually asked to function at the concrete stage on assignments, they will most certainly become bored with the work. Similarly, if the teacher tries to get the students to a symbolic level before they are ready to proceed, the students might be able to demonstrate the skill on paper but will still have significant gaps in their understanding of the concept. Maybe you have heard someone say, "I could do it and got through the class, but I'm not sure I really learned very much, and I don't even remember what we did anymore!" It is likely that this student was rushed through the stages without enough time to allow the concepts to fully develop.

Historically, the lack of conceptual understanding has been a major problem in mathematics education. Perhaps you were taught this way and, before reading this section, would have been hard pressed to visualize what it means to combine similar terms. For many students, mathematics is simply a set of rules and procedures because they have been taught almost entirely on the symbolic level or in a classroom in which *getting the answer* was valued over *making sense* of the mathematics. A unit on similar terms that progresses through the phases allows the child to reason out *why* terms are added together, to communicate the process through the use of models and pictures as representations, and to connect the idea of place value to algebra. This unit goes beyond procedural knowledge to an understanding of the process. And although some students can be taught at the symbolic level and be successful in school, many cannot and are in need of other representations of problems. Bruner stated that students with well-developed symbolic systems might be able to bypass the first two stages when studying some concepts, but he warned that their teachers take a risk because these students will not possess the visual images on which to fall back if the symbolic approach is not working (Bruner, 1966).

The van Hiele Model

A considerable amount of research has been conducted to specifically study the way that children learn about geometry. The most well-known theory of geometric development is the **van Hiele model.** This cognitive theory was developed in the 1950s by a husband-and-wife team of mathematics teachers in the Netherlands, Pierre van Hiele and Dina van Hiele-Geldof. They attempted to explain why students have so much difficulty with high school geometry even if they have been successful in other mathematics experiences. After a considerable amount of quantitative and qualitative research (see the NCTM monograph on the van Hiele model by Fuys et al., 1988), they theorized that children pass through five stages, or levels, of geometric reasoning. Determining the level on which students function can help teachers understand how to meet the needs of their students.

The first level, Level 0, is the *visualization* phase. At this stage, a child will look at a square and identify it as a square. When asked how the child knows this, a typical response would be, "Because it looks like one," but the student will not know the properties of a square. The child simply recognizes the shape. At the second level, Level 1 or the *analysis* stage, students begin to recognize the attributes or properties of a shape. A child at Level 1 might say, for example, that a square has four sides, opposite sides that are parallel, and four right angles. However, the child will not be able to relate two geometric figures to one another. Looking at the diagram in Figure 2–5, the child generally will say that the figure on the left is a square, that it has four equal sides, and so forth. The student will also say that the figure on the right is a parallelogram, that it has two pairs of opposite parallel lines, and so on, but the child at Level 1 will not be able to recognize that the square is a special case of the parallelogram. The figures are seen as seemingly unrelated geometric shapes, although each has its own important properties.

Figure 2–5 A Square and a General Parallelogram

When a child advances to Level 2, *informal deduction,* the student will begin to compare geometric shapes and construct simple proofs. At this level, the child will be able to recognize that the square is a special case of a parallelogram or that a parallelogram does not necessarily have to be a rhombus and why this is the case. However, at Level 2, the child is still unable to construct significant proofs. The ability to accept postulates and theorems and write proofs emerges at Level 3—*deduction.* This is the level at which we have historically taught high school geometry, which focuses on the assumption of various postulates and emphasizes two-column, paragraph, or indirect proofs of theorems. The highest level, Level 4, is *rigor.* This level is associated with the student's ability to work in other geometric systems such as non-Euclidean geometry, in which virtually all of the work is done on an abstract, proof-oriented level.

If you browse through several traditional high school geometry textbooks, you will often find an emphasis on postulates, theorems, and two-column proofs. Perhaps you used these texts in high school geometry. These textbooks assume that the student is ready to function at Level 3; however, research has shown that over 70 percent of students enter into high school geometry functioning at Level 0 or 1 and, furthermore, that only those students who are at Level 2 or above are prepared well enough to be successful at writing proofs in the course (Shaughnessy & Burger, 1985). In short, there is a serious mismatch between the students' ability level coming into a geometry course and what the teacher is expecting them to do. It's no wonder so many people have negative memories of high school geometry classes. Brumfield (1973) conducted a study with 52 high school students who had just completed an accelerated geometry course. When asked to pick one interesting theorem and prove it, 42 of them did not even attempt to prove the theorem they stated, and of the remaining 10 students, only 1 was able to write a correct proof. So, even for the best students in the school, the traditional geometry course did little for their mathematical development.

The van Hieles also found that the geometric development of students was sequential: One had to pass through Levels 0 and 1 to get to Level 2. They recognized that students can slip back to a lower level and need to work their way back up. Finally, and most importantly for our purposes, they determined that the quality of mathematics *instruction* and not simply the chronological age of the student determined advancement. The van Hieles pointed out that some levels of thought may not even be accessible to students, because of the lack of effective teaching at these levels.

The research of the van Hieles has brought about several recommended changes in the teaching and learning of school geometry. Elementary school textbooks and curricula have begun to include a greater emphasis on geometry so that students have more time to develop their understanding, and the NCTM has emphasized the role of geometry in *Principles and Standards for School Mathematics* for grades Pre-K–2, 3–5, 6–8, and 9–12. But although the van Hiele model has existed since the 1960s, we still see many traditional, proof-oriented high school texts and courses. Clearly, there is much to be done in this area if we are to truly embrace the notion of mathematics for *all* students. Fortunately, many current secondary and middle school textbooks emphasize hands-on geometry lessons, in which students discover theorems for themselves rather than being "given" a theorem and asking for a two-column proof (see, for example, Serra's popular *Discovering Geometry* textbook).

The Inquiry Approach and Constructivist Model

Authors of recent texts and resources, even beyond the study of geometry, have reflected an effective implementation of learning theory in the design of their lessons. Let's look at an example of a hands-on problem and see how it can be used to help students arrive at their own conclusions.

Take a sheet of paper and fold it in half. Then, take the half sheet and fold it in half again, and again, and again. How many times can you continue to fold the paper in half before it becomes impossible to fold it again? Is this true for all

Students use hands-on materials as an aid to construct their understanding of mathematical principles.

pieces of paper or just the one you were folding? What if your "piece" of paper was a 25-foot stretch of cash register tape? What if it was a sheet of newspaper? What patterns do you see?

If you have actually tried this, you might have found it simple to make the first and second folds, but by the fourth or fifth fold, it becomes difficult. Regardless of what kind of paper you used, you were probably unable to fold it more than about 8 times. Why does this happen? Let's organize the data in Table 2–2:

Table 2–2 Paper-Folding Data

Number of Folds	Number of Layers of Paper
0	1
1	2
2	4
3	8
4	16
5	32
6	64
7	128
8	256
9	512
10	1,024

As is evident in this table, by the time you try to fold the paper for the fifth time, you are folding 32 pieces of paper, and by the eighth time, you are folding over 250 sheets. A standard phone book is about 900 pages, so folding the piece of paper in half 12 times would be like attempting to fold a stack of two phone books in half. But let's look at the problem with some more depth. How would we determine the number of thicknesses of paper if we only knew the number of folds? Students may recognize the numbers in the right-hand column of the table as powers of 2 and determine that the fold number, n, used as the exponent, determines the thickness in terms of the number of sheets of paper (e.g., sheets = 2^n). So, if we wanted to fold the paper in half 17 times, we would find that it requires $2^{17} = 131,072$ layers of paper, which is the thickness of about 145 phone books—a stack of paper that is over 25 feet (7.6 m) high. Looking at the table again, what do we get when we take 2^0? Because the exponent tells us how many times to fold the paper, and the simplified result equals the number of thicknesses of paper, it is logical to assume that $2^0 = 1$, and now we have a *reason* for *why* this is true. If we trust the structure of mathematics and the consistency of patterns in problem solving, then raising to the zero power makes sense. Perhaps when you were in high school or middle school, you were *told* that any number raised to the zero power is equal to 1 but could not explain why this is the case. A simple paper-folding activity such as this can help students reach that conclusion for themselves.

Now, let's continue to probe even deeper into the mathematical implications of the problem. Suppose that you were to extend the table further, in both directions:

Table 2–3 Extended Table for the Paper-Folding Problem

n	2^n
−3	$0.125 = \frac{1}{8}$
−2	$0.25 = \frac{1}{4}$
−1	$0.5 = \frac{1}{2}$
0	1
1	2
2	4
3	8
4	16
5	32
6	64
7	128
8	256
9	512
10	1,024
11	2,048
12	4,096

What patterns do you see as the n values decrease in Table 2–3? Think about it before reading on. Students may recognize that the values double as you move up the table, but they are divided in half as you move down the table. We can compare, for example, the fact that $2^2 = 4$ but $2^{-2} = \frac{1}{4}$, and that $2^3 = 8$ but $2^{-3} = \frac{1}{8}$. Can we predict the relationship between taking 2^4 and 2^{-4}? Using the logical order of mathematics, students will *discover*—without being told—that negative exponents produce reciprocals and will be able to generalize this to simplify, for example, 5^{-3}. Again, the effect of negative exponents does not need to be taught as a rule to be memorized; instead, the relationship can be discovered by students as they explore patterns in a table.

The paper-folding problem is used to teach an **inquiry lesson** in which students work through the activity and essentially invent their own mathematical rules. The teacher's role is not to provide direct instruction but to select a rich task and to guide the students in their exploration of that problem. An inquiry lesson can produce deeper and longer-lasting conceptual understanding than traditional lecture-type methods. It is consistent with a theory of teaching and learning known as the **constructivist model**. The constructivist model is an outgrowth of the work of Jean Piaget, although he did not use the term himself. A constructivist believes that knowledge cannot be passively transmitted from one individual to another. Rather, knowledge is built up or constructed from within as we have experiences in our lives. In addition, a constructivist believes that children create knowledge not just by *doing* but by *reflecting* upon and discussing what they have done. A hands-on lesson is not inherently constructivist—it only becomes so when accompanied by significant discourse or processing along the way. Finally, a constructivist generally views learning as a social process, in which students compare and contrast their ideas about the patterns they see and what they believe about particular problems or concepts.

In a way, constructivism appeals to common sense. Most people would agree that it is more desirable, for example, for a middle school student to discover the need for common denominators when adding fractions than to be told that "you must find a common denominator any time you add two fractions." There are many mathematical rules, such as "invert and multiply," "count up the total number of decimal places and move it over that many in the answer," "FOIL to multiply the binomials," and "multiply the exponent and the coefficient and reduce the exponent by 1 to find the derivative," that many people have memorized, but few can explain why they work, because most of us were educated in a traditional, lecture-oriented environment. Most people's mathematical knowledge, thus, relies on rote, pencil-and-paper procedures rather than on conceptual understanding.

However, putting constructivist research into practice requires a great deal of skill, both in selecting appropriate activities and in guiding students as they explore new concepts. Paul Cobb, in his research on the constructivist model of teaching and learning, stated that "although constructivist theory is attractive when the issue of learning is considered, deep-rooted problems arise when attempts are made to apply it to instruction" (1988, p. 87). Because using an inquiry approach is generally more difficult than "teaching as telling," more classroom teachers are still using traditional approaches even though they often acknowledge that the teaching techniques are not working. A publication from the Association for Supervision and Curriculum Development (ASCD) (Brooks & Brooks, 1993) outlines the difference between what might be observed in the traditional classroom versus what is seen in the constructivist classroom (Table 2–4):

Table 2–4 Comparison of Traditional and Constructivist Classrooms

Traditional Classrooms	Constructivist Classrooms
Curriculum is presented part to whole, with emphasis on basic skills.	Curriculum is presented whole to part with emphasis on big concepts.
Strict adherence to fixed curriculum is highly valued.	Pursuit of student questions is highly valued.
Curricular activities rely heavily on textbooks and workbooks.	Curricular activities rely heavily on primary sources of data and manipulative materials.
Students are viewed as "blank slates" onto which information is etched by the teacher.	Students are viewed as thinkers with emerging theories about the world.
Teachers generally behave in a didactic manner, disseminating information to students.	Teachers generally behave in an interactive manner, mediating the environment for students.
Teachers seek the correct answer to validate student learning.	Teachers seek the students' point of view in order to understand students' present conceptions for use in subsequent lessons.
Assessment of student learning is viewed as separate from teaching and occurs almost entirely through testing.	Assessment of student learning is interwoven with teaching and occurs through teacher observations of students at work and through student exhibitions and portfolios.
Students primarily work alone.	Students work primarily in groups.

(Brooks & Brooks, 1993. Reprinted by permission.)

It should be noted that the constructivist classroom can and should include some individual work, pencil-and-paper tests, and even lectures. In fact, the model is often misconstrued as one in which it is "never appropriate to lecture or provide direct instruction," but that is simply not the case. The issue is the *frequency* with which various teaching techniques are used and whether the student and the student's thinking processes are the focal point of the classroom. Essentially, while the curriculum has been historically content centered, the constructivist approach is student centered. The examples used throughout this textbook are rooted in constructivist theory, because it underlies much of the reform effort in curriculum, teaching, and assessment.

Inductive versus Deductive Teaching

Each time that a teacher prepares a lesson, consideration of how the students learn and how to best meet their needs should be the foundation of that lesson. Research supports the work of Bruner and the van Hieles and the constructivist model, and if you concur, these theories should drive your teaching decisions. Suppose, for example, that you were teaching a review lesson on subtracting fractions and pose the following problem:

> *You have a cookie recipe that calls for $2\frac{1}{3}$ cups of flour. If you have a bag with 6 cups of flour in it, how much flour will be left after making the cookies?*

First, students must recognize this as a problem requiring subtraction. Then, they need a basic knowledge of fraction subtraction. Most of us have been shown how to take 6 and change it to $5\frac{3}{3}$, then subtract to get the solution of $3\frac{2}{3}$. But any teacher with some classroom experience has observed many students doing the problem $6 - 2\frac{1}{3}$ by taking away 2 from the 6 to get $4\frac{1}{3}$ as an answer. The student has forgotten the rule and made essentially the same mistake a primary child makes when taking $30 - 19$ to get an answer of 29 (i.e., taking the 1 from the 3 to get 2, and because the 9 is being subtracted from nothing, just bringing it down). If the teacher wants to intervene, as we discussed earlier in the chapter, the student may have no concrete or pictorial images on which to fall back.

Suppose, instead of teaching a rule, we had given the student the problem and a set of **pattern blocks**. Pattern blocks are wooden or plastic sets of geometric shapes that are used for a variety of purposes in the mathematics classroom, including, but not limited to, teaching fractions, similarity, congruence, symmetry, numerical and visual patterns, angles, and graphing. A set of pattern blocks consists of six shapes as shown in Figure 2–6—a small rhombus (tan), a larger rhombus (blue), a square (orange), an equilateral triangle (green), a trapezoid (red), and a hexagon (yellow).

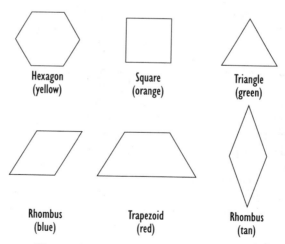

Hexagon (yellow) Square (orange) Triangle (green)

Rhombus (blue) Trapezoid (red) Rhombus (tan)

Figure 2–6 Six Pattern Block Shapes

Each of the six pieces has sides of the same length, except for the base of the red trapezoid, which is twice the standard length. We will let the hexagon represent a unit, so that the trapezoid is $\frac{1}{2}$ of the unit and so on. The student can model the cookie problem by laying out six hexagons to represent the 6 cups of flour. Then, $2\frac{1}{3}$ hexagons need to be taken away. Removing 2 of the hexagons leaves 4, but an additional $\frac{1}{3}$ must also be removed. Trading three blue rhombi for one of the hexagons, the student can then remove one blue rhombus, leaving three hexagons and two blue rhombi, or $3\frac{2}{3}$, as shown in Figure 2–7.

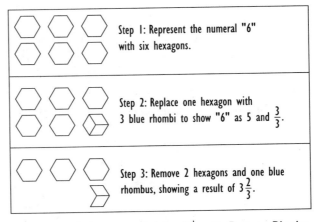

Step 1: Represent the numeral "6" with six hexagons.

Step 2: Replace one hexagon with 3 blue rhombi to show "6" as 5 and $\frac{3}{3}$.

Step 3: Remove 2 hexagons and one blue rhombus, showing a result of $3\frac{2}{3}$.

Figure 2–7 Representing $6 - 2\frac{1}{3}$ with Pattern Blocks

In the constructivist model, the children will do several problems like this one, using the pattern blocks as needed until they eventually invent a rule for doing problems that require some form of regrouping. A student will recognize that three of the thirds can be traded for one of the wholes and will be able to do similar examples such as $12 - 5\frac{4}{5}$ by applying the same procedure. In this way, not only has the student created a rule that is more likely to be remembered than if the teacher told the class what to do, but the student also has formed a visual image that ultimately enhances understanding. According to Bruner, pattern blocks and picture drawing on problems of this type should be utilized long before any pencil-and-paper abstractions are initiated.

This method is often referred to as **inductive teaching** because the student thinks through several examples and then generalizes a rule at the end. The more traditional form of teaching, in which the teacher states a rule or definition and then expects the student to apply it to a worksheet or set of problems is called **deductive teaching,** meaning that a generalization serves as the starting point, and specific examples are applied later. Many teachers of traditional geometry courses in high school have relied on deductive thinking—give the students a definition and see if they can apply it—rather than inductive methods, which place the students at the center of the process and expect them to invent some of their own rules and procedures.

One classroom technique that promotes inductive thinking is the **concept attainment** method. This strategy was actually devised by Bruner as a way to help students make their own generalizations. Consider the 18 geometric figures in Figure 2–8:

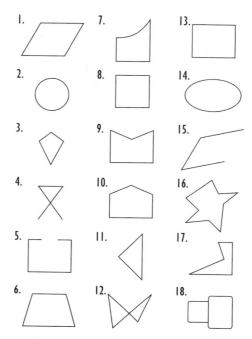

Figure 2–8 Using Concept Attainment to Define "Polygons"

The teacher would begin the lesson by telling the class to remain silent and not share ideas with anyone until instructed to do so. Then, the teacher would tell the class, for example, that #3 is a "yes," but #15 is a "no"; #11 is a "yes," but #2 is a "no." The class should be challenged to start to think about the rule that the teacher is using to classify the "yes" and "no" pictures. At this point, the class can be given one more example, such as #9 is a "yes," but #18 is a "no." If a member of the class appears to have the rule figured out, that student should give an example of a "yes" and a "no" to the rest of the class with no explanation of why this is the case. Eventually, the class would be asked to list some common characteristics of "yes" figures versus "no" figures. Students realize that the "yes" figures have line segments as sides, that the segments must be joined at their endpoints, and that the figures must be closed or connected. Of course, the class has just defined a *polygon,* and the teacher can write this word on the board after the definition has been invented.

The concept attainment method tends to be challenging and fun for the students while giving them the responsibility for creating the definition. They have looked at a series of examples and nonexamples to generalize a rule, so the teaching method is said to be inductive. Contrast this teaching episode with the traditional geometry lesson in which the teacher turns on the overhead projector and writes "A POLYGON is a geometric figure in which . . . " and asks the students to copy it down. Later, the class in this traditional situation is generally presented with some drawings and asked whether they represent polygons. Because the teacher started with a definition or generalization and then attempted to have students apply it to specific examples, the lesson is deductive. Most teachers would agree that the inductive lesson is preferable and embodies the current learning theories just discussed. But, again, the inductive approach often requires more time and creativity on the part of the teacher than does simply giving a definition on the chalkboard. In making instructional decisions, we try to think about what is best for the student, which is not necessarily what is easiest for the teacher. Someone once said that recent reform efforts in mathematics education were not intended "to make teaching easier; they were meant to make learning easier and more meaningful."

Motivation

An activity such as the concept attainment polygon lesson is often enjoyable and memorable for students. Clearly, if the teacher can capture the imagination of the students, the potential for a successful lesson is much greater than if the class appears disinterested with the same old routine. Although psychologists do not have a universal definition of **motivation,** we know that it is an affective attribute that influences the degree to which students want to engage in some activity or choose to become involved. A student who is *motivated* to do a mathematics activity has a desire to do the work, for a variety of reasons. Three interacting components constitute the psychological construct called motivation according to Ford's model (1992)—goal orientations, emotions, and self-confidence.

Individuals are motivated by either ego goals or mastery goals. Students who have primarily **ego goal** orientations do their work to gain favorable judgments from other people. They work for extrinsic rewards, such as grades or teacher approval, and they measure their success according to whether they have outperformed their peers. Suppose that a senior in high school scores 92 percent on a Calculus test and is initially excited by the grade. If a student who has an ego goal orientation discovers that many other students in the class scored above 95 percent, that student's excitement will typically turn to disappointment as a result of a perceived inability to outdo everyone else. On the other hand, students with a **mastery goal** orientation emphasize the intrinsic value of learning and self-improvement. These students value learning for its own sake, and success depends on how much effort they put into a project. If a student with mastery orientation works as hard as possible and learns a great deal from a unit, then a test grade of a C may be as acceptable as a B or an A because it was not the grade that the person sought in the first place. Although the mastery goal orientation is certainly more desirable, students with ego goals are more commonly found in mathematics classrooms.

Although many students enter our classrooms with ego goal orientations, one of our challenges as educators is to help them to develop a mastery goal orientation—to show them that mathematics can be inherently interesting and that they should want to learn. A teacher can do specific things in the classroom to make this happen. For example, if teachers select problems and activities for the classroom that elicit participation and spark debate, students will solve the problems not only because they are required to but because they view the work as worth doing. Another strategy that teachers can use to promote mastery goal orientations is to keep student grades confidential at all times. Posting grades by code number, reading test scores aloud, or in any way comparing grades of students in the classroom feeds ego goals and only reinforces the drive of students to learn so that they can avoid looking stupid in front of their peers. Seemingly innocent teaching techniques, such as board races or writing the class average for a test on the chalkboard, can seriously undermine efforts to get students to be self-motivated. Teachers need to examine what they do in their classrooms and whether their actions promote an intrinsic desire to do mathematics.

A second component of motivation in the classroom is **emotion.** Ford (1992) pointed out that interest and curiosity are two of the important emotions that constitute this component of motivation. We say that a student has *interest* in an academic topic when the individual believes that the study of that topic will be beneficial in some way. Hidi (1990) defined two types of interest—personal and situational. Personal interests are those that we have all the time, such as stamp collecting or watching football. Situational interests, on the other hand, can be evoked by posing a problem or reading a book. You may not have any inherent interest in coins, but you might become interested if you were asked whether the Empire State Building or a stack of one million pennies is higher. Students can become interested in the study of mathematics when teachers identify problems and projects that either appeal to the personal interests of the students or that pose eye-catching puzzles to solve or present problems that students find meaningful. In fact, the constructivist approach emphasizes that students work at their optimal level when presented with tasks that are *meaningful and relevant* because they will choose to expend effort on that which interests them.

Two types of curiosity are addressed in the research literature—cognitive and sensory. Cognitive curiosity results when a student realizes that there is a difference between what was expected and what actually happened. For example, cognitive curiosity may be evoked by posing the birthday problem in Chapter 1, in which the students try to figure out how the teacher was able to determine their birthdate and ask, "How did the teacher know that?" Sensory curiosity can be thought of as inherent curiosity triggered by something in the environment. This is the curiosity we see when a student is handed a set of pattern blocks or a graphing calculator for the first time and wants to play with them and figure out how they work. In a sense, the tools themselves serve as the motivators just as the visual and auditory appeal of a handheld baseball game might entice a person to want to play it. Posing paradoxical problems and using manipulatives and technology can evoke curiosity in the classroom, thus motivating the student to want to work on some problem or activity.

The third component of motivation is **self-confidence** or self-efficacy. This refers to the degree to which students believe that they will be able to succeed at a task or in a class. If a student has been historically unsuccessful in a mathematics class and is posed a problem that is even moderately difficult, that student is likely to think, "I can't do this" and may almost immediately give up. This student believes that the work will be impossible to complete successfully and that the ability to do it is lacking. Research has shown that individuals tend to choose tasks that are neither impossibly difficult nor overly simple—within their comfort zone (Malone and Lepper, 1987; Nicholls, 1984). This point is important for planning instruction in the classroom, as students will appear unmotivated if a task appears easy and a waste of their time, and they may refuse to attempt a task or simply give up if it appears to be too difficult. The teacher's role, then, is to select tasks that challenge and build self-confidence for more difficult concepts later in the semester or school year.

The effective teaching of mathematics, then, depends on appealing to the needs of students in a way that motivates them. Motivating students means helping them to develop a mastery goal orientation, appealing to their interests and curiosity, and building their confidence so that they will be successful in the class. The effective teacher must pay attention to how the child develops and how that student can be motivated to complete the tasks. If a teacher displays enthusiasm and attempts to appeal to the interests and curiosity of the students, then we would also hope that students would develop not only their mathematical content knowledge but also their positive attitudes and beliefs about mathematics. The National Council of Teachers of Mathematics has referred to the affective (feeling) side of mathematics as mathematical **disposition.**

The authors of the Evaluation Standards (NCTM, 1989) stated that "learning mathematics extends beyond learning concepts, procedures, and their applications. It also includes developing a disposition toward mathematics and seeing mathematics as a powerful way for looking at situations. *Disposition* refers not simply to attitudes but to a tendency to act in positive ways" (p. 233). Evaluation Standard 10 challenges teachers to find ways to assess the development of student dispositions. It states:

> The assessment of students' mathematical disposition should seek information about their
>
> - confidence in using mathematics to solve problems, to communicate ideas, and to reason;
> - flexibility in exploring mathematical ideas and trying alternative methods in solving problems;
> - willingness to persevere in mathematical tasks;
> - interest, curiosity, and inventiveness in doing mathematics;
> - inclination to monitor and reflect on their own thinking and performance;
> - valuing of the application of mathematics to situations arising in other disciplines and everyday experiences;
> - appreciation of the role of mathematics in our culture and its value as a tool and as a language (p. 233).

These dispositions develop in students most effectively when teachers model the dispositions. For example, research both in the K–12 arena (Zimmerman and Ringle, 1981; Zimmerman and Blotner, 1979) and at the college level (Brown and Inouye, 1978) has shown that when teachers model persistence in problem solving, their students become more persistent in solving problems as a result. Again, this may be a commonsense issue because we would expect that when teachers frequently use real-life, applied problems, their students will begin to appreciate the usefulness of mathematics. Similarly, teachers who are enthusiastic about the topics they are presenting are likely to instill the same interest in their students. Ask students who "like math" where this feeling came from, and you'll often find that one teacher at one particular grade level got them excited about math, and that excitement impacted their attitudes for the rest of their lives. Unfortunately, the same situation can be and often is true for those who dislike mathematics or even fear it—the math-anxious students.

One semester, one year, or a lifetime of undesirable experiences in mathematics courses can produce what is referred to as **mathematics anxiety.** Although this term is defined differently by various researchers, mathematics anxiety is generally thought of as both a fear of mathematics and a negative attitude toward its study. This fear often exhibits itself as the test-taking anxiety of a student in a mathematics class, but it may also surface as an unwillingness to volunteer answers or function in a learning team in the classroom or a fear of doing so. Research shows that this anxiety is ordinarily the result of low academic performance in mathematics and can be treated, in part, by attempting to change the beliefs of students about the nature of mathematics (Hembree, 1990). When we consider the high incidence of mathematics anxiety in our world, it becomes critical that we, as teachers, not only deliver content but become actively involved in the shaping of attitudes and beliefs—dispositions—toward mathematics in the classroom every day.

■ CONCLUSION ■

The National Council of Teachers of Mathematics publishes the quarterly *Journal for Research in Mathematics Education,* which disseminates the latest research findings for educators to consider when making curricular, teaching, and assessment decisions. Other organizations have similar publications or feature articles that address the need to put research into practice. As mathematics teachers, it is our responsibility to stay current with the latest research and its implications. Just as physicians are expected to attend conferences and update themselves on the current research on prescribing proper medications, a teacher needs to know what classroom strategies are supported by data and attempt to put them into practice. We address the issue of ongoing professional development in Chapter 10.

In this chapter, several current learning theories and their implications in the classroom have been described. Steffe and Cobb (1988) wrote that "the teacher will be far more successful in accommodating children's growth in conceptual understanding if he or she has some notion of what the child's present structures and ways of operating are" (p. viii). Indeed, what we do as teachers on a day-to-day basis will be rooted in what we believe about the way that our students learn. If

we accept the notion that learning is an active process that involves discussion and allowing students to reach their own conclusions, then we will organize our classroom in an inquiry mode that emphasizes cooperative learning and active, hands-on lessons. An administrator who spends even twenty minutes in your classroom should not have to ask you what you believe about mathematics education; it will be evident by virtue of the lesson you teach and the role you assume in the classroom.

It has been said that the teacher who accepts the constructivist theory of teaching and learning is a "guide on the side" rather than a "sage on the stage." But being a guide is not as easy as it sounds. If you look closely at the examples described in this chapter, such as the polygon-definition activity or the inquiry lesson on exponents, you will see that the questions that the teacher asked and the way in which the lessons were organized were key to implementing the lessons. Although the students were actively engaged in the activities, the teacher played a critical role in selecting and organizing the tasks, guiding the process through careful questioning techniques, and assessing student progress along the way. One hope that, as they take part in active lessons that involve the invention or discovery of mathematical concepts, the students will develop a view of mathematics that includes more than its content. They should also come to recognize the important role of problem solving, reasoning, communicating, connecting, and representing mathematics and the notion that mathematics can be thought of as a verb—something one *does*. As their dispositions toward mathematics change, we should also see a decline in the level of mathematics anxiety and an increase in appreciation for the study of mathematics.

In Chapters 3 and 4, we turn our attention to the mathematics curriculum. We examine what topics are studied in secondary and middle school mathematics, how the material is sequenced, and how those decisions are made while keeping in mind that all curricular decisions should be based on research.

■ GLOSSARY ■

Algebra Tiles: Algebra tiles are manipulatives that are used to model variable expressions and equations. A standard set of tiles contains three shapes as shown:

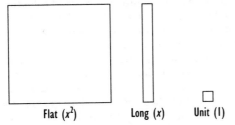

Flat (x^2)   Long (x)   Unit (1)

Most commercially available algebra tiles are a different color on each side: One color represents a positive term, and the other color represents a negative term. Mathematical processes from solving equations to simplifying expressions can be modeled with algebra tiles to enhance visualization skills and to promote conceptual understanding.

Base Ten Blocks: Base ten blocks are manipulatives that are frequently used to model numbers and number relationships. A standard set of blocks contains three shapes as shown:

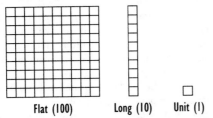

Flat (100)   Long (10)   Unit (1)

Most commercially available base ten blocks have standard measurements: A unit cube measures 1 cm on a side; a long is 10 cm long; and a flat measures 10 cm by 10 cm. Mathematical concepts from place value to decimal operations can be modeled with base ten blocks to enhance visualization skills and to promote conceptual understanding.

Bruner's Stages: Jerome Bruner, an educational theorist, described cognitive development as passing through three stages: enactive, iconic, and symbolic. His theory emphasizes the importance of hands-on, concrete experiences in the early stages of learning a new concept. These experiences provide a foundation upon which more abstract concepts can be built at a later time. He is also recognized for having developed the concept attainment teaching strategy.

Concept Attainment: Concept attainment is a teaching strategy developed by Jerome Bruner. Students inductively create their own definitions as they are presented with a series of "yes" and "no" examples and counterexamples. The teacher's role in the process is to carefully select the examples that will allow students to invent their own definitions and rules. The students must reflect on the common characteristics of elements in a set and make generalizations.

Constructivist Model: The constructivist model is a teaching and learning theory in which educators view students as active participants who construct their own understanding of concepts rather than empty vessels into which someone can transfer knowledge. The teacher in a constructivist classroom places student interests at the center of the curriculum and tends to use cooperative learning strategies and a variety of assessment techniques. The roots of constructivism are found in the research and publications of Jean Piaget.

Curiosity: Curiosity is an emotion and an important mathematical disposition that students usually develop over time. Two types of curiosity are addressed in the literature—cognitive and sensory. Cognitive curiosity results when students realize that there is a difference between what they expected and what actually happened, and sensory curiosity can be thought of as an inherent curiosity that is triggered by something in the environment.

Deductive Teaching: A teacher who uses a deductive teaching strategy tends to provide students with rules or generalizations and expects the students to apply those rules to particular cases. Deduction is a process that moves from the general to the specific. Emphasis is placed on students being able to use a rule in specific cases.

Descriptive Research: Descriptive research is undertaken for the purpose of generating statistics and information for discussion but not necessarily for comparison. Descriptive research efforts do not ordinarily make claims that one method is more effective than another as is the case with experimental research.

Disposition: Disposition refers to the affective (feeling) side of the teaching of mathematics. It is important not only to teach students mathematical concepts but also to promote positive attitudes toward the content area. The National Council of Teachers of Mathematics noted that disposition refers to "a tendency to act in positive ways" (1989, p. 233).

Ego Goal: A student is said to have an ego goal orientation when the individual considers a performance to be successful if it is better than that of the others in the class. The student is generally more interested in earning extrinsic rewards, such as grades or teacher approval, than actually learning the mathematical concepts.

Emotion: An emotion is an affective attribute—a feeling—that is considered one of the elements of motivation. Ford (1992) pointed out that interest and curiosity are two of the important emotions that constitute this component of motivation. A student who is *interested in* or exhibits *curiosity about* a problem or lesson in the mathematics classroom will appear to be motivated to learn.

Experimental Research: Experimental research is undertaken to attempt to prove that one teaching or assessment strategy is more effective than another. Generally, this research effort utilizes a control group that receives no treatment and an experimental group that experiences a unique teaching approach, and a statistical comparison of effectiveness is used to argue in favor of one strategy over another.

Inductive Teaching: A teacher who uses an inductive teaching strategy tends to provide students with many specific examples and expects the students to generalize the examples into broad rules or definitions. Induction is a process of going from the specific to the general. Emphasis is placed on students inventing their own rules and definitions that are consistent with presented examples or counterexamples.

Inquiry Lesson: A teacher employing an inquiry lesson will typically pose a problem to a class and allow students to investigate and explore rather than to provide direct instruction through lecture methods. Students involved in an inquiry lesson ordinarily use induction to generalize patterns and rules that arise while conducting the investigation. Teachers who adhere to the constructivist theory of teaching and learning usually employ inquiry lessons.

Interest: Interest is an emotion associated with motivation and a disposition that develops in students over time. We say that a student has *interest* in an academic topic when the individual believes that the study of that topic will be beneficial in some way. Hidi (1990) defines two types of interest—personal and situational. Personal interests are those that we have all the time, while situational interests can be evoked by, for example, posing a problem or reading a book.

Manipulatives: Manipulatives are hands-on materials used as tools in the mathematics classroom to promote understanding of a concept or to explore a problem. Algebra tiles, base ten blocks, and pattern blocks are examples of mathematics manipulatives. According to the cognitive theory of Jerome Bruner, students should have concrete experiences with manipulatives when they begin to learn new concepts.

Mastery Goal: A student is said to have a mastery goal orientation when the individual places an intrinsic value on learning and self-improvement. For students possessing mastery goals, learning is valued for its own sake, and success depends on how much effort they expend on a project.

Mathematics Anxiety: Mathematics anxiety is both a fear of mathematics and a negative attitude toward its study. This fear often manifests itself as the test-taking anxiety of a student in a mathematics class, but it may also surface as an unwillingness to volunteer answers or function in a learning team in the classroom or a fear of doing so.

Motivation: Motivation can be thought of as an affective attribute that influences the degree to which students want to engage in some activity or choose to become involved. Motivation has three components—goals (ego and mastery), emotions (such as interest and curiosity), and self-confidence (or self-efficacy).

Pattern Blocks: Pattern blocks are manipulatives that are used to model geometric designs and patterns. A standard set of pattern blocks contains six shapes as shown:

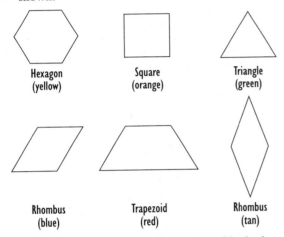

Hexagon (yellow) Square (orange) Triangle (green)

Rhombus (blue) Trapezoid (red) Rhombus (tan)

Most commercially available pattern blocks have standard colors, and the lengths of the sides are all the same, except for the base of the trapezoid that is twice the standard length. Mathematical concepts from fraction skills to angle measurement can be studied through the use of pattern blocks, which enhance visualization skills and promote conceptual understanding.

Qualitative Research: Qualitative research involves the collection and analysis of non-numerical data such as videotapes of classroom episodes, scripts of student-teacher conversations, audio recordings of interviews, or written summaries of student journal entries. Descriptive studies often use qualitative data to paint a picture of a classroom situation or to enhance numerical data with quotes from a student interview.

Quantitative Research: Quantitative research involves the collection and analysis of numerical data, such as test scores or the number of times a person behaves in a particular way. Experimental studies often rely heavily on quantitative data to demonstrate the effectiveness of one teaching strategy over another.

Self-Confidence: Self-confidence or self-efficacy refers to the degree to which students believe that they will be able to succeed at a task or in a class. It is an important component of motivation, because students who perceive an inability to complete a mathematical task may simply give up and appear unmotivated.

Van Hiele Model: The van Hiele model describes the stages a student passes through in learning geometric concepts. The van Hieles—a Dutch couple—theorized that students pass through five levels of development—visualization, analysis, informal deduction, deduction, and rigor. Advancement from one level to the next appears to be heavily dependent upon effective instruction rather than maturity or chronological age.

■ DISCUSSION QUESTIONS ■

1. Obtain several recent articles from the *Journal for Research in Mathematics Education* published by the NCTM. Scan the article abstracts and describe some of the issues that are currently being studied. Does most of the recent research appear to be qualitative or quantitative? Descriptive or experimental?

2. Not all research is necessarily conducted in a formal manner, and a current trend is to view the teacher as a researcher. On a practical level, discuss what kinds of research can be carried out by a teacher in the classroom, including questions the teacher might try to answer and what kind of data could be collected to answer those questions.

3. Obtain a secondary or middle school mathematics textbook. Choose a unit or chapter and review it in light of current learning theory. Does the book, for example, appear to follow Bruner's stages of learning by suggesting an ini-

tial concrete experience? Does the book provide student activities that appear to be inquiry based or constructivist in nature?

4. Describe your own experiences with high school geometry. In light of the van Hiele model, discuss the degree to which your geometry course addressed your needs as a learner.

5. We have all heard the expression that practice makes perfect. Discuss the role of rote practice of skills in the mathematics classroom. Is there a place for the traditional worksheet in a classroom that emphasizes inquiry and an inductive approach to teaching?

6. When a student chooses not to complete required assignments or refuses to pay attention in class, we often hear it said that the student lacks motivation. In light of the three components of motivation described in Chapter 2, identify several possible reasons why the student might be failing to do the necessary work. Discuss some practical strategies that a teacher might use in an attempt to motivate the student.

7. Having chosen mathematics as your teaching field, you probably have a very positive disposition toward the content area. Identify and discuss experiences that you have had over the years that influenced your attitudes and dispositions toward mathematics. What specific strategies can you use in the classroom to improve the dispositions of your mathematics students?

8. Obtain copies of the 1989 *Curriculum and Evaluation Standards for School Mathematics* in hard copy or by visiting <http://www.enc.org> on the Web and read Evaluation Standard 10 on disposition (pp. 233–237). Discuss the various components of a student's disposition and how a teacher can assess the degree to which a student is developing a positive disposition.

9. Conduct some additional research on the topic of mathematics anxiety. Describe some of the factors that cause individuals to become math anxious, and find some research-based suggestions on how to help students counter mathematics anxiety.

■ BIBLIOGRAPHIC REFERENCES AND RESOURCES ■

Albrecht, M., Bennett, D., & Block, S. (Eds.). (1997). *Discovering geometry with the Geometer's Sketchpad*. Berkeley, CA: Key Curriculum.

Ball, D. L. (1990). The mathematical understandings that preservice teachers bring to teacher education. *Elementary School Journal, 90,* 449–466.

Beaton, A. E., Mullis, I. V. S., Martin, M. O., Gonzalez, E. J., Kelly, D. L., & Smith, T. A. (1997). *TIMSS: Mathematics achievement in the middle school years*. Chestnut Hill, MA: Boston College.

Brooks, J. G. & Brooks, M. G. (1997). *Constructivism: An ASCD professional inquiry kit*. Alexandria, VA: Association for Supervision and Curriculum Development.

Brooks, J. G. & Brooks, M. G. (1993). *In search of understanding: The case for constructivist classrooms*. Alexandria, VA: Association for Supervision and Curriculum Development.

Brown, I., Jr. & Inouye, D. K. (1978). Learned helplessness through modeling: The role of perceived similarity in competence. *Journal of Personality and Social Psychology, 36,* 900–908.

Brumfield, C. (1973). Conventional approaches using synthetic Euclidean geometry: In K. B. Hen-

derson (Ed.), *1973 Yearbook of the NCTM: Geometry in the mathematics curriculum* (pp. 95–115). Reston, VA: National Council of Teachers of Mathematics.

Bruner, J. S. (1973). *Beyond the information given*. New York, NY: W. W. Norton.

Bruner, J. S. (1973). *The relevance of education*. New York, NY: W. W. Norton.

Bruner, J. S. (1966). *Toward a theory of instruction*. New York, NY: W. W. Norton.

Bruner, J. S. (1960). *The process of education*. New York, NY: Vintage.

Cai, J. (1995). *JRME Monograph number 7: A cognitive analysis of U.S. and Chinese students' mathematical performance on tasks involving computation, simple problem solving, and complex problem solving*. Reston, VA: National Council of Teachers of Mathematics.

Cobb, P. (1988). The tension between theories of learning and instruction in mathematics education. *Educational Psychologist, 23* (2), 87–103.

Davis, R. B., Maher, C. A., & Noddings, N. (Eds.). (1990). *JRME Monograph number 4: Constructivist views on the teaching and learning of mathe-

matics. Reston, VA: National Council of Teachers of Mathematics.

Fennema, E. & Franke, M. L. (1992). Teachers' knowledge and its impact. In D. Grouws (Ed.), *Handbook of research on mathematics teaching and learning* (pp. 147–164). Reston, VA: National Council of Teachers of Mathematics.

Ferrini-Mundy, J. & Schram, T. (1997). *JRME Monograph number 8: The recognizing and recording reform in mathematics education project: Insights, issues, and implications.* Reston, VA: National Council of Teachers of Mathematics.

Ford, M. E. (1992). *Motivating humans: Goals, emotions, and personal agency beliefs.* Newburg Park, CA: Sage.

Fuys, D., Geddes, D., & Tischler, R. (1988). *JRME Monograph number 3: The van Hiele model of thinking in geometry among adolescents.* Reston, VA: National Council of Teachers of Mathematics.

Grouws, D. A. (Ed.). (1992). *Handbook of research on mathematics teaching and learning.* Reston, VA: National Council of Teachers of Mathematics.

Hembree, R. (1990). The nature, effects, and relief of mathematics anxiety. *Journal for Research in Mathematics Education, 21,* 33–46.

Hidi, S. (1990). Interest and its contribution as a mental resource for learning. *Review of Educational Research, 6,* 549–571.

Linchevski, L. & Kutscher, B. (1998). Tell me with whom you're learning, and I'll tell you how much you've learned: Mixed-ability versus same-ability grouping in mathematics. *Journal for Research in Mathematics Education, 29,* 533–554.

Malone, T. W. & Lepper, M. R. (1987). Making learning fun: A taxonomy of intrinsic motivations for learning. In R. Snow & M. Farr (Eds.), *Aptitude, learning and instruction volume 3: Cognitive and affective process analyses* (pp. 223–253). Hillsdale, NJ: Lawrence Erlbaum.

Miller, L. D. (1992). Teacher benefits from using impromptu writing prompts in algebra classes. *Journal for Research in Mathematics Education, 23* (4), 329–340.

Millroy, W. L. (1992). *JRME Monograph number 5: An ethnographic study of the mathematical ideas of a group of carpenters.* Reston, VA: National Council of Teachers of Mathematics.

National Council of Teachers of Mathematics. (1989). *Curriculum and evaluation standards for school mathematics.* Reston, VA: National Council of Teachers of Mathematics.

National Research Council. (1989). *Everybody counts: A report to the nation on the future of mathematics education.* Washington, DC: National Academy.

Nicholls, J. G. (1984). Achievement motivation: Conceptions of ability, subjective experience, task choice, and performance. *Psychological Review, 91* (3), 328–346.

Rogers, K. B. (1998). Using current research to make 'good' decisions about grouping. *NASSP Bulletin, 82:* 38–46.

Serra, M. (1997). *Discovering geometry: An inductive approach* (2nd ed.). Berkeley, CA: Key Curriculum.

Serra, M. (1994). *Patty paper geometry.* Berkeley, CA: Key Curriculum.

Shaughnessy, J. M. & Burger, W. F. (1985). Spadework prior to deduction in geometry. *Mathematics Teacher, 78,* 419–428.

Skemp, R. R. (1979). *Intelligence, learning, and action: A foundation for theory and practice in education.* New York, NY: Wiley.

Skemp, R. R. (1971). *The psychology of learning mathematics.* Middlesex, England: Pelican.

Slavin, R. E., Madden, N. A., Karweit, N. L., Livermon, B. J., & Donaln, L. (1990). Success for all: First-year outcomes of a comprehensive plan for reforming urban education. *American Educational Research Journal, 27,* 255–278.

Steffe, L. P. & Cobb, P. (1988). *Construction of arithmetical meanings and strategies.* New York, NY: Springer-Verlag.

Stiggins, R. J. (1988). Revitalizing classroom assessment: The highest instructional priority. *Phi Delta Kappan, 69,* 363–372.

Teppo, A. R. (1998). *JRME Monograph number 9: Qualitative research methods in mathematics education.* Reston, VA: National Council of Teachers of Mathematics.

Tymoczko, Thomas. (Ed.). (1998). *New directions in the philosophy of mathematics: An anthology.* Princeton, NJ: Princeton.

Whitman, B. S. (1976). Intuitive equation solving skills and the effects on them of formal techniques of equation solving (Doctoral dissertation, Florida State University, 1975). *Dissertation Abstracts International, 36,* 5180A. (University Microfilms No. 76–2720)

Zimmerman, B. J. & Blotner, R. (1979). Effects of model persistence and success on children's problem solving. *Journal of Educational Psychology, 71*, 508–513.

Zimmerman, B. J. & Ringle, J. (1981). Effects of model persistence and statements of confidence on children's self-efficacy and problem solving. *Journal of Educational Psychology, 73*, 485–493.

The Mathematics Curriculum

Decisions about the mathematical content of K–12 courses—the curriculum—are not easy to make. Indeed, it is difficult, if not impossible, to reach universal agreement on the mathematics that every student should learn. If 10 people sit at a table and each makes a list of the most important mathematical concepts for, say, a seventh grader to master, you can expect inconsistencies in the lists because different people believe that different skills and processes are more critical. Fortunately, curricular models exist at the national level and, generally, at the state and local levels as well. These models provide direction for curriculum planners and classroom teachers. In Unit II, we explore the issue of content selection and what it is important for all students to know and be able to do. Chapter 3 describes the role of national and state models and addresses different approaches to designing the curriculum. Chapter 4 focuses on curriculum at the local level—how goals and objectives for school districts are designed and implemented by teachers.

Curricular Models

After reading Chapter 3, you should be able to answer the following questions:

- What are the NCTM curriculum Standards of 1989 and 2000? Why and how were they developed?

- What are the similarities and differences between a state curricular model and a set of national Standards?

- Why is it becoming increasingly important for *all* students to have a significant mathematical background?

- What is the core curriculum concept, and what are the models that schools may follow to achieve this?

- What are the advantages and disadvantages of the traditional versus an integrated sequencing of mathematical content?

Take a piece of paper and write down 10 things that you believe every student should know after completion of a Pre-K–12 mathematics program. Keep in mind that, because your list can only contain 10 items, you need to focus in on the skills and concepts that you believe are critical for success in life beyond high school (which may or may not include college). Then, ask a friend to do the same and compare your lists. Although you may agree on simple issues, such as the need to be able to add and subtract, you will probably put several items on your list that are not on your friend's and vice versa. For example, does your list include the Pythagorean Theorem or the use of right-triangle trigonometry? Is it important that every person be able to use a ruler to accurately measure the length of an object? Should every student become proficient with using a calculator for problem solving, or should all critical outcomes require only the use of a pencil and a piece of paper?

Some people argue that it is important to learn to factor trinomials in algebra, but others believe this skill is a waste of time more efficiently done by a hand-held computer. Some believe that every student should be well grounded in topics from the area of discrete mathematics, but others contend that a comprehensive exploration of calculus (a study of continuous functions) is more important. As you travel from district to district and state to state, you may find that what people consider to be significant content varies greatly. Some countries, such as Russia and Japan, have a national curriculum with a set list of topics that every child must master in mathematics; this is not the case in the United States. The authority to write curricula, by virtue of the U.S. Constitution, is delegated to the states. Therefore, each state and, sometimes, each school district within that state, is free to determine its own curriculum, which means that each state has the power to draw up its own list of critical objectives that every student should master in a Pre-K–12 mathematics program.

■ NCTM CURRICULUM STANDARDS

Recognizing the differences in curricula from state to state and the need for the reform of mathematics education programs, the NCTM initiated a process of developing national Standards for mathematics curriculum. A standard is a benchmark against which a state or local school district's curriculum can be compared to determine the degree to which the curriculum addresses nationally recognized critical outcomes. The first Standards-writing process began in the mid-1980s with a writing team drafting a document that was scrutinized and eventually endorsed by thousands of educators, business leaders, and other professionals and organizations throughout the United States. In 1989, the NCTM *Curriculum and Evaluation Standards* were published, and they served as the driving force behind curricular reform at the national, state, and local level for over ten years. In 1998, the NCTM updated and refined the document into a new working draft to continue the reform efforts. The final document, *Principles and Standards for School Mathematics,* with a spring 2000 release date, is designed to be consistent with the efforts of the previous Standards documents.

In the 1989 *Curriculum and Evaluation Standards,* the NCTM recognized that our society was shifting from an industrial age to an information age—driven by computers, calculators, and a host of other technology. In the information age, there are four goals for our educational system that the traditional curriculum has not adequately addressed. First, there is a need for a *mathematically literate workforce.* The assembly line, on which the role of each worker is to place a bolt in a hole, has all but disappeared and been replaced by a workplace that requires an understanding of computers and an ability to problem solve when a system breaks down. Studies such as that conducted by the Bell Laboratory (Pollack, 1987) have shown that, above all else, businesses need employees who can solve problems.

MATHEMATICAL EXPECTATIONS OF EMPLOYEES IN INDUSTRY

- The ability to set up problems with the appropriate operations
- Knowledge of a variety of techniques to approach and work on problems
- Understanding of the underlying mathematical features of a problem
- The ability to work with others on problems
- The ability to see the applicability of mathematical ideas to common and complex problems
- Preparation for open problem situations, since most real problems are not well formulated

(NCTM, *Curriculum and Evaluation Standards,* 1989.)

The second societal goal is *lifelong learning* for the workforce. In our rapidly changing society, employees frequently undergo additional schooling and training. Businesses consolidate or refocus their direction, and workers must adapt to the changes and learn new skills. The days in which a person would take a job, work the job for 30 years, and then retire are all but gone, so one needs to prepare for a lifetime of education. The third goal is an *opportunity for all*. Historically, the white male has been most successful in school mathematics. With the significant rise in minority populations comes the social responsibility to prepare all children—minorities and females equally included—to be successful in this changing world. The final goal is the need for an *informed electorate*. It has long been the goal of education to prepare citizens to make reasoned choices and contribute effectively to the democracy. Decision making in a complex world requires the consideration of a vast amount of data and the ability to construct logical arguments with supporting data.

Thirteen years of mathematics worksheets containing isolated skill-based practice such as fraction addition, denominator rationalizing, two-column proofs, and distance = rate × time problems are simply not sufficient to meet the goals identified by the NCTM. Consequently, the NCTM set five general mathematical goals for all students to help to achieve the four overarching societal goals for all of education: (1) learning to value mathematics, (2) becoming confident in one's own ability, (3) becoming a mathematical problem solver, (4) learning to communicate mathematically, and (5) learning to reason mathematically (NCTM, 1989, pp. 5–6).

SOCIETAL GOALS FOR ALL OF EDUCATION

- Mathematically literate workers
- Lifelong learning
- Opportunity for all
- Informed electorate

(NCTM, *Curriculum and Evaluation Standards*, 1989.)

MATHEMATICAL GOALS FOR ALL STUDENTS

- Learning to value mathematics
- Becoming confident in one's own ability
- Becoming a mathematical problem solver
- Learning to communicate mathematically
- Learning to reason mathematically

(NCTM, *Curriculum and Evaluation Standards*, 1989.)

We can see that the first two of these goals—learning the value of mathematics and developing confidence—are dispositions toward mathematics as discussed in Chapter 2. The other three goals—problem solving, communication, and reasoning—are mathematical process skills that were discussed at length (along with representation) in Chapter 1. In these goals, we can see an emphasis on developing students' ability to think and problem solve—what we have previously described as the capacity to do mathematics—as well as to nurture positive beliefs about the nature and usefulness of mathematics. With these goals in mind, the writing committee, with input from thousands of reviewers, took two years to draft 13 curriculum Standards for Grades 5–8 and 14 curriculum Standards for Grades 9–12 (as well as 13 curriculum Standards for Grades K–4, which are beyond the scope of this book). Subsequently, a set of 10 curriculum Standards for grades Pre-Kindergarten through 12 was released in *Principles and Standards for School Mathematics.*

For the first time in U.S. history, a national organization had developed a list of recommended curricular topics with a broad base of support from within and outside of the group. It is important to remember that these Standards were not written as *mandatory* curricular benchmarks but as a list of recommendations for states and school districts to voluntarily use as a basis for determining student outcomes at each grade level. As such, it was assumed that not every state or district would necessarily adopt every detail of the Standards but that at least a framework with a solid research base would be available for deliberation and decision-making processes. However, in the years that followed, virtually every state adopted a model curriculum that aligned with the Standards (we will discuss state models later in the chapter), and other professional organizations, such as the National Science Teachers' Association, began to write their own sets of Standards with the NCTM process as their model.

Table 3–1 lists the 1989 curriculum Standards for Grades 5–8, and Table 3–2 lists the Standards for Grades 9–12. Notice that the first four Standards—problem solving, communication, reasoning, and connections—are the same for both grade clusters, as we discussed in Chapter 1. These are often referred to as the **process Standards;** whereas, the 9 or 10 Standards that follow them in each cluster are the **content Standards,** a list of recommended areas of mathematical content to be addressed at each grade level within that cluster. The authors of the 1989 *Curriculum and Evaluation Standards for School Mathematics* noted that these topics were not intended to be course titles, per se, but rather a list of content areas that could be addressed each year that a child is in that grade cluster.

Table 3–1 1989 NCTM Curriculum Standards for Grades 5–8

Standard Number	Standard Topic	
Standard 1:	Mathematics as Problem Solving	
Standard 2:	Mathematics as Communication	
Standard 3:	Mathematics as Reasoning	
Standard 4:	Mathematical Connections	
Standard 5:	Number and Number Relationships	
Standard 6:	Number Systems and Number Theory	
Standard 7:	Computation and Estimation	
Standard 8:	Patterns and Functions	
Standard 9:	Algebra	
Standard 10:	Statistics	
Standard 11:	Probability	
Standard 12:	Geometry	
Standard 13:	Measurement	

Table 3–2 1989 NCTM Curriculum Standards for Grades 9–12

Standard Number	Standard Topic
Standard 1:	Mathematics as Problem Solving
Standard 2:	Mathematics as Communication
Standard 3:	Mathematics as Reasoning
Standard 4:	Mathematical Connections
Standard 5:	Algebra
Standard 6:	Functions
Standard 7:	Geometry from a Synthetic Perspective
Standard 8:	Geometry from an Algebraic Perspective
Standard 9:	Trigonometry
Standard 10:	Statistics
Standard 11:	Probability
Standard 12:	Discrete Mathematics
Standard 13:	Conceptual Underpinnings of Calculus
Standard 14:	Mathematical Structure

In the revised version of the *Standards—Principles and Standards for School Mathematics*—the curriculum Standards for all grade levels were refined into 10 more succinct Standards, making it easier for the reader to observe how content and processes are intended to be developed over a fourteen-year span of time in a child's life. The 10 curriculum Standards from the 1998 *Principles and Standards for School Mathematics* are listed in Table 3–3.

Table 3–3 2000 NCTM Curriculum Standards for Grades Pre-K–12

Standard Number	Standard Topic
Standard 1:	Number and Operation
Standard 2:	Patterns, Functions, and Algebra
Standard 3:	Geometry and Spatial Sense
Standard 4:	Measurement
Standard 5:	Data Analysis, Statistics, and Probability
Standard 6:	Problem Solving
Standard 7:	Reasoning and Proof
Standard 8:	Communication
Standard 9:	Connections
Standard 10:	Representation

In the revised *Standards*, the mathematics curriculum is still defined in terms of content and processes. Standards 1 through 5 focus on content issues, and Standards 6 through 10 encompass the mathematical processes discussed in Chapter 1. Notice that a process of representation emerged in the revised version even though it was not included in the 1989 *Curriculum and Evaluation Standards*. Also, although the 1989 *Curriculum and Evaluation Standards* were designed for grade clusters of K–4, 5–8, and 9–12, the *Principles and Standards for School Mathematics* are more carefully aligned to the developmental needs of students and are clustered for grades Pre-K–2, 3–5, 6–8, and 9–12.

Appendix A includes a complete reprint of Standard 2 for Grades 6–8 on Patterns, Functions, and Algebra and Standard 3 for Grades 9–12 on Geometry and Spatial Sense, taken from *Principles and Standards for School Mathematics* (1998). The 1989 NCTM *Curriculum and Evaluation Standards* can be accessed on the World Wide Web at the Eisenhower National Clearinghouse site at <www.enc.org> by following links to Standards and Frameworks. Updates and information on the updated Standards can be accessed through the website of the National Council of Teachers of Mathematics at <www.nctm.org>.

The content and process Standards for each grade cluster in both documents not only outline mathematical topics for student exploration but also illustrate the major concepts through classroom vignettes and examples that have a constructivist, student-centered approach at their core. Therefore, the documents not only provide direction on mathematical topics but also include insights on how to present these topics in a manner that would be meaningful and relevant to students. The Standards also present a major challenge to curriculum planners who have historically offered algebra or geometry courses primarily to the more advanced students, leaving only general mathematics courses for the non-college-bound population. The Standards essentially assert that *every* student needs to explore topics from algebra, geometry, discrete mathematics, probability, and so forth, regardless of academic ability, gender, or culture. The notion of "math for all students" is very difficult for many educators to accept or put into practice. Yet, this has always been the challenge of the teacher, even back in the days of the one-room schoolhouse—to select activities that address the needs of all of the learners in the classroom while maintaining the basic belief that all students are capable of achieving.

■ STATE MODELS

The NCTM *Curriculum and Evaluation Standards* present an achievable philosophy of mathematics education, given the school's resources and willingness to support the programs. As such, they are characterized by broad, theoretical statements of what students should be able to achieve in each grade-level cluster. However, what the *Standards* do not do is to prescribe *exactly* what a student should know or be able to do *at each grade level*. This task is left up to each state or district that chooses to use the *Standards* as their overarching model. Essentially, if a state chooses to embrace the vision of the *Standards,* then its task is to write a grade-by-grade, sequenced curricular model that provides districts within the state with a more specific design for each grade level.

When reading a state model rooted in the *Standards,* one should be able to recognize the spirit and intent of the national view, despite the need to be more specific about objectives for each grade level. For example, Standard 3 on Geometry and Spatial Sense for Grades 9–12 in the 1998 *Standards* document states that "all students should connect geometry to other strands of mathematics (e.g, . . . trigonometry), relate it to other areas of interest (e.g., art, architecture), and use it to solve problems" (NCTM, 1998, p. 291). A state model based on the *Standards* might take this statement further by specifying that, in Grade 11, students "will be able to use the right triangle relationships, the Law of Sines, and the Law of Cosines to solve real-life problems." In this respect, the strategies that the students are to develop are clearly delineated and attached to a particular grade level. State models are created to provide curricular direction to the local districts, so they tend to be much more specific about content and grade levels than do the Standards documents.

In some states, there is a statewide curriculum or course of study that is intended to be followed by every district in that state. In others, the State Department of Education provides a model to follow, and each district or county within that state is responsible for drafting its own curriculum for local implementation. Objectives for these models and local courses of study are generally grouped together in logical content categories or **strands,** such as patterns and algebra, number sense, geometry and measurement, and probability and statistics and may also include strands emphasizing the mathematical processes. Examples of state curricular models are readily available on the Internet and in libraries. For example, the Eisenhower National Clearinghouse website displays numerous state-level frameworks and models from around the United States. The Data Analysis and Probability content strand from one state for grades K–12 is reprinted in Appendix A as an example of how specific objectives are outlined for each grade level to ensure the long-term development of important concepts. States that have some type of competency or proficiency testing program, then, draw the objectives for these assessments from their state models. The issue of assessment and its implications are discussed in more detail in Chapters 8 and 9.

Ultimately, as a state develops a model curriculum, the important mathematical concepts to be mastered by all students must be identified. At the high school level, prescribing a curriculum can be particularly difficult because historically a number of "tracks" of mathematics study have been made available, depending on student interests, future needs, and ability. In the next section, we explore the issues surrounding establishment of a common core curriculum for all students.

■ THE CORE CURRICULUM

Suppose that two students each decided to take four units of high school mathematics courses and followed the sequence shown in Table 3–4:

Table 3–4 Possible Curricular Sequences for Secondary Students

	College Bound	Non-College Bound
Grade 9	Algebra One	General Mathematics
Grade 10	Geometry	Applied General Math
Grade 11	Algebra Two	Technical/Vocational Math
Grade 12	Pre-Calculus	Pre-Algebra

Upon graduation, each student's transcript would indicate that he or she had taken four years of mathematics. But how do you believe they would compare if given a standard achievement test or an SAT or ACT exam? Are their mathematics backgrounds equivalent? Clearly not. The college-bound students have a distinct advantage in having studied a more diverse and higher-level set of concepts than other students. Yet, this sequence and all of its inequities were very common in schools around the country even into the late 1980s; in fact, in some places, they still exist. Interestingly, in the 1970 NCTM *Yearbook,* the authors, speaking of changes in mathematics between 1920 and 1945, stated that it became an "increasingly common requirement that everyone take at least one year of mathematics in grades 9–12" and that "this new general mathematics [course] developed as the most popular alternative to algebra in the ninth grade. Down to the present day this course has been ill-defined and often poorly, or at least unwillingly, taught" (Jones & Coxford, 1970, p. 53). The General Mathematics course, indeed, still exists today—some 75 years later! The Standards documents, however, challenged us to reconsider what mathematical topics were being developed with whom and to think of ways to make mathematics accessible to all students as we have discussed. But why is this so important? Why not keep the curriculum the way it has always been?

As the world has moved into the information age, physical skills have been replaced by technical and problem-solving skills, and the workforce continues to require updating as industry changes. The average worker will change jobs at least four or five times over a 25-year period (NCTM, 1989), and most experts agree that a job stays the same for only about five years, so a need for retraining is inevitable (Meiring et al., 1992). The National Research Council (1989) reported that 75% of all available jobs require at least a basic understanding of algebra and geometry. And the need for students to be exposed to discrete mathematics topics, such as recursion and graph theory, is rapidly increasing due to the growth of the computer industry and the relevance of discrete mathematics in industry (Dossey, 1991). It is unrealistic to believe that one segment of the population needs algebra "and beyond," and another segment will never need more than basic arithmetic; this simply does not appear to be the case anymore.

Consequently, the NCTM has strongly encouraged schools to establish a core curriculum—a three-year high school sequence with common objectives or outcomes—for *all* students. This notion is discussed at length in one of the Standards addenda books entitled *A Core Curriculum: Making Mathematics Count for Everyone* (Meiring et al., 1992). The authors make the case for developing a curricular model that would ensure that every secondary student has exposure to important mathematical topics that extend well beyond arithmetic. They suggest that the college-bound and higher-achieving students will visit many concepts in greater depth than some of their peers but that at least the curriculum would ensure equal access to various areas of mathematics for all students. Meiring et al. suggest three possible models for schools to consider in restructuring their curriculum: the crossover, enrichment, and differentiated curriculum models.

The crossover model is probably the easiest to adopt if the school is currently on a very traditional tracking system. Two parallel tracks are established, one for college-bound students and one for students not planning to go to college. There is a three-year sequence of courses with basically identical content objectives in both tracks. However, although the college-bound students may visit the topics at an advanced level with plenty of abstraction, including the exploration of some optional topics, the student not planning to attend college will explore these concepts at a more concrete level with, perhaps, an increased emphasis on the use of technology. This is the "crossover" model because if a student decides, after a year or two of high school, to go to college after all but has not been in the college-bound track, that student can still switch to the other sequence and know that classmates have explored essentially the same objectives. Compare this situation to more traditional models in which the student in a low-average mathematics class visits less material in a watered-down fashion, making it virtually impossible for that student to ever get out of a low track. The minute a teacher, parent, counselor, or administrator labels the student as below average, the door is shut on the student's chances for exposure to significant mathematics. In traditional basic math courses, often reserved for low-achieving students, the classes do no more than review elementary and middle school arithmetic. Also, in the crossover model, the student who is not successful on the college track can switch to the other without a loss of continuity. Finally, the model suggests a fourth-year advanced course for college-bound students. Figure 3–1 illustrates this with a simple flow chart.

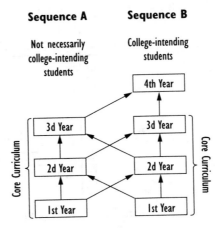

Figure 3–1 The Crossover Model
(Meiring et al., 1992. Reprinted with permission.)

Let's suppose, for example, that a freshman mathematics class had an objective involving the multiplication of polynomials. The students not planning to attend college might begin with a concrete experience involving algebra tiles. An analogy could be expressed as follows: *Think of what it means to multiply 12 × 13*. Geometrically, this multiplication problem can be expressed as the process of finding the area of a rectangle measuring 12 by 13. The tens and units pieces have been separated for emphasis in Figure 3–2.

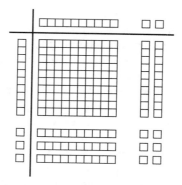

Figure 3–2 Area Model of 12 × 13

Think of the traditional algorithm. Four multiplications take place: 10 × 10, 10 × 2, 3 × 10, and 3 × 2. The diagram shows one flat that represents 100, 5 longs that represent 50, and 6 units, modeling the product of 156. Using base ten blocks, a child can visualize what it means to multiply. Similarly, the secondary class might consider $(x + 2)(x + 3)$. This problem is nothing more than a generalization of 12 × 13, where $x = 10$. So, with algebra tiles, as described in Chapter 2, the polynomial multiplication would look like the diagram in Figure 3–3.

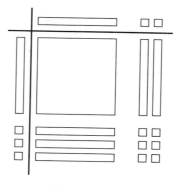

Figure 3–3 Area Model of $(x + 3)(x + 2)$

The area of the rectangle is made up of one x^2 tile, five x tiles, and six unit tiles, so the product would be $x^2 + 5x + 6$. Students can work through several examples of polynomial multiplication problems like this, involving positive and negative numbers, without having to memorize a rule of any kind. Actually, every student should be exposed to this visual model, because many leave high school knowing "how to FOIL" without realizing that FOIL (First, Outside, Inside, Last) has no mathematical meaning beyond serving as a mnemonic for remembering an algorithm and without being able to explain *why* the problem is done that way. Eventually, the non-college-bound students will be able to move on to an iconic level, according to Bruner, and sketch free-hand pictures of tiles that represent polynomial multiplication problems. Finally, the student will learn the procedure without using concrete materials or drawing pictures. But the series of lessons that develop the abstract symbol manipulations are appropriate to the students and allow them to generalize their own rules, based on observations, which is at the core of the constructivist model for learning and teaching, as described in Chapter 2. They might also try their hand at writing a function that describes the orange-grove problem from Chapter 1 to see an application of binomial multiplication.

In the college-bound track, the students will explore the same concept but may be ready to move from concrete to abstract levels within a couple of days, thus leaving them additional time to explore extensions of the concept, such as how to develop a rule for multiplying and factoring the difference of squares or perfect cubes. They may also begin solving higher-level applied problems such as those that involve maximizing volume. Perhaps you have solved the problem in which you are given an $8\frac{1}{2}$" × 11" sheet of paper and asked how big should the four squares you cut off from the corners be in order to maximize the volume of the resulting open-top box formed when the sides are folded up. Figure 3–4 helps you to visualize this.

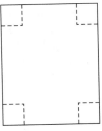

Figure 3–4 Making a Box from an $8\frac{1}{2}$" × 11" Sheet of Paper

If the original dimensions of the paper were $8\frac{1}{2}$" × 11," and the squares cut out measure $x \times x$, then the volume of the resulting box could be found by examining the function $y = x(11 - 2x)(8.5 - 2x)$, where x represents the height of the box, and the expressions $(11 - 2x)$ and $(8.5 - 2x)$ represent the length and the width of the base, respectively. Students can readily view the function's graph (Figure 3–5) on a graphing calculator.

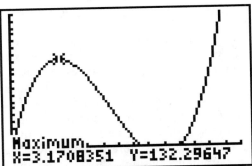

Figure 3–5 Finding the Maximum Volume with a Graphing Calculator

By tracing the curve using the TRACE function or using the CALC (calculate) button, they can locate the local maximum of the function at about $x = 1.59$ and calculate the volume by taking $1.59(11 - 3.18)(8.5 - 3.18) \approx 66.15$ cubic inches. This entire problem represents a rich, realistic application of polynomial multiplication that would engage the college-bound classes and extend their understanding of the use of variables for generalizing and solving problems. But again, in the crossover model all students still visit the same major core objectives.

A second curricular alternative suggested in *A Core Curriculum* is called the enrichment curriculum model. Under this model, students are arranged into small groups at the beginning of each unit throughout the three-year common core. If a group completes the core content of a particular unit before the rest of the class, it can be assigned an enrichment topic to explore. These enrichment topics may include historical considerations of the content, such as the history of π, further exploration of a concept, such as studying fractals in a unit on area and perimeter, or looking at new situations, such as an application of a mathematical concept to a career area. In this way, all students are assured of a common core of mathematical concepts, but students who are more able have the opportunity to expand their knowledge even further. The enrichment model, like the crossover model, provides a common three-year core. But these models differ in that classes are heterogeneously (mixed) grouped in the enrichment model, with small groups formed within class, whereas students choose one of two tracks in the crossover model. Figure 3–6 provides a visual description of the enrichment model.

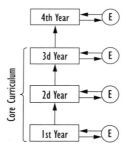

Figure 3–6 The Enrichment Model
(Meiring et al., 1992. Reprinted with permission.)

The third curricular sequence suggested by the NCTM is the differentiated model. As in the enrichment model, students are heterogeneously mixed into a common three-year core of mathematics courses, with a possible common fourth-year experience as well. Within each class, students are organized into small groups at the beginning of each unit. However, instead of all students completing a core of objectives and some moving on to additional topics, all students explore the same topics but at a variety of levels as was described in the crossover model. So, there might be one group of students working on multiplying polynomials with algebra tiles while another group is devising a short cut for finding the square of a binomial in a more abstract manner. Both groups would be learning to multiply polynomials, but the content would be at a level appropriate to each particular group. Figure 3–7 illustrates how all students explore the same core of objectives but at a different level of depth in the differentiated model.

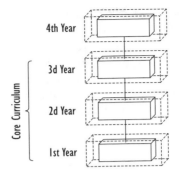

Figure 3–7 The Differentiated Model
(Meiring et al., 1992. Reprinted with permission.)

The differentiated model organizes classes in a heterogeneous manner like the enrichment model but structures the work of each group by depth of coverage as the crossover model does.

Common to all three models, however, is the notion that every student deserves to explore a common core of objectives regardless of perceived ability level or future plans. Lessons should be rich in the use of hands-on materials (manipulatives) and technology and are taught with the students' needs in mind. The idea of a core curriculum for all, however, can be difficult to implement because it requires a radical change from the curriculum of the past—the idea that the "best" students get algebra, geometry, and pre-calculus, and the less-able students take basic math and, perhaps,

Cooperative learning strategies are used to promote interaction among students.

a pre-algebra or algebra course. In a core curriculum, algebra, geometry, and discrete mathematics topics are given equal weight, so the secondary and middle school curriculum should provide experiences in all of the content areas. In order for a wide array of mathematical topics to make sense to students and to appear to be connected, many schools have dropped the traditional Algebra I-Geometry-Algebra II sequence and replaced it with an integrated high school mathematics program. The next section explores the traditional and integrated curricular sequences.

■ TRADITIONAL VERSUS INTEGRATED SEQUENCES

If you peruse the table of contents of a fairly traditional Algebra I textbook, you will usually find a couple of sections near the end of the book that address the Pythagorean Theorem and then introduce the distance formula based on that theorem. Generally, the section on the Pythagorean Theorem exists only to set up a proof to justify why the distance formula works. However, as we know, there are many interesting spin-offs to a discussion of triangles and the lengths of their sides. For example, students can draw pictures of obtuse triangles, measure the sides, and try to apply the Pythagorean Theorem, only to discover that $c^2 > a^2 + b^2$ and possibly conjecture that the reverse is true for acute triangles. Using computer software, such as Geometer's Sketchpad or Cabri Geometry on a hand-held computer, the student can further explore these relationships and generate corollaries to the Pythagorean Theorem. It is important to note that some calculators have large viewing screens and are able to sketch graphs of functions and be programmed; they are generally referred to as *graphing calculators*. However, other hand-held technology allows students not only to sketch curves and write programs but also to perform symbolic manipulations (such as solving equations or simplifying expressions), and it contains built-in software (such as interactive geometry software); these machines are ordinarily called *hand-held computers*.

In Figure 3–8, the student is using a TI-92 hand-held computer to compare the square of the length of the longest side of an obtuse triangle to the sum of the squares of the lengths of the shorter sides.

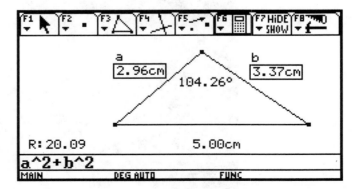

Figure 3–8 Exploring Triangle Relationships on a TI-92 Hand-Held Computer

When the student realizes that the sum of the squares—20.09—is less than the square of the length of the longest side (25), a conjecture or hypothesis can be made about the lengths of sides in obtuse triangles and the way to determine whether a triangle is obtuse when given the lengths of its three sides.

Furthermore, because algebra is, in part, a study of patterns, students often enjoy exploring Pythagorean Triples and searching for number patterns in the context of an algebra course. Take a look at this ordered list of triples:

3, 4, 5

5, 12, 13

7, 24, 25

Each list of numbers is referred to as a Pythagorean Triple because the sum of the squares of the legs equals the square of the hypotenuse or longest side (e.g., $3^2 + 4^2 = 5^2$), and all of the lengths are integers. Can you predict the fourth triple in the sequence? Take a few minutes to do this before reading ahead. How did you find the next triple, and what patterns did you notice? You might have noticed that the shortest leg is always an odd number, that the longest leg and the hypotenuse always differ by 1, and that you can find rules for generating triples, such as noticing that the 12 of 5–12–13 comes from adding the 3 and 4 on the first triple to the 5 of the second triple. Similarly, the 24 of the third triple comes from adding 5 and 12 of the previous to the 7 of that triple. Some other discoveries actually made by students in a ninth grade mathematics course are the following:

Sarah: I looked at the triple 3–4–5 and took the first number, 3. If you add 1, then divide by 2, and then subtract 1, you get 1, which, when you multiply it by the (3 + 1), gives you the second number of the triple. In other words,

3 + 1 = 4

4 ÷ 2 = 2

2 – 1 = 1, and

1 × 4 = 4

The last number of the triple is one more, so it would be 5. For the next triple, I know that it starts with the next odd number after 3, which is 5. Using the same process:

5 + 1 = 6

6 ÷ 2 = 3

3 – 1 = 2, and

2 × (5 + 1) = 2 × 6 = 12

The last number is one more than the middle number, so the triple would be 5–12–13.

Klaus: I noticed that the first numbers of the triples are consecutive odd numbers. If you take the length of the shortest leg, add 1, and multiply that sum by the number of the triple, it gives you the length of the longest leg. Then, the hypotenuse is always one more unit longer than the leg. So,

Triple 1: 3–4–5 because $(3 + 1) \times 1 = 4$

Triple 2: 5–12–13 because $(5 + 1) \times 2 = 12$

Triple 3: 7–24–25 because $(7 + 1) \times 3 = 24$

Jessica: Earlier in the year, we learned about **triangular numbers** and how they follow the sequence of 1, 3, 6, 10, 15, and so on. I noticed that if you multiply 4 times each consecutive triangular number, you always get the length of the longest leg in the next triple. Then, the hypotenuse is 1 more than that. The first number is always the next largest odd number, based on the previous triple. So,

Triple 1: 3–4–5. Then, $4 \times 3 = 12$ tells us that the next triple is 5–12–13.

Triple 2: 5–12–13. Then $4 \times 6 = 24$ tells us that the next triple is 7–24–25.

Triple 3: 7–24–25. Then $4 \times 10 = 40$ tells us that the next triple is 9–40–41.

Notice how these students made use of prior knowledge, such as triangular numbers, and their ability to identify and extend patterns to solve a rich problem. Many of the issues surrounding acute and obtuse triangles, as well as Pythagorean Triples, are typically found in a high school Geometry course. However, the context for discussing these topics may be more appropriate when the Pythagorean Theorem is first introduced and, in a sense, it may not be educationally sound to make the student wait until that chapter in the following course before making some of those connections. In fact, some schools place the Algebra II course immediately after Algebra I, and these students may explore the Pythagorean Theorem while learning the distance formula in Algebra I and not even encounter Pythagorean Triples or acute or obtuse triangles again for at least two more years!

Similarly, students in a high school Geometry course ordinarily study reflections, rotations, and translations. And although the topic of matrices is often deferred until Algebra II or a Discrete Mathematics course (if brought up at all), the geometry student is in a position to discover that you can represent the coordinates of the vertices of a triangle, such as $\triangle ABC$ with the coordinates (3, 7), (5, –1), and (–2, 4), by a matrix:

$$A = \begin{bmatrix} 3 & 5 & -2 \\ 7 & -1 & 4 \end{bmatrix}$$

If matrix **A** is added to the matrix **B**, the result is a matrix whose entries represent a triangle that is translated 2 units to the right on the x-axis, as shown in Figure 3–9.

$$B = \begin{bmatrix} 2 & 2 & 2 \\ 0 & 0 & 0 \end{bmatrix}$$

Similarly, multiplying matrix **C** by matrix **A** results in a matrix representing another new triangle, $\triangle A''B''C''$.

$$C = \begin{bmatrix} 0 & 1 \\ -1 & 0 \end{bmatrix}, \text{ so } C \times A = \begin{bmatrix} 7 & -1 & 4 \\ -3 & -5 & 2 \end{bmatrix}$$

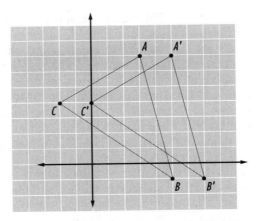

Figure 3–9 Matrix Addition Translating △ABC 2 Units to the Right

If you draw a ray from the origin through point A in Figure 3–10 and another ray from the origin through point A″, you will find that the rays form a 90° angle. The same relationship is true for the other two points of the triangles as well. Therefore, multiplication by matrix C results in a clockwise rotation of 90°.

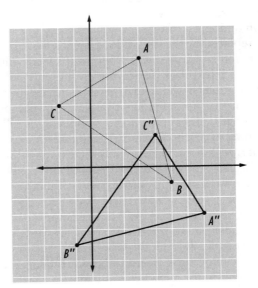

Figure 3–10 Matrix Multiplication Rotating △ABC Clockwise 90°

With the aid of a graphing calculator, matrix operations can be done quickly and accurately and allow students to discover how adding or multiplying matrices can affect a geometric shape. Yet, students rarely, if ever, make this interesting and natural connection in traditional mathematics course sequences.

The topical areas of algebra, geometry, discrete mathematics, and so forth, are merely content organizers that were never intended to build walls between those areas of study. Virtually any algebra problem can be represented geometrically, and geometry problems can be represented by algebraic expressions or equations. For example, we used algebra tiles to create a geometric representation of similar terms in Chapter 2 and to relate area to polynomial multiplication in this chapter. Furthermore, although the study of combinatorics is a typical discrete mathematics topic, the patterns generated when studying combinations and permutations can lead to the generation of some interesting algebraic formulas and graphs. Yet topics such as probability and combinatorics have been historically absent from most secondary and middle school curricula. The NCTM Standards documents not only call for a robust set of concepts to be taught in the Pre-K–12 mathematics program, but they also encourage the exploration of connections along the way. In an attempt to make connections and help students recognize that boundaries between content topics are generally artificial, many schools have begun to move from a traditional sequence of Algebra I to Geometry to Algebra II to an **integrated curriculum.** In an integrated curriculum, all of the major mathematics areas—generally, algebra, geometry, probability and statistics, and discrete mathematics—are visited every year from the middle through the high school levels.

While the major advantage of an integrated sequence of content is that students can make connections between topics, it has other benefits as well. As students learn the mathematics in context, they continue to sharpen skills such as order of operations, graphing lines, and so forth, along the way. Consequently, the traditional notion of doing a chapter on square roots and then moving on to something else might be replaced by the idea of looking at square roots in the context of a quadratic equation and revisiting them a few weeks later when determining a geometric mean. Integrated textbook series and resource books tend to contain regular, ongoing applications of mathematical skills rather than entire chapters, units, or worksheets focusing on an individual topic. Finally, because the integrated topic includes ongoing review and application, less time tends to be spent reviewing material at the beginning of a school year or semester. A quick look at a traditional Algebra II book will reveal that approximately the first one third of the text is devoted to content that students already visited in Algebra I and are being asked to brush up on before moving forward. And this should not be a surprise, given that many students study geometry for a year between algebra courses and have forgotten many of the concepts. With less time lost on extensive reviews and a broader range of topics to be explored, the student in an integrated sequence tends to visit more mathematical topics than has historically been the case. Topics such as probability, recursion, and matrix algebra can become the norm for *all* students rather than being relegated to an upper-level course for a few select students.

So, why wouldn't a school or district choose to use an integrated approach? There are several possible reasons, three of which we will discuss here—tradition, lack of research, and availability of resource materials. Probably nothing gets in the way of reform more powerfully than does tradition—the way it has always been done. Imagine a school district with a mathematics department made up of five teachers who have been teaching a traditional sequence of courses out of the same textbook series for 20 years. Unless some incredible staff development program comes along to convince them otherwise, they will assume that their way is best and continue to do it despite trends or research to the contrary. Simply put, it is safer and easier to continue to do something the old way than to change. That is why innovations from automatic transmissions in automobiles to compact disc players didn't catch on right away; people needed time to adjust and rethink.

Tradition is an interesting player in the change process, however. The State of New York, for example, has used a unified or integrated approach to teaching mathematics since the early 1970s. So, to a teacher in that state, the tradition over the past 30 years has been to teach an integrated sequence, and it may be difficult to convince that educator that it could be done differently. A mathematics education student from New York recently asked her classmates in another state, "Did you really just study algebra for a whole year?" and added, "I can't imagine doing that!" But there is some history here too, as the traditional sequence of algebra and geometry has not always been the norm. In the 1940s, for example, many schools in the United States were using an integrated approach. A report published by the Joint Commission to Study the Place of Mathematics in Secondary Education in the 1930s "emphasized the spiraling of instruction by including a grade-placement chart that displayed the attention given in *each grade* [emphasis added] to each of what were called major subject fields, namely: number and computation, geometric form and space perception, graphic representation, logical thinking, relational thinking, and symbolic representation and thinking" (Jones & Coxford, 1970, p. 55). However, a discriminatory system eventually developed in which vocational students were relegated to integrated courses, whereas college-bound students took the algebra-geometry sequence. By the early 1960s, the New Math reform movement had emerged, and the integrated approach fell to the wayside. So, when someone talks about this "new idea" of integrating the mathematics content, we need to realize that it's not really new at all—it's a return to the past. A look at historical perspectives in any curricular area will reveal a pendulum effect—the tendency to try something for a few years and then abandon it for another trend, only to return to the original plan several years later. Some educators choose to maintain the status quo and hope that, eventually, the pendulum will swing back to what they believe.

The second reason why a school district may choose to follow an algebra-geometry program is that there is not a significant amount of research to support that integrated mathematics sequences impact students more effectively than the traditional course sequences. A 1979 study conducted in New York showed no measurable difference between students who were enrolled in an integrated sequence and those in a traditional sequence (Paul & Richbart, 1985). This study confirmed others that have shown that the integrated approach was not harming students, but it didn't appear to be helping them significantly either. Recently, work done with curriculum projects funded by the National Science Foundation (discussed at length in Chapter 4) has shown several positive effects of integrating content. However, the absence of a consistent, long-term body of research to support the change makes many educators hesitant to move toward an integrated approach. Chapter 2 discussed the importance of making educational decisions based upon research, and there is simply not enough evidence to convince many mathematics teachers or administrators that a change will benefit them and their students.

The last drawback to an integrated approach to the mathematics curriculum is a lack of resource materials. Since the traditional sequence has been with us for so long, most schools have texts, software, resource books, videos, and other media that support this approach. Moving toward an integrated program would require not only a great deal of time for faculty reorientation but the selection and purchase of thousands of dollars worth of books and materials. Because the materials are not as abundant in the integrated sequence, teachers feel they have fewer choices in decision making and this, together with the cost, can hold a school district back from making a change. When the *Curriculum and Evaluation Standards* were first published in 1989, some states adopted models that called for an integrated approach, but textbooks did not yet exist to support the Standards. Now that several National Science Foundation (NSF) projects have produced some outstanding materials, schools are able to at least view the resources in their decision making deliberations.

■ CONCLUSION ■

In order to move toward a core of mathematics outcomes for all students, there must first be some agreement on the objectives that are critical. Identifying these objectives, however, is not an easy task—as we said at the beginning of the chapter, any two people making a list of important content issues are likely to come up with different objectives. Another quick look at some history as we close this chapter will again reveal the pendulum effect—that the more things change, the more they stay the same.

In the *Curriculum and Evaluation Standards* (1989), the NCTM stated that "decreased emphasis" should be placed on trinomial factoring, simplifying radicals and complex fractions, and solving quadratic equations by hand. Compare this to a statement made by William Reeve in the *Fourth Yearbook of the NCTM* in 1929. Reeve, speaking of "recent" changes in the U.S. curriculum, stated that "among the first topics to be eliminated from elementary algebra were the highest common factor [of polynomials] by division . . . complex fractions of a difficult type . . . and complicated radicals. . . . One might here raise the question why the study of quadratic equations beyond the pure type such as $x^2 = 4$ should any longer be required of everybody in the ninth grade . . . those who do not [continue the study of mathematics] will never have any use for the kind of work that is traditionally given. It is artificial and ought to be omitted" (Reeve, p. 159). He went

on to note that the 1930 syllabus for the State of New York made trinomial factoring optional and that, while using factoring and completing the square to solve quadratic equations were in the 1910 syllabus, the study of quadratics was made optional in 1930 as well. As you can see, curricular changes never come easy, and determining a common list of core objectives for a state or school district can be much more difficult than it may appear on the surface. However, if a discussion does not begin on this issue at some point, the mistakes of the past that have created generations of individuals with poor mathematics skills and attitudes will continue to perpetuate themselves.

In this chapter, we have examined the nature of the mathematics curriculum at the secondary and middle school levels. The *Curriculum and Evaluation Standards* of the National Council of Teachers of Mathematics in 1989 and again in 1998 were described as visionary guides for states to follow as specific objectives are written for each grade level in a school district. The *Standards* are somewhat radical in that they promote mathematics for all students, which includes a significant background in algebra, geometry, and discrete mathematics. At the secondary and middle school levels, the *Standards* recommend an integrated approach to the content rather than the traditional sequence of Algebra I, then Geometry, and so forth. To achieve this end, three curricular models of implementation were suggested, including the crossover, enrichment, and differentiated models. The chapter included a discussion of the fact that many of the general principles embraced in the *Standards* are not entirely new and that suggestions from curricular content to sequencing of courses have been with us for nearly 100 years.

In the second chapter of this unit—Chapter 4—we discuss the process by which a school district drafts a course of study, including the selection and writing of general goals and more specific objectives. Because the curriculum is heavily influenced by textbooks and resource materials, we also describe how teachers can use these sources to plan and implement curriculum. As you read the remainder of this textbook and ponder your position on the purposes of mathematics education, try to focus on these questions: Why do we teach mathematics, and what are the most important outcomes from a Pre-K–12 mathematics education? Do you view mathematics as a process, as content, or both? If you were on a curriculum committee, appointed to determine the core objectives for a secondary and middle school program, which objectives would you select and why? Thinking about these issues will lead you to a philosophy of mathematics education and define your place in the classroom.

■ GLOSSARY ■

Content Standards: Content Standards are national (or state) benchmarks associated with mathematics content that should be addressed in a school mathematics program, including number sense, algebra, geometry, measurement, and probability and data analysis. The NCTM released national content Standards in 1989 and 1998.

Core Curriculum: The core curriculum is a three-year secondary mathematics program designed to ensure that all students have equal access to a variety of mathematics topics, regardless of future plans, ethnicity, gender, or perceived ability. In an addendum to the NCTM *Standards,* three possible curricular models were outlined, the crossover, enrichment, and differentiated models.

Crossover Model: In the crossover model, all high school students address the same set of objectives in a three-year sequence. The school has one sequence for college-bound students and another for students not planning to attend college, but both tracks feature the same core mathematics outcomes.

Differentiated Model: In the differentiated model, all high school students address the same set of objectives in a three-year sequence. However, within a classroom, each learning team of students might address the same outcomes in different ways. Teachers may use manipulatives, technology, or deeper applied problems, depending on the readiness and needs of students in the class.

Enrichment Model: In the enrichment model, all high school students address the same set of objectives in a three-year sequence. However, a team of students who have mastered a set of outcomes might be given an enrichment extension that goes beyond the common core. Enrichment topics would be optional in a class and explored only by those students who initially demonstrate an understanding of the common objectives.

Integrated Curriculum: An integrated curriculum is a sequence of mathematics courses that include the development of algebra, geometry, discrete mathematics, and probability and statistics each year that a student is in school. The integrated approach is an alternative to following a sequence of Algebra I, Geometry, Algebra II, and so forth.

Process Standards: Process Standards are national (or state) benchmarks of process skills that should be addressed in a school mathematics program, including problem solving, reasoning, communication, connections, and representation. The NCTM released national process Standards in 1989 and 1998.

Strand: A strand is a content area that is developed over a period of time. For example, if geometry is viewed as a content strand (rather than a course title), it is thought of as an area of the curriculum that is developed each year that a student is in school, and a district or state determines what content is developmentally appropriate within that strand for each grade level.

Triangular Numbers: The triangular numbers are a sequence of numbers that, geometrically, refer to the number of dots required to build successively larger triangles, as shown in Figure 3–11:

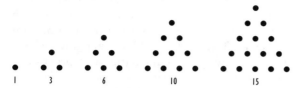

Figure 3–11 Geometric Representation of the Triangular Numbers

Therefore, the sequence of triangular numbers is 1, 3, 6, 10, 15, 21, 28, 36, 45, 55, and so on, where the nth term is $\dfrac{n(n + 1)}{2}$. Triangular numbers frequently occur in problems that involve patterns or sequences and, when recognized, can be extremely useful in solving problems.

■ DISCUSSION QUESTIONS ■

1. Obtain a copy of the 1989 NCTM *Curriculum and Evaluation Standards* (or access them on the Internet at <www.enc.org>) and compare this book to the *Principles and Standards for School Mathematics* document. Discuss the similarities and differences in terms of content, style, and purpose.

2. Using a copy of the 1989 or 1998 NCTM Standards on probability and data analysis, compare the national Standards to the sample state model strand in Appendix A. How would you characterize the differences and similarities between a national and a state model? To what degree does the model reprinted in Appendix A follow the recommendations of the national *Standards*?

3. Obtain a copy of your state's model curriculum or standards. Review and discuss the document and determine the mathematical content and processes that your state believes to be important by virtue of the outcomes emphasized in the model.

4. Divide into small groups and have each group generate a list of 10 mathematical outcomes that are critical for *every* high school graduate. Then, compare the lists with other groups and with a list of critical outcomes in your state (which may include a list of graduation or proficiency exam objectives). Discuss the processes that might be used by a state or local school district in reaching consensus on what is important for students to know and be able to do in mathematics.

5. Divide into three teams and assign each team to one of the core curriculum models—crossover, enrichment, and differentiated. Each group should identify at least two major benefits of their model over the others and at least two potential drawbacks to adopting that particular model. The three groups should, then, be prepared to compare the advantages and possible disadvantages of the three models in depth.

6. The topic of multiplying polynomials was used as an example of how to deliver the same content at different levels for students at a variety of levels. Select another example of a secondary or middle school topic and show how that content area can be addressed through the use of manipulatives, technology, or applied problems.

7. Compare the textbooks of a somewhat traditional Algebra I course and a first-year integrated mathematics course. Identify the algebra content included in the integrated text and discuss the degree to which all areas of the mathematics curriculum—including geometry, discrete mathematics, and probability and data analysis—are addressed in the book. What are the advantages and disadvantages of the design of each course?

8. Invite the mathematics department chairs or principals of two schools—one having a traditional mathematics curricular sequence and one having an integrated sequence—and conduct a panel discussion on the practical benefits and drawbacks of each model.

9. "The more things change, the more they stay the same." Discuss how trends in education have come and gone over the course of history and how this pendulum effect impacts the implementation of innovative curricular changes.

■ BIBLIOGRAPHIC REFERENCES AND RESOURCES ■

Alper, L., et al. (1996). Problem-based mathematics—not just for the college-bound. *Educational Leadership, 53* (8), 18–21.

Anderson, R. D. (1995). Curriculum reform: Dilemmas and promise. *Phi Delta Kappan, 77* (1), 33–36.

Battista, M. T. (1994). Teacher beliefs and the reform movement in mathematics education. *Phi Delta Kappan, 75* (6), 462–63, 466–68, 470.

Bliss, L. (1996). Six keys to the 22nd century high school. *School Planning and Management, 36* (5), 22–27.

Chard, D. J. & Kameenui, E. J. (1995). Mathematics instruction for students with diverse learning needs: Heeding the message of the Cheshire cat. *Focus on Learning Problems in Mathematics, 17* (2), 24–38.

Dossey, J. A. (1991). Discrete mathematics: The math for our time. In M. J. Kenney (Ed.), *1991 Yearbook of the NCTM: Discrete mathematics across the curriculum, K–12* (pp. 1–9). Reston, VA: National Council of Teachers of Mathematics.

Eisenhower National Clearinghouse. (1999). Eisenhower National Clearinghouse website. Retrieved August 20, 1999 from the World Wide Web: <http://www.enc.org>

Garet, M. S. & Mills, V. L. (1995). Changes in teaching practices: The effects of the curriculum and evaluation standards. *Mathematics Teacher, 88* (5), 380–88.

Hiebert, J. (1999). Relationships between research and the NCTM standards. *Journal for Research in Mathematics Education, 30* (1), 3–19.

Hirsch, C. R. (Ed.). (1985). *1985 Yearbook of the NCTM: The secondary school mathematics curriculum.* Reston, VA: National Council of Teachers of Mathematics.

Hirschhorn, D. B. et al. (1995). Rethinking the first two years of high school mathematics with the UCSMP. *Mathematics Teacher, 88* (8), 640–47.

Jones, P. S. & Coxford, A. F. (1970). Abortive reform—depression and war. In *The thirty-second yearbook of the NCTM: A history of mathematics education* (pp. 46–66). Washington, DC: NCTM.

Meiring, S. P., Rubenstein, R. N., Schultz, J. E., Lange, J., & Chambers, D. L. (1992). *A core curriculum: Making mathematics count for everyone.* Reston, VA: National Council of Teachers of Mathematics.

National Council of Teachers of Mathematics. (1998). *Principles and standards for school mathematics* (working draft). Reston, VA: National Council of Teachers of Mathematics.

National Council of Teachers of Mathematics. (1989). *Curriculum and evaluation standards for school mathematics.* Reston, VA: National Council of Teachers of Mathematics.

National Research Council. (1989). *Everybody counts: A report to the nation on the future of mathematics education.* Washington, DC: National Academy.

Parmar, R. S. & Cawley, J. F. (1995). Mathematics curricula frameworks: Goals for general and special education. *Focus on Learning Problems in Mathematics, 17* (2), 50–66.

Paul, F. & Richbart, L. (1985). New York state's new three-year sequence for high school mathematics. In C. R. Hirsch (Ed.), *1985 Yearbook of the NCTM: The secondary school mathematics curriculum* (pp. 200–210). Reston, VA: National Council of Teachers of Mathematics.

Pollack, H. Notes from a talk given at the Mathematical Sciences Education Board. Frameworks Conference, May 1987, at Minneapolis, MN.

Reeve, W. D. (1929). United States. In W. D. Reeve (Ed.), *The fourth yearbook of the NCTM: Significant changes and trends in the teaching of mathematics throughout the world since 1910* (pp. 131–186). New York, NY: Teachers College, Columbia University.

Robicheaux, R. (1996). Professional development: Caring teachers can realize the vision on the standards. *Mathematics Teaching in the Middle School, 1* (9), 738–42.

Smith, S. Z., et al. (1993). What the NCTM standards look like in one classroom. *Educational Leadership, 50* (8), 4–7.

Steen, L. A. (Ed.). (1997). *Why numbers count: Quantitative literacy for tomorrow's America.* New York, NY: College Entrance Examination Board.

Steen, L. A. (Ed.). (1990). *On the shoulders of giants: New approaches to numeracy.* Washington, DC: National Academy.

Thornton, C. A. & Bley, N. S. (1994). *Windows of opportunity: Mathematics for students with special needs.* Reston, VA: National Council of Teachers of Mathematics.

Implementing a Course of Study

After reading Chapter 4, you should be able to answer the following questions:

■ What is a state or local course of study, and what does it generally contain?

■ What is the process by which a state or local course of study is written?

■ What is the difference between a goal and an objective? Provide examples illustrating the levels at which objectives are written.

■ What are the criteria by which textbooks are often chosen in a school district or state?

■ What are some examples of alternative sources of problems and activities, outside of a textbook? Provide examples on how to organize a resource file of teaching ideas.

Congratulations! You have just been hired to teach seventh grade mathematics at Oak Knoll Middle School in Monroe, Iowa. It is your first teaching position, and you walk into the department chair's classroom, excited about your new job, two weeks prior to the start of the school year.

You: So, what am I supposed to teach the seventh graders?

Chair: Well, it's really up to you. Teach them whatever you think they need to know. Oh, and feel free to teach and emphasize the things you're interested in. That's how I make my decisions.

You: You mean if I don't enjoy a topic like probability or three-dimensional geometry, I can just choose not to deal with it in my classes?

Chair: Yeah, that's correct. I mean, why not? If you've made it this far in your life without knowing much about a certain area of the math curriculum, they probably don't need to know much about it either. Teach what's in the book but leave out the stuff you don't want to do. Like I said, it's up to you.

A bit confused, you walk out of the room shaking your head and thinking, "This is my first job. I was really hoping that someone would give me at least a little bit of direction here."

As strange as this scenario appears, states and school districts have not always had models and prescribed curricula for teachers to follow. Remember that the

United States did not have a widely accepted set of national curriculum standards prior to 1989. In fact, as recently as the early 1980s, it was not unusual for mathematics teachers to be told that they would be teaching pre-calculus but be given little, if any, details of what it is that pre-calculus students are supposed to know or be able to do. In many cases, teachers were handed a textbook for a course, and the book *became* the curriculum, because it was the only guide that was provided. Imagine the power that a textbook publisher has when a book *defines* the curriculum, from mathematical content to the sequence in which it is taught. But if you have no other assistance or guidelines, either a textbook or an educated guess may be all you have on which to base curricular decisions.

However, with more recent sweeping changes toward accountability—making local school districts responsible for student achievement—came the development of the **course of study**. A course of study is a document that prescribes the curriculum, by grade level, for a state, county, or individual school district. Instead of having a conversation like the one with the chair of the department, teachers are now generally handed a copy of a graded (by grade level) course of study to serve as the basis for instruction. The course of study should clearly define what a student should feel, know, and be able to do at each grade level. Chapter 3 addressed the general issues surrounding the NCTM Standards documents and the process of selecting appropriate curriculum, and this chapter focuses specifically on the writing and implementation of a course of study in a state or a local school district. We begin by looking at how the course of study is developed and then focus our attention on how one effectively uses resources such as a textbook or the Internet to support the course of study.

■ THE COURSE OF STUDY

As we have seen, the NCTM *Principles and Standards for School Mathematics* contains broad statements of what a student should be able to do across grade-range bands of Pre-K–2, 3–5, 6–8, and 9–12. But what if you are teaching a seventh grade class and want the students to explore some geometry? How do you know, specifically, what a seventh grader should know about two- or three-dimensional geometry? In most cases, you consult the course of study that has been written for a state, county, or local school district. The level at which a course of study is written varies by location. In some cases, a state or a county within a state may have a curriculum that is shared by many school districts. In other locations, each school district may have its own document, based upon some standards, framework, or model written at the state level. Because the Constitution gives states the power to make educational decisions, there is no national curriculum in the United States. Some argue that there *is* a national curriculum—defined by textbooks used in the schools—but there is no federally produced set of outcomes to which all states must adhere.

Suppose that your state has a model or framework that provides guidance to local school districts for writing their courses of study. Generally, at the local level, a curriculum committee is assembled to study national and state standards and to determine how to use them for writing a grade-by-grade document for teachers to follow. The curriculum committee might consist of central office administrators, principals, department chairs, guidance counselors, classroom teachers, curriculum supervisors, community members, or any combination of individuals representing various viewpoints. The curriculum committee usually begins the writing process by defining a **district philosophy** or statement of beliefs that are held by educators in that system. This philosophy serves as a the underlying foundation from which the rest of the document flows. It usually describes the role of mathematics in our society and establishes the need for students in the district to be well versed in the content area. Based on this philosophy, the committee then produces a series of overarching **goals** of mathematics education. Goals are broad statements about what a student should be able to accomplish as a result of participating in the district's program. A course of study may have three or four major goals or may contain a page or two of general statements of student outcomes. From these goals, curriculum writers define **objectives,** which are very specific statements that describe what a student should feel, know, or be able to do at each grade level. Finally, any of these objectives that are intended to be mastered by students at a particular grade level have an associated **pupil performance objective (PPO),** which is an even more specific description of what a student should be able to do under a given set of conditions. These PPOs are often used to write classroom or districtwide assessment items, which may take the form of problems, questions, or projects.

Let's consider a specific example. Suppose that the curriculum committee decides that it is important for every seventh grader to study the topic of probability, because the NCTM recommended it in Standard 5 for grades 6–8 (NCTM, 1998). The course of study, then, may contain a goal that says "The student will explore probability and its applications." Once this goal is stated, the classroom teacher knows that probability is important but is likely to ask, "What, specifically, do you want seventh graders to know about probability?" Consequently, the course of study is written to contain objectives that fall under the general goal of probability. For example, the course of study might say that "The student will be able to determine the number of combinations and permutations for a set of concrete items." Furthermore, if this objective is to be mastered by a seventh grader, the document may state a PPO such as, "Given a set of five or fewer concrete objects such as colored cubes, the student will be able to demonstrate and list the possible permutations of the cubes and the number of ways that 1, 2, 3, 4, or 5 of the cubes can be chosen from the set." The sequence of outcomes is set forth in Figure 4–1.

What did you notice about the wording of the objective versus that of the PPO? How are they similar? How do they differ? You might have noticed, for example, that neither the objective nor the PPO says anything about students being able to use formulas. Although the number of permutations of three items can be found by calculating 3! ($3 \times 2 \times 1 = 6$), the course of study recognizes that it is inappropriate for twelve-year-olds to be memorizing factorial formulas at the possible expense of misunderstanding the concept of permutations. Instead, the document emphasizes visualization skills, which is consistent with the learning theories discussed in Chapter 2. Similarly, the number of ways that 2 objects can be pulled from a set of 5 can be determined by using a familiar formula and calculating $\frac{5!}{3!2!}$. However, developmentally, it makes more sense for the student to think of having 5 choices, then 4 more choices, so 5×4 will need to be calculated. And the student should recognize that

The student will explore probability and its applications.
(Goal)

↓

The student will be able to determine the number of combinations
and permutations for a set of concrete items.
(Objective)

↓

Given a set of five or fewer concrete objects, such as colored cubes, the student
will be able to demonstrate and list the possible permutations of the cubes and
the number of ways that 1, 2, 3, 4, or 5 of the cubes can be chosen from the set.
(Pupil Performance Objective)

Figure 4–1 Sample Seventh Grade Goal, Objective, and PPO

the order in which you select the two blocks does not matter, so 20 can be divided by 2 to find a solution of 10 combinations (that is, it doesn't matter whether you pull the red block, then the green block or the green and then the red, so the number of combinations can be divided in half). At this point, it is more important for a student to know what it means to find all of the permutations of a set or to pull two blocks from a set of five than to possess the skill of using formulas to calculate a number of permutations or combinations.

To assess this PPO, a teacher might give the student three blocks—blue, red, and green—along with three colored pens and a piece of paper, and ask the student to move the blocks around on the desk to find all of the permutations and sketch them on paper. The child, then, is responsible for identifying the set of six permutations as illustrated in Figure 4–2.

Permutation 1	R	B	G
Permutation 2	R	G	B
Permutation 3	B	R	G
Permutation 4	B	G	R
Permutation 5	G	R	B
Permutation 6	G	B	R

Figure 4–2 Colored Blocks Representing Permutations

The child can also be asked to describe the strategy used in listing the permutations and how to be certain that all of the permutations have been listed. This type of teaching and assessment emphasizes conceptual understanding over procedural knowledge—an important and critical distinction. You might have also recognized that the goal is only useful inasmuch as it informs you that students should be studying the topic of probability at this grade level. But the objective and the PPO clarify in a very specific way what a student should know (the objective) and be able to do (the PPO) to demonstrate understanding of probability-related concepts in the seventh grade—specifically, permutations and combinations.

Under the same goal dealing with probability, we might expect the school district to include an outcome in, say, a First-Year Integrated course, stating that "the student will be able to determine simple permutations and combinations" as a way of extending the related seventh grade outcome. The PPO for the course could state that, "Given a problem requiring permutations or combinations, the student will be able to use multiplication or Pascal's Triangle to find the solution." The sequence of outcomes for seventh grade is summarized in Figure 4–3.

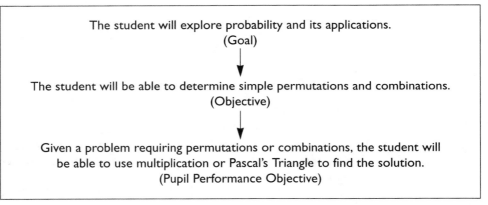

Figure 4–3 Sample First-Year Integrated Goal, Objective, and PPO

In this First-Year Integrated course, if the student is asked to determine how many ways a subcommittee of 3 individuals can be selected from a board having 8 members, the student should be able to generate eight rows of **Pascal's Triangle,** as shown in Figure 4–4.

```
                    1
                 1  2  1
               1  3  3  1
             1  4  6  4  1
           1  5  10 10  5  1
         1  6  15 20 15  6  1
       1  7  21 35 35 21  7  1
     1  8  28 56 70 56 28  8  1
```

Figure 4–4 First 8 Rows of Pascal's Triangle

The numbers in the eighth row indicate, in order, how many ways 0, 1, 2, 3, 4, 5, 6, 7, or 8 items can be chosen from a collection of 8 items. So, there are 56 ways to select 3 individuals from a board consisting of 8 people. (Note that there are also 56 ways to select 5 individuals from the board. Can you explain why?) Students would be expected to use Pascal's Triangle to find this combination, which is more complex than concretely counting blocks, as illustrated in the seventh grade example, but not to use any particular formula for completing a calculation for combinations.

Finally, as shown in Figure 4–5, by the time the student is in a Third-Year Integrated course or, perhaps, Algebra II or Pre-Calculus, the objective might read, "the student will be able to use formulas to compute permutations and combinations." The PPO might state, "given a problem requiring permutations or combinations, the student will accurately use factorials and formulas to find a solution."

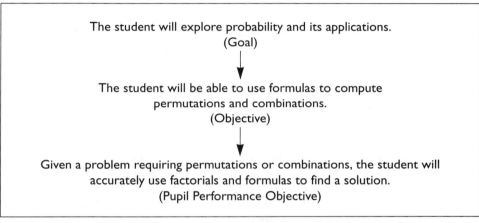

Figure 4–5 Sample Third-Year Integrated Goal, Objective, and PPO

Consequently, a high school junior or senior should be able to solve a problem such as this:

A state lottery is run in the following manner: 36 balls are placed in a container, numbered from 1 to 36. Six of the balls are pulled out at random. If an individual correctly guesses the six numbers on the balls, in any order, that person wins a grand prize of one million dollars. What is the probability that the person who pays $1.00 and guesses one set of six numbers will win the grand prize?

For a student who has moved through the curricular sequence described in this section, it should be apparent that this problem can be solved by determining how many ways six balls can be selected from a group of 36 without replacement. However, the problem is far too complex to be drawn by hand as was the seventh grade problem with colored blocks, and it is also unrealistic for a student to write out 36 rows of Pascal's Triangle. However, by using the formula for combinations, the number can be calculated, as follows:

$$C_r^n = \frac{n!}{(n-r)!r!}$$

so, using the numbers from this problem,

$$C_6^{36} = \frac{36!}{(36-6)!6!} = \frac{36!}{30!6!} = 1,947,792$$

Therefore, the probability of winning the lottery in this state is nearly one in two million. We can expect that this state will take in almost $2,000,000 in revenues to play the game for every $1,000,000 that it gives back in prize money. Also, a careful examination of the formula reveals that there are 36 numbers to select on the first draw, 35 on the second, then 34, 33, 32, and 31. Because the order does not matter, the product of $36 \times 35 \times 34 \times 33 \times 32 \times 31$ needs to be divided by the number of ways to arrange six items, which is 6! The student might even be required to explain *why* the formula works as well as actually being able to use it to complete the calculation and solve the problem.

Perhaps, after reading how the topics of permutations and combinations can evolve over a five-year period, you, too, have become more comfortable with these concepts as you have looked at them through a number of developmental lenses. The point is that the local course of study serves as an important guide in that it describes what is *valued* at each grade level and helps the teacher to think about the ongoing development of important mathematical ideas as students progress from one course to the next.

In the process of writing curriculum, committees often deliberate for several months, thinking about what is appropriate mathematics content for each grade level. The committees participate in staff development presentations, view videos, read curricular models and other documents, explore the Internet, and review possible textbooks and resources while making their decisions. Disagreements among committee members are common and are part of the decision-making process as they wrestle with deciding what is important, as we discussed in Chapter 3. When the document is completed, the course of study is submitted for approval to a governing body, such as the state, and it essentially becomes a legal document—a contract that school districts have with their communities in terms of what will be taught at each grade level. And to some degree, because the document contains PPOs that may refer to small groups of students, calculator or computer explorations, or the use of manipulatives, the course of study has implications for teaching strategies in the classroom as well. One of the most important tasks of a teacher who is new to a school district is to obtain a copy of the mathematics course of study so as to become familiar with *what* is to be learned and, often, *how* it is suggested that students in that district are to learn the mathematical content and processes. Because a local course of study consists of goals and objectives, we will explore these elements in some depth.

■ WRITING GOALS AND OBJECTIVES

A goal is a general outcome that is addressed through a lesson, a series of lessons, a course, or even an entire Pre-K–12 mathematics program. Goals are stated broadly in terms of what a student is to achieve. The following statements are examples of goals in mathematics education:

- The student will appreciate the use of algebra in solving real-life problems.

- The student will develop a positive disposition toward the study of mathematics.
- The student will understand the connection between geometry and probability.

Suppose that you were in charge of assessing students in your school to ensure that they met each of the outcomes listed above. Determining whether a student "appreciates," "develops," or "understands" is virtually impossible. Hence, goals are not necessarily statements that one can measure in some way to see if they have been accomplished. Instead, they provide a general direction for a lesson or even a program.

On the other hand, an objective is a very specific statement of what a student should feel, know, or be able to do. Sometimes, such statements are referred to as behavioral objectives because they reflect the behaviors that a student should display to demonstrate an understanding of the skill or concept. The following statements are examples of objectives:

- Given the original cost and a percent discount, the student will calculate the sale price.
- Given a compass and straightedge, the student will draw an angle and construct its angle bisector.
- Given the equation of a function, the student will determine the derivative of the function at a particular point and explain the meaning of the derivative at that point.

In contrast to the goals listed earlier, these objectives are very specific in terms of what a student should know and be able to do; furthermore, the degree to which the student has met these objectives can be measured through a variety of assessment techniques. A behavioral objective should be measurable, meaning that the statement should be clear enough so that a teacher can readily assess whether the student has mastered or met the objective. Objectives also generally contain a condition under which the student should perform. The conditions in the list just provided are the phrases that begin with "given . . . " so that the reader knows the conditions under which a student should be able to do something. These conditions often include specific directions in terms of materials the student should use (e.g., a compass and straightedge, pattern blocks, etc.) or whether technology is required to meet the outcome. Notice how the objectives also contain action words, such as calculate, draw, explain, show, contrast, and so forth. Finally, objectives sometimes contain criteria by which one knows whether a student has mastered it. For example, the first objective in the presented list could read, "Given the original cost and a percent discount, the student will correctly calculate the sale price 80 percent of the time." This means that if the student can accurately determine a sale price at least four out of five times, the teacher can check off the objective and conclude that the student has mastered that skill. However, keep in mind that this criteria-setting process is dangerous because a student can get 80 percent of the questions right and still not understand the skill, just as another student can fully comprehend the concept but make careless errors and miss 50 percent of the assessment items. This issue is pursued in depth in Chapters 8 and 9 that deal with assessment.

Classifying Objectives

Educators usually group objectives into three categories—affective, cognitive, and psychomotor. **Affective objectives** refer to attitudes or feelings; **cognitive objectives** reflect skills and concepts the student should understand; **psychomotor objectives** refer to things that a student should be physically able to do. When a curriculum is written, committees try to include a variety of objective types. We will elaborate on affective and cognitive objectives in this section, because both are common in the mathematics curriculum; whereas, psychomotor objectives are more common in physical education and the arts.

Affective Objectives

Although we often think of most mathematics objectives as being cognitive—something the student should know or be able to do—it is common for a mathematics curriculum to include affective objectives. In Chapter 2, we discussed mathematical disposition as described in the NCTM *Standards*. If we want our students to develop positive attitudes and beliefs about mathematics, such as interest, curiosity, perseverance, and an appreciation for the usefulness of mathematics, then those attitudes should be spelled out in a curriculum document. Therefore, it is not unusual to see a course of study display objectives such as:

- The student will appreciate the historical development of Pascal's Triangle.
- The student will display interest and curiosity in problem solving.
- The student will exhibit confidence in using technology to solve mathematics problems.
- The student will recognize the value of a mathematical background in virtually all career areas.

These statements can be difficult to measure (e.g., it is not easy to know whether a student has developed an appreciation for something), but they prompt the teacher to consider the affective side of the mathematics classroom. The role of the teacher is not only to help the student to learn skills and concepts but also to develop important attitudes and beliefs about mathematics along the way. As was pointed out in Chapter 2, the best way that a teacher can foster positive dispositions toward mathematics is to model those dispositions in the classroom. When students observe a teacher who is persistent, curious, and flexible in problem solving, the student is likely to develop similar dispositions. So, if the course of study and individual lesson plans contain affective outcome statements, the objectives serve as a reminder that attitudes are important in the mathematics classroom.

Cognitive Objectives

Cognitive objectives are generally subdivided into three categories—knowledge and skills, concepts, and applications. As you look at the examples that follow, think about what differentiates these objective categories from one another. Take a piece of paper and pencil and make note of the characteristics of objectives that might typically fall into each of the three categories.

Knowledge and Skill

- Given a protractor and a diagram of a triangle, the student will measure each of the angles to within 5°.
- Given a piece of graph paper and a ruler, the student will accurately draw the graph of a linear function nine out of ten times.
- Given the length of one side of a 30-60-90 triangle, the student will determine the lengths of the other two sides without the use of a calculator.

Concept

- Given the general equation $y = A\sin(x + B) + C$, the student will describe the effects on the shape and position of the sine curve when values for A, B, and C are changed.
- Given a trinomial such as $x^2 - 5x + 4$ and a set of algebra tiles, the student will demonstrate geometrically what it means to factor the trinomial.
- Given a set of data, the student will determine whether the mode, median, or mean is the most appropriate measure of central tendency for that set and justify the response.

Application

- Given an object such as a cereal box or a cylindrical oatmeal container, a ruler, and a calculator, the student will determine the surface area and volume of the object.
- Given a problem involving probability, the student will devise a way to model the problem, collect data, and compare or contrast the experimental results with a calculated theoretical probability for the problem.
- Given an open-ended question involving computation with fractions, the student will respond to the question with explanations and diagrams and score at least a 3 on the district's rubric of 0 to 4.

After reading these examples, how did you characterize each of the three categories? You might have noticed, for example, that the knowledge and skill level is the simplest, the most straightforward, and the easiest to measure. If you want a class to be able to add a list of numbers containing decimals, you can give the students some exercises and see if they can add four out of five of them correctly. Keep in mind that the results of this assessment do not necessarily imply that the student understands *why* decimals are added this way, but understanding may not be the focus of that particular objective either. If, on the other hand, the objective is that "given a list of numbers with decimals and a set of base ten blocks, the student will show why the algorithm of lining up decimal places works," the objective has moved up a notch to the concept level. In general, concept-level objectives involve higher thinking levels and are used to emphasize understanding a process, rather than just being able to do it. Most calculus students can differentiate a function, but far fewer can explain what the answer means or why the procedure works. In our discussion of learning theories in Chapter 2, we have already made the case that we live in a world in which people can perform mathematical skills but not necessarily understand *why* they are done that way or *when* one would have to use that particular skill. As a result, curriculum writers can and should write objectives so that particular levels of achievement are expected.

Consider, for example, the general outcome that students should be able to find the area of a circle. Table 4–1 illustrates how the same outcome might be translated at the three different objective levels.

Table 4–1 Comparison of Circle Area Objective at Three Different Levels

Knowledge and Skill Level	Given the diameter or radius of a circle, the student will be able to compute its area.
Concept Level	Given the formula for area of a circle, the student will be able to justify the formula by using a diagram and written explanation.
Application Level	Given a diagram of a figure containing rectangles, triangles, and fractional parts of circles, the student will determine the area of a shaded region.

At the skill level, nothing more is required than students' ability to substitute numbers into the formula $A = \pi r^2$ and to find a numerical answer. However, at the concept level, students are expected to know where the formula comes from so that it makes sense. Students might, for example, use a previously proven formula such as

$$\text{Area of a Regular Polygon} = \frac{1}{2} \times \text{Apothem} \times \text{Perimeter}$$

to explain how the apothem (the distance from the center of a circle circumscribed about a regular polygon to a side of the polygon) approaches the length of the radius, and the perimeter of the polygon approaches the circumference of the circle when the number of sides of the polygon tends to infinity. That is,

$$A = \frac{1}{2}a \times p \to \frac{1}{2}r \times C$$

And, because $C = 2\pi r$,

$$\frac{1}{2}r \times C = \frac{1}{2}r \times (2\pi r) = \pi r^2$$

Finally, it requires yet another level of understanding and application to use the formula for area of a circle, together with the area of a rectangle, to find the area of the shaded region in Figure 4–6.

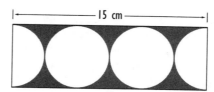

Figure 4–6 Find the Area of the Shaded Region

A teacher often asks, "In how much depth do my students need to understand this concept?" But a careful look at the course of study will generally answer this question and simplify the planning process. Objectives written at the skill level require students to perform some mechanical task or memorize a set of definitions, but objectives written at the concept and application levels emphasize the underlying reasons for mathematical processes and the consideration of when they are used.

As in the case of the circles-within-a-rectangle problem in Figure 4–6, an objective written at the application level requires the student to apply some concept to a problem-solving situation. In the following problem, a student not only needs to know how to weigh an object to the nearest gram on a balance but must also be able to use this skill in context to answer the questions:

There is an ancient story that says a man was put in prison for committing a crime, and the king said he would honor one wish for the man. The prisoner showed the king a checkerboard and asked that he put one grain of rice on the first of the 64 squares, 2 grains on the second, 4 grains on the third, 8 grains on the fourth, and so on. Then, he asked the king to give all of this rice to his family so that they would be well fed. Is his request reasonable? Will his family have enough to eat for the rest of their lives? Why or why not?

To solve this problem, one might begin by looking at the pattern of numbers representing the number of grains of rice on each square. The numbers are 1, 2, 4, 8, 16, 32, . . . , 2^{63}. So, the total number of grains of rice could be found by taking $1 + 2 + 4 + 8 + \ldots + 2^{63}$. Alternatively, students might use a spreadsheet containing the following commands as is shown in Figure 4–7:

	A	B	C
1	Square Number	Grains on the Square	Total Number of Grains
2	$=1$	$=2\wedge(A2-1)$	$=B2$
3	$=A2+1$	$=2\wedge(A3-1)$	$=C2+B3$
4	$=A3+1$	$=2\wedge(A4-1)$	$=C3+B4$

Figure 4–7 Spreadsheet Formula Representation of the Grains-of-Rice Problem

By using the FILL DOWN command on a standard spreadsheet program, the student can immediately have the computer calculate the number of grains of rice on each of the 64 squares and the total for all of the squares combined. The spreadsheet display would look like Figure 4–8.

But how much rice is this? How much does it weigh, and how much space would it occupy? First, one might want to weigh, say, 100 grains of rice and then use a proportion to determine an estimate of the total weight of all of the rice. Incidentally, the amount of rice produced is a quantity considerably greater than the total worldwide rice production for an entire year. The critical point is that this problem cannot be solved unless the student has the skill of being able to use a balance and can apply the skill of using the tool to solve the rice problem. An application-level objective

	A	B	C
1	Square Number	Grains on the Square	Total Number of Grains
2	1	1	1
3	2	2	3
4	3	4	7
5	4	8	15
6	5	16	31
7	6	32	63
8	7	64	127
9	8	128	255
10	9	256	511
11	10	512	1023

Figure 4–8 Spreadsheet Calculations for the Grains-of-Rice Problem

often requires a student to explain how or why a problem was solved in a particular way so that the teacher can gain a sense of the student's ability to use a skill in context. Also, open-ended questions—questions that may have several possible solutions or problem-solving approaches—are often scored on a rubric, a grading scale that is discussed fully in Chapter 8.

You might have noticed that several references to assessment have been made throughout this chapter. This is not a coincidence; in fact, it is difficult to discuss the ideas of goals and objectives without referring to assessment. These terms are related because an objective should serve as a focus for a lesson or series of lessons, and teachers use assessment techniques such as written tests, interviews, projects, and journal writing to determine the degree to which students have mastered those objectives. When you think about the objectives you are addressing in a lesson or a longer-term plan known as a unit (discussed in Chapter 5), you should also think about what students should be able to do to demonstrate their understanding of a skill, concept, or application. Objectives that are vague are often difficult to measure and are not of much use in planning. Here are some examples of poorly written objectives:

- Given a teacher-constructed board game, the students will win the game to show that they understand fractions.
- Given a set of algebra tiles, the student will show how to use them.
- Given a series of questions about triangles, the students will answer them with 75% accuracy.

In the first of these objectives, the emphasis is placed on the board game and not on the important mathematics. We know that the students are learning about frac-

An application-level objective on problem solving might incorporate a skill such as using a balance.

tions, but the objective does not specify what the students should be able to do with fractions (e.g., add, subtract, find common denominators, represent fractional parts with pattern blocks, etc.). In the second example, the focus is on the manipulatives and not on the mathematics. One might ask, "show how to use them *for what*?" Without being specific about the mathematical content, we have to assume that the purpose of the lesson will be to instruct the students on how to use algebra tiles and not necessarily to learn a polynomial or equation-solving skill. In the last example, we are not given any clues as to what kinds of questions students should be able to answer about triangles. The objective could apply to angle measures, lengths of sides, classification, area of the triangle, whether a triangle has symmetry, and so forth. Each of these three objectives is vague and would not give the teacher enough information about what students should know and be able to do to be helpful when planning a lesson. Keep in mind that objectives should reflect the mathematical content that the student is supposed to be mastering or the disposition that the student should be developing.

In many cases, teachers do not write objectives on a day-to-day basis. In reality, curriculum committees write objectives for a district, county, or state, and all of the teachers in that locale select objectives for lessons from the same list to achieve a continuity across grade levels and courses. Otherwise, when a student enters a sophomore-level Geometry course, the content and processes explored when that student was a freshman in Algebra I would be completely dependent upon the instructor and the book used for the class. But with a course of study, the instructors and their strategies can vary, but at least teachers throughout the district know what is intended to be taught in other courses. The skilled teacher, however, should not only know how to write an objective but should be adept at interpreting the meaning of objectives written by another person in a course of study. For this reason, some course-of-study writing committees even provide examples of problems throughout the document to key in on the types of questions that students should be able to answer at a particular grade level or in a certain course. These clues are also intended to keep teachers from "teaching the book" and, instead, turn them to teaching the students, using the textbook as a resource. We now explore the use of a textbook in the mathematics classroom and its role, from writing the course of study to making day-to-day instructional decisions.

■ SELECTION AND ORGANIZATION OF RESOURCES

Textbooks

Let's listen to three mathematics teachers discussing the progress of their students:

Loretta: How far is your math class?

James: We're about halfway into Chapter 5. How about you?

Loretta: That's what I had heard from my kids who talk to yours . . . we're barely into Chapter 4. My class is moving so slowly this year.

Juanita: You two had better speed up if we're all going to make it to Chapter 7 by the end of the semester. We've already got that departmental exam made up for all of us to give our students in January, but you have to finish Chapter 7 to be able to use it.

Loretta: I know. But my students always get hung up on the section that starts at page 115. By the time I give them a few worksheets on it and move on, we end up behind everybody else. That section gets them every year. And it kinda gets me, too, because I'm not sure why the book throws in those puzzle problems; my students always have a hard time with them.

James: That's why I've decided not to even bother with the worksheets. If they don't get it, they should see me for help. Otherwise, I'll slow down too much, and we'll never make it to Chapter 7 by January.

Juanita: It gets worse from there, too . . . it's impossible to finish the book by June unless you get to Chapter 7 by the end of the semester. But I'm determined to do it, and I've already warned my students to "hold on to their hats"!

Can you figure out what grade level or which course these three individuals teach? Do you know what the content is that they have been exploring with their students? Of course not. This conversation is so focused on *the book* that the relevant mathematics and the needs of the learners have been put aside. This is a very real problem in education that occurs anytime the users of a textbook decide that the book itself is the cornerstone of a class. In an attempt to gain consistency and to be thorough, educators sometimes forget that their purpose is to teach mathematics to real students. And if learning is not entirely linear (i.e., it is not important for every student to master Concepts A and B before exploring Concept C)—as suggested by the constructivist model in Chapter 2—we almost have to believe that it is sometimes appropriate to work problems in the back of a textbook before exploring some of the issues in earlier chapters. Finally, because no two classrooms of learners are exactly the same, why should we believe that three classes in a school would move at exactly the same pace, ending at the same chapter by the end of a semester? Decisions to follow a set program of timing for a course are often made for the convenience of the instructors, not for the benefit of the students they teach. We need to think of learning particular mathematical concepts as the constant and the amount of time it takes to do the learning as the variable, rather than making the historical error of viewing time as the constant and learning as the variable. So, what is the purpose for a textbook in mathematics?

A textbook is a resource and a guide. It is a resource in that it serves the purpose of an encyclopedia—we may not need it every day, but when a visual or written explanation is needed or when a set of practice exercises is sought, the book can provide these items. But the book can also serve as a worthwhile guide for instruction. Particularly, the novice teacher can look to a textbook for direction in terms of how to sequence content and how much time one might need to spend on a particular concept. Instructors' manuals frequently contain charts that include teaching hints and field-tested timelines of teaching that can be very valuable to the less-experienced teacher. The book and its manual can be helpful for providing insights on how students might link previous knowledge to new concepts and for thinking about what types of activities and problems the students should pursue. We often hear of veteran teachers who are teaching mathematics without a book, and this is very possible—in fact, in the constructivist model of teaching and learning, it's almost a necessity because a textbook can tie the hands of the teacher and make it difficult to follow the lead of student interests and questions. But most of these individuals are experienced teachers who used a textbook for several years previously to learn how students progress and how to address their needs.

However, we must be careful not to allow a mathematics textbook to *define* the curriculum. If you compare a typical course of study to the textbook used in that course, you will find that most books contain more content than is required in a course of study, and that many courses of study require that students visit topics that are not present in the text for that particular class. Therefore, it is appropriate and even desirable for teachers to skip sections of a book that contain material not included in the course of study and to supplement the book with activities from other resources that address topics not included in the text.

One way to make effective use of the textbook is to sit down with the course of study and textbook and compare each objective in the curriculum with what is in the textbook. By placing a checkmark next to each section of the book that addresses an objective in the course of study and a star next to any objective in the curriculum for which there does not appear to be a related section in the book, the teacher can quickly recognize which sections or units in the book can be omitted and which objectives will require resources beyond the textbook. Another suggestion on textbook use is to set up a meeting with a veteran teacher in the department, if possible, who has used the textbook in the past. Even one year of using a book can generate a great deal of insight into its strengths and shortcomings, and there is often no substitute for the personal advice of another individual who has actually worked with the text.

On the other hand, it may not be helpful to pick the brain of an instructor who tends to rely entirely on the book for teaching a course.

A teacher at a workshop, during some active hands-on lessons, once said, "These lessons are nice, but I've got a 400-page book to cover." In reality, the teacher didn't have a book to cover at all; instead, this person had a classroom full of students to teach and had lost the focus of the course because the book had become more important than the students themselves and the course of study. Teachers are not expected to cover every page of every book. Instead, they are encouraged to use the book as a guide and a resource to help them teach to the objectives listed in the course of study. It has been said that the best way to cover a book is to have students sit on it!

A curriculum committee frequently writes a course of study and defines the objectives with several possible textbooks as guides. That way, it can be comfortable that most of the objectives in the course of study are supported by text materials. So, one difficult decision of the committee—and, sometimes, of mathematics teachers within a particular building—is how to choose a textbook for a course. How do you know a potentially effective text from a weaker one? The following list of questions that can be asked when selecting a textbook is only a sample and is not intended to be exhaustive, but it will provide some ideas to think about when reviewing textbooks for their relative strengths and weaknesses.

MAKING A MATHEMATICS TEXTBOOK SELECTION— SOME QUESTIONS TO CONSIDER

1. Does the book place the mathematical process skills (problem solving, reasoning, communication, connections, representation) as major focal points? How do the authors of the textbook do this?
2. Do the authors approach mathematics holistically with investigations and problem solving as the context in which skills are developed, or is the book more skill oriented with occasional investigations suggested?
3. Do the problems and exercises, as well as assessments, throughout the book adequately address a mix of knowledge and skill-, conceptual-, and application-level objectives?
4. Does the book take into account the developmental level of the students, using language and providing examples accordingly?
5. Is there evidence of a progression from concrete to pictorial to more abstract means of learning concepts as is consistent with current learning theories? Do the problems presented make effective use of manipulatives as tools for exploring and discovering mathematical principles?
6. How is technology used in the book? Do problems involve the regular, integrated use of calculators, computers, and other technologies for exploring concepts? Or are suggestions for how to use technology generally placed in special locations, such as the end of each chapter or the book?
7. How close is the match between the objectives stated in the course of study and the contents of the textbook? Are the course of study and textbook compatible enough to limit the need to "skip" sections or to supplement the text?

8. Does the book appear to be free from gender bias and provide examples that demonstrate cultural diversity and acceptance of disabilities? How effectively have the authors addressed the issues of equity and equal access to mathematics for all students?

After questions such as these have been addressed, curriculum committees or the faculty within a school make a textbook selection and adopt a book for a course or grade level. Depending on the budget of a school district, a textbook may be used for many years, so a careful choice is critical. But the effective teacher will not only use the textbook as a reference and a guide; the teacher will also look to resources beyond the textbook, including general resource activity books, journals, and the Internet. We discuss the use of these ancillary materials in the instructional process in the sections that follow.

Print Resources

Suppose that you were preparing to teach a series of lessons (a unit) on graph theory, a discrete mathematics topic. The textbook you are using is from a high school program that has a unit on discrete mathematics embedded in it. You look through the textbook and decide that students need more than the book provides—more hands-on experiences and richer problems to solve. You decide to go searching for additional teaching ideas. Fortunately, the National Council of Teachers of Mathematics published an annual yearbook on *Discrete Mathematics across the Curriculum, K–12* (1991) that contains a number of practical classroom ideas and a book of discrete teaching ideas in 1998 that can be used to supplement textbook ideas. Furthermore, a nonprofit organization known as The Consortium for Mathematics and Its Applications (COMAP) publishes a number of videos and teaching units, several of which key in on graph theory and contain reproducible masters and hands-on activities for classroom use. If you consult some of these sources as well as another textbook or two on discrete mathematics that you do not use for your course, you can suddenly find yourself equipped with dozens of problems and teaching ideas from which to choose. Remember that teaching ideas are like recipes—the more you have to choose from, the more likely it is that you'll find one that is practical and effective. After all, a powerful activity or lesson is worth sharing, and an important role of the teacher is to seek out the most popular recipes, while recognizing that an activity which works for one teacher in a class may not work for another. When a teacher fails to seek out additional resource books, the result is a short menu of textbook-driven ideas that may be acceptable but are not nearly as powerful as is possible when additional sources are considered.

Of course, these books and videos are only useful if you know that they exist and know how to obtain copies of them. So, how do you find out about these resource books? Here are five suggestions to consider:

- Make sure that you are on the mailing list of several commercial publishers of teaching ideas. As new resources become available, the publishers will highlight them in the catalogs. Many of these catalogs are available on the World Wide Web, and having your name on a company's database is generally free. Often, resource books can be purchased on a thirty-day trial basis, during which time you can determine whether the source is worth the money. In many school districts, the school or department has a budget for these resources. If not, tell your family and friends that the books make a great birthday gift.

- Talk to your colleagues and friends in mathematics education. It is likely that a teacher down the hall or in a neighboring district has used a particular resource for years, and you have never heard of it. The more you talk with people about what they do and what they use, the more often exemplary resources will surface. And, in many cases, the teacher who owns an effective resource will be willing and excited about sharing it with you—borrowing one another's books is common among classroom teachers.

- Attend local, state, and national conferences of mathematics teachers. At these sessions, presenters often cite sources of effective teaching ideas that you can pursue when you return home. Also, there is generally an exhibition area at conferences at which publishers display their teaching aids and resource books. These exhibitions give the teacher an opportunity to browse the many resources available. The issue of professional development is discussed at length in Chapter 10.

- Pay a visit to curriculum libraries at universities or for local school districts. Often, libraries have places set aside for featuring the latest in teaching resource books that can be browsed or even checked out for use as supplementary sources of ideas. Curriculum supervisors at the district level frequently receive complimentary copies of new resource books and keep them on file in a curriculum library or holding area. These supervisors are generally very accommodating about allowing teachers to browse the sample copies for possible purchase.

- Look for teaching ideas in the feature articles of the professional journals such as *The Mathematics Teacher* and *Mathematics Teaching in the Middle School* by the NCTM. These articles often include classroom-tested ideas from other teachers, complete with reproducible masters and step-by-step instructions on how to carry out a lesson. Also, these journals regularly review the latest resource books. These reviews describe available resources in some detail and point out strengths and weaknesses.

Remember that teachers are the best when it comes to "stealing" ideas from one another. And why shouldn't they be? Many teaching ideas have been around for decades and continue to re-surface in slightly reworked formats. The better you are at locating the resources and selecting the best teaching ideas, the more proficient you will become at supplementing the activities and problems in your textbook.

The Internet

Over the past several years, the growth of the World Wide Web has been phenomenal. Teachers who had no Internet access a few years ago are, today, using the Web extensively to find lesson plans and ideas for their classes. Let's say, for example, that you wanted to use the Internet to locate some additional teaching ideas on graph theory. By going to the AltaVista website at <www.altavista.com>—one of the popular search engines for locating websites—and running a search for "graph theory," the site locates Web page "hits" that contain something about your topic of interest. Figure 4–9 shows a search for graph theory at the AltaVista site that located 15,818 Web pages relating to the topic. Of course, use of the World Wide Web requires patience because few of us have the time to actually view thousands of Web pages.

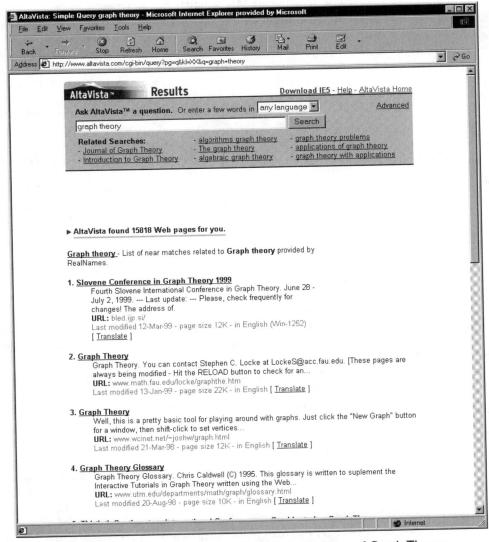

Figure 4–9 A World Wide Web Search on the Topic of Graph Theory
(Reproduced with the permission of AltaVista. AltaVista and the AltaVista logo
are trademarks of AltaVista Company.)

So, the skilled teacher will quickly browse the titles of the sites and only click on those that appear to have a high probability of being useful in planning and teaching. Sometimes, searches can be narrowed by typing, for example, "lesson plan + graph theory," rather than just "graph theory," so the site will only identify those Web pages containing lesson plans. But like seeking out useful books in a library, the ability to efficiently and effectively locate sources is developed primarily by practice.

Several journals and most professional organizations now have websites that allow you to access supplemental teaching ideas from any computer with Internet access. If you are relatively new to the Internet, you may first want to visit the National Council of Teachers of Mathematics at <www.nctm.org>. At this website, you will obtain information about the NCTM and its affiliates and gain access to articles and ideas for teachers. You may also want to visit the Eisenhower National Clearinghouse at <www.enc.org>, which features examples of standards and state models, hundreds of lesson plans, and reviews of resource materials for teachers of mathematics and science. The popular Math Forum website at <www.forum.swarthmore.edu> has teaching ideas, problems of the week, links to other mathematics websites, and even a button that allows students to leave questions to be answered by a mathematician, Ask Dr. Math. In fact, the future of teacher resources may very well reside with the Internet, as more materials are being made available every day and are easy to access with the click of a mouse. Some professional organizations have already begun to make their journals available on-line. For more details on the use of the Internet in secondary and middle school mathematics instruction, see Chapter 7. Also, a list of useful websites, including short descriptions and addresses, has been organized for your use in Appendix E.

Organizing a Resource File

Ultimately, most teachers accumulate a great deal of resource materials. It is not unusual for teachers to collect exemplary lesson plans, activities, classic problems, assignment ideas, useful handouts, and a wealth of other teaching resources from books, journals, the Internet, professional conferences, and colleagues. But although collecting these ideas is relatively simple, organizing them in a useful manner is not always so easy. We often hear teachers saying, "I know I have it somewhere because I took notes on that topic during a conference one time, but I have no idea where I put it." Therefore, it is important—particularly for teachers who are new to the profession—to establish a useful method for collecting and organizing resource materials. After all, what good is an exemplary hands-on activity if you can't find it on the day that you want to use it in class? Here are three practical suggestions for organizing a resource file:

- Obtain a box of file folders. Each time that you find a good problem, activity, or lesson, place a master copy in one folder and title the folder by writing a descriptor (such as "Grains of Rice" or "Orange Grove") on the label. Then, organize the file folders in alphabetical order by content area. For example, you may place the grains-of-rice problem under Measurement because it involves weighing a sample of rice to estimate the total weight of the rice. You may file the orange-grove problem under Algebra and Functions because the problem involves patterning and writing an equation that represents the problem. It is important, however, that you use a filing scheme that works for you. The grains-of-rice problem, for example, could just as easily be filed under Algebra and Functions because the solution can include an analysis of exponential functions. Consequently, some teachers file all of the problems and activities alphabetically. However you choose to organize the resources, it is important to place only *one* idea in each file folder. Otherwise, you may spend a great deal of time rummaging through a file to find one teaching idea that has been mixed in with a dozen others. And the process becomes simple: Each time that you encounter an idea that you think will be useful, give it a title on a file folder, place the idea in the folder, and file it in an appropriate location.

- Obtain several three-ring binders and a plastic storage tub or a small file cabinet. Label each binder for a particular content strand, such as the five content areas in *Principles and Standards for School Mathematics*—number and operation, patterns/functions/algebra, geometry and spatial sense, measurement, and data analysis/statistics/probability. Then, each time that you locate a useful teaching idea, three-hole-punch the pages, and place the idea in the appropriate binder. If you store all of the binders in a plastic tub or file cabinet, you will always know where to look for the teaching ideas. As new ideas are added, you may choose to change the organization scheme, and this is very easy when using binders and three-hole-punched pages. For example, if you decide to create a new binder on problem solving that includes some ideas you have already collected, you only need to label a new binder and either move some activities from their former location to the new one or make a second copy of the activity and place one copy in each binder.

- Obtain a set of index cards and an index card file box or use a computer database program. Each time that you discover a new teaching idea, write the idea title at the top of the card, a short description of the idea on the card, and file it in a file box by content topic (or by chapter of the textbook if your class uses a particular one over a period of time). Then, keep one master file of all of the teaching ideas on paper in alphabetical order, titled at the top to match the titles on the index cards. Whenever you are going to teach a lesson on a particular topic, you can quickly thumb through the short descriptions on the index cards to locate a useful idea. Then, go to the master file of ideas and pull it out for duplication or use in your class. It is often quicker and easier to locate a problem or lesson by looking through a small box of index cards than by flipping through binders filled with papers. Similarly, you can save the content area, title of the activity, short description, and even the source or date on a computer disk. The database would facilitate a rapid search for a key word such as "rice" to find a problem.

Whatever method you choose—including, perhaps, some other scheme that is not listed here but makes sense to you—it is important to seek out exemplary problems, activities, and lessons from resource books, journals, the Internet, and other sources and to organize them for easy reference. These resources will facilitate your ability to meet the mathematical goals and objectives set forth by the school district for your grade level.

■ CONCLUSION ■

The teaching and learning process begins with a very specific set of statements about what a student should feel, know, and be able to do at each grade level in a Pre-K–12 program. While national standards and state models provide a framework for teaching, a local course of study is written to prescribe the details of what students should be exploring each year they are in school. The course of study is essentially the contract between the school and the community in that it provides direction for the instructional process. Objectives within the course of study document vary from simple knowledge-level items to conceptual and higher-order application situations. The wording of these objectives can also suggest the type of teaching methods that are expected in a district, including the use of hands-on materials and technology.

But, although the active, hands-on engagement of students in the learning process makes sense on paper, this type of teaching only becomes possible when the teacher has access to lessons and activities that support a more constructivist approach. And although a textbook can be a valuable tool for providing direction and serving as a source for problems, often many additional ideas are found in resource books and on the Internet. Ideally, the teacher will use the textbook as a general guide for instruction but will supplement the book with a multitude of ideas from other sources. The thoughtful collection and organization of these resources is an important skill for an effective mathematics teacher.

When the NCTM *Curriculum and Evaluation Standards* were released in 1989, the National Science Foundation provided millions of dollars in competitive grants for colleges and universities to develop instructional programs consistent with the vision of the *Standards*. Several of these projects resulted in textbooks, websites, and print materials for general use. The real strength of these programs is that they were field-tested and researched for years prior to their publication in a final form. At the middle school level, for example, Michigan State University developed a three-year program known as the Connected Mathematics Project or CMP, which was later published by Dale Seymour Publications for Grades 6–8. Likewise, Encyclopedia Brittanica published a program for grades 5–9 entitled Mathematics in Context, and Creative Publications released an NSF-supported middle school program known as MathScape. Similarly, at the high school level, several integrated core curriculum projects were developed and published. The Core Plus Mathematics Project or CPMP was created at Western Michigan University. In addition, the high school level has seen the publication of the Interactive Mathematics Program (IMP) and Project ARISE as well as their predecessor, the University of Chicago School Mathematics Project (UCSMP). All of these programs—and others not discussed here—provide educators with teaching units that are rooted in real-life problems so that students can explore mathematical concepts in the context of problem solving. The materials emphasize the connections between content subjects and the use of technology in problem solving.

When the *Standards* of 1989 were first released, educators said that they wanted details on how to implement the reformed curriculum and teaching vision. Now that these NSF-funded materials have become available, teachers have specific lessons that can be used in the classroom to support the *Standards* documents. For details and examples of the secondary NSF-funded curricula, visit the COMPASS (Curricular Options in Mathematics Programs for All Secondary Schools) website at <http://www.ithaca.edu/compass>. A similar website for middle school curricula is available at <http://showmecenter.missouri.edu>. These sites offer listings of available project materials, samples of lessons and activities, and interactive opportunities for the user to compare the contents of the projects. A list of these projects and their publishers is included in the Resources section at the end of this chapter.

This chapter concludes our discussion of the Mathematics curriculum. Chapter 3 explored the NCTM *Curriculum and Evaluation Standards,* the use of state models, and the notion of a core curriculum. In this chapter, we have discussed the issues of writing courses of study, the use of goals and objectives in curriculum planning, and the selection, use, and organization of supplementary resource materials. In the three chapters that make up Unit III, we turn our attention to the art of *teaching* mathematics. In Chapter 5, we discuss how daily lesson plans and long-term unit plans are prepared to meet the goals and objectives set forth in a course of study, and Chapter 6 deals with organization of the classroom and the role of the mathematics teacher. Finally, in Chapter 7, we look at the use of technology—computers, calculators, visual media, and the Internet—in the instructional process.

■ GLOSSARY ■

Affective Objective: An affective objective is a statement of an outcome referring to attitudes or feelings that should be displayed by a student after experiencing a lesson, series of lessons, course, or mathematics program.

Cognitive Objective: A cognitive objective is a statement of an outcome referring to skills and concepts the student should understand after experiencing a lesson, series of lessons, course, or mathematics program. Cognitive objectives are generally subcategorized as knowledge and skill, concept, and application level outcomes.

Course of Study: A course of study is a document that prescribes the curriculum, by grade level, for a state, county, or individual school district. It includes a district philosophy, overarching goals, a list of objectives for each grade level, and pupil performance objectives for mastery-level outcomes.

District Philosophy: A district philosophy is a broad statement of beliefs held by educators in that system. The philosophy should provide the underlying foundation upon which specific objectives are written.

Goals: Goals are broad statements about what a student should be able to accomplish as a result of participating in a district's mathematics program. The goal statement should follow logically from the district's philosophy and provide a framework for more specific grade-level objectives.

Objective: An objective is a very specific statement that describes what a student should feel, know, or be able to do at a particular grade level. Objectives are the intended outcomes of a lesson or series of lessons. Objectives can be subcategorized as affective, cognitive, and psychomotor.

Pascal's Triangle: Pascal's Triangle is a triangle made up of progressively longer rows of numbers as shown:

```
            1
          1   1
        1   2   1
      1   3   3   1
    1   4   6   4   1
  1   5  10  10   5   1
1   6  15  20  15   6   1
1  7  21  35  35  21  7  1
1  8  28  56  70  56  28  8  1
```

The numbers in each row come from adding the two numbers directly above and to the right and left of the location. Pascal's Triangle was named in honor of Blaise Pascal, a seventeenth-century French mathematician, although there is evidence that the triangle existed long before Pascal's lifetime. Patterns in Pascal's Triangle are numerous as one views numbers vertically, horizontally, and diagonally. Determining binomial distributions, finding combinations, and locating famous number patterns such as the triangular numbers are just a few of the uses of this valuable tool.

Psychomotor Objective: A psychomotor objective is a statement of an outcome referring to things that a student should be physically able to do after experiencing a lesson, series of lessons, course, or mathematics program. An example of a psychomotor objective is, "the student will be able to successfully do at least ten consecutive jumping jacks," where the emphasis is on a physical activity required of the student. Psychomotor objectives are common in the areas of physical education and the arts and not generally associated directly with mathematics education.

Pupil Performance Objective (PPO): A pupil performance objective is a specific description of what a student should be able to do at a particular grade level. PPOs flow naturally from the objectives for a grade level, generally reflect those objectives, and are often used to write classroom or district-wide assessment items, which may take the form of problems, questions, or projects. A PPO often contains a condition under which the student should perform as well as criteria that are used to determine the degree to which a student has mastered the outcome.

■ DISCUSSION QUESTIONS ■

1. Obtain a copy of the mathematics course of study for a school district near you. Examine the document, looking for the philosophy, goals, objectives, and pupil performance objectives. How effectively does the document communicate to the teacher exactly what is to be taught at each grade level?

2. Discuss the potential advantages and disadvantages of including broad representation on a course of study writing committee. Why might a school district choose to have a curriculum supervisor and a small committee of mathematics teachers write the document rather than select a larger representative committee including administrators, guidance counselors, and community members?

3. Suppose that a school district's goal is that "the student will apply the use of algebra and functions to solve problems." List several objectives that you might expect to see in a course of study based on this goal.

4. One of the problems with including affective objectives in a course of study is that it can be difficult to assess the development of dispositions. Discuss some possible alternatives that teachers have for measuring affective outcomes in a lesson or throughout a course.

5. Suppose that you want students to become proficient at working with square roots. Write three objectives involving the use of square roots—one at the knowledge and skill level, one at the concept level, and one at the application level.

6. Divide the class into small groups and have each group write a pupil performance objective that might accompany each of the following content objectives if mastery of the outcome is expected: (a) The student will determine the arithmetic mean of a set of numbers. (b) The student will graph a linear function. (c) The student will classify quadrilaterals. (d) The student will find the zeros of a polynomial function. Compare objectives and discuss the variety of ways that an individual can interpret a given cognitive objective.

7. Obtain two available textbooks for a particular course or grade level. Using the questions and criteria described in this chapter, prepare a criticism of each book and a comparison that would allow an educator to select one text over the other.

8. Discuss some of the advantages and disadvantages of teaching mathematics without a textbook. Under what conditions might a novice teacher have success at teaching a course without a textbook?

9. Obtain copies of several resource books, such as the NCTM Addenda Series or other commercially available books of teaching ideas. How are the books organized, and what features might make one resource book more desirable to the classroom teacher than another?

10. Using a computer with Internet access and a search engine such as AltaVista, run a search for teaching ideas on the mathematical topic of your choice. Then, discuss the difficulties that may have confronted you while running the search and the practicality of using the Internet to find teaching ideas.

11. In a small group, discuss the options for organizing a resource file listed in this chapter. Which one appeals the most to you and why? What other ideas do you have for organizing resources?

12. Obtain a copy of one of the NSF-funded curriculum materials listed in the Resources section of this chapter. Browse through the text materials and discuss the similarities and differences between this curriculum and a more traditional curriculum that you may have experienced. What are the benefits and possible drawbacks to using the NSF-funded curricula?

■ BIBLIOGRAPHIC REFERENCES AND RESOURCES ■

AltaVista. (1999). AltaVista Search Engine website. Retrieved August 20, 1999 from the World Wide Web: <http://www.altavista.com>

COMAP. (1999). COMAP website. Retrieved August 20, 1999 from the World Wide Web: <http://www.dc.net/pthomas/comap/>

Educational Resources Information Center. (1999). AskERIC Lesson Plans. Retrieved August 20, 1999 from the World Wide Web: <http://ericir.syr.edu/Virtual/Lessons/>

Eisenhower National Clearinghouse. (1999). Lesson Plans and Activities. Retrieved August 20, 1999 from the World Wide Web: <http://www.enc.org/classroom/lessons/index.htm>

Ithaca College. (1999). COMPASS: Curricular Options in Mathematics Programs for All Secondary Students. Retrieved August 20, 1999 from the World Wide Web: <http://www.ithaca.edu/compass>

Kenney, M. J. (Ed.). (1991). *1991 Yearbook of the NCTM: Discrete mathematics across the curriculum, K–12.* Reston, VA: National Council of Teachers of Mathematics.

National Council of Teachers of Mathematics. (1999). NCTM website. Retrieved August 20, 1999 from the World Wide Web: <http://www.nctm.org>

National Council of Teachers of Mathematics. (1998). *Principles and standards for school mathematics.* Reston, VA: National Council of Teachers of Mathematics.

National Council of Teachers of Mathematics. (1989). *Curriculum and evaluation standards for school mathematics.* Reston, VA: National Council of Teachers of Mathematics.

Rosenstein, J. G., Franzblau, D. S., & Roberts, F. S. (Eds.). (1998). *Discrete mathematics in the schools.* Reston, VA: National Council of Teachers of Mathematics.

Southeast Missouri State University. (1999). Show-Me Center: Supporting Standards-Based Middle Grades Mathematics Curricula. Retrieved August 20, 1999 from the World Wide Web: <http://showmecenter.missouri.edu>

Swarthmore University. (1999). The Math Forum. Retrieved August 20, 1999 from the World Wide Web: <http:// www.forum.swarthmore.edu>

■ NCTM ADDENDA SERIES RESOURCE BOOKS ■

Secondary School Addenda Series

Burrill, G., Burrill, J. C., Coffield, P., Davis, G., de Lange, J., Resnick, D., & Siegel, M. (1992). *Data analysis and statistics across the curriculum.* Reston, VA: National Council of Teachers of Mathematics.

Coxford, A. F., Burks, L., Giamati, C., & Jonik, J. (1991). *Geometry from multiple perspectives.* Reston, VA: National Council of Teachers of Mathematics.

Froelich, G., Bartkovich, K. G., & Foerster, P. A. (1991). *Connecting mathematics.* Reston, VA: National Council of Teachers of Mathematics.

Heid, M. K., Choate, J., Sheets, C., & Zbiek, M. R. (1995). *Algebra in a technological world.* Reston, VA: National Council of Teachers of Mathematics.

Meiring, S. P., Rubenstein, R. N., Schultz, J. E., de Lange, J., & Chambers, D. L. (1992). *A core curriculum: Making mathematics count for everyone.* Reston, VA: National Council of Teachers of Mathematics.

Middle School Addenda Series

Curcio, F. R., Bezuk, N. S., et al. (1994). *Understanding rational numbers and proportions.* Reston, VA: National Council of Teachers of Mathematics.

Geddes, D. (1994). *Measurement in the middle grades.* Reston, VA: National Council of Teachers of Mathematics.

Geddes, D., Bove, J., Fortunato, I., Fuys, D. J., Morgenstern, J., & Welschman-Tischler, R. (1991). *Geometry in the middle grades.* Reston, VA: National Council of Teachers of Mathematics.

Phillips, E., Gardella, T., Kelly, C., & Stewart, J. (1991). *Patterns and functions.* Reston, VA: National Council of Teachers of Mathematics.

Reys, B. J., et al. (1991). *Developing number sense in the middle grades.* Reston, VA: National Council of Teachers of Mathematics.

Zawojewski, J. S., et al. (1991). *Dealing with data and chance.* Reston, VA: National Council of Teachers of Mathematics.

■ SAMPLE RECOMMENDED RESOURCE BOOKS ■

Bezuszka, S., D'Angelo, L., Kenney, M. J., & Kokoska, S. (1980). *Perfect numbers.* Chestnut Hill, MA: Boston College.

Bezuszka, S., Kenney, M., & Silvery, L. (1977). *Tesselations: The geometry of patterns.* Palo Alto, CA: Creative Publications.

Bezuszka, S., D'Angelo, L., & Kenney, M. J. (1976). *Applications of finite differences.* Chestnut Hill, MA: Boston College.

Bezuszka, S., D'Angelo, L., & Kenney, M. J. (1976). *Fraction action: Booklet 6.* Chestnut Hill, MA: Boston College.

Bezuszka, S., D'Angelo, L., & Kenney, M. J. (1976). *Fraction action: Booklet 5.* Chestnut Hill, MA: Boston College.

Bezuszka, S., D'Angelo, L., & Kenney, M. J. (1976). *The wonder square.* Chestnut Hill, MA: Boston College.

Carlson, R. J. & Winter, M. J. (1993). *Algebra experiments II: Exploring nonlinear functions.* Menlo Park, CA: Addison-Wesley.

Edwards, E. L. (1990). *Algebra for everyone.* Reston, VA: National Council of Teachers of Mathematics.

Farrell, M. A. (1988). *Imaginative ideas for the teacher of mathematics, grades K–12: Ranucci's reservoir.* Reston, VA: National Council of Teachers of Mathematics.

Hirsch, C. R. & Laing, R. A. (Eds.). (1993). *Activities for active learning and teaching: Selections from the "Mathematics Teacher."* Reston, VA: National Council of Teachers of Mathematics.

House, P. (1997). *Mission mathematics: Grades 9–12.* Reston, VA: National Council of Teachers of Mathematics.

Hynes, M. C. (Ed.). (1996). *Ideas: NCTM standards-based instruction, grades 5–8.* Reston, VA: National Council of Teachers of Mathematics.

Kenney, M. J. (1976). *The incredible Pascal's triangle.* Chestnut Hill, MA: Boston College.

Kenney, M. J. (1976). *The super sum.* Chestnut Hill, MA: Boston College.

O'Connor, V. F. & Hynes, M. C. (1997). *Mission mathematics: Grades 5–8.* Reston, VA: National Council of Teachers of Mathematics.

Saunders, H. (1981). *When are we ever gonna have to use this?* Palo Alto, CA: Dale Seymour.

Souviney, R., Britt, M., Gargiulo, S., & Hughes, P. (1992). *Mathematical investigations: Book three.* Palo Alto, CA: Dale Seymour.

Souviney, R., Britt, M., Gargiulo, S., & Hughes, P. (1992). *Mathematical investigations: Book two.* Palo Alto, CA: Dale Seymour.

Souviney, R., Britt, M., Gargiulo, S., & Hughes, P. (1990). *Mathematical investigations: Book one.* Palo Alto, CA: Dale Seymour.

Willcutt, B. (1995). *Cubes: Building algebraic thinking with progressive patterns.* Pacific Grove, CA: Critical Thinking Press & Software.

Willcutt, B. (1995). *Pattern blocks: Building algebraic thinking with progressive patterns.* Pacific Grove, CA: Critical Thinking Press & Software.

■ COMAP "HI-MAP" (HIGH SCHOOL MATHEMATICS) TEACHING MODULES ■

Bennett, S., DeTemple, D., Dirks, M., Newell, B., Robertson, J. M., & Tyus, B. *Module 9: Fair divisions: Getting your fair share.*

Bennett, S., DeTemple, D., Dirks, M., Newell, B., Robertson, J. M., & Tyus, B. *Module 8: The apportionment problem: The search for the perfect democracy.*

Brown, S. I. *Module 7: Student generations.*

Chavey, D. *Module 21: Drawing pictures with one line: Exploring graph theory.*

Cozzens, M. B. & Porter, R. *Module 6: Problem solving using graphs.*

Cozzens, M. & Porter, R. *Module 2: Recurrence relations—"counting backwards."*

Crowe, D. *Module 4: Symmetry, rigid motions, and patterns.*

Djang, F. C. *Module 11: Applications of geometrical probability.*

Francis, R. L. *Module 10: A mathematical look at the calendar.*

Francis, R. L. *Module 13: The mathematician's coloring book.*

Growney, J. S. *Module 5: Using percent.*

Kumar, G. S. *Module 14: Decision making & math models.*

Lucas, W. F. *Module 19: Fair voting: Weighted votes for unequal constituencies.*

Malkevitch, J., Froelich, G., & Froelich, D. *Module 18: Codes galore.*

Malkevitch, J. & Froelich, G. *Module 22: Loads of codes.*

Malkevitch, J. & Froelich, G. *Module 1: The mathematical theory of elections.*

Martin, W. B. *Module 12: Spheres and satellites.*

Metallo, F. R. *Module 17: The abacus: Its history and applications.*

Meyer, R. W. *Module 16: ExploreSorts.*

Rogers, J. R. *Module 15: A uniform approach to rate and ratio problems: The introduction of the universal rate formula.*

Sriskandarajah, J. *Module 20: Optimality pays: An introduction to linear programming.*

Zagare, F. C. *Module 3: The mathematics of conflict.*

■ NSF-FUNDED CURRICULAR MATERIALS ■

Secondary Materials

Applications/Reform in Secondary Education (ARISE)

Grades: 9–12
Publisher: South-Western
Contact: South-Western Educational Publishing, 5101 Madison Rd., Cincinnati, Ohio 45227 or (1-800-824-5179) or <http://www.swep.com>

Core-Plus Mathematics Project (CPMP)

Grades: 9–12
Publisher: Everyday Learning Corporation
Contact: 1-800-322-6284 or <http://www.everydaylearning.com>

Interactive Mathematics Program (IMP)

Grades: 9–12
Publisher: Key Curriculum
Contact: 1-800-995-MATH or <http://www.keypress.com/>

MATH Connections

Grades: 9–12
Publisher: It's About Time, Inc.
Contact: 1-888-698-TIME or <http://www.Its-About-Time.com/MC1a.html>

Systemic Initiative for Montana Mathematics and Science (SIMMS)

Grades: 9–12
Publisher: Simon & Schuster Custom Publishing
Contact: 1-800-693-4060

University of Chicago School Mathematics Project (UCSMP)

Grades: 6 (or 7)–12
Publisher: Scott Foresman/Addison-Wesley

Contact: 1-800-552-2259 or <http://www.scottforesman.com>

Middle School Materials

Connected Mathematics Project (CMP)

Grades: 6–8
Publisher: Dale Seymour Publications
Catalogue Sales: Scott Foresman/Addison-Wesley (1-800-552-2259) or <www.cuisenaire-dsp.com>

Mathematics in Context Curriculum (MiC)

Grades: 5–8 or 6–9
Publisher: Encyclopedia Brittanica
Contact: 1-800-554-9862 or <www.ebmic.com>

MathScape Curriculum

Grades: 6–8
Publisher: Creative Publications
Contact: 1-800-624-0822 or <www.creativepublications.com>

MathThematics (STEM)

Grades: 6–8
Publisher: McDougal Littell
Contact: 1-800-289-2558, Ext. 5441 or <www.mcdougallittell.com/math>

Middle School Math Through Applications Curriculum (MMAP)

Grades: 6–8
Publisher: Modules are available through self-publishing
Contact: 1-415-614-7900 by phone or 1-415-614-7900 by fax

Teaching Mathematics

The art of teaching is difficult to capture on paper. Every day, teachers make decisions regarding the directions in which to guide their students, both outside of classtime and in the midst of a lesson. Questions arise in the classroom that a teacher can choose to pursue at length or to push aside for the time being. As we discussed in Chapters 3 and 4, teachers also make decisions about how to sequence experiences for students and how to try to meet the needs of a diverse population in the classroom. Unit I focused on the the field of mathematics and how the student learns; Unit II looked at the curriculum and how decisions are made about the mathematical content and processes that students should explore in school. In Unit III, we examine the teaching process itself. Chapter 5 describes how teachers attempt to address the goals and objectives of a course of study through the planning process, from writing daily lesson plans to organizing long-term plans or units. Chapter 6 discusses the role of the classroom teacher as outlined in the Standards documents of the National Council of Teachers of Mathematics. Finally, Chapter 7 features an explanation of how technology, from simple calculators to the integration of computer software, can be used to enhance classroom experiences.

Planning for Instruction

After reading Chapter 5, you should be able to answer the following questions:

- What is a unit plan and what factors need to be considered when writing one?

- What are the essential components of a lesson plan? Describe each component.

- What features make one lesson plan better than another? Discuss some lesson-planning tips that increase the likelihood of success.

- What is the difference between a *lesson plan* and a *lesson image,* and how does teaching experience change the way that lessons are prepared?

- What are examples of key questions that can be addressed during reflection on a lesson, and why is it important for teachers to reflect on their teaching practice?

Suppose that you were an architect overseeing the construction of a new home. Prior to drawing up any plans, you would want to see the site and measure it, so you would know what kind of space is available and what it is realistic to build on the plot of land. Then, you might carefully map out the project, scheduling each step of the process in an organized manner. It wouldn't make any sense, for example, to have the roofers show up with shingles on the same day the masons are laying the foundation, and you had better make sure that the carpenters have constructed the walls before the electrician comes in to wire the home. So, you design a general sketch of the process, including each of the major components of construction. And, although a general plan guides the building of the home, daily needs must be addressed. For example, if the carpenter is going to put on a roof on a Monday, then the plan must include not only a goal for what can be accomplished that day but the personnel and a list of supplies needed to construct the roof. The carpenter will have to secure plywood, nails, hammers, saws, tapemeasures, and so forth, and know, in advance, which step of the process will require which tools. Finally, when the house is completed, an inspector will need to visit to approve the construction and wiring before a family moves in.

The process of building a home is similar to the process that teachers go through each time they develop a series of learning experiences for students in a mathematics class. In a very general way, the teacher needs to identify a series of goals and objectives (discussed in detail in Chapter 4) and construct an all-encompassing plan. After all, the point of teaching a lesson or series of lessons is to attempt to address issues and concepts stated in a course of study. But, specifically, the teacher must also write detailed plans for how each day within the unit will be conducted, including daily objectives, materials, procedures, and a way to assess the degree to which students are understanding the major mathematical concepts. A well-engineered home-building project can save time and money and result in an excellent structure. Similarly, a carefully planned series of learning experiences for students can make all the difference as to whether students understand the outcomes in the course of study. In this chapter, we explore the major issues to be considered when planning long-term units and daily lesson plans.

■ UNIT PLANNING

A **unit** is a carefully planned set of learning experiences that are designed to address one or several goals and objectives over time. Generally, units are long term in that they may take several class periods or even several weeks to complete. However, there is no rule for the length of a unit—a unit may be taught in a couple of days, but it is not unusual for one to be planned so that it takes three or four weeks to complete. For example, a teacher may choose to insert a three-day mini-unit on fractals in a geometry course but design a four-week unit on similar and congruent triangles later in the same course. A unit will contain a few or several daily lesson plans, carefully sequenced to develop the goals and objectives of the unit. Following are some examples of secondary and middle school mathematics units and the topics of daily lessons within them. The individual topics may take one or more days to develop within the unit:

Sample Unit 1:

UNIT TOPIC: Probability

DAILY LESSON TOPICS INCLUDE:

Introduction: explorations involving experimental probability

Probabilities in a real-world setting (e.g., weather forecasts and games)

Permutations and combinations to determine sample spaces

Calculating theoretical probabilities

Independent and dependent events—conditional probabilities

A geometric look at probability

Wrap-up: review and discussion of the misuse of data in society

Sample Unit 2:

UNIT TOPIC: Geometry/Right Triangles

DAILY LESSON TOPICS INCLUDE:

Introduction: Review of classification of right, obtuse, and acute triangles

Exploring right triangles (acute angles are complementary, etc.)

The Pythagorean Theorem
Converse and corollaries of the Pythagorean Theorem
Pythagorean Triples and patterns
Simple right-triangle trigonometry (sine, cosine, tangent relationships)
Wrap-up: Review and stage-setting for next unit on congruent triangles

Sample Unit 3:

UNIT TOPIC: Discrete Mathematics/Graph Theory
DAILY LESSON TOPICS INCLUDE:
Introduction: Konigsberg Bridge problem and networks
Explorations to determine whether or not a path is traversible
Euler Paths
Hamiltonian Circuits
Traveling Salesperson problem (i.e., counting the number of possible paths)
Representing circuits as adjacency matrices
Wrap-up: review and stage setting for the next unit on matrix algebra

As you read through these samples, you may have noticed that the first lesson in the unit sometimes begins by posing a problem or set of problems to get the students to begin to explore the topic at hand. Other times, a unit will begin with a brief review to help the student make connections between what is already known and what will be studied over the next several lessons. The last lesson of a unit often provides an opportunity for the teacher to review and to help the students make the connection between the current unit and the next topic to be explored. In a sense, a unit represents a block of teaching time, and it is important to remember that learning took place prior to the block and will continue after that block of lessons. Consequently, any time that a teacher designs a unit for a class, it is critical to consider (1) the knowledge that students will bring to the new topics and (2) how the current unit will connect to the next one. These tasks are not as easy as they may appear on the surface, and, unless they are considered, a unit may be destined to fail.

Let's suppose that you were going to teach a unit on graphing lines in a ninth grade mathematics course (Algebra I or First-Year Integrated Mathematics). The first question you need to ask is, "What kinds of things do I expect students to know and be able to do by the end of the unit?" Although this inquiry may eventually result in the formulation of specific outcomes or objectives as described in Chapter 4, it is generally desirable to first think about the types of problems that students should be able to solve by the time they complete the unit. For example, you might look through the teacher's manual of your textbook or some other resource materials and decide that students should recognize the following situations as examples of linear functions:

- The cost of going to see a movie is $5.50. How much does it cost to see x movies?
- You agree to pay back a $250 loan at the rate of $15 per month. How much do you owe on the loan after m months?

- Create a table that relates the temperature in degrees Fahrenheit to the temperature in degrees Celsius.
- Draw a graph that shows how the circumference of a circle, C, depends on the diameter, d.
- Graph the function $y = 2x - 5$.

Once you have identified the skills and attitudes the students should possess by the end of the unit, you can begin to think about what they should already know—a starting place—and how you might get them to the desired outcomes. You can begin by asking, "What types of experiences have they already had with linear functions, even if they have not specifically labeled them as such?" You may realize, for example, that every student has at least had exposure to graphing in the coordinate plane and to using a table of values to explore the relationship between two variables. Perhaps a study of the Cartesian plane was even the focus of a previous unit or chapter. The key issue here is to decide what **prerequisite knowledge** the students will need prior to studying the new unit. For the unit we are discussing, it may be necessary for the student to know how to graph in the plane, how to construct a value table, and how to use a variable to generalize a relationship. As long as you are confident that the students in your class possess those skills, you are ready to proceed. If not, they will need some additional preparation before moving into the new content.

Assuming that your class has the prerequisite knowledge to learn about graphing linear functions, you can ask, "As we explore this unit, what are the key concepts and skills the students will encounter and need to understand?" Often, this analysis is done in the form of a **conceptual map** or a graphic organizer of how the content in a lesson, unit, semester, course, or even an entire program fits together as a whole. Figure 5–1 presents an example of a conceptual map for the linear function unit:

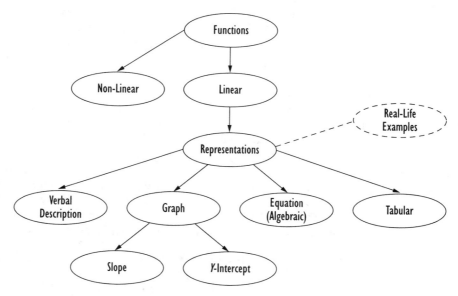

Figure 5–1 Conceptual Map for a Unit on Linear Functions

This conceptual map provides a visual "feel" for how all of the pieces of the unit fit together. The map is not only useful for planning, but students often find this type of graphic helps them to appreciate the whole unit, as students tend to get caught up in the details of a unit and lose the forest for the trees. A map may be presented at the beginning of the unit, as a review, or as an assignment to encourage students to think about the connections among content areas they have been studying. In the map in Figure 5–1, the unit focuses on linear functions and their multiple representations. In the unit, the student will develop the notion that some functions are linear, but others are not and that a linear function can be represented through a verbal description, in tabular form, as an equation, or as a graph. Furthermore, students will explore the concepts of slope and y-intercept of a linear function and will make connections to the real-life uses of linear functions throughout the unit.

Once the unit is mapped out on paper, several questions become relevant and may be dealt with in no particular order:

- In what order should the key concepts be sequenced?
- What kinds of experiences should the students have to help them learn these concepts?
- How many lessons do I estimate it will take to accomplish the goals and objectives for the unit?
- What materials and tools will I need to support the lessons in this unit?

After reflecting on the map, you may decide that the sequence and timing for the unit would be:

- Introduction: an exploration of real-life functions (two days)
- Expressing linear functions as tables and graphs by hand (two days)
- Exploring linear functions on the graphing calculator (one day)
- Writing equations to describe linear functions (two days)
- What is the slope of a line? (one day)
- Discovering slope-intercept form (one day)
- Linear versus non-linear functions (one day)
- Putting the pieces together: four representations of a function (two days)

This rough sketch of the unit provides the teacher with some important information. You can anticipate, for example, that the unit will take from about ten to fifteen class days to accomplish. It is important, however, to realize that the unit plan provides a skeletal framework, and it is very possible that the first topic may only take one class period, but the discussion of linear and non-linear functions may expand—as a result of student interest—into three days rather than one. Remember that the focus of the unit needs to be on the *student* and not the *content* as we have emphasized throughout this book. Another advantage to creating a rough sketch of the unit is that you can start to research your textbook, the Internet, and other resources to locate ideas for each of the lessons in the unit. As you begin to decide what those lessons might look like, you can list the tools that will be needed, such as graphing calculators, graph paper, and hands-on materials that may generate data for the study of functions.

The next step of the unit-planning process is to ask, "How am I going to know if my students really understand what I will teach them in this unit?" This question raises the issue of assessment and how it will be conducted in the unit. Are students going to write in journals throughout the unit? Will there be any quizzes along the way? Do you plan to take any observational notes? Will students be assessed on a team project on linear functions, or will all of the work be done individually? Will there be a final test at the end of the unit? If there is a final test, are you certain that it will show you who has really mastered the objectives? A plan for assessing student progress should be roughed out as part of the planning process, keeping in mind that the best way to get a total picture of student understanding is to use multiple methods of assessment rather than restricting student assessment to a quiz or final test. Assessment is discussed in detail in Chapters 8 and 9.

The final decision to be made when crafting the total unit plan is to consider where students will move after its completion. You should ask yourself, "Once we have completed this unit, what is the next logical step in the students' learning sequence?" You have several options, and one is not necessarily better than another. For example, students in this unit on graphing linear equations might move on to study non-linear functions, such as quadratics and exponential functions. On the other hand, you may choose to take them into a study of simultaneous equations, beginning with a graphing method and working toward more symbolic approaches, such as substitution or addition and subtraction methods. Or, you may want to use this unit as a springboard to the study of function notation (e.g., $f(x)$) and to make generalizations about graphs of a variety of function types. To help you make this decision, you have a number of resources available to you, not the least of which is the textbook. However, considerable caution should be used here, as a textbook is useful for providing direction and ideas but should not be considered the final word, as was emphasized in Chapter 4. Just because your ninth grade textbook moves from graphing linear functions to studying simultaneous equations does not necessarily mean that your class has to go there. When all is said and done, you are the curricular leader in the classroom, and much is left to you in terms of deciding what sequence is appropriate for your class. Administrators are generally not as concerned with how you are sequencing the content and using the book as they are with ensuring that you are teaching to the concepts and skills outlined in your course of study. Throughout the unit, keep your eyes and ears open—often, students ask leading questions that can assist the teacher in making decisions. For example, they might ask, "Do you ever need to graph two functions on the same set of axes?" You may be able to use this question to lead the class into a unit on simultaneous equations.

The following chart summarizes the major types of questions a teacher needs to ask when planning a unit of study:

UNIT-PLANNING QUESTIONS

- What kinds of things do I expect students to know and be able to do by the end of the unit? (goals and objectives)
- What types of experiences have they already had with this topic, even if they have not specifically labeled them as such? (prerequisite knowledge)

- As we explore this unit, what are the key concepts and skills the students will encounter and need to understand? (goals and objectives)
- In what order should the key concepts be sequenced? (sequencing)
- What kinds of experiences should the students have to help them learn these concepts? (lessons)
- How many lessons do I think it will take to accomplish my goals for the unit? (sequencing and timing)
- What materials and tools will I need to support the lessons in this unit? (tools)
- How am I going to know if my students really understand what I want them to know after completing this unit? (assessment)
- Once we have completed this unit, what is the next logical step in the students' learning sequence? (sequencing)

As a final note, it is important to realize that teachers do not necessarily go through this type of detailed unit planning for every unit in every class—time simply doesn't always allow it. Many textbook authors have already carefully considered the design of units included in the books, and teacher's manuals frequently discuss prerequisite knowledge, a suggested sequence, a list of outcomes, and so forth, so that a teacher is not really starting from scratch when planning a unit. In fact, the NSF-funded curricular materials described in Chapter 4 are generally packaged in predesigned units that have already been field tested to ensure that students make the connections, provide accurate estimates for the amount of time the units will take, and describe the possible concerns that students will raise when they encounter the content of the unit. However, keeping in mind that a textbook's objectives are unlikely to be a perfect match for the course of study in your district, it is important not to assume that a preplanned unit is usable as is—modifications are inevitable as you consider the background of *your* students and the content of *your* course of study. A key to effective teaching is to work in harmony with the textbook, supplementing it with activities from outside resources when necessary and omitting sections or problems that do not advance objectives in the course of study. Similarly, teacher's manuals and resource books feature tips and suggestions for individual lessons, but they need to be regarded as just that—ultimately, teachers should tailor the ideas to fit the needs of their classes. In the next section, we explore the process of writing individual lesson plans.

■ LESSON PLANNING

Imagine inviting twenty-five children to your house to celebrate a younger sibling's birthday without having thought through what you wanted them to do. They arrive at your house to find that there are no organized games, few decorations, a cake but no forks or napkins, and no set ending time. What would happen? Most likely, you would end up with twenty-five screaming children looking for things to do and getting into a lot of trouble. Although the party may have been well intentioned, and the focus of the day was clear—to celebrate a birthday—the fact that it was not organized and prepared for in detail could very well have led to disaster. Similarly, when we walk into the classroom each day as teachers, we not only need a focus in terms of what we want the students to accomplish and be able to do, but we are also in need of a blueprint for the class period—a road map of sorts—with details on how to most effectively spend class time. The document that details our objectives and the day's activities is referred to as the **lesson plan.** As we discussed in the previous section, the lesson plan should fit into a longer-range unit plan, flowing logically from the previous day's activities and preparing the students for future lessons. The effectiveness of a lesson depends significantly on the care with which the lesson plan is prepared. Although an excellent plan does not ensure a powerful lesson, you can be almost certain that the lack of a focused, detailed lesson generally spells disaster for the classroom teacher.

Let's think further about the road map analogy. When you set off in a car to travel from City A to City B, you have a route in mind. However, the actual route traveled may be very different from what was intended as shown in Figure 5–2.

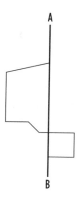

Figure 5–2 A Road Map Leading from Point A to Point B

We often encounter detours that force us off of the intended path or sideroads that are too tempting to be ignored. Consequently, we may begin at City A and eventually end up at City B, but the roads driven are sometimes unplanned. Likewise, a good lesson plan sketches out a beginning point and an objective or set of objectives for the class period as well as a set of instructions for how to get a class to where the teacher wants them to go. However, the teacher needs to be flexible enough to recognize that there may be changes along the way—detours caused by unplanned student misconceptions or sidetrips suggested by questions or comments from the students. Midstream in a lesson, a student may ask a question that leads to a **teachable moment**—a point at which the timing is perfect for addressing an issue other than what was intended in the lesson. Consider the classroom situation mentioned briefly in Chapter 3.

A class of high school sophomores has been studying right triangles and leading up to a discussion of the Pythagorean Theorem. The teacher, Mr. Marks, has asked students to draw five right triangles and to measure the lengths of their sides to the nearest millimeter, square the lengths of the sides, and see if they can find a pattern developing. After about fifteen minutes, Josette raises her hand:

Student participation is critical to the success of a lesson and can bring about teachable moments.

Josette: I think I found it! When you add two of the numbers together, after you square them, you almost get the square of the third side.

Mr. Marks: Almost? What do you mean?

Josette: Well, it's like I get the feeling that it should be equal to the square of the third side, but the numbers aren't perfect.

Mr. Marks: Why not?

Sam: We noticed that too . . . it's because our rulers aren't exact enough, so you'll always miss it by a little.

Mr. Marks: How many people saw that pattern? (several students raise their hands)

Terri: We noticed that it didn't work for just "any" two sides . . . it's always the hypotenuse that when you square it equals the squares of the other two added together.

At this point, Mr. Marks feels as though his lesson has gone as intended. Time is running short, and he has planned to assign several practice problems for homework in which students will be given two sides in a right triangle and asked to calculate the length of the third side. Then, Jason raises his hand:

Jason: Okay, so when we know it's a right triangle, we can square each of the sides, and the two legs added together will equal the hypotenuse squared, right?

Mr. Marks: Is that the pattern you were all seeing?

Jason: Yeah, but we were wondering . . . what if it's not a right triangle?

Sarah: Then, they wouldn't be equal anymore. So, it would be an acute triangle!

Jason: How do you know it wouldn't be obtuse?

Sarah: Well, I guess it could be, but I don't know.

Josette: That's a good point. We know that if it's a right triangle, $a^2 + b^2 = c^2$, but what if we discover that $a^2 + b^2 > c^2$?

Mr. Marks: Good question. Does anyone have any ideas?

Randy: I don't know, but it's possible that the sum could be less than the c-squared too, you know. But I'm not sure if that has any significance. I guess I'm a little confused now.

At this point, there are only five minutes remaining in the period. Mr. Marks can either work through an example with the class in which they are given two sides of a right triangle and have to calculate the third, or he can let go of his lesson plan to focus on student interests. He decides to choose the latter:

Mr. Marks: Well, you have certainly hit on an interesting idea here, group. Tonight, I would like for you to draw three different acute triangles and three different obtuse triangles on a piece of paper. Measure and square the sides on all six of your triangles, and see if you notice any patterns for these. Maybe in tomorrow's class we can draw some conclusions about what happens when we have something other than a right triangle to work with.

As the bell rings, and the class leaves the room, Mr. Marks knows that his objective for the day was not met. He had intended to make the point about how the Pythagorean Theorem could be used and allow students to practice the skill as an assignment. Instead, he took advantage of a teachable moment and allowed the students to lead the lesson in a direction in which they were interested. In the homework assignment, which he created on the spot, students will explore and most likely discover two important corollaries to the Pythagorean Theorem—that when the sum of the squares of the shorter sides is greater than the square of the longest side, the triangle is acute, and when the opposite is true, the triangle is obtuse. This can also be demonstrated with a simple model of two straws connected with a twist tie. As Figure 5–3 illustrates, when the straws are at a 90° angle, the Pythagorean Theorem holds true. If the angle is made greater than 90°, but the lengths of the short sides are fixed, the long side gets longer; therefore, the obtuse angle makes $c^2 > a^2 + b^2$. But when the angle is collapsed to less than 90°, the acute angle makes the third side smaller, so $c^2 < a^2 + b^2$. Thus, the students visually prove these corollaries for themselves.

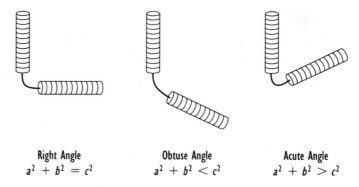

Right Angle	Obtuse Angle	Acute Angle
$a^2 + b^2 = c^2$	$a^2 + b^2 < c^2$	$a^2 + b^2 > c^2$

Figure 5–3 Corollaries to the Pythagorean Theorem

The important question is: How do you feel about Mr. Marks switching his direction midstream and following the student questions rather than his lesson plan? The answer probably depends on whether you are teaching a lesson plan or teaching real students in a mathematics class. When interest and curiosity have been generated, it is desirable to follow the path that the students view as important and worth exploring. So, we need to keep in perspective that a lesson plan is just that—a plan. It must be focused, with objectives and specific activities, but also be flexible enough to allow for modifications as students react to the activities. And, as we discuss in the next chapter, the real issue in this example is the task that the teacher provided for the class. It was during the process of working on the task of drawing and measuring five right triangles and generating subsequent classroom discussion (discourse) that students began to raise questions of their own. Instead of the teacher telling students what they were supposed to know, student opinions and questions were valued and used to redirect the instruction. Mr. Marks' lesson plan for the next day will need to be carefully crafted to give students an opportunity to discuss their conjectures about acute and obtuse triangles, while also taking the time to put some closure to a statement of the Pythagorean Theorem and explore some of its applications. So, in the end, Mr. Marks' objectives will be met, but like the road map analogy, the class will not follow the roads that he had intended.

There is no universal structure or framework for lesson planning; however, most teachers use the following **components of a lesson plan:** goals, objectives, materials, motivation, lesson procedure (including transition statements), closure, and, sometimes, extensions. After teaching a lesson, a teacher should reflect on its implementation. Many lesson plans also include a statement on assessment, but this topic is discussed at length in Chapters 8 and 9. We now explore each of the components.

Goals and Objectives

As we discussed in Chapter 4, every effective instructional episode begins with clearly stated goals and objectives that delineate exactly what it is that the student is expected to feel, know, or be able to do at the end of a lesson or unit. Ordinarily, these goals and objectives are not actually written by the teacher; instead, they are pulled from the district-adopted graded course of study. The goals are big-picture statements of learning outcomes; objectives are specific statements of what a student should feel, know, or be able to do. The goals and objectives should be the bases of all unit and lesson planning, and everything from the activities or tasks selected to the way that the class is run should flow from a statement of what is expected of students. The goals and objectives provide direction for a lesson and are intended to keep both the teacher and the students focused on the key issues. It is not unusual for a teacher to explain the main goals and objectives to a class when initiating a new unit or lesson to make it clear to everyone what is expected of them and what they are intended to learn. The objectives stated in the lesson plan should always focus on the mathematical content and processes that you are trying to teach.

Materials

When an activity is selected for a lesson, it is likely to involve the use of tools, such as calculators, rulers, graph paper, a videotape, and so forth (see Chapter 6 for a further discussion of tools). The lesson plan, therefore, should completely describe the materials necessary for the presentation. When appropriate, it should also refer to the location of materials and how many are required per class, per learning team, or per student. For example, a plan may state that the lesson requires "6 sets of algebra tiles (one for each group of 4 students), graph paper (one sheet per student), and 6 graphing calculators (one for each group of 4 students)." This listing helps ensure that the activity will be organized and smooth. There is nothing worse than getting to the middle of a lesson and realizing that each student needs a pair of scissors, but you didn't bring a box of scissors today because it wasn't in the plan. As a result, the lesson falls apart, and so does the behavior of your students. So, be prepared by including a detailed listing of materials in the lesson plan.

Motivation

Every good lesson should open with an attention-grabber that gets students thinking about the topic for the day's lesson while also sparking their curiosity and interest, making them want to engage in the learning process. Let's face it: How excited do you get when the teacher walks in and says, "Good morning. Open your books to page 147 and take out your homework"? If students are invited to engage in an interesting lesson right away, you have them in the palm of your hand. Otherwise, your students may shut down within the first five minutes, and you will have lost them for the entire period. So, a critical task of the planning process is to think of a short activity that will motivate the lesson.

Sometimes, the **motivation**—also referred to as an initiatory activity or a springboard—can be a book that is displayed or partially read to a class; at other times, it's a problem that is posed, a newspaper clipping that is displayed, or some other visual aid or activity that evokes interest and curiosity. For example, one teacher who was about to conduct a lesson on three-dimensional geometry brought in a sack of mineral crystals, leading the students to a discussion about how geologists classify minerals based on the shape of their crystals as they occur in nature. The students were fascinated by the shape of calcite and quartz crystals and were immediately drawn into the geometry lesson introduced by the solids. Another teacher, wishing to motivate a discussion of the trigonometric functions, presented the class with a graph of the average monthly high temperatures in their area over the course of five years. As the students viewed the graph of the temperatures, they recognized the cyclic behavior of the weather, and the teacher had set the stage for the discussion of the sine curve as a periodic function. A third teacher brought in an ad from a local department store and, displaying it to the class, asked what it means for the store to "take off an additional 20% on all sale items."

The motivation for a lesson can be brief, sometimes only lasting a couple of minutes, but it should be linked to the lesson content and give the students a reason for studying what they are about to encounter. The rest of the lesson becomes considerably easier to teach if the students are engaged from the beginning. However, most experienced teachers find the motivation to be the most difficult part of the lesson to plan because you have to know your students enough to understand what will get their attention and make them want to engage in the lesson for the day. This is one of many reasons why it is important for teachers to have a firm grasp of adolescent development and learning psychology. Keep in mind that opening a lesson by stating that "today, we're going to study rational functions," or "we're going to study polygons today, and I think you'll find them interesting," or, simply, "take out your homework" is not motivational, and you will probably turn off your students from the start.

Lesson Procedure

The **lesson procedure,** a set of instructions for the teacher, is the heart of the lesson plan. Generally, the lesson procedure is an outline, a step-by-step description of what the teacher and the students will do in the lesson. The procedure should be detailed enough to give the teacher very specific directions on what to do and flexible enough to allow for student interactions and redirections along the way. The teacher writes a lesson plan for personal use in the classroom. However, particularly when you are first learning to write lessons, it is often useful to think of the audience as the principal or a supervisor, who may walk into class that day and want to read about what you are doing. Or, think of the audience as a substitute teacher, who will be called upon to teach your lesson if you are ill. You certainly can't make any major assumptions about a principal or substitute's ability to read into a lesson and ad lib. The plan needs to contain carefully written procedures so that one could pick it up and teach it without wondering what the writer meant by a particular step. Consequently, vague phrases such as "show the students how the distance formula works" should be avoided, as this statement does not help the teacher to prepare for *how* to develop the distance formula with a class. Likewise, instead of a step that says "ask the students some questions about the diagram," the plan should include a list of specific questions to ask the class during that step of the lesson. Veteran teachers become very adept at writing plans as outlines in less detail, but beginning teachers need to spell out specific examples, questions, and comments to make the lesson flow. We will discuss how veteran teachers "lesson image" instead of lesson plan later in this chapter.

Transition Statements

It is important that students recognize the connection between parts of the lesson and the sequencing of examples and experiences. Therefore, the lesson plan should include **transition statements** throughout the lesson procedure that are used by the teacher to assist students in moving from one activity to the next. Something as simple as saying, "Let's see how the game we just played relates to number theory" can help students recognize that the discussion will shift from a game to a discussion about the Real Numbers. If you just say, "Take out your notebooks" after playing a game, students will have no idea what will be the focus of the next discussion. The beginning teacher often includes transition statements throughout the lesson plan, before and after each major activity, so that the plan progresses smoothly and coherently. Without these transition statements, the lesson can feel very choppy to the students, who might see it as nothing more than a series of disconnected activities and pieces.

Closure

When the bell rings as the teacher is in the middle of an example, the class is left hanging, and the teacher does not always know whether the students understood the major concepts. Just as an effective lesson begins with a motivational activity, the lesson should be carefully planned to conclude with a logical wrap-up activity known as the closure. The closure gives the teacher an opportunity to assess the progress of the students through a series of specific questions, a journal prompt, or one final problem to solve. In many cases, the closure is a problem or set of questions that is linked to the original issue or problem posed in the motivation at the beginning of the lesson. Students view the lesson as a unified whole, if the opening and closure are related in some way. For example, the teacher who began the lesson with an ad from the local department store might close the lesson by displaying three actual prices from the ad, asking the students to determine the new price after an additional 20% discount.

In other cases, teachers use the closure as a time to raise a final thought or question that may set the tone for the next class period. For example, a teacher who is concluding a lesson on measures of central tendency—mean, median, and mode—might put up a transparency bearing this statement:

A person can drown in a lake with an average depth of one inch.

Then, either students could be invited to comment on the statement in the last five minutes of class, or they could be asked to reflect on it in a journal entry as a homework assignment. Class ending statements such as "close your books," "your homework is . . . ," or "see you tomorrow" should not be confused with the closure of the lesson; they are statements a teacher might make *after* the lesson has been concluded.

Sample Lesson Plans

In order to make you think about the issue of lesson planning, two plans are presented here. Lesson Plan 1 is an example of a flawed plan. As you read it, think about the components of effective lesson planning as discussed and make a list of potential weaknesses in this plan. Lesson Plan 2 is an example of a well-constructed lesson plan. Again, think about what makes the plan useful and complete. In both cases, a standard lesson planning format has been used.

SAMPLE LESSON PLAN 1

Name: Brian Pack
Date: 11/11/99
Course: Seventh grade mathematics
Number of Students: 23

I. **Goal(s):**
   • To develop the concepts of perimeter/circumference and area

II. **Objective(s):**
   • The student will learn about π.
   • The student will work with another student.
   • The student will use string to measure circles.
   • The student will use a calculator to find the ratio of circumference to diameter.
   • The student will complete a worksheet involving the measurements taken from several circles.

III. **Materials:**
- Several circular objects
- Pieces of string
- Calculators

IV. **Motivation**
1. Hold up a piece of string and say, "What do you think we'll use this string for today?"
2. Explain to the class that they will be using it to measure the circumferences of several circles today.

V. **Lesson Procedure**
3. Have students work in pairs. Give each pair of students a piece of string, a ruler, and a calculator.
4. Pass out a copy of the worksheet that contains lines on which to record the diameters and circumferences of the circles. Show the students where the circles are and tell them to measure the diameter and circumference of each. Then they should write those numbers down on the worksheet and use their calculators to figure out the ratio of the two numbers.
5. Ask if there are any questions.
6. After the students have finished collecting all of their data, ask the class several questions to see what they noticed.
7. Tell the class that the actual value of π is about 3.14. Do several examples of circumference problems using π.

VI. **Closure**
8. Give the class their homework assignment. They will do page 89, numbers 1–22. If they don't understand how to do the problems, do a couple of them on the board.
9. Ask if there are any final questions before the period is over.

VII. **Extension**
VIII. **Reflections** (after the lesson)

SAMPLE LESSON PLAN 2

Name: Katherine Bronson
Date: 10/2/00
Course: Algebra 1
Number of Students: 27

I. **Goal(s):**
- To develop an understanding of functions as applied to authentic data

II. **Objective(s):**
- The student will collect and organize real-life data from an experiment.

Continued

- The student will represent a function as a table, an equation, a graph, and with a verbal description.
- The student will describe the meaning of the slope and *y*-intercept for a linear function involving real-life data.

III. **Materials:**
- Each team of 3 students will need (1) a meter stick, (2) a superball, a golf ball, a ping-pong ball, and a tennis ball, (3) a sheet of centimeter graph paper, and (4) a ruler.
- Each student will need a graphing calculator.
- The teacher will need a superball and 27 playing cards—one each of a 6, 7, 8, 9, 10, jack, queen, king, and ace in the suits of hearts, diamonds, and clubs.

IV. **Motivation**
1. Bounce a superball on the floor and tell the class about how "we used to skip these off the elementary school building when I was a kid" and how the older children would try to throw them on the roof.
2. Raise the question, "But I'm wondering . . . just how 'super' is a superball, really? Does it have more bounce than, say, a golf ball?" (Let the class discuss how they think a superball bounce compares to the bounce of a golf ball.)
3. Ask the class how we might design an experiment to find out. (Lead them to think about how a number of different balls could be dropped from a given height to determine how high they bounce.)

Transition: Explain to the students that they will be working in teams, so I will randomly hand out playing cards to establish the working groups.

V. **Lesson Procedure**
4. Deal out one card to each student, randomly. Ask the students who received the same card to sit together (e.g., a 10-team, a king-team, etc.).
5. Describe the experiment that the class is to conduct, as follows: Each team will be given a superball, a golf ball, a ping-pong ball, and a tennis ball as well as a meter stick. Placing a meter stick along the wall, each team should drop each ball from at least five different heights, and each height should be attempted twice for accuracy. Each time, the height from which the ball was dropped and the height to which it bounced should be recorded in a table until four data tables—one for each ball—have been produced. Before beginning, each team should have one person in charge of dropping the ball (the one holding a heart), one person to help measure the heights (holding a diamond), and one person to record the data in a table (holding a club).
6. Ask the class if they have any questions about the procedure before moving ahead.
7. Ask the person in charge of dropping the ball to come to the front table and pick up a meter stick and one of each of the four balls. After the team has collected all necessary data, it should return to the front of the room

for further instructions. Teams should now collect their data. (Circulate through each of the teams, listening to comments and keeping students on task. It may be helpful to prompt teams to re-try some of the drops and/or to attempt more than five drops of the ball to more accurately depict the characteristics of the ball. Record anecdotal notes of significant comments made by individuals or discussions within teams.)

8. As each team returns to the front of the room, give the data recorder a piece of centimeter graph paper and a ruler. The person who recorded the data is to draw a graph of each set of data points, where x is the height from which the ball was dropped and y is the height to which it bounced. All four balls' data should be recorded on the same sheet. The other two team members should enter the data into their graphing calculators so that the technology can display the picture as well. The team should, then, come up with a linear equation to describe the bounce of each of the four balls. When all of the groups have finished, each will be asked to identify which ball had the "best bounce" and how they knew that.

9. Allow each of the nine groups to briefly present its picture and findings to the class. Encourage debate among the class by asking appropriate questions, such as, "Why do you suppose that their golf ball bounced better than yours?" or "Why didn't we all find the same ball to have the best bounce?" (Flexibility will be important here because the data from all five groups may be very similar or very different and require much discussion.)

Transition: "Let's compare the class's data a little more formally now."

10. On the chalkboard, make a table:

	Super	Golf	Ping-pong	Tennis
Team 1				
Team 2				
Team 3				
Team 4				
etc.				

Ask each group to write down the slope of their equation for each of the four balls. As a class, compute the mean slope for each ball and discuss how the class results may have deviated from what individual teams have found.

11. Ask the class to state the equations describing the bounce of each ball. What is the meaning of the slope? (They should note that the slope is a ratio, in this case, comparing the amount of bounce per unit of height dropped. Thus, the greater the slope, the steeper the line, and the more bounce the ball has.) What is the y-intercept? (The y-intercepts should all be 0 or very close to 0. This means that if the ball isn't dropped, it doesn't bounce.) Can you use the equation to predict the height each ball would bounce if it were dropped from higher than you actually measured? How?

Continued

Is this prediction realistic? (Students should recognize that dropping the ball from a mile-high cliff may not have the same result because the data may change dramatically with extremely high or low numbers.)

VI. **Closure**

12. We started the class today by asking if a superball is really all that super. Do you think so now? Why or why not? Take out your journal and spend the last five minutes of class writing a paragraph that starts with the phrase, "The most interesting mathematical idea that I learned today was . . ."

VII. **Extension**

If time allows, prior to 11, have students look at the data on their graphing calculators. Using an overhead, enter the class averages for the slopes and have the calculator draw the four graphs. Switch back and forth between the equations, tables, and graphs, and use the graphs to trace each function to make predictions about dropping the ball from heights other than those used in the experiment.

VIII. **Reflections** (after the lesson)

These lessons both use a standard format, as we have discussed in this chapter, but the lessons are very different in terms of what they tell the reader and how they are written. What did you notice as you read through them? Suppose that you were a substitute and were called upon to teach either of these lessons. Would you consider one to be more clearly written and easier to follow? You might have noticed that both lessons are hands-on and actively involve students in the learning process. The intent here was not to differentiate between teaching philosophies but to illustrate the different ways that lessons are actually written.

Let's look at Lesson Plan 1. Mr. Pack is teaching a middle school class about circumference and the value of π. Although his overall goal appears reasonable, the objectives are far less useful. For example, the first objective, "The student will learn about π," is vague. What does it mean to "learn about" something? If the purpose of the objective is to say that "the student will define π as the ratio of circumference to diameter in a circle," then it should have been stated as such. Otherwise, we are left to wonder what the student is actually supposed to know and how the objective would be assessed. As we discussed in Chapter 4, objectives need to be clear and are usually measurable. The other four objectives listed in Mr. Pack's lesson are not really worthwhile either. They are simply statements about what the student will *do* in the activities for today's class—work in pairs, use string, use a calculator, and complete a worksheet—rather than statements of what the student should *know* by the end of the lesson. In reality, this lesson only has two major objectives. The first is the student's ability to define π and use it to determine the circumference of a circle, and the second, which should have been included, is that "the student will collect and analyze real-life data from an experiment."

A substitute (or even the teacher who wrote the plan) might find the materials section confusing. First, we do not know what the writer means by "several circular objects." If this item is to include plastic container lids, a pie tin, a bicycle tire, and a quarter, then they should be listed. Otherwise, the teacher would have no idea about which items to gather, how many items to use, and so forth. Also, the materials section does not say how many pieces of string and calculators will be needed. Later in the lesson, we find out that students work in pairs, and because there are 23 students in the class, we can determine that 12 pieces of string and 12 calculators will be needed, but this should have been included in the materials section. Also, the lesson later tells us that students will use a ruler and a worksheet, but neither of these items have been included in the materials listing.

What did you think of the motivation for Lesson 1? Did it capture your imagination and make you eager to proceed with the lesson? Probably not. The teacher could have given the class the diameter of the earth and asked them if they could figure out the distance around the earth, given this information. When the class realizes that they have no method of doing this, the teacher could proceed by explaining that today's experiment will give them the power to do this by the end of the period and return to that question in the closure. In the lesson procedure, students are to work in pairs, but the reader is not told how those pairs are formed. Are students already seated in pairs, or are they to select their own partner? Or will the teacher assign them to a partner? This needs to be spelled out in the lesson plan. In general, the lesson procedure is vague. For example, in step 6, the reader is told to "ask the class several questions," but the plan does not list any possible questions. If the teacher plans to ask, for example, "What was the smallest ratio value that anyone found?", then this question should be specifically stated; otherwise, the teacher is likely to forget to ask the question while teaching the lesson. The direction to "do several examples" is another common error of lesson planning by novice teachers. It is not a useful step because the specifics of which examples, how many, and in what sequence are critical to the success of the lesson. If the teacher plans to work two sample problems with the class, then those problems should be written and sequenced in advance, included in the plan, and not left to chance.

Finally, the closure for Lesson 1 does not really close the lesson at all; it is simply a statement of the homework assignment. How does the teacher know whether the students understood the main message for the day? And what does "do a couple of them on the board" mean? The closure is unclear and does not allow the teacher to assess the progress of the students over this lesson. Finally, the lesson does not include transition statements at all. The class abruptly moves from a discussion about a piece of string to measuring circles to a homework assignment and is in need of teacher statements to ease students from one step of the lesson into the next. Flawed because of a lack of detail, the lesson would be very difficult to implement, and it leaves more questions unanswered than it provides direction for a principal conducting an observation or a substitute replacing an ill teacher.

Lesson Plan 2 is a high school lesson prepared by Ms. Bronson for 27 Algebra I students, focusing on functions and, specifically, the slope and y-intercept of a linear function. The objectives are clear in that they contain action statements, with words such as "collect," "organize," "represent," and "describe the meaning." There is enough detail in the materials section to make it useful, including a description of the tools that each student and team will need to conduct the activity. The motivation for Lesson 2 is almost certain to gain the attention of adolescents, as the teacher bounces a superball on the floor and asks students to design an experiment to determine just how "super" it is. This motivation is clearly intended to hook the students and involve them in the lesson that follows. In step 3, the teacher has made a note to herself in terms of where she wants to lead the students in the discussion, so that the stage is set for the lesson procedures that follow. Placing a hint or reminder into a lesson plan can be very helpful, particularly for the novice teacher.

The lesson procedure is very specific in terms of what the teacher intends to do. For example, playing cards are used to determine randomly selected teams and to assign responsibilities in the project. Contrast this to Lesson 1 in which we were not told how the pairs were selected, nor were we told what the role of each person was to be in the experiment. Notice, also, how step 7 gives the teacher a specific direction about what she is to do as the class is conducting the experiments. By noting that she will "record anecdotal notes," the teacher is reminding herself of the assessment strategy to be used during the class period to ensure that students are on-task and are comprehending the major concepts.

The steps that follow serve as a logical extension to the collection of data. After the students have collected their team data, the lesson is completed by compiling class data and looking for patterns. Again, in step 11, the teacher has provided herself with a note of what she hopes that students will realize about slopes and y-intercepts, which will be helpful in leading the class discussion. The last step of the lesson is a logical closure, which links the end of the lesson to the first question raised in step 2 and allows students to reflect in their journal as a means to assessing their understanding. Finally, the teacher of Lesson 2 has included an extra component to the lesson, an extension. The extension is a statement of what students (or the teacher) can do if there is extra time left in the period. The extension may provide an optional, expanded way to handle the lesson, or it may be used to lay an additional foundation for the next day's lesson. As a teacher of secondary or middle school students, the last thing you want to do is to run out of problems and ideas with 15 minutes remaining in the period. Planning an optional extension can relieve you of the pressure by providing you with an additional teaching idea if there is time or the class leads you in that direction. Ms. Bronson has included it in her lesson to increase her flexibility.

Looking at these two lesson plans, you can see how, on the surface, they both appear to be mathematically solid. They both use an appropriate planning format, key in on a couple of major mathematical ideas, and use hands-on, minds-on instructional strategies and technology. However, a careful study of the details reveals that one lesson is vague and leaves much to the imagination of the reader and the other is clear, coherent, and very user-friendly. As is true for a blueprint for a house, the more detail we put into the planning process, the more likely it is that we will teach a successful lesson. Someone once said, "Show me a classroom in which the students are misbehaving and off-task, and I will show you a teacher who does not know how to write a lesson plan." While we cannot attribute all classroom management problems to planning, we can certainly curtail a great deal of potential classroom disruption through effective planning. So, why is it that veteran teachers can plan very effective lessons without writing out all of the details? What happens when you practice detailing procedures, including specific questions and transitions? The answer is simple: You gain experience. Schoenfeld (1998) and others have written about how experienced teachers generate "lesson images" rather than "lesson plans," something we discuss in the next section.

■ LESSON IMAGING VERSUS LESSON PLANNING

Suppose that Mr. Pack attempts to implement his lesson on circumference of circles, using Lesson Plan 1 as his guide. As the class period progresses, he realizes that his plan is not detailed enough and that his students are off-task and missing the point of the lesson. At the end of the day, he briefly writes a reflection on his experience in a journal that he maintains throughout the year:

I just wasn't pleased with my lesson this morning. First of all, I realized that the motivating question did not motivate the class much at all, and I wish I had posed a real-life question that involved circumference instead. Then, I had several vague steps in my lesson, and I wasn't prepared enough to know what examples to explore with my class. I think they missed the point and still don't understand the formula for circumference or how to use it. I will need to approach the topic again tomorrow but from a different angle. Finally, we have a computer lab across the hall, and I have access to several TI-92 hand-held computers. I never thought about it at the time, but I could have used Geometer's Sketchpad or Geometry Inventor in the lab or the TI-92 in my classroom to have students measure circumferences and diameters on the screen—they really enjoy using technology—I could have played to their interests. There is so much I would change next time around.

You can bet that before Mr. Pack teaches the lesson again, he will rethink the examples he uses and, perhaps, attempt to use technology to help him make his point. If the students use a TI-92 hand-held computer to explore circle relationships, the screen might resemble Figure 5–4.

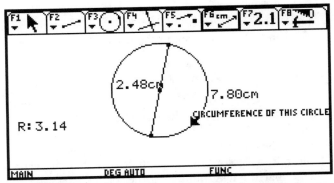

Figure 5–4 Estimating the Value of π with a TI-92 Hand-Held Computer

In Figure 5–4, the student has created a circle, and the TI-92 has measured the circumference to be 7.80 cm and the diameter to be 2.48 cm. Using the Calculate command, the student can find the ratio of circumference to diameter to be about 3.14 and test circles of other sizes to see if the relationship is always true. If Mr. Pack has success with the revised lesson, it may become incorporated as part of his routine. Consequently, it will be much easier to plan in the third year because he has seen that the lesson worked much better on the second try when technology was used in addition to hands-on measuring of circular objects. But experience is the key, and after you have written and rewritten a lesson a number of times, you begin to picture the lesson in your mind.

This mental picture of the lesson includes the kinds of comments that the teacher needs to make in order to clarify the task and help students identify the major mathematical ideas; it includes the errors that students are likely to make and concrete ways to respond to those misconceptions, and it includes a sense of how long the lesson will take and what parts can be shortened or lengthened. The mental picture is often referred to in the literature as a **lesson image,** the sense that a teacher carries into the classroom of what to expect from students, how they are likely to react, and what the teacher can do to make the lesson work. The lesson image differs from a lesson plan, which is a written document that guides instruction. But although a plan can be prepared by the novice teacher, it takes an experienced educator to image a lesson, and the more experience you gain with teaching a particular lesson or teaching toward a certain concept, the closer you will come to being able to create a lesson image. Individuals who have had considerable experience can write a fairly sketchy lesson plan on paper and still teach the lesson with artistry because they carry a mental image into the classroom. As you teach, over the course of several years, you will watch your skills progress from planning lessons to creating lesson images, but only experience can teach you how to do that.

It is important to realize the distinction between plans and images, however, because novice teachers are often surprised by the brevity of lesson plans of veteran teachers and wonder why they are being asked to write out every step. Like a musician who has learned which song to save for last after seeing how audiences respond to that song throughout an entire tour, anticipating audience reactions in the classroom also becomes much easier when you have an experience base. It's necessary not only to have the experience of teaching a lesson but to take the time to reflect on its effectiveness, as we saw when Mr. Pack wrote his journal entry. In the next section, we discuss the final step in the teaching of a lesson—reflection.

■ REFLECTING ON A LESSON

As we discuss further in Chapter 6, one of the things that good teachers of mathematics do is reflect on the effectiveness of their lessons. Perhaps you have heard the statement that "nothing ever goes as planned," and this is often the case with planning a lesson in mathematics. One day, a teacher organizes what appears to be a simple review lesson and then discovers that the class has very little or none of the anticipated background. Another day, the lesson contains a seemingly complex task that the students complete in half the time allotted, leaving the teacher without a plan for fifteen minutes or more. Earlier in the chapter, we discussed the issue of how to deal with student questions or misunderstandings, which, in some cases, may cause a teacher to put the plan aside and pursue a totally different direction. Of course, if we place students at the center of the teaching, we can expect and anticipate that their questions and concerns will often change the direction of our lessons. At the conclusion of the lesson, however, the teacher needs to return to the plan, think about how the class actually reacted to it, and ask three key questions:

1. What did I set out to do in this lesson, and why did I plan to do it that way?
2. Did I accomplish my goals and objectives for the lesson? How do I know (i.e., how did I measure the success of my lesson)?
3. What have I learned about myself and my students that will help me to be a better teacher tomorrow, next month, or next year?

The answers to these questions will lead the teacher to write an even more effective lesson the next day and, certainly, the next year when another class studies the same content.

After the implementation of a lesson plan, the teacher should always reflect on or assess the plan and its effectiveness. If the students appeared to understand the content, was it because of the lesson itself or something that wasn't even in the plan? If the class was restless, confused, or off-task, can this be attributed to the students, or was it a flaw in the planning? While it is sometimes difficult to be self-critical, examination of the plan may reveal gaps that could have been avoided or opportunities that should have been pursued. Over time, with experience, teachers create a collection of "best lessons" that work with their classes. Although some of these best lessons can be found in resource books or on the Internet, teachers begin to "own" a lesson only after planning, teaching, reflecting upon, and reteaching it. As a result, the teacher becomes increasingly proficient in lesson imaging, anticipating student responses, and attaining the desired flow and success of the lesson. A well-planned set of lessons, then, becomes the cornerstone of coherent, meaningful units.

■ CONCLUSION ■

The ability to plan a good lesson is one of the most fundamental of all teaching skills. In this chapter, we have explored the role of planning both long-term units and daily lessons. Frameworks for the construction of units and lessons have been presented, with examples and analyses of poorly written and well-written lesson plans. We acknowledged that the textbook and local course of study often drive the planning process but noted that teachers can supplement these with additional resources to make lessons more meaningful for students. We have also emphasized that it is important to assess the strengths and weaknesses of the plan and its implementation. We only improve when we look back at previous work and ask ourselves how it could have been done better. Using our experience in in the classroom, we move from planning lessons extensively on paper to imaging lessons in our minds, and our organizational skills progress from the need to write out details to the ability to sketch outlines.

Throughout your career as a student of mathematics, you have inevitably experienced some very interesting and worthwhile lessons. Perhaps those lessons involved you actively in a cooperative learning team or required that you use manipulatives or technology in the learning process. Maybe you were challenged with thought-provoking questions and were expected to struggle somewhat to try to make sense of a problem. However, behind every one of those worthwhile lessons was a caring teacher who was responsible for planning, implementing, and reflecting on your

classroom activities. So, what is a "good" teacher, and what kinds of experiences do they provide for their students? These questions are pursued in Chapter 6 as we continue Unit III with a detailed discussion of the role of the mathematics teacher in the classroom.

■ GLOSSARY ■

Closure: Closure is the final step of a lesson plan during which the teacher wraps up a lesson. Often, the closure includes an opportunity to assess student understanding of the lesson and may tie back to an issue raised in the lesson's motivation or pose a question for students to consider for the next class period.

Components of a Lesson Plan: Although there is no universal agreement on a structure for all lesson plans, this simple outline and components may be helpful in constructing plans:

    I. Goal(s)
    II. Objective(s)
    III. Materials
    IV. Motivation
    V. Lesson Procedure (including Transition Statements)
    VI. Closure
    VII. Extensions (optional activity or teaching idea)
    VIII. Reflection (completed after the lesson has been taught)

Lesson plans generally also include a plan for assessing student understanding of the outcomes.

Conceptual Map: A conceptual map is a graphic organizer of how the content of a lesson, unit, semester, course, or even an entire program fits together as a whole. The diagram indicates how various concepts are connected and suggests a possible instructional sequence.

Lesson Image: A lesson image is a mental picture that is held by an experienced teacher of what is expected of students in a lesson, how the lesson is likely to progress, and what the teacher's role will be in the teaching and learning process. Novice teachers spend most of their time writing lesson plans in detail on paper, but veteran teachers are more likely to be able to "image" a lesson and work from a more general outline for a plan.

Lesson Plan: A lesson plan is a written document that details the goals and objectives, the necessary tools, and the activities to be used in a particular classroom teaching episode. It is a road map that can be used by the teacher to provide structure to the lesson. The main components generally found in a lesson plan include goals, objectives, materials, motivation, lesson procedure (including transition statements), closure, and extensions. Assessment is also generally included as part of the lesson plan, and formal or informal reflections should follow the implementation of the plan. Prospective and less-experienced teachers must write extensive lesson plans that detail their classroom activities and attempt to anticipate student questions and misconceptions.

Lesson Procedure: The lesson procedure is a set of instructions for the teacher, generally written as an outline, with step-by-step descriptions of what the teacher and the students will do in a lesson. The procedure should feature specific instructions but be flexible enough to allow the teacher to move in a different direction if the students raise questions or concerns during the lesson.

Motivation: As it pertains to lesson planning, the motivation is an activity used at the beginning of a lesson to gain the attention of the students. Taking the form of a problem, a visual aid, or an activity, the motivation is intended to set the stage for the lesson and to evoke interest and curiosity in the intended topic. The motivation is often the most difficult part of a lesson to plan because it depends on the teacher knowing the students well enough to understand what will get their attention. Sometimes, the motivation is also referred to as an initiatory activity or a springboard.

Prerequisite Knowledge: Prerequisite knowledge refers to the competencies and skills that students should already possess, prior to the beginning of an instructional unit. It is important for a teacher to identify the prerequisite knowledge of students prior to designing a unit so that the students can connect the new content to concepts they have developed in the past.

Teachable Moment: A teachable moment is a class situation in which a student has answered a question in a particular way or raised a certain concern that leads the teacher naturally into the discussion of an unplanned example or topic. Students indicate their interest in the topic by making comments in class, and the teacher decides that it is better for the class to pursue the issue than to leave it alone.

Transition Statements: Transition statements are statements included in a lesson plan that are intended to help students recognize how the activities in the lesson are connected. These statements are generally included in the lesson procedure are are often written as direct quotes for the teacher to say so that the plan progresses smoothly.

Unit: A unit is a set of learning experiences that are designed to address one or several goals and objectives over time. Generally, units are long term in that they may take several class periods or even several weeks to complete. A unit may contain several individual lesson plans with a common theme or general topic.

■ DISCUSSION QUESTIONS ■

1. Choose a general unit topic, such as exponential growth or total surface area and volume of three-dimensional solids, and create a conceptual map indicating the possible components of the unit and how they are connected.
2. Examine a textbook unit in a small group and discuss the length of time it might take to explore the unit and the degree to which your group agrees with the suggested sequence of topics.
3. Sample Lesson Plan 1 was presented as an example of a poorly written lesson. Rewrite the lesson to address the weaknesses described in this chapter.
4. Obtain a copy of a teacher's manual for a mathematics textbook. Identify and discuss the suggestions for lessons that are described in the manual. How helpful is the manual in the lesson-planning process for a novice teacher?
5. Run a search for mathematics lesson plans on the World Wide Web in a topic area of your choice (or locate a resource book containing sample lessons). Evaluate the strengths and weaknesses of the lesson plans based on the criteria described in this chapter. To what degree do the lessons illustrate the lesson-plan components discussed in the chapter?
6. View a videotape of a mathematics lesson. Then, in a small group, try to sketch out the teacher's lesson plan. Identify the goals, objectives, materials, motivation, lesson procedure, closure, and extensions, if any. What transitional statements did the teacher use, and how was assessment conducted in the lesson? Describe anything in the lesson that appeared to be unplanned or in which the teacher pursued a student concern.
7. View a videotape case or read a case study of a classroom teaching episode. Play the role of the teacher in the case study and write a reflection on the lesson. Be sure to include the three components of lesson reflection described in this chapter.
8. It has been said that there are teachers with 20 years of experience and teachers who have one year of experience, repeated 20 times. What does this statement suggest about the reasons for reflecting on lessons in the teaching and learning process?

■ BIBLIOGRAPHIC REFERENCES AND RESOURCES ■

The Annenberg/CPB Projects. (1999). The Annenberg/ CPB Projects Learner Online. Retrieved August 20, 1999 from the World Wide Web: <http://www. learner.org>

Austin, J. D., et al. (1992). Coordinating secondary school science and mathematics. *School Science and Mathematics, 92* (2), 64–68.

Ball, D. L. & Schroeder, T. L. (1992). Improving teaching, not standardizing it. *Mathematics Teacher, 85* (1), 67–72.

Bitter, G. (1997). *Understanding teaching: Implementing the NCTM professional standards for teaching mathematics CD-ROM series.* Tempe, AZ: Arizona State University (available through the Association for Supervision and Curriculum Development).

Borich, G. D. (1996). *Effective teaching methods.* New York, NY: Merrill.

Classroom Connect. (1997). *Teaching grades K–12 with the Internet: Internet lesson plans and classroom activities.* Lancaster, PA: Classroom Connect.

Duquette, G. (Ed.). (1997). *Classroom methods and strategies for teaching at the secondary level.* Lewiston, NY: Edwin Mellen.

Gronlund, N. E. (1995). *How to write and use instructional objectives.* Englewood Cliffs, NJ: Merrill.

Gronlund, N. E. (1985). *Stating Objectives for classroom instruction.* New York, NY: Macmillan.

Harris, D. E., Carr, J. F., Flynn, T., Petit, M., & Rigney, S. (1996). *How to use standards in the classroom.* Alexandria, VA: Association for Supervision and Curriculum Development.

Henak, R. M. (1984). *Lesson Planning for meaningful variety in teaching.* Washington, DC: National Education Association.

Joseph, L. C. (1995). Eisenhower National Clearinghouse—an online bonanza for math and science resources. *Technology Connection, 2* (4), 17.

New York City Board of Education. (1986). *How does a lesson plan?* New York, NY: New York City Board of Education.

Ornstein, A. C. (1990). *The systematic design of instruction.* New York, NY: HarperCollins College Publishing.

Public Broadcasting System. (1999). Mathline. Retrieved August, 20 1999 from the World Wide Web: <http://www.pbs.org/teachersource/math/>

Ridley, L. L. (1995). When a lesson bombs: Hints and suggestions for teachers. *Teaching Exceptional Children, 27* (4), 66–67.

Roberts, P. (1996). *A guide for developing an interdisciplinary thematic unit.* Englewood Cliffs, NJ: Merrill.

Schoaff, E. K. (1993). How to develop a mathematics lesson using technology. *Journal of Computers in Mathematics and Science Teaching, 12* (1), 19–27.

Schoenfeld, A. H. (1998). On theory and models: The case of teaching-in-context. In S. Berenson, K. Dawkins, M. Blanton, W. Coulombe, J. Kolb, K. Norwood, & L. Stiff (Eds.) *Proceedings of the Twentieth Annual Meeting of the North American Chapter of the International Group for the Psychology of Mathematics Education, 27–38.* Columbus, OH: ERIC Clearinghouse for Science, Mathematics, and Environmental Education.

Schroeder, M. L. (1996). Professional development: Lesson design and reflection. *Mathematics Teaching in the Middle School, 1* (8), 648–652.

Tyson, P. (1991). Talking about lesson planning: The use of semi-structured interviews in teacher education. *Teacher Education Quarterly, 18* (3), 87–96.

Activities—Selected Lesson Plan Ideas from *The Mathematics Teacher*

Bezuk, N. S. & Armstrong, B. E. (1993). Activities: Understanding division of fractions. *Mathematics Teacher, 86* (1), 43–46, 56–60.

Coes, L. (1994). Activities: The functions of a toy balloon. *Mathematics Teacher, 87* (8), 619–622, 628–629.

Craine, T. V. (1996). Activities: A graphical approach to the quadratic formula. *Mathematics Teacher, 89* (1), 34–38, 44–46.

DeTemple, D. W. & Walker, D. A. (1996). Activities: Some colorful mathematics. *Mathematics Teacher, 89* (4), 307–312, 318–320.

Disher, F. (1995). Activities: Graphing art. *Mathematics Teacher, 88* (2), 124–128, 134–136.

Kennedy, J. B. (1996). Activities: An interest in radioactivity. *Mathematics Teacher, 89* (3), 209–214, 228–230.

Mack, C. W. (1995). Activities: Exploring three- and four-dimensional space. *Mathematics Teacher, 88* (7), 572–578, 588–590.

Reinstein, D., Sally, P., & Camp, D. R. (1997). Activities: Generating fractals through self-replication. *Mathematics Teacher, 90* (1), 34–38, 43–45.

Schultz, H. & Bonsangue, M. V. (1995). Activities: Time for trigonometry. *Mathematics Teacher, 88* (5), 393–396, 405–410.

Van Dyke, F. (1996). Activities: The inverse of a function. *Mathematics Teacher, 89* (2), 121–126, 132–133.

Westegaard, S. A. (1998). Activities: Stitching quilts into coordinate geometry. *Mathematics Teacher, 91* (7), 587–592, 598–600.

Wood, E. (1995). Activities: Gas-bill mathematics. *Mathematics Teacher, 88* (3), 214–218, 224–227.

Responsibilities of the Professional Teacher

After reading Chapter 6, you should be able to answer the following questions:

- What are the NCTM Professional Teaching Standards and the related Principles of the *Principles and Standards for School Mathematics* document? Why and when were they developed?

- What are the criteria according to which a teacher selects activities and problems for the classroom?

- What are some of the tools of mathematics instruction, and how are they helpful in the teaching and learning process?

- How can the teacher use questioning skills and cooperative learning to enhance the level of discourse in the classroom?

- What are some specific strategies that teachers can use to develop a positive learning environment in the classroom and create community? Discuss these strategies.

- What is the role of reflection in the teaching and learning process?

In a mathematics class, Anne Kelley is helping her students estimate the value of the square root of a number and compare the estimate with an answer on the calculator.

Ms. Kelley: Can anyone give me an estimate of $\sqrt{52}$?

Luke: It's about 7.5.

Ms. Kelley: Explain your thinking on that, Luke.

Luke: Well, I know that $\sqrt{49}$ is 7 and that $\sqrt{64}$ is 8. So, I knew it had to be between those, since 52 is between 49 and 64.

Elise: That's true, but 52 is a lot closer to 49 than it is to 64, so I would guess it would be more like 7.2 or 7.3.

Ms. Kelley: Does anyone else have any thoughts on this one?

Terry: Well, look at it this way . . . the average of 49 and 64 is 56.5. So, we can figure that $\sqrt{56.5}$ is halfway between 7 and 8 . . . um . . . 7.5, right?

Ms. Kelley: How can we check to see how close 7.5 is to the answer?

Luke: Find 7.5^2 and see if it's 56.5.

Ms. Kelley: Good. Why don't you go ahead and find 7.5^2 on your calculators. (The class keys 7.5 into their calculators and squares the number.)

Joshua: No, 7.5^2 is equal to 56.25, not 56.5.

Terry: Close enough, wouldn't you say, Ms. Kelley?

Ms. Kelley: I don't know. Why don't you go ahead and take $\sqrt{52}$. (The class finds the square root with their calculators.)

Elise: I knew it! It's only 7.21-something. It's like I said; it's closer to 7 than to 8.

Ms. Kelley: Do we know "exactly" what it's equal to?

Luke: Yea, it's exactly 7.211102551. That's what my calculator shows anyway.

Terry: So does mine. But I still think it's close enough if we call it 7.21.

Lakisha: Does it go any further than 7.211102551? I'm just wondering because we've seen other times where the calculator cuts a number off because it doesn't have enough space . . . like that one time we tried to change a fraction to a repeating decimal that had, like, 12 decimal places before it started to repeat.

(The students in the class start to look confused and wonder if Lakisha is on to something. They look up at Ms. Kelley and wait for her response.)

Now, put yourself in Anne Kelley's position. How would you handle this situation? Think about what you would do before reading ahead. In this short episode, a couple of significant issues have surfaced—let's discuss each of them.

First, Terry has the misconception that the square of a number should fall exactly between the square of the two numbers that bound it. Ms. Kelley could run with this point and, for example, show that while 11^2 is 121 and 12^2 is 144, 11.5^2 is 132.25 and not 132.5, as Terry might predict. But this might result in a question as to whether the average of the squares of two consecutive integers is always 0.25 more than the square of the average of the two integers (in this case, 132.5 − 0.25 and in the classroom situation, 56.5 − 0.25). This conjecture is correct and could be proven as follows:

Let x be an integer and $x + 1$ be the next consecutive integer. Then, the squares of the two numbers would be x^2 and $(x + 1)^2 = x^2 + 2x + 1$. The average of the two original numbers would be $\frac{x + (x + 1)}{2} = \frac{2x + 1}{2} = x + \frac{1}{2}$. Therefore, the square of the average of the original numbers would be $(x + \frac{1}{2})^2 = x^2 + x + \frac{1}{4}$. But the average of the squares of the original numbers would be $\frac{x^2 + (x + 1)^2}{2} = \frac{2x^2 + 2x + 1}{2} = x^2 + x + \frac{1}{2}$, which is exactly $\frac{1}{4}$ or 0.25 larger than the square of the averages. So, although this conjecture is true and the class might be able to prove it, Ms. Kelley has to decide whether she wants to pursue the issue.

Second, the class may be on the brink of discovering that the square root of a number that is not a perfect square is irrational, and Lakisha's question about whether the calculator is actually displaying the entire number is interesting. Ms. Kelley could, for example, ask the class to key π into their calculators. If they have some background with π, they might already know that it neither terminates nor repeats, yet the graphing calculator displays only "3.141592654." This may prompt students to ask about how many digits the calculator actually has for π in its memory. But how can we find out? One simple approach is to key in 10*π on the calculator and then subtract 30. The display will be as follows:

π	3.141592654
10π	31.41592654
−30	1.415926536

Subtracting 30 gives the student's calculator the room to display another digit of the decimal because it can only display 10 digits at a time. Now, the students know that it originally rounded 3.1415926536 to 3.141592654. So, the question might be, "If you multiply by 100 more and subtract 140, can we find out if the calculator knows even more digits?" Repeating this process again and again, students will find that their particular calculators "know" π up to 3.1415926535898. Finally, the same process could be used for determining an approximation for $\sqrt{52}$, and students can discover whether the decimal repeats or terminates within the first 13 decimal places. When they discover that it neither terminates nor repeats, the stage is set for a discussion of square roots as irrational numbers. Again, this is an interesting problem-solving excursion, but Anne Kelley has to make an on-the-spot decision about whether it is worth the class time to pursue Lakisha's question, particularly if it was unexpected and not part of her lesson plan or the curriculum as described in her course of study.

Although it would be relatively easy to dismiss Terry's answer as "close enough" and Lakisha's question as "interesting, but something you'll look at in another class in high school," this may also be a perfect opportunity for exploring something about which a student has expressed interest—what educators often call a teachable moment as discussed in Chapter 5. But the decision about how to proceed is up to Anne Kelley, and the master teacher knows whether the students can handle a further investigation and whether the time would be productively used before proceeding. Just as two musicians can perform the same song very differently, each having a different interpretation of the music, the implementation of a teacher's lesson plan depends on the teacher's ability to pick up on student interactions and adjust the plan in a meaningful way. In this chapter, we discuss the art of teaching and the role of the teacher in posing problems and orchestrating discussions that challenge and interest the students. We will begin with a discussion of the NCTM *Professional Standards for Teaching Mathematics* and the related Principles from the *Principles and Standards for School Mathematics* publication.

■ TEACHING STANDARDS AND GUIDING PRINCIPLES

The NCTM Professional Teaching Standards

Two years after the National Council of Teachers of Mathematics issued the *Curriculum and Evaluation Standards,* it released a second volume entitled *Professional*

Standards for Teaching Mathematics (1991) to assist those individuals involved in preparing or inservicing classroom teachers. The *Professional Standards* painted a picture of effective teaching and encouraged readers to think about the degree to which their teaching skills were aligned with the suggested benchmarks.

The *Professional Standards* put forth the need for five major reorientations or shifts to occur in mathematics education:

Table 6–1 Suggested Reorientations in Mathematics Instruction

Recommended Shift	Traditional Model
• toward classrooms as mathematical communities	• away from classrooms as simply a collection of individuals
• toward logic and mathematical evidence as verification	• away from the teacher as the sole authority for right answers
• toward mathematical reasoning	• away from merely memorizing procedures
• toward conjecturing, inventing, and problem solving	• away from an emphasis on mechanistic answer-finding
• toward connecting mathematics, its ideas, and its applications	• away from treating mathematics as a body of isolated concepts and procedures

(Reprinted from NCTM, *Professional Standards for Teaching Mathematics*, 1991, p. 3.)

Looking at the list of recommendations in Table 6–1, you might notice the emphasis on the student's ability to think and reason as opposed to a teacher-directed environment in which skills and procedures are emphasized. This model is consistent with the constructivist theory of teaching and learning described in Chapter 2, in which the student is the center of focus in the classroom.

The *Professional Standards* is divided into four major sets of Standards. The first set is the Standards for Teaching Mathematics, which we will use as an organizer for much of this chapter, as they are concerned with the way that a teacher conducts a class and analyzes student progress. The second set of Standards, the Standards for the Evaluation of the Teaching of Mathematics, presents a vision of how administrators should determine the degree to which instructors of mathematics are teaching in a manner that is consistent with the philosophy of the two Standards volumes. The third set of Standards, the Standards for the Professional Development of Teachers of Mathematics, describes how teachers should be initially prepared and, later, developed throughout their teaching careers. Specifically, the Professional Development Standards discuss what teachers should know about mathematics, the nature of the learner, and teaching pedagogy. Finally, the last group of Standards, the Standards for the Support and Development of Teachers and Teaching, details the responsibilities of the decision-makers who impact the teaching of mathematics.

So, what does it mean to be a "good teacher" of mathematics? Think back to your school experiences and jot down five things that your best teachers were able to do. Perhaps you remember the types of activities or projects in which you were engaged in the class, the conversations that took place during the class, or the classroom climate that felt inviting and made you want to learn. In its efforts to define what good teaching is all about, the NCTM set forth six Standards for professional teaching: worthwhile mathematical tasks, teacher's role in discourse, students' role in discourse, tools for enhancing discourse, learning environment, and analysis of teaching and learning. As you read through the text of these six Standards throughout this chapter, think about whether your mathematics teachers measured up to each of the benchmarks. A complete reprint of the worthwhile mathematical tasks Standard is featured in Appendix B.

Guiding Principles

In *Principles and Standards for School Mathematics* (1998), the NCTM extended their discussion of effective teaching practices by proposing that educators consider several underlying Guiding Principles when making decisions about mathematics education from the state or district level to the individual classroom. Among others, these Principles included the equity Principle (reprinted in its complete form in Appendix B), the mathematics teaching Principle, and the learning Principle. The authors stated in the equity and learning Principles that mathematics programs should give all students the opportunity to develop mathematical literacy. Furthermore, they asserted in the mathematics teaching Principle that "mathematics instructional programs depend on competent and caring teachers who teach all students to understand and use mathematics" (NCTM, 1998, p. 30).

As we think about the design and implementation of lesson plans and units, we need to determine how closely our efforts as mathematics teachers measure up to the Guiding Principles. While exploring the role of the classroom teacher in this chapter, we use the *Professional Standards* dealing with tasks, tools, discourse, learning environment, and reflection on practice and intersperse comments on how the Guiding Principles can be addressed.

■ SELECTING ACTIVITIES AND PROBLEMS

As we discussed in Chapter 5, lesson planning should always begin with the process of identifying and clearly stating the goals and objectives that the teacher intends to address. At the same time, it is critical to consider the various problems and activities that can be used in teaching the lesson and to carefully select the type of experiences that the teacher believes to be the most effective in developing the relevant mathematics. Standard 1 of the *Professional Standards* outlines a description of how a teacher can go about selecting appropriate activities for lessons.

Standard 1: Worthwhile Mathematical Tasks

The teacher of mathematics should pose tasks that are based on:

- sound and significant mathematics;
- knowledge of students' understandings, interests, and experiences;
- knowledge of the range of ways that diverse students learn mathematics;

and that

- engage students' intellect;

- develop students' mathematical understandings and skills;
- stimulate students to make connections and develop a coherent framework for mathematical ideas;
- call for problem formulation, problem solving, and mathematical reasoning;
- promote communication about mathematics;
- represent mathematics as an ongoing human activity;
- display sensitivity to, and draw on, students' diverse background experiences and dispositions;
- promote the development of all students' dispositions to do mathematics.

(NCTM, *Professional Standards for Teaching Mathematics*, 1991, p. 25.)

Let's look at a specific example. Suppose that the teacher wants the class to think about the graph of an absolute value function such as $y = |x|$. The instructor can ask the students to construct a table of values and sketch a rough, simple graph as shown in Figure 6–1:

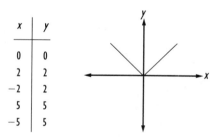

x	y
0	0
2	2
−2	2
5	5
−5	5

Figure 6–1 Table and Hand-Drawn Sketch of the Absolute Value Function

Then, the students can be given additional functions, such as $y = 2|x - 3| + 5$, and challenged to sketch their graphs by hand as well. In the end, students gain experience with making tables and sketching graphs, but the teacher has to wonder whether the students actually understand *why* the graphs have a V-shaped appearance. Additionally, the students may or may not have developed enough of an understanding to allow them to graph more complicated absolute value functions.

If the students have access to graphing calculators or computers with a graphing utility, they can be asked to use technology to draw graphs of such functions as:

$$y = |x|$$
$$y = |x| + 3$$
$$y = |x| - 5$$
$$y = -|x|$$
$$y = -|x| - 3$$

By observing graphs such as the one in Figure 6–2, students can look for patterns and make generalizations about how the parameter changes affect the shape of each graph.

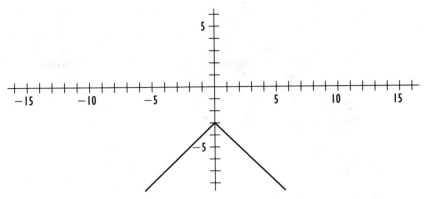

Figure 6–2 Computer Graphing Utility Sketch of $y = -|x| - 3$

Figure 6–2 was generated using a desktop graphing utility in a student computer lab. Again, students are likely to recognize characteristics of graphs that, for example, have negative coefficients multiplying the absolute value term, but they may or may not appreciate why the graph is shaped in this manner.

The teacher might also ask students to construct the graph of $y = |x|$ with graph paper and a straightedge and compare it with the graph of the line $y = x$. Students will recognize that the portion of the graph lying in Quadrant III has been flipped over the x-axis and can discuss the fact that the absolute value function takes all of the coordinates of the points and makes the y-coordinates (ordinates) positive. Then, students can use a manipulative known as a **mira**, an I-shaped plastic tool that, when laid on a piece of paper containing a picture, allows one to see the reflection of the picture in its window. Students can lay the mira on the x-axis and see how the Quadrant III piece of the line $y = x$ is reflected up to Quadrant II in the graph of $y = |x|$.

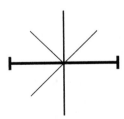

Figure 6–3 A Mira Used to Show a Reflection in the Absolute Value Graph

In Figure 6–3, the mira, placed on the x-axis, allows the reflection of the line $y = x$ to be viewed.

The advantages of using the mira are threefold. First, the students have a visual image of how the absolute value function is generated from the related linear function. Second, a geometric connection can be made, allowing students to appreciate the role of reflection in an algebraic context. And third, the stage is set for students to graph other absolute value functions by starting with their linear "parent." For example, the student can be asked to graph the function $y = |2x - 3|$ by sketching $y = 2x - 3$ on graph paper, using the mira to locate the reflected part, and completing the

A carefully selected task will generate interest and actively engage students.

sketch of the absolute value graph. After concretely laying the groundwork with a manipulative such as a mira, additional explorations on a graphing calculator might follow so that, in a short period of time, students can appreciate how the parameters A, B, C, and D affect the graph of the function $y = A|Bx + C| + D$.

Therefore, by choosing to conduct a hands-on investigation of how absolute value functions are related to linear functions, the teacher can encourage visualization and the use of geometry in an algebra problem. The decision to take this route, rather than to simply sketch a few absolute value functions by using a value table, gives the students a considerably richer experience and allows them to make significant connections to previous learning. Because the lesson addresses the needs of the visual learner, it also promotes the equity and learning Principles, which call for mathematics instruction that reaches out to all students, regardless of their learning styles. However, the teacher needs to carefully select tasks and problems that actively engage students and play into their interests. Even an objective that appears to be rather mechanical, like sketching an absolute value graph, can become an enticing activity for students if it is planned carefully. As we discussed in Chapter 4, there are a number of resources that a teacher can use to find these types of problems and activities, including, but not limited to, the textbook, resource books, journal articles, and the Internet. Whenever an activity or problem is posed, you should look for a stimulus to evoke curiosity and interest on the part of the students. Also, keep in mind that a carefully selected classroom task may take students five minutes to complete or may be designed to take one or several days.

■ CLASSROOM TOOLS

Hands-on Manipulative Materials

Any good carpenter knows that if a nail is to be driven into wood, not only is a tool required, but it makes more sense to drive the nail with a hammer than with a screwdriver. To hit a screw with a hammer doesn't make much sense either, but most people would never choose to drive a screw into wood with their bare hands. The problem-solving process in the classroom often lends itself to the use of tools such as calculators and computers, but you must choose the proper tool for the task. Professional Teaching Standard 4 is stated as follows:

Standard 4: Tools for Enhancing Discourse

The teacher of mathematics, in order to enhance discourse, should encourage and accept the use of

- computers, calculators, and other technology;
- concrete materials used as models;
- pictures, diagrams, tables, and graphs;
- invented and conventional terms and symbols;
- metaphors, analogies, and stories;
- written hypotheses, explanations, and arguments;
- oral presentation and dramatizations.

(NCTM, *Professional Standards for Teaching Mathematics*, 1991, p. 52.)

Notice that Standard 4 does not limit tools to "technology"; it also includes such items as manipulatives, pictures, diagrams, and oral presentations. Just as the carpenter chooses between a hammer and a screwdriver, the classroom teacher must decide which tools are most appropriate for exploring mathematical concepts. There are times when the use of hands-on materials, such as pattern blocks or miras, is important and other times when manipulatives may actually inhibit the classroom conversations. Sometimes, students get so caught up in determining what the physical model looks like that they lose the mathematical intent in the process. Likewise, there are times when a graphing calculator is appropriate in solving a problem and other times when the problem is more readily solved with pencil and paper. So, teachers need to think about the concept to be presented and determine which tools might be most useful to the students.

Let's suppose, for example, that you were going to teach a series of lessons on decimals in a middle school classroom. In getting students to think about what it means to add 3.25 + 5.7, you could choose to use a calculator. When the students key the numbers into the machine, it will deliver an answer of 8.95, and the problem is solved. But is this the best way for students to explore the concept of adding decimals? Probably not, unless considerable discussion takes place afterward about how the calculator arrived at that answer. Instead, the teacher may choose to use base ten blocks as a manipulative to drive the exploration. The unit cube can represent $\frac{1}{100}$, so the long represents 10 of these or $\frac{1}{10}$, and the flat would represent 10 of the longs, or 1. Therefore, the problem could be represented as in Figure 6–4:

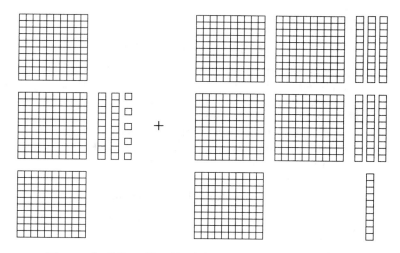

Figure 6–4 Base Ten Block Representation of 3.25 + 5.7

By putting together the flats, the longs, and the units, the student can visualize the sum as 8.95. Furthermore, the class can discuss why the 0.7 needed to be added to the 0.2, which will generally cause students to devise their own rule about lining up decimal places to ensure that proper place values are being added.

As an alternative to base ten blocks, the teacher might choose to give the students a piece of graph paper and have them shade a 10 × 10 grid to represent the number 1. Similarly, a student can shade a 1 × 10 grid to represent 0.1 and a single square to represent 0.01. The problem could be modeled just as with the base ten blocks but by drawing the pictures on the graph-paper grid instead. This approach might benefit a student who is better served by creating a model than by being handed a commercial set of materials. It is also a low-cost alternative for a school that does not have an adequate supply of base ten blocks.

Another teacher may choose to use money as a model for the problem. By viewing the problem as $3.25 + $2.70, the students can use a visual such as the one in Figure 6–5:

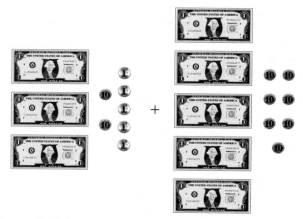

Figure 6–5 Representation of 3.25 + 5.70 with Currency

Recognizing that the dollars, the dimes, and the pennies can be combined, the student will see that the sum of the money is $8.95. Once again, students can discuss why the dimes cannot be combined with the pennies and justify the need for aligning decimal points when adding decimal fractions.

Making connections to an earlier measurement unit, still another teacher might give each student a ruler marked with decimeters, centimeters, and millimeters (see Figure 6–6). Because there are 10 millimeters in each centimeter and 10 centimeters in each decimeter, students could represent the number 3.25 with a line segment whose length is 3 dm, 2 cm, and 5 mm—the unit is 1 decimeter. Similarly, another line segment would have the length of 5 dm and 7 cm. When these two segments are placed side by side, the total length can be read off of the ruler as 8 dm, 9 cm, and 5 mm, or 8.95.

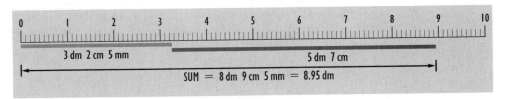

Figure 6–6 Measurement Representation of 3.25 + 5.7

The measurement model works for many students because it relates to reading a ruler, a skill that is very familiar to most students by the secondary and middle grade levels.

So, which tool is the best for getting a student to visualize and think about a decimal addition problem—calculators, base ten blocks, graph paper sketches, money (dollar bills, dimes, and pennies), or a ruler? You may have guessed by now that there is rarely a best way to teach a concept, one that will work for all students. Because a mathematics classroom is made up of many individuals, who each think in a different way, one model may be more effective for some people, and another works better for others. If students have had enough exposure to money problems prior to this class period to visualize coins in their heads, they may feel most comfortable with modeling the problem in terms of dimes and pennies. Another student who has been successfully thinking about whole number addition using base ten blocks may prefer to stay with that model. As teachers, we need to be prepared to use any of a number of different tools to promote learning and equity in our classrooms. Each time that we plan a lesson, we ask ourselves, "What is my class like this year, and what do I know about how they've responded to the use of various tools that might help me choose the best place to start?" For example, if you have just completed a series of lessons on metric measurement, and the students had a very difficult time with the material, probably the last thing you would want to do is to begin the unit on decimal operations with a ruler. On the other hand, introducing the metric model later in the unit might be just the reinforcement that your students need to help them view measurement in a different context—one that allows them to make a connection between number sense and measurement. Finally, it is important to acknowledge that what worked last year in your class or what works for another teacher in another classroom may not be effective in your current situation.

Think of the classroom tools as a collection in a carpenter's toolbox. Sometimes, carpenters reach in and pull out a pair of needle-nose pliers, but if that doesn't work, they may reach back into the box and try a bolt cutter instead. You might begin a lesson with base ten blocks and very quickly realize that the manipulative you have selected is not working and that you need to pull back and display a set of coins on an overhead projector instead. This decision is generally made during class—a real-time choice—and is based upon an assessment of the degree to which students are mastering your planned objective. Consequently, flexibility is crucial; we must be prepared to shift gears in the middle of a lesson or to work individually with a student who appears to need a different tool than the rest of the class. As was pointed out in Chapter 5, our lesson-planning process should allow for the possibility that a particular model may not work for all of the students in a class.

Throughout the book, we have referred to a number of different classroom materials available to the secondary and middle school mathematics teacher, such as base ten blocks, pattern blocks, algebra tiles, miras, rulers, and play money. Keep in mind that these tools do not automatically ensure a successful lesson. As we mentioned earlier, hands-on materials can, in some cases, actually get in the way of learning. Students may, for example, get so involved in trying to properly model a fraction-addition problem with pattern blocks that they become proficient at using blocks but miss the major mathematical concepts of the lesson. In a sense, the proper use of the manipulatives can almost become more important in the student's eyes than mastering the mathematical content. We need to be very careful in selecting and using hands-on manipulative materials and recognize that their proper use in the classroom is a teaching skill that is developed over time. A surgeon can spend years studying books about how to repair a damaged liver, but the first time the physician is handed a scalpel, everything goes back to zero—the skill of actually using the scalpel is much different from having memorized the properties of the scalpel and its proper use. And as a surgeon spends several years learning to use the scalpel properly to make incisions, the mathematics teacher needs time to learn how to properly use manipulatives in the classroom.

The list that follows contains a series of recommendations and practical suggestions for the use of manipulatives in the secondary and middle school mathematics classroom. It includes both a summary of the discussion in this chapter and a few additional ideas to take into account when deciding whether to use hands-on materials in the classroom:

GENERAL TIPS ON MANIPULATIVE USE

1. Always *allow students "freeplay" time* with manipulatives the first couple of times that they are distributed. Students often need up to 15–20 minutes the first time that they encounter manipulatives such as pattern blocks or technology such as a graphing calculator just to explore and experiment with them. Giving students time for free play will reduce the likelihood that they will be exploring the materials while you are trying to teach the lesson.

2. It is important to realize that manipulatives can tempt students to exhibit off-task behavior. Therefore, it is important to *establish specific rules* for the use of hands-on materials. For example, you might specify that students cannot touch the materials during a whole-class discussion unless the teacher says that they may. Furthermore, if a student throws a manipulative such as a base ten block, there must be a consequence. The consequence may be that the student loses the privilege of using hands-on materials for a week, and the second offense results in a phone call to parents.

3. *Establish a routine for distributing and collecting materials.* For example, if students are working in learning teams, one person should be designated to get the materials, and another student should be responsible for cleaning up and returning the tools to their storage space.

4. *Don't ask students to memorize procedures with the manipulatives.* The hands-on materials should be used as a teaching aid but not as another process to be memorized. Students have enough problems with learning the mathematics without worrying about whether they are modeling the problem with the manipulatives in a way that satisfies the teacher.

5. *Remember that manipulatives are tools but are not the focus of instruction.* Lessons that teach students "about" pattern blocks or calculators are not useful in and of themselves. Instead, the materials should be used as a means to promote some mathematical idea.

6. Remember that students learn the mathematics as they discuss what they are doing with the materials; *they do not inherently learn simply because they use manipulatives.* In Chapter 2, the processes of reflection and communication were described as critical in the learning process. We cannot assume that the students mastered an outcome just because they used hands-on materials; instead, the tools should promote the discussion and interaction that brings about the learning.

7. *Not every child will find manipulatives the easiest or the best way to solve certain problems.* Hands-on materials are merely an aid for those students who tend to learn best visually or tactilely and provide a concrete experience.

8. *Work with other teachers in the building to determine a central location for storage of manipulatives.* When teachers need a set of graphing calculators or metric rulers for a lesson, they often don't know where the tools are located in the building. Consequently, some people avoid hands-on problems because it hardly seems worth the effort to try to find the materials. A tools closet with a sign-out system makes the use of manipulatives much more practical.

Use of Technology

The NCTM teaching Standards listed calculators, computers, and other technology as crucial tools for generating discussions in the mathematics classroom. Furthermore, one of the Guiding Principles from the *Principles and Standards for School*

Mathematics is the technology Principle, which states that "mathematics instructional programs should use technology to help all students understand the mathematics and should prepare them to use mathematics in an increasingly technological world" (NCTM, 1998, p. 40). Throughout this book, a number of references have been made to the use of technology to support everything from curve sketching to exploring rational and irrational numbers. As is the case with manipulatives, there are times when a calculator or computer is appropriate, and times when they are not useful. In fact, the *Curriculum and Evaluation Standards* states that a major objective for students in the new millennium is to be able to look at a problem and determine whether that problem is most efficiently solved by using paper and pencil, technology, or a mental estimation or computation. Teachers need to model this decision-making process in the classroom for students to get the idea. Let's say, for example, that a student in a high school mathematics course is solving a linear system such as:

$$\begin{cases} 2x + 5y = -3 \\ y = -3x + 15 \end{cases}$$

If the student chooses to solve the system by addition and subtraction, the individual may begin by adding $3x$ to both sides of the second equation and multiplying the bottom equation by 5. When doing this multiplication, the student must determine 5×15. At this point, we often see students reaching for a calculator to find the product. It then becomes the teacher's responsibility to step in and say, "Let's see if we can do that one in our heads. Can anyone think of how we might do that without having to reach for a calculator?" Using the Distributive Property, students can then be led to think of 5×15 as $5(10 + 5)$ and can mentally add $50 + 25$ to get 75. Not only does this discussion teach students how to do simple mental arithmetic, but it also provides a context in which to review the power of the Distributive Property. The point here is that most would agree that it is inappropriate for students to use a calculator to find the answer to 5×15, and it is the teacher's job to model the mental processes that will enable the student to do the calculation without technology.

The same argument could be made about the use of the Internet in problem solving. Although a student might be able to use the World Wide Web to find the price of a car for a project on budgeting, it may be easier just to pick up a phone, call the local auto dealership, and ask. When high-powered technology is at our fingertips, we need to carefully consider how to make the best use of it in the classroom. The next chapter, Chapter 7, will explore this issue in much more depth and will also discuss the use of computers, graphing calculators, video and CD-ROM, and the Internet in mathematics instruction.

Diagrams, Graphs, and Other Discussion Starters

The final classroom tool that we will discuss here is the use of a picture to generate a classroom discussion. Often, students can be motivated by a graph, a diagram, a picture, or some such visual image that involves mathematical principles. Consider this problem as illustrated in Figures 6–7 through 6–9, adapted from the University of Hawaii Geometry Learning Project (Curriculum Research and Development Group, 1997):

Jill's mother asked her to move a heavy metal table. Its top view is shown, with the positions of its legs at the vertices.

Figure 6–7 Picture Representation of a Table

After moving the table, Jill sees to her horror that the lower right leg of the table has made a deep scratch mark on the wooden floor, as shown.

Figure 6–8 Picture of the Scratch Made by Moving a Table

Draw the position of the table before and after Jill moved it.

How would you draw the picture? Make a sketch before reading ahead. Figure 6–9 illustrates three different possible interpretations that students may have of the image.

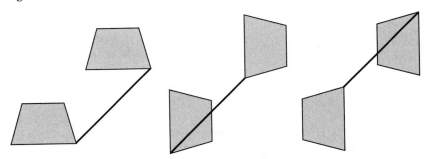

Figure 6–9 Interpretations of How the Scratch Was Made

(Figures 6–7, 6–8, and 6–9 from the Geometry Learning Project, Curriculum Research and Development Group, University of Hawaii. Reprinted with permission.)

Students may also argue about whether the table started at the upper right and was pushed down and to the left or whether it started from the lower left and was pushed up and to the right. They may eventually conclude that there are an infinite number of solutions to the problem because the table can also be rotated around 360°, pivoting on the lower right leg. The point here is that, although the lesson focuses on the geometric notions of a translation (slide) and a rotation (turn), the picture lends itself to considerable discussion in the classroom, as students try to determine how the scratch might have been created. As such, the picture and its related problem become tools that have the potential to generate a classroom debate and discussion.

A similar problem for a mathematics class is to present the students with a line segment as shown in Figure 6–10 and ask the following question:

Draw a rectangle such that this segment is one of its diagonals.

———————

Figure 6–10 Find the Rectangle for Which This Line Segment Is a Diagonal

Some students will often immediately jump to the conclusion that there is only one answer to the problem and draw a rectangle such as the one shown in Figure 6–11:

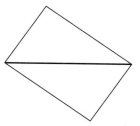

Figure 6–11 Rectangle with the Segment as Its Diagonal

But, upon further inspection, they will realize that there are some other solutions, such as the general rectangle and the square illustrated in Figure 6–12:

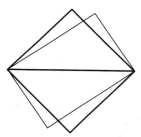

Figure 6–12 Other Possible Rectangles with the Same Diagonal

Continuing the generalizing process, students may recognize that a diagram of several possible solutions will include points on a circle representing the vertices of the rectangles as shown in Figure 6–13:

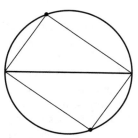

Figure 6–13 Vertices of All Possible Rectangles Lie on the Circle

Interestingly, a typical high school geometry theorem states that angles inscribed in a semicircle such that the sides pass through the endpoints of a diameter form right angles. (This theorem follows from another theorem stating that the measure of an inscribed angle is one half the measure of its intercepted arc. Since the intercepted arc is a semicircle, it measures 180°, so the inscribed angle must measure 90°.) By exploring this problem, students are likely to discover the theorem for themselves. In this case, we see that a single drawing of a line segment serves as a tool for a rich classroom discussion about rectangles, right angles, and, eventually, circles and inscribed angles.

The tools that teachers choose to employ—manipulatives, technology, diagrams, or others—are intended to serve as the basis for discussion of important mathematical topics. The tools, therefore, are not inherently valuable. Tools *become* valuable when they are carefully selected and effectively used to generate classroom discussion or discourse. In the next section, we look at what it means to promote discourse in the classroom.

■ CLASSROOM DISCOURSE

Student and Teacher Roles

At the beginning of the chapter, we presented Anne Kelley's discussion about square roots with her students. After she had posed a problem to the class, several points were raised by students, forcing her to decide what to pursue and what to leave alone. In a contemporary mathematics classroom atmosphere that invites student opinions and emphasizes conjecture and validation of thinking, the teacher has an important role in directing the communication process. In the *Professional Standards* (NCTM, 1991), the authors noted that "discourse is both the way ideas are exchanged and what the ideas entail: Who talks? About what? In what ways? What do people write, what do they record and why? What questions are important? How do ideas change? Whose ideas and ways of thinking are valued? Who determines when to end a discussion?" (p. 34). The authors of the document also point out that discourse in the classroom is largely driven by the tasks and tools selected by the teacher and the learning environment that has been established. Two teaching Standards involve discourse—Standard 2: The Teacher's Role in Discourse, and Standard 3: The Student's Role in Discourse. The text of those Standards reads as follows:

Standard 2: Teacher's Role in Discourse

The teacher of mathematics should orchestrate discourse by

- posing questions and tasks that elicit, engage, and challenge each student's thinking;
- listening carefully to students' ideas;
- asking students to clarify and justify their ideas orally and in writing;
- deciding what to pursue in depth from among the ideas that students bring up during a discussion;

- deciding when and how to attach mathematical notation and language to students' ideas;
- deciding when to provide information, when to clarify an issue, when to model, when to lead, and when to let a student struggle with a difficulty;
- monitoring students' participation in discussions and deciding when and how to encourage each student to participate.

Standard 3: Student's Role in Discourse

The teacher of mathematics should promote classroom discourse in which students

- listen to, respond to, and question the teacher and one another;
- use a variety of tools to reason, make connections, solve problems, and communicate;
- initiate problems and questions;
- make conjectures and present solutions;
- explore examples and counterexamples to investigate a conjecture;
- try to convince themselves and one another of the validity of particular representations, solutions, conjectures, and answers;
- rely on mathematical evidence and argument to determine validity.

(NCTM, *Professional Standards for Teaching Mathematics*, 1991, pp. 35 & 45.)

Although the teacher often directs the discourse in a mathematics classroom, students must realize that they have an important role in the process as well (as emphasized in Standard 3). They need to learn to listen to one another, to share their thinking, and to counter or affirm the thinking of others. In Chapter 2, we discussed how learning often happens in a social environment as students affirm or refute the mathematical reasoning of others. As students listen to one another and say, "yes, that's what I think, too" or "no, I disagree because . . . ," they are engaged in the type of discourse that brings about learning. Students have a responsibility to actively engage in classroom discussions and problem solving, and teachers are charged with the task of assessing student interactions to determine whether the students are fulfilling that obligation. Assessing students in team interactions by the use of checklists and self-evaluations is discussed in Chapter 8.

Questioning Skills

Much of the discourse in the classroom is the result of effective questions raised by the teacher. In fact, the difference between a strong lesson and a weaker one often lies in the teacher's ability to raise clear but critical questions with artistry. Entire books have been written on questioning skills in the classroom because the way that teachers ask questions determines whether students actively engage in a discussion or shy away from it. For example, a teacher exploring permutations with a class could ask, "How many ways can you arrange six pictures on a fireplace mantel?" Students should respond that there are 6! or 720 possible arrangements. This question is **closed** in that it only has one expected and correct response. Now, suppose that the teacher had said, "I have six pictures to arrange on the fireplace mantel. I'll bet there are at least 500 ways to do that. I need you to prove that I'm right or to prove that I'm wrong." If a student raised a hand and responded, "There would be 6! ways to arrange them, so there are more than 500," the teacher might reply, "Why should I believe that there are 6! arrangements? How do you know that?" With these questions, the student is pressed to explain *why* the formula works. The teacher can then direct the class in a discussion that leads to the conclusion that there are six choices for the first location, then five for the second, and so forth. And, even when the students have drawn this conclusion, the teacher can ask, "But why do you multiply 6 × 5 × 4 × 3 × 2 × 1 rather than adding those numbers together?" This pushes students even further as they defend why multiplication makes sense, perhaps by drawing a tree diagram to convince the teacher and one another. In this second line of questioning, we refer to the questions as **open** or **open ended** because responses are not limited to one correct answer. Students may react in a variety of ways, and the teacher can use those responses to make related points about permutations. In fact, open-ended questions in the classroom may have one correct response but several ways of explaining how to get to it, or the questions may have several acceptable answers.

In the *Professional Standards*, the NCTM pointed out five different purposes for asking questions in the classroom, together with examples. These purposes and two examples of each are represented as follows.

PURPOSES FOR QUESTIONS IN THE CLASSROOM

1. **Helping students work together to make sense of mathematics**
   "What do others think about what Janine said?"
   "Can you convince the rest of us that makes sense?"
2. **Helping students to rely more on themselves to determine whether something is mathematically correct**
   "Why do you think that?"
   "How did you reach that conclusion?"
3. **Helping students to learn to reason mathematically**
   "Does that always work?"
   "How could you prove that?"
4. **Helping students learn to conjecture, invent, and solve problems**
   "What would happen if . . . ? What if not?"
   "Can you predict the next one? What about the last one?"
5. **Helping students to connect mathematics, its ideas, and its applications**
   "How does this relate to . . . ?"
   "What ideas that we learned before were useful in solving this problem?"

(NCTM, *Professional Standards for Teaching Mathematics*, 1991, pp. 3–4.)

In Chapter 4, we discussed that objectives are often written on four different levels—knowledge and skill, concept, application, and problem solving. Similarly, questions raised by the classroom teacher are on a variety of different levels, and the key to good questioning is to vary the depth of questions raised. Cathy Cook and Claudette Rasmussen (1991) have provided some examples of classroom questions that require increasingly higher levels of thinking. These examples may serve as a helpful checklist of question levels that you can keep in mind as you watch a videotape of your teaching or observe that of another teacher.

EXAMPLES OF QUESTIONING FOR SPECIFIC TYPES OF THINKING

Knowledge: remembering, reciting, recognizing
"Who/what/when/where is ___?"
"What do you remember about ___?"

Comprehension: understanding, translating, estimating
"Given ___, what would you predict?"
"What is meant by ___?"

Creative thinking: elaborating, taking another point of view, brainstorming
"In what other ways can you ___?"
"What details can you add to ___?"

Application: using, demonstrating, solving
"How can you solve this (similar situation)?"
"How could you use ___?"

Analysis: comparing and contrasting, inferring, attribute listing
"How is this ___ like/different from this ___?"
"What are the characteristics of ___?"

Synthesis: hypothesizing, planning, creating
"How would you create a ___?"
"What plan can you develop for solving ___?"

Evaluation: justifying, rating, judging using criteria
"What criteria would you use to ___?"
"Why do you agree/disagree with ___?"

(Cook & Rasmussen, 1991. Reprinted with permission.)

When orchestrating classroom discourse, it is important to pay attention to the levels of questioning. You might ask yourself, "If someone was keeping track of my questions, placing each question I ask into one of the categories suggested in this chapter, how much variety would they observe? Am I asking frequent knowledge-level questions at the expense of higher-level analysis and synthesis questions? Or is it the other way around?" Students will only respond to a question in the depth that is expected; that is, if you ask a simple knowledge-level question, you'll get a simple answer back. If you expect to generate a meaningful discussion about a mathematical concept, you need to ask a significant question.

On a very practical level, the seemingly slightest change in the way that a question or statement is phrased can make a dramatic difference in the way that students respond. For example, strange as this may sound, teachers should always ask questions that can be answered. As an illustration, consider these two statements that a teacher might say to the entire class when distributing paper and scissors for a hands-on activity:

Statement 1: Did everyone get a sheet of paper and a pair of scissors?

Statement 2: Raise your hand if you did not receive both a piece of paper and a pair of scissors.

Which statement is preferable and why? You should recognize that Statement 1 is a well-intended question, but it has no answer. If you were a student in the class and were asked that question, how would you respond? How do you know whether the other 25 students in the class got paper and a pair of scissors? The question is vague and will lead to confusion about how to respond, and the confusion often leads to behavioral problems. On the other hand, Statement 2 is a very specific direction that each person in the class can respond to. If you did not receive, for example, a pair of scissors, you will raise your hand. Teachers often make this type of mistake when they work through a mathematics problem with the class and conclude the example by asking, "Does everyone understand this now?" Similarly, the teacher tells students to take out a homework assignment and asks, "Were there questions on the assignment?" The students don't know whether to raise their hands, to shout, "Yes" or "No," or just to look around and see how other people are responding. Again, the response is entirely different when the teacher concludes an example and asks, "May I have a volunteer to come up to the board and re-explain this problem in your own words?" Upon telling students to take out their homework assignments, the teacher can ask, "How many of you found that at least one problem confused you on the assignment last night?" These direct questions provide the teacher with valuable information and are clearly stated so that students know how they are to respond.

Through a teacher's modeling, the students can also learn to ask questions of one another that have considerable depth and clarity. With time, the students should rely less on the teacher to raise the important questions and begin asking one another for justifications of their thinking. Learning teams or cooperative learning strategies can facilitate this process. Cooperative (or collaborative) learning can also greatly enhance the level of discourse that takes place in the classroom.

Cooperative Learning

John Goodlad's (1984) research showed that, on the average, 80 percent of a typical class period is devoted to "teacher talk"; the other 20 percent of the class time, students are actually talking. Consider a typical fifty-minute mathematics class: Out of this fifty minutes, 20 percent amounts to ten minutes of student talk. If you consider that a classroom typically has twenty or more students, this means that the average student is allotted about thirty seconds per day to speak in your class. If we assume that knowledge is, in some way, constructed by the learner, often through interactions with others, then thirty seconds per day is simply not acceptable for student talk time. By using cooperative learning, teachers achieve what is referred to as **simultaneous interaction,** when several students in the classroom share their thinking at the same time. If a classroom of twenty-eight students is divided up into teams of four students, and each team is given time to discuss a problem, seven students can communicate simultaneously. This situation generates seven times as much student talk time as can be achieved in a traditional classroom setting. The mathematics of talk time is simple, but the results can be striking.

A summary of research studies on cooperative learning published in *Social Education* in 1991 (Guyton) showed that the appropriate use of cooperative learning in the classroom results in:

- increased achievement and long-term retention
- development of higher-order processing skills
- improved attitude toward school and subject area
- development of collaborative competencies and an increased ability to work with others
- improved psychological health
- liking for fellow classmates, including respect for students with different racial or ethnic backgrounds or disabilities
- increased self-esteem

So, not only is the student's academic achievement generally enhanced through cooperative learning, but a variety of social and psychological goals can be addressed as well. The key issue here is the appropriate use of cooperative learning in the classroom.

Suppose that Mr. Read poses this problem:

If I were to roll a number cube and toss a fair coin at the same time, what is the probability that I will roll a 6 and toss a head on the same trial?

He gives each table of students a number cube and a coin and tells the students to "figure it out in your groups." Typically, the highest achiever at the table will take the materials, roll the number cube and toss the coin, and tell the rest of the group what is happening. Or, even worse, this student might reason out the sample space—a head with a 1, 2, 3, 4, 5, or 6 or a tail with a 1, 2, 3, 4, 5, or 6—and announce to the group that the probability has to be 1 in 12, eliminating any need for the group of students to actually conduct an experiment and make a conjecture. This traditional way of handling group assignments is often referred to as "group work," and it is *not* equivalent to cooperative learning as defined in the contemporary classroom. We often hear seasoned educators say, "I have used group work for years," which translates as "I give a problem to four students and tell them to work on it together." But we know exactly what happens—the best student does all the work, and everyone else gets credit for it.

In a cooperative learning environment, the activity should be structured so that every student has no choice but to be actively involved in the problem-solving process. Also, each student has **individual accountability,** which means that even though the work is done as a team, in the end, each student is required to individually demonstrate an understanding of the concepts through an interview, a written test, or some other means. So, in the number cube and coin problem (adapted from NCTM, *How to Use Cooperative Learning in the Mathematics Class,* 1997), the teacher might divide the class into learning teams of three. In each team, one person is assigned the task of rolling the number cube; one person tosses the coin, and one person records the results on paper. Then, after the team has collected the data and come to a conclusion, the teacher randomly selects one person on the team to be responsible for sharing the results of the experiment and explaining the conclusions for the team. By using a random selection at the end, the teacher emphasizes that *every* student on the team must understand the problem because no one knows who will be selected to discuss the results. You will notice how this approach to cooperative learning is entirely different from simply telling a few students to work together. The structure for *how* the students are required to work as a team is provided, so there are no free riders in the process—every student gets involved in the process and is accountable for learning the mathematics.

You may have heard it said that you never completely understand a concept unless you can explain it to someone else, and that is where cooperative learning can be particularly powerful. When students explain their thinking to others, the result is "win-win" in that the student who is confused gets to hear an explanation from someone other than the teacher, and the students who are helping their peers clarify their own thinking by having to explain it to someone else. Students working in pairs can be a powerful strategy for checking homework assignments as well. Too often, several students go to the chalkboard to demonstrate a number of problems that most other people already know how to do, and valuable class time is wasted. Instead, students can compare and discuss homework solutions at a table and correct one another's errors so that class time is spent only on those items with which students need help. The topic of assigning and checking homework is discussed in more depth in Chapter 9.

Following is a list of practical tips and suggestions for implementing cooperative learning strategies:

PRACTICAL TIPS ON IMPLEMENTING COOPERATIVE LEARNING STRATEGIES

1. Rarely, if ever, should a teacher use student-selected or random grouping for learning teams. Instead, a teacher should carefully assign the members to each team. Sometimes, teams of four students are made up of a high achiever, a low achiever, and two average students. Other times, it may be more appropriate to group students of similar ability or performance levels when, for example, a teacher is implementing an enrichment or differentiated curricular model as described in Chapter 3. Whenever possible, a learning team should include a mix of males and females.

Continued

2. Once learning teams are established in a class, they should stay together for at least four to six weeks. A team generally needs a couple of weeks just to learn how to work together and deal with each others' personalities. Teams should also be changed periodically, as students need opportunities to work with others and can grow tired of always working with the same individuals.

3. The process of changing to a cooperative environment can be difficult for some students and should be gradual. If a ninth grader has rarely worked in cooperative teams in middle school, then that student is likely to resist, may prefer to work alone, and will need time to adjust to a collaborative environment.

4. Reading a manual or going to a short workshop on cooperative learning can be helpful in preparing a teacher to use the techniques effectively. However, nothing is more helpful than regular practice and acceptance of the idea that cooperative structures often require several "trials" before the teacher and the class begin to feel comfortable with this way of organizing the classroom.

5. Be prepared for some chaos and disorder when you initially introduce cooperative assignments. Cooperative learning is frightening to many teachers because they feel that they are losing control. Keep in mind that the teacher's role in a cooperative classroom is to guide and not to dispense knowledge.

Classroom discourse, therefore, needs careful analysis by the teacher in terms of the roles of the student and teacher, the effectiveness of questions that are being asked, and the ways in which students interact in a cooperative classroom. And, as we have mentioned, the way that the teacher runs the classroom—the environment—is critical to enhancing the discourse that occurs within it. Next, we discuss a few of the issues related to the establishment of a nurturing classroom environment.

■ LEARNING ENVIRONMENT

Try to visualize some mathematics classrooms that you have visited. When you looked around the rooms, what did you see? Were they cluttered and messy with stacks of books and papers? Did you see posters on the wall, suggesting mathematical themes, or were the walls antiseptic, with nothing on them? Were the desks arranged in neat parallel rows of individual workstations, or were tables or sets of desks arranged into groups of four or six? Were there tables with chairs, or were there individual desks? Were the bulletin boards colorful and suggestive of mathematical topics and themes, or were they bare or simply displaying calendars or homework assignment listings? Was the teacher shouting at the class to remain quiet, or were students on-task, with the teacher helping those who needed it? Did it feel like the type of room that invited you in and made you want to be a member of the class, or were you happy to get out the door and leave the room behind?

All of these factors, from the physical layout to the attitudes of the teacher and students, constitute the **learning environment**. The *Professional Standards* (1991) state that "more than just a physical setting with desks, bulletin boards, and posters, the classroom environment forms a hidden curriculum with messages about what counts in learning and doing mathematics: Neatness? Speed? Accuracy? Listening well? Being able to justify a solution? Working independently?" (p. 56). Furthermore, the authors declared that the environment should foster whatever type of learning the teacher believes is important. We generally don't need more than a ten-minute visit to a mathematics classroom to know exactly what the teacher is valuing in that room. What we are absorbing as we look around and listen is the environment.

The NCTM teaching Standard on the learning environment is as follows:

Standard 5: Learning Environment

The teacher of mathematics should create a learning environment that fosters the development of each student's mathematical power by

- providing and structuring the time necessary to explore sound mathematics and grapple with significant ideas and problems;
- using the physical space and materials in ways that facilitate students' learning of mathematics;
- providing a context that encourages the development of mathematical skill and proficiency;
- respecting and valuing students' ideas, ways of thinking, and mathematical dispositions;

and by consistently expecting and encouraging students to

- work independently or collaboratively to make sense of mathematics;
- take intellectual risks by raising questions and formulating conjectures;
- display a sense of mathematical competence by validating and supporting ideas with mathematical argument.

(NCTM, *Professional Standards for Teaching Mathematics*, 1991, p. 57.)

The physical environment in the classroom can be a very important motivator. When students walk into a classroom and see a poster showing the first 2,000 digits of π or an unsolved problem such as the triangle-trisection problem, students often can't help but get caught up in the wonder of mathematics. One of the features of an attractive classroom is the bulletin board. Bulletin boards are often used for utilitarian purposes, such as posting announcements, bulletins, schedules, homework assignments, and calendars, but they can also be used to promote mathematical understanding. For example, the bulletin board could display the ancient Egyptian numeration system, with the symbols that represent a few numbers. Underneath might be a series of questions, such as "How does this differ from our system?" and "How would you write 1,247 in hieroglyphics?" This type of bulletin board is interactive in that students learn something from reading it and might be challenged by a problem posed on it.

Similarly, some teachers put a "Problem of the Week" on the bulletin board. Changing the problem each week, they challenge students to turn in a solution by the end of the week, often offering extra credit points or some other incentive. Several excellent World Wide Web sites (see, for example, <http://forum.swarthmore.edu/pow/>)

can be used as resources from which to draw problems of this type for a bulletin board. In fact, a simple search of the Internet for "Problem of the Week" can reveal more than 2,000 Web pages of problems. Also, students often solve problems as part of classroom projects and can display their solutions on a bulletin board. The displays not only showcase student work but are attractive reminders of the work that has been taking place in the classroom. A simple piece of corkboard can generate excitement in the mathematics classroom.

The physical arrangement of desks in the classroom is also an environmental issue to consider. Historically, desks are placed in straight, parallel rows. However, the straight rows suggest a lecture-style lesson and send a message that students should not be talking to one another. If the teacher values teamwork, student interaction, and hands-on lessons, desks are rarely placed in rows. You might consider putting four desks together to form a "table," so that all four students face one another.

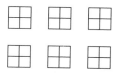

Figure 6–14 Classroom Design of Desks Arranged in Tables of Four

The arrangement shown in Figure 6–14 promotes student interaction, while, at the same time, it creates more floor space around tables and makes the room feel more open and inviting.

Some teachers find it useful to arrange the room with rows of desks placed in pairs as shown in Figure 6–15.

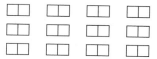

Figure 6–15 Classroom Design of Desks Arranged in Pairs

In this configuration, each student has a buddy with whom to work during routine classroom activities, and, whenever needed, two pairs of students can be joined to form a team of four.

Teachers who frequently employ cooperative strategies sometimes find it best to leave individual desks in straight rows and ask students to move the furniture before a cooperative activity. This method has students sitting by themselves for some teacher-led lessons, which is conducive to classroom management and positive discipline. In addition, students are less prone to copy others' papers in quiz and testing situations if their desks are separated. On the other hand, one must weigh this factor against the amount of time spent moving desks around and the noise and distractions of desks being dragged across the floor into pairs or groups of four. Most importantly, the teacher needs to think about the message sent about the nature of the mathematics class and the invitation to learning by the placement of the furniture within the room. Maybe that's why kindergarten teachers often have rugs on the floor and few, if any, desks.

As we discussed in Chapter 2, in the sections on motivation and disposition, students develop their attitudes toward mathematics by virtue of how the classrooms are structured. A sixth grader who was asked to "write a letter to a friend, explaining to that friend how we add $\frac{1}{3} + \frac{1}{4}$" responded to the teacher, "You've got to be kidding! That's what you do in English class; it's not what you're supposed to do in math!" Why did the student respond that way? Probably because it was the first time a teacher had ever expected that student to write in a mathematics classroom. As soon as the teacher begins to require that students justify their thinking in words and with pictures, the students understand that this is what will be expected of them within the particular classroom environment. Indeed, the types of questions the teacher asks, the way they are asked, and the way in which a teacher responds to correct and incorrect answers will all affect the classroom environment. Let's look at a simple example.

Ms. Barry is leading a discussion on Pascal's Triangle in her third period Math 3 course for juniors. She has just looked at the first row containing 1, 1, the second row containing 1, 2, 1, and the third row containing 1, 3, 3, 1.

Ms. Barry: Does anyone know what numbers will be in the fourth row? Pat?
Pat: 1, 4, 4, 4, 1?
Ms. Barry: No, that's not it. Anyone else?
Juan: 1, 4, 6, 4, 1.
Ms. Barry: Very good, Juan. That's it!

In this situation, Pat was incorrect but was neither rewarded for attempting the solution nor revisited to see if Juan's answer made sense. And, in the end, the class now knows the correct answer but may still wonder how Juan solved the problem. Now, look at the possibility for a discussion in another way:

Ms. Barry: Does anyone know what numbers will be in the fourth row? Pat?
Pat: 1, 4, 4, 4, 1?
Ms. Barry: How did you get that, Pat?
Pat: In the second row, we put a 2 in the middle, and in the third row, we put a 3, 3, so I figured that the next row should have three 4's. It fits the pattern, doesn't it?
Ms. Barry: Can others see how Pat found that pattern? What other kinds of patterns did you find? Juan?
Juan: I got 1, 4, 6, 4, 1.
Ms. Barry: What pattern did you notice, Juan? How did you get that?
Juan: Well, the 3 came from the sum of 2 + 1 above it, so in the fourth row, the 4 comes from 1 + 3 above it; the 6 comes from 3 + 3, and the other 4 comes from 3 + 1 above it. That's the pattern I saw.
Ms. Barry: Hmmm . . . that pattern seems to work too. How many others got the same answer and pattern that Juan found? (Several students raise their hands.) Did anyone else get the solution that Pat got? (Two other students raise their hands.)
Brian: I actually got them both and couldn't decide when to raise my hand. I think it works either way.
Melissa: Me, too. I wasn't sure which was right.

Ms. Barry: Did anyone else get a third solution or see another pattern? (No hands are raised.) Well, let's go back to the coin-tossing problem we looked at the other day and see if we can figure out which answer would fit the real-life problem we were working on.

At this point, Ms. Barry would return to a previous day's problem and have students look at the possible outcomes for tossing four coins. Once students realize that they can get four heads (one way), three heads and one tail (4 ways), two heads and two tails (6 ways), one head and three tails (4 ways), or four tails (one way), they will recognize that Juan's solution fits the real-life problem and can argue that Pat's version fits a reasonable pattern but would not actually be the next row of the triangle. The point here is that in the first version of this classroom scenario, the teacher was exhibiting a value on correct answers over student thinking. In the alternative version, however, the students' thinking took the center stage, and Ms. Barry allowed her students to explain their reasoning and encouraged them to defend their solutions. In the second case, the classroom environment is much more open and supportive of student interaction and thinking. If teachers want students to actively participate and share ideas, they must model a willingness to listen to student responses and value interactions.

The following list was distributed to students and posted by a mathematics teacher as a way to help students to think about the importance of building a supportive, nonthreatening mathematical community in the classroom.

BUILDING A MATHEMATICAL COMMUNITY

It is important to view a mathematics classroom as a supportive group of learners who depend on one another for success. In order to build the feeling of community, the following guidelines are recommended for our class:

- View our class as a community in which each person wants all of the others to be successful in their learning experiences. Try not to see the classroom as a competitive environment in which your role is to outdo others.
- Criticize ideas, not people (e.g., say, "I disagree with the way you solved that problem because . . . ," rather than, "You're so stupid; I can't believe you got that answer!")
- Make frequent contributions to classroom discussions by asking questions, answering questions, and reaffirming or disagreeing with comments made by others
- Take responsibility for the learning of other students. If you understand a concept, take it upon yourself to help others (at your table or in the whole class) to understand it as well.
- Ask questions and let the teacher and teammates know when you don't understand something. Remember that no one can read your mind—you will need to communicate your lack of understanding to get someone to help you.
- Encourage classmates to participate. Don't let individuals sit, day after day, without contributing their thoughts (e.g., encourage the person sitting next to you to raise the question with the class that the individual has expressed to you).

- Recognize that there is no such thing as a wrong answer in a mathematics classroom. It has been said that students never give a wrong answer; they just answer a question different from what the teacher intended. Seemingly wrong answers are actually opportunities for the class to explore new ideas.
- Realize that it is natural to fear failure in the classroom, but recognize that your classmates have this same fear and that risk-taking is important for success. For this reason, never laugh at the response of a classmate: laughter erodes confidence and feeds that fear. Also, you may be in the same position on the next day.
- Use first names. It creates a much more supportive environment when you say, "I think Frances is correct, but I disagree with Joseph's answer, and here's why . . ." than to refer to classmates simply as "he" and "she."
- Support one another. When you respond in a class discussion, make use of previous points made by saying, "I agree with Mark. And I also think that. . . ." If someone comes up with a unique approach or solution to a problem, it is appropriate to applaud and affirm that person.

Keep in mind that any time students are encouraged to contribute and debate their ideas, the teacher is likely to have some discipline concerns and classroom management issues, particularly when the classroom's desks are arranged in pairs or groups of four. However, we find that in many cases, if the students are provided with a combination of a nurturing environment and worthwhile, hands-on problems to solve, the disciplinary concerns are kept to a minimum. Simply put, students are much more likely to act out and be uncooperative when they are asked to do repetitive worksheets in a lecture-style classroom than when they are allowed to solve interesting problems in learning teams. However, some simple strategies can promote an orderly classroom.

First, as was mentioned previously, students need specific directions for the use of classroom materials. If they are to measure circles with string, tell them up front that the string and rulers are the tools of the mathematician and are not toys. If students know, in advance, that the teacher expects appropriate use of the tools, this awareness will go a long way in curtailing management problems. As teachers, we need to anticipate potential misbehavior so that we can address our concerns with students prior to beginning an activity. Then, if students do not follow the prescribed rules of the classroom, the materials can be taken away or the student told to work alone on the project as a consequence. When students are working in learning teams, they need to be reminded that they are expected to speak no louder than they would if they were just sitting at the kitchen table, talking to their parents. Although it seems simplistic to tell seventeen-year-olds to keep their voices down in small-group interactions, just explaining what you want prior to an activity can significantly reduce problems.

When distributing materials for use in a hands-on activity, always try to explain to the students what they will be doing and walk through the directions *prior to* handing out the materials. If you hand a set of algebra tiles to a student and then start to explain what the class will be doing with them, the student will often start building a castle with the materials before you even finish explaining that you don't want the class to do that. Finally, if your room is arranged in pairs or fours, have the students pull their desks apart and face them forward before handing out test papers. You can more easily monitor the classroom, and students are much less likely to attempt to cheat. Remember that each class is different, so the management strategy that works for one group using hands-on materials or cooperative learning may or may not work for another class or another teacher. However, the "good teacher" reflects on what works and what doesn't and uses the experience to improve classroom situations in the future.

■ REFLECTIVE PRACTICES

The final component of effective teaching that we discuss in this chapter is reflection on practice. We discussed this issue in Chapter 5, because reflection should be the final step after implementing a lesson plan. Reflection is revisited here because the analysis of teaching and learning is one of the six NCTM professional teaching Standards.

Standard 6: Analysis of Teaching and Learning

The teacher of mathematics should engage in ongoing analysis of teaching and learning by

- observing, listening to, and gathering other information about students to assess what they are learning;
- examining effects of the tasks, discourse, and learning environment on students' mathematical knowledge, skills, and dispositions;

in order to

- ensure that every student is learning sound and significant mathematics and is developing a positive disposition toward mathematics;
- challenge and extend students' ideas;
- adapt or change activities while teaching;
- make plans, both short- and long-range;
- describe and comment on each student's learning to parents and administrators, as well as to the students themselves.

(NCTM, *Professional Standards for Teaching Mathematics,* 1991, p. 63.)

As we have noted, a piece of conventional wisdom is that many teachers have 20 years of experience and others have 1 year of experience, repeated 20 times. One of these teachers learns from successes and challenges, and the other ignores the past and tends to make the same mistake over and over. But learning from experience does not happen automatically; it is part of the teaching and learning process known as reflection.

The effective classroom teacher develops the ability to look back on a lesson or teaching episode and analyze it from every angle, thinking about what worked and what didn't. Specifically, you might look at the task you chose and determine whether students viewed it as worthwhile and if it fit within the overall scope of the curriculum. Second, you might consider the tools that students used in the lesson—were they appropriate? Should you have selected an additional tool or simply used another? For example, if students used graphing calculators to sketch quadratic functions, might the lesson have been more effective if they had drawn a few hand sketches first? Third, you can reflect on the classroom interactions. How did the discourse flow? What type of questions did you ask? What kind of questions did the students ask? Finally, you might think, in a more general way, about the learning environment that has been established. Do students feel free to participate? What are they learning about the nature of mathematics because of being a member of your class? How might you have managed the classroom more effectively to maintain better discipline?

As you reflect on these questions, you want to think about the three major lesson-planning questions that were raised in Chapter 5: (1) What did I set out to do in this lesson, and why did I plan to do it that way? (2) Did I accomplish my goals and objectives for the lesson? If so, how do I know (i.e., how did I measure the success of the lesson)? (3) What have I learned about myself and my students that will help me to be a better teacher tomorrow, next month, or next year? In other words, how might I complete this statement: Now that I have been through this lesson with my class, I have learned that in the future I need to . . . ? These rather loaded questions constitute what we refer to as **reflection**, the process of thinking through what we have done in the classroom to improve our practice in the future. Ideally, reflection is carried out with colleagues who share their hits and misses with us as we attempt to grow together as a staff. Some details on the issue of interacting with colleagues are included in Chapter 10 in a section on professional development.

■ CONCLUSION ■

Near the beginning of this chapter, the question was raised as to what it means to be a "good teacher." Unfortunately, despite centuries of educational practice and countless books, we still don't have a working definition of good teaching. But we do have research on best practices of classroom teachers as well as guidelines set forth by professional organizations to guide us in the teaching and learning process. As you continue to develop your picture of the good teacher, think about what the *Professional Standards* of the NCTM promote—selection of worthwhile tasks, the use of classroom tools, promotion of teacher and student discourse, establishment of an effective learning environment, and ongoing analysis of the teaching and learning process. Furthermore, *Principles and Standards for School Mathematics* emphasizes the importance of the caring teacher in promoting the learning of mathematics for all students.

It has been said that "good teaching is 75 percent planning and 25 percent theater" (Godwin, 1974). When we think about that, it makes sense. Many "B" movies have become major box-office hits, not because the script was very interesting but because the acting and theatrics were appealing to the audience. Conversely, many potential blockbusters have lost a considerable amount of money because, although they had a great script, the actors and actresses didn't excite the audiences. Similarly, a well-written, interesting activity can still be a bomb if the classroom teacher doesn't carefully orchestrate the discourse in the classroom. On the other hand, a simple question, such as, "Can anyone give me an estimate of $\sqrt{52}$?," can generate a classroom discussion that continues in depth for an hour or more. In the end, it is neither the content nor the lesson alone that makes the difference; it is the way that the teacher guides the process that matters.

Recently, classroom teachers have had the opportunity to use a number of technological innovations as tools to promote discourse in the classroom, from the simple four-function calculator to computers, CD-ROMs, and the Internet. In Chapter 7, we complete Unit III with an exploration of ways of using technology as a tool in the mathematics classroom.

■ GLOSSARY ■

Closed Question: A question is said to be closed if it has only one expected and correct response. Closed questions have their place in the classroom, but they rarely lead to an in-depth discussion because such questions do not generally invite speculation or differences in reasoning.

Discourse: Discourse is the exchange of ideas in the classroom. Discourse can take place between the teacher and the students or within a group of students. It involves conversation, conjecturing, and sense-making of mathematical ideas and is closely related to the tools used by the teacher and the environment established in the classroom.

Individual Accountability: In using cooperative learning, individual accountability means that, although the work may be done as a team, each student is ultimately required to individually demonstrate an understanding of the concepts through an interview, a written test, or some other means.

Learning Environment: The learning environment is the classroom atmosphere in which a student is immersed. The environment includes both the physical features, including the arrangement of the classroom, and the mood or tone that is set by the teacher.

Mira: A mira is an I-shaped plastic manipulative tool that, when laid on a piece of paper containing a picture, allows one to see the reflection of the picture in its window. A mira is helpful in exploring geometric properties such as symmetry and reflection and studying the graphs of functions such as absolute value.

Open (or Open-Ended) Question: A question is said to be open (or open-ended) when it has several possible answers or one correct answer with several ways to reach the solution. The use of open-ended questions in the classroom can lead to rich discourse as students attempt to make and defend conjectures.

Reflection: Reflection is the process by which a teacher carefully analyzes a lesson, a unit, a teaching episode, or student progress to determine whether the stated goals and objectives are being met. The "lenses" of worthwhile tasks, tools, classroom discourse, and learning environment can be helpful in reflecting on the teaching practice. Over time, reflection should enable a teacher to fine tune skills and determine what strategies tend to work best.

Simultaneous Interaction: In cooperative learning situations, simultaneous interaction refers to the idea that many students can interact or share ideas within the classroom at the same time. Simultaneous interaction is a major benefit of cooperative learning. In a traditional model, only one person in a classroom can speak at a given time.

■ DISCUSSION QUESTIONS ■

1. Observe a mathematics class or view a videotape of a teacher in the classroom. Assess the strengths and weaknesses of the lesson by discussing the tasks with which students are engaged, the flow of discourse in the classroom, the use of tools, and the perceived learning environment.

2. Select a topic such as measuring angles or determining a limit. Consult at least three different sources, such as journals, the Internet, resource books, or a textbook, and choose what you consider to be the best activity for developing the concept. Support your choice by explaining what makes it more worthwhile than other possible activities.

3. Select a classroom manipulative from the following list: algebra tiles, base ten blocks, color tiles, Cuisenaire rods, fraction pieces, geoboards, miras, pattern blocks, and tangrams. Research the proper use of the selected manipulative and find examples of lessons and activities that make effective use of the tool. Demonstrate your selected materials to a small group.

4. The *Professional Standards* state that tools that enhance classroom discourse include more than manipulatives and calculators. Locate several examples of other tools—pictures, tables, diagrams, and graphs—that can be used to enhance classroom discourse. Discuss the context in which each of these tools might be used in the classroom.

5. Observe a mathematics lesson or view one on tape. While watching the lesson, record the level of questions asked by both the teacher and the students, using the questioning levels described in this chapter. What patterns do you notice in the type of questions typically asked by teachers and students? How could those questions be changed to enhance the level of discourse in the classroom?

6. Locate an example of a lesson plan or activity in a textbook or other resource that is written for students working alone. Rewrite the lesson plan or activity in a format that incorporates cooperative learning. Be sure to structure the lesson so that every student is actively involved.

7. The suggestions for implementing cooperative learning recommended that, when possible, learning teams should include a mix of males and females. Why is this important? What are the possible benefits of occasionally organizing single-sex groups?

8. List several specific ideas that teachers can use to help establish a positive learning environment—including both physical and psychological environments. When making the list, reflect on your own experiences as a student and the characteristics of mathematics classrooms that were particularly inviting for you.

9. Observe a mathematics class and interview the teacher and a sample of students from the class. Ask both the teacher and the students what they thought was the greatest strength of the lesson and what should have been changed. Compare the responses of the teacher to the opinions of the students in the class. How well does the teacher appear to be aware of the needs of the students in the room?

10. In this chapter's conclusion, the following quote was cited: "Good teaching is 75% planning and 25% theater." What does this quote say to you about the art of teaching?

■ BIBLIOGRAPHIC REFERENCES AND RESOURCES ■

Alper, L., et al. (1995). Implementing the professional standards for teaching mathematics: What is it worth? *Mathematics Teacher, 88* (7), 598–602.

Andrini, B. (1991). *Cooperative learning & mathematics: A multi-structural approach.* San Juan Capistrano, CA: Resources for Teachers, Inc.

Artzt, A. F. & Newman, C. M. (1997). *How to use cooperative learning in the mathematics class, second edition.* Reston, VA: National Council of Teachers of Mathematics.

Arvold, B., et al. (1996). Implementing the professional standards for teaching mathematics: Analyzing teaching and learning: The art of listening. *Mathematics Teacher, 89* (4), 326–329.

Becker, J. P. & Shimada, S. (1997). *The open-ended approach: A new proposal for teaching mathematics.* Reston, VA: National Council of Teachers of Mathematics.

Cauley, K. M., & Seyfarth, J. T. (1995). Curriculum reform in middle level and high school mathematics. *NASSP Bulletin, 79* (567), 22–30.

Chuska, K. R. (1995). *Improving classroom questions: A teacher's guide to increasing student motivation, participation, and higher-level thinking.* Bloomington, IN: Phi Delta Kappa Educational Foundation.

Cook, C. J. & Rasmussen, C. M. (1991). *Cues for effective questioning.* Evanston, IL: Self-Published.

Cooney, T. J. (Ed.). (1990). *1990 Yearbook of the NCTM: Teaching and learning mathematics in the 1990s.* Reston, VA: National Council of Teachers of Mathematics.

Curriculum Research and Development Group. (1997). *Geometry learning project, version 7.1.* Honolulu, HI: University of Hawaii.

D'Ambrosio, B. S. (1995). Implementing the professional standards for teaching mathematics: Highlighting the humanistic dimensions of mathematics activity through classroom discourse. *Mathematics Teacher, 88* (9), 770–772.

Davis, R. B. & Maher, C. A. (Ed.). (1993). *Schools, mathematics, and the world of reality.* Boston, MA: Allyn & Bacon.

Dockterman, D. A. (1994). *Cooperative learning and technology*. Watertown, MA: Tom Snyder Productions, Inc.

Erickson, T. (1989). *Getting it together: Math problems for groups grades 4–12*. Berkeley, CA: Lawrence Hall of Science.

Feldt, C. C. (1993). Becoming a teacher of mathematics: A constructive, interactive process. *Mathematics Teacher, 86* (5), 400–403.

Glasser, W. (1986). *Control theory in the classroom*. New York, NY: Harper & Row.

Godwin, G. (1974). *The odd woman*. New York, NY: Berkley.

Goodlad, J. (1984). *A place called school: Prospects for the future*. New York, NY: McGraw-Hill.

Guyton, E. (1991). Cooperative learning and elementary social studies. *Social Education, 55* (5), 313–315.

Holubec, E. J. (1992). How do you get there from here? Getting started with cooperative learning. *Contemporary Education, 63* (3), 181–184.

Johnson, D. W. & Johnson, R. T. (1984). *Circles of learning: Cooperation in the classroom*. Alexandria, VA: Association for Supervision and Curriculum Development.

Johnson, D. W., Johnson, R. T., & Holubec, H. J. (1987). *Structuring cooperative learning: Lesson plans for teachers*. Edina, MN: Interaction.

Kagan, S. (1994). *Cooperative learning*. San Clemente, CA: Kagan Cooperative Learning.

Leiva, M. A. (1995). Implementing the professional standards for teaching mathematics: Empowering teaching through the evaluation process. *Mathematics Teacher, 88* (1), 44–47.

Lindquist, M. M. (1993). Tides of change: Teachers at the helm. *Arithmetic Teacher, 41* (1), 64–68.

The Math Forum. (1999). Problem of the Week. Retrieved August 20, 1999 from the World Wide Web: <http://forum.swarthmore.edu/pow/>

Middleton, J. A. & Goepfert, P. (1996). *Inventive Strategies for Teaching Mathematics: Implementing standards for reform*. Washington, DC: American Psychological Association.

Mousley, J. & Sullivan, P. (1996). *Learning about teaching*. Reston, VA: National Council of Teachers of Mathematics (distributor).

National Council of Teachers of Mathematics. (1998). *Principles and standards for school mathematics* (working draft). Reston, VA: National Council of Teachers of Mathematics.

National Council of Teachers of Mathematics. (1991). *Professional standards for teaching mathematics*. Reston, VA: National Council of Teachers of Mathematics.

National Council of Teachers of Mathematics. (1989). *Curriculum and evaluation standards for school mathematics*. Reston, VA: National Council of Teachers of Mathematics.

Prevost, F. J. (1993). Implementing the professional standards for teaching mathematics: Rethinking how we teach: Learning mathematical pedagogy. *Mathematics Teacher, 86* (1), 75–79.

Schifter, D. (Ed.). (1996). *What's happening in math class? Envisioning new practices through teacher narratives*. New York, NY: Teachers College Columbia University.

Shotsberger, P. G. (1999). INSTRUCT: Standards for Teaching Mathematics. Retrieved August 20, 1999 from the World Wide Web: <http://instruct.cms.uncwil.edu/standard.html>

Slavin, R. E. (1988). Cooperative learning and student achievement. *Educational Leadership, 45,* 31–33.

Integrating Technology in Mathematics Instruction

After reading Chapter 7, you should be able to answer the following questions:

- How is the use of technology in the mathematics classroom consistent with the NCTM *Professional Standards for Teaching Mathematics* and *Principles and Standards for School Mathematics*?

- What are some examples of technology that can be used at the secondary and middle school levels for teaching mathematics? Describe them.

- What are some examples of how computers, graphing calculators, laser discs, CD-ROMs, and videos can be used as tools in the mathematics classroom?

- How can teachers and students use the Internet, in general, and the World Wide Web, specifically, in teaching and learning mathematics?

- What are some of the advantages and disadvantages of the use of technology in the mathematics classroom?

Ms. Lucas is teaching a middle school mathematics class and poses the following problem:

> A local video store offers the following options for renting videos: Under Option A, customers join the Rental Club for $20.00 per year and can rent each video for $1.50. Under Option B, the customer does not have to pay an annual fee but must pay $2.95 for each movie rental. Under what conditions is Option A better than Option B? Which would you choose and why?

Seated at tables of four, the students begin to work together to solve the problem. Ms. Lucas immediately realizes that most of the teams are using a guess-and-check approach. She gives them a few minutes to work and then asks if anyone can explain the team's insights on the problem. Leslie raises her hand.

Leslie: We began the problem by assuming that the person was planning to rent 10 videos per year. Under Option A, the cost would be $20 + 10(1.50) = \$35.00$. But with Option B, the cost would be $10(2.95) = \$29.50$. So, we decided that if you rent 10 videos a year, you should use Option B.

Manuel: We did about the same thing except we decided that a typical family rents two videos a month, which would be 24 videos a year. If you use 24 videos, then the cost for Option A is $56, but Option B costs about $71. So, if you rent more like 24 videos a year, rather than just 10, you're better off with Option A.

Frederick: Yeah, we decided that people who rent lots of movies should use Option A, and everyone else should stick with Option B.

Ms. Lucas: What did the rest of you think?

Tina: Well, we agreed except that we decided there's probably some kind of break-even point where, if you rent more than that many videos, you should switch to Option A. But we didn't have enough time to figure out what it was.

Ms. Lucas: That's an interesting conjecture, Tina. Did anyone find that break-even point?

Manuel: I don't know what it is, exactly, but I know it's more than 10 and fewer than 24. I guess we would have to try out all of the possibilities to figure it out.

At this point, Ms. Lucas realizes that no one has found the break-even solution and decides to let technology take over to explore the problem further. In the next two sections of this chapter, we discuss some of the technological options she has for exploring the problem. With the improvements in computers, calculators, and other forms of technology in recent years, students have an opportunity to investigate problems that might not have been practical activities in years past. In fact, the National Council of Teachers of Mathematics (1997, p. 34) stated that

- Some mathematics becomes *more important* because technology *requires* it
- Some mathematics becomes *less important* because technology *replaces it*
- Some mathematics becomes *possible* because technology *allows* it

Furthermore, the NCTM *Professional Standards for Teaching Mathematics* (1991) highlights technology as a tool that has the potential to enhance classroom discourse. *Principles and Standards for School Mathematics* listed the use of technology as one of the six underlying Guiding Principles of teaching mathematics. The document stated that technology "offers the potential for students to engage in significant ways with mathematical ideas" and that "technology can make mathematics and its applications accessible in ways that were heretofore impossible" (NCTM, 1998, p. 40).

One of the many benefits of using technology, such as computers or graphing calculators, is that students can work with "ugly"-number problems that may have been avoided in the past because the solutions did not work out evenly. Scanning a textbook from the 1970s or earlier, you are likely to find a number of problems that have simple integral solutions primarily because it was unrealistic to ask students to solve problems that had fractions in the solutions or numbers that were too large or too small to manipulate effectively. But with a calculator, finding the area of a rectangle that measures 13.385 cm by 26.197 cm is just as reasonable as determining the area of a rectangle measuring 13 cm by 26 cm. The former problem has historically been avoided to save students from having to perform a long calculation by hand.

Computers and calculators also allow students to visualize parameter changes on their resulting calculations and graphs, again, making it possible to explore many problems in a relatively short period of time. From the 1960s through the early 1980s, it was not unusual for a teacher to assign long-term, pencil-and-paper projects in which students compared characteristics of the graphs of functions such as $y = x^2$, $y = 2x^2$, $y = -x^2$, $y = -\frac{1}{2}x^2$, and so on. But today, thanks to computers and graphing calculators, this exploration can be conducted easily in a forty-five-minute class period, because the students can change parameters and make conjectures along the way.

However, teachers need to use technology carefully in the teaching and learning process because it is important not to treat technology as an "add-on." Instead, a class that uses graphing calculators should take an entirely different approach to problem solving and symbol manipulation than a class that uses no technology at all. Many teachers have fallen prey to the trap of using calculators as a nice Friday afternoon diversion; others use them only as a way for students to check answers. Some teachers believe that the purpose of a computer in the classroom is to allow students to play games when they finish worksheets ahead of schedule. Technology, however, should be woven into everything we do in the classroom. Students can explore problems in a variety of ways and decide when it is appropriate to use technology and when it is better to work a problem with pencil and paper. The issue of when to use technology will be discussed near the end of the chapter.

This chapter explores the potential uses of different types of technology through several examples and discussion. Keep in mind that not every teacher will use every form of technology discussed; in fact, budget and time constraints will keep most people from using some of the tools. Instead, the purpose is to provide an overview of what is possible and allow you to make some choices about what might work best in your own situation. Let's begin with a section on computer technology and return to Ms. Lucas's classroom.

■ COMPUTER TECHNOLOGY

After hearing about the variety of ways the students approached the video-rental problem, Ms. Lucas decided to have her students explore the problem further on the classroom computers. She has arranged the room so that every four students can gather around a computer screen. She has the students open a spreadsheet application program (such as Excel or the spreadsheet option in Claris Works or Microsoft Works). Students input the number of video rentals into Column A, a formula for calculating the total cost of video rentals using Option A in Column B, and a formula for the cost using Option B in Column C, as illustrated in Figure 7–1.

	A	B	C
1	VIDEOS	Option A	Option B
2		0	= 20 + (A2*1.5)	= A2*2.95
3	= A2 + 1		

Figure 7–1 The Video Problem Solved on a Spreadsheet

By using the Fill Down option on the spreadsheet, the students can create a table (see Figure 7–2) that shows the relative cost of renting from 0 to 25 videos in a year, which will allow them to see what happens between 10 and 24 rentals, a point that was raised by students in the class.

Students can scan the table to look for patterns and to draw conclusions. They should notice, for example, that the values for the cost of Option A and Option B are $35.00 and $29.50, respectively, for 10 video rentals as was pointed out in class. Also, for 24 video rentals, they can see how Option A is nearly $15.00 cheaper. But, most importantly, the values in the spreadsheet allow them to compare the relative costs of the options and find the break-even point. They should notice that Option B is cheaper until about 14 video rentals, at which point the costs are almost the same. At 14 videos or more, Option A becomes the less expensive choice. In fact, continuing the table even further, if a family rents an average of one movie per week, Option A will save them over $50 per year in rental fees, despite the $20.00 membership fee.

The spreadsheet, then, serves as a tool for comparing the costs of the options, given a particular number of video rentals. Students gain experience in setting up and reading a table, looking for patterns, and using algebraic symbols to define the spreadsheet formulas. The last of these activities is extremely important, because a significant amount of time is generally spent on the representation of patterns and functions with variables at the secondary and middle school levels. In addition, the spreadsheet saves the students from having to guess and check their way through 14 different video rental scenarios to find the break-even point. Once the cost of an option has been calculated, the spreadsheet allows the calculation to be mechanically repeated to display a wide variety of possibilities. Finally, the spreadsheet option allows the teacher to ask such a question as, "What if the video store raised the membership fee to $30 but dropped the cost of renting tapes to $1.25 for members? What is the new break-even point?" With a quick change in the spreadsheet formula, students will discover that members will need to rent 18 or more videos to make the new Option A the better choice. The spreadsheets essentially allow a class to play out a number of scenarios to gather data and draw conclusions, with the computer doing each of the individual calculations. The focus of the problem, then, becomes the analysis of data and the formulation of an answer rather than computation.

A significant amount of drill-and-practice software on the market allows students to practice the addition of integers and the like, and there is a place for these programs. However, drill-and-practice software does not provide the dynamic, interactive type of experience that will promote the active involvement of students in the classroom as was discussed in Chapter 6. In general, effective computer software allows students to conjecture and to explore in mathematics. Spreadsheets are just one simple example. Another popular software category for the secondary and middle school levels allows the students to explore geometric concepts. Common programs include Geometer's Sketchpad and Geometry Inventor (a somewhat simpler version of the Sketchpad, more commonly used at the middle school level). This software is **dynamic** because students interact with it, playing out various scenarios and making observations before drawing conclusions.

	A	B	C
1	VIDEOS	Option A	Option B
2	0	$20.00	$0.00
3	1	$21.50	$2.95
4	2	$23.00	$5.90
5	3	$24.50	$8.85
6	4	$26.00	$11.80
7	5	$27.50	$14.75
8	6	$29.00	$17.70
9	7	$30.50	$20.65
10	8	$32.00	$23.60
11	9	$33.50	$26.55
12	10	$35.00	$29.50
13	11	$36.50	$32.45
14	12	$38.00	$35.40
15	13	$39.50	$38.35
16	14	$41.00	$41.30
17	15	$42.50	$44.25
18	16	$44.00	$47.20
19	17	$45.50	$50.15
20	18	$47.00	$53.10
21	19	$48.50	$56.05
22	20	$50.00	$59.00
23	21	$51.50	$61.95
24	22	$53.00	$64.90
25	23	$54.50	$67.85
26	24	$56.00	$70.80
27	25	$57.50	$73.75

Figure 7–2 Comparison of Plan A and Plan B for 25 Video Rentals

Let's suppose, for example, that a teacher wanted students to examine the relationship of a radius of a circle drawn perpendicular to a chord in the circle. Using the dynamic geometry software, students can construct Circle A, with A as its centerpoint. Then, radius $\overline{AB}$ and chord $\overline{CE}$ can be constructed such that $\overline{AB} \perp \overline{CE}$. Students can label the intersection point of the radius and chord D and use the software to measure the lengths of CD and DE. They will discover that these segments are congruent and can conjecture that a radius drawn perpendicular to a chord also bisects the chord.

The image in Figure 7–3 was constructed with the Geometry Inventor software. The measuring tools indicate that $\overline{CD} \cong \overline{DE}$, because their lengths are both 1.67 units and that $m\angle ADC = 90$.

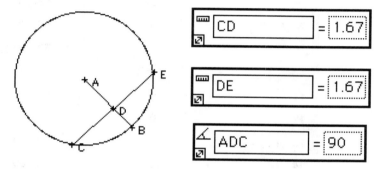

Figure 7–3 Radius Drawn Perpendicular to a Chord

By placing a pointer on point C and then on point B, students can slide the points around the circle and discover that wherever the chord lies, as long as the radius is perpendicular (a 90° angle is formed), the chord is always bisected. As a result, students make their own conjecture—a theorem—and can then prove it as a generalization ($\triangle ACD \cong \triangle AED$ because they are right triangles that share side $\overline{AD}$ and have congruent hypotenuses since $\overline{AC}$ and $\overline{AE}$ are radii of the same circle. The triangles are congruent by the Hypotenuse-Leg Theorem, and $\overline{CD} \cong \overline{DE}$, because they are corresponding parts of congruent triangles).

Many resource books that accompany texts highlight the uses of software such as spreadsheets and dynamic geometry programs. Again, the power of these software packages lies in the fact that students can make conjectures, look for patterns, and manipulate pictures and data to test their ideas. In this way, students are actively involved in generating the mathematics—in a sense, they are re-inventing theorems and properties rather than being told that the properties exist. Even something as simple as finding that the three angles of a triangle always sum to 180° can be exciting when the students construct their own triangle on the computer screen, have the computer find the sum of the three angles, and then manipulate a vertex to stretch and move the triangle around the page before conjecturing that the sum is a constant. These investigations are made possible by contemporary software.

One of the most significant drawbacks to the use of computers in mathematics education is the lack of both hardware and software in many schools. Some schools, for example, house all of the computers in a laboratory that is shared by teachers in all subject areas. So, when Ms. Lucas wants her class to go to the lab to explore the problem on a spreadsheet, the English teacher may have the lab reserved for the entire week so that students can learn some keyboarding skills and write essays. Even if she is able to get her class into the lab, the software may not be available, or the lab may be equipped with computers in a platform that is unfamiliar to her (Macintoshes instead of IBM-compatibles, for example).

As a result, some school districts have decided to try to put computers into the individual classrooms. Teachers organize the classroom into pods, in which a small group of students can access a computer right in the room when it fits into the lesson. In addition, the teacher may also have a computer that can be projected on a screen or displayed on a television screen for demonstration purposes. Although this arrangement is certainly convenient, it also often means that each teacher receives two or three computers per classroom. If you have twenty-five students in a geometry class, you must be very creative in working with small rotating groups in order to keep twenty-five students busy on two or three machines. Also, even if teachers choose not to employ computer technology, they are often given the computers anyway (the administrator hopes that if they have easy access to computers, they are more likely to use them), so a dozen or more computers may sit in classrooms, literally collecting dust

Interactive software can help students use computers to pursue conjectures and to validate their thinking.

when they could be used by other teachers. There is an interesting ongoing debate as to whether students are best served by a central computer laboratory or a few computers in each classroom, and in the end, it's probably best if the school has both—a couple of computers easily accessible in the classroom *and* a lab to which an entire class can go for an exploration when needed. But because of the cost of computers and the scarcity of funds in many schools, compromises are often made.

Scarcity of funds also forces teachers to carefully choose the **hardware** (computers, printers, modems, etc.) and **software** (programs that are run on the computers). Often, a school or district appoints a committee of teachers and administrators to preview and recommend hardware and software options. A site license for a software package can cost hundreds of dollars, so these committees should select programs that are actually *requested* by the teachers and have a high probability of being *used* frequently. There are many different forms and criteria available for evaluating software. An example of a software preview form by Jodi Haney and Nancy Brownell (1999) is reprinted in Figure 7–4 (side 2 below, side 1 on the following page).

Program Description:

I. Briefly describe the program (What happens when it's run? What user interaction? etc.):

II. Describe the instructional objectives met by this program:

III. Are additional software-related instructional materials available?
_____ Yes _____ No   Describe these materials:

IV. Describe any teacher management options in the program (scores recorded, etc.):

V. In your opinion, what are the strengths of the program? Explain.

VI. In your opinion, what are the weaknesses of the program? Explain.

VII. How would you use this program in your classroom (For instance, with what lesson would you use it? what activities would integrate it with your curriculum? use in a lab, or in a learning center? in groups or individually? etc.)

VIII. Additional comments regarding this program:

Software Evaluation

General Information:

Name of Program: _____ –

Producer/Publisher: _____

Copyright date: _____ Grade Level Range: _____

Subject Area(s): _____

How to Order:

Company: _____

Address: _____

Phone: _____

Price: _____

Hardware Required:

Computer: _____
Memory (RAM): _____ MB
Hard Disk Space: _____ MB
System: _____
Peripherals Needed (CD ROM, printer, etc.): _____

Processing Skills Required:

_____ Recalling	_____ Questioning
_____ Observing	_____ Hypothesizing
_____ Interpreting	_____ Solving
_____ Communicating	_____ Inferring
_____ Comparing	_____ Generalizing
_____ Measuring	_____ Inventing
_____ Organizing	_____ Creating
_____ Classifying	_____ Other (specify):
_____ Relating	_____

Type of Software:

_____ Tutor Mode:
　_____ Simulation
　_____ Demonstration
　_____ Drill & Practice
　_____ Instructional Game
　_____ Problem Solving
　_____ Other_____
_____ Reference (Specify Type): _____
_____ Other (Check with instructor before reviewing): _____

Evaluator:

_____

Date: _____

_____ Highly Recommended
_____ Recommended
_____ Not Recommended

Evaluation criteria:

Rate (Check) 1 to 4 (1 = poor; 4 = excellent　)　　Comments:

1 2 3 4 N/A	
0 0 0 0 0	Clarity of directions
0 0 0 0 0	Ease of operation (user friendly)
0 0 0 0 0	Free of errors
0 0 0 0 0	Graphics
0 0 0 0 0	Sound
0 0 0 0 0	Readability of text & graphics
0 0 0 0 0	Motivation
0 0 0 0 0	Appropriate use of technology
0 0 0 0 0	Interaction with user
0 0 0 0 0	Feedback to students
0 0 0 0 0	Management component
0 0 0 0 0	Promotion of high order thinking skills
0 0 0 0 0	Free of stereotypes (racial, ethnic, gender)
0 0 0 0 0	Teacher documentation
0 0 0 0 0	Additional student materials

Figure 7–4 Sample Software Evaluation Form
(Haney & Brownell, 1999. Reprinted with permission.)

The good news is that, in recent years, many of the functions previously performed only by computers are now available on a hand-held graphing calculator. Graphing calculators were introduced in the classroom in the mid-1980s and have revolutionized the teaching and learning of mathematics for many school districts. More recent hand-held computers, in fact, have built-in geometry programs that allow students to do the types of investigations that were previously possible only on a computer. For example, the TI-92 from Texas Instruments contains dynamic geometry software known as Cabri Geometry that does much of the sophisticated manipulation of shapes that is usually done on a computer screen. In the next section, we explore the potential impact of the graphing calculator in the mathematics classroom.

■ GRAPHING CALCULATORS

Ms. Lucas may choose to use the video-rental problem as a springboard to discuss equations of lines and the solutions of simultaneous equations. Historically, systems of linear equations in textbooks have looked much like the following:

Find the solution to the system by graphing:

$$\begin{cases} y = 2x + 1 \\ y = -\frac{2}{3}x - 7 \end{cases}$$

Of course, the system was contrived in that it didn't include any real-life application. Also, the slopes and y-intercepts were kept small and simple so that students could readily sketch them on graph paper. Finally, the solution worked out evenly at the point $(-3, -5)$, so that students could easily read the intersection point on a piece of graph paper. But with the advent of graphing calculator technology, a whole new approach to the topic becomes possible. Ms. Lucas could ask her students to represent Options A and B as functions and sketch them on the graphing calculator screen. Students can define the functions as:

$$Y_1 = 20 + 1.5x$$
$$Y_2 = 2.95x$$

Graphing these two equations generates a picture like the one in Figure 7–5.

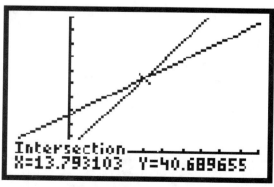

Figure 7–5 Graphing Calculator Display of the Video Problem

After students have generated the graphs, the teacher can lead a high-level discussion by asking questions such as the following:

- Which line is the steepest? Why is it steeper than the other? What does the slope represent? *Students can conclude that Option B's graph is steeper because the slope represents the amount of money spent each time a video is rented, and 2.95 is greater than 1.50. In this way, the slope as a rate of change becomes something "real" and relevant to the problem.*
- What are the y-intercepts of these lines? What do these numbers represent? *The y-intercept represents how much money the person has to pay whether renting a movie or not. In Option A, there is an automatic $20.00 fee, so the y-intercept at (0, 20) represents a cost of $20 with 0 video rentals. On the other hand, Option B has a y-intercept at the origin because if no movies are rented, there is no fee. Again, students can explore and discuss the real-life meaning of the y-intercept.*
- If we change Option A to an annual fee of $30 but a rental fee of $1.25, how will it change the look of the graph? Why? *Students can discuss how the y-intercept will move up from 20 to 30, but the line will be less steep because 1.25 is less than 1.50. The line is less steep because the cost per movie has decreased. Again, when students think of the slope as cost per movie, they can appreciate slope as a rate of change and not just a number.*
- On the CALC menu, choose "intersect." Where do the two lines intersect? What does this point tell you? *Students will find that the lines intersect at approximately (13.8, 40.7), as shown in Figure 7–5. This is technically the break-even point: More than 13.8 video rentals will result in Option A being cheaper than Option B. Note that this problem does not work out evenly like most textbook problems because technology makes it possible to explore ugly solutions. Students will have to recognize that it is not possible to rent 13.8 videos, so, realistically, it is better to use Option B for 13 or less videos, but a family renting 14 or more videos should select Option A. This is the same conclusion they drew when considering the spreadsheet representation, but students are now able to see a picture or graph that displays the data in a different way. This display, then, leads to some other questions the teacher can ask, such as the following:*
- From $x = 0$ to the intersection point, which line is under the other? What is the significance of the relative positions of the lines? *Students can discuss how the lower line segment represents a lower cost for the movie rentals.*
- To the right of the intersection point, what happens to the lines? What does this show? *Beyond the intersection point, the lines reverse in that Option B becomes more expensive, and Option A is now below the other line and becomes the better choice. The geometric meaning of the positioning of these two lines can lead to a rich discussion of the comparative costs.*
- Press the TRACE key, enter the number 20 and ENTER. What is displayed, and what does it mean? Press the up arrow and explain the meaning of this display. *When students TRACE at x = 20, they locate the point (20, 50) on the Option A line. This point indicates that 20 movie rentals will cost a person $50.00 under Option A. But by pressing the up arrow, they find that 20 rentals will cost $59.00 under Option B, making it more expensive. Toggling*

back and forth between lines for any x-value can give students a glimpse of the difference in cost between the two options.

- Press "2nd" and TABLE. What do you see? *Students will discover that the graphing calculator can be used like a spreadsheet in that the TABLE function will generate a table of values where the first column are x-values (rentals) and the other two columns represent the relative cost of x rentals when using Option A and Option B. Technically, the entire investigation could be done with a graphing calculator using the TABLE function because the computer spreadsheet is really not necessary. The choice is up to the teacher and may include a decision on how important it is for students to learn to use a spreadsheet on a computer as an outcome in the course.*

As you can see, what appears to be a relatively simple problem involving the comparison of two payment plans can be transformed into a rich investigation employing geometry and algebra by using a graphing calculator. Similarly, students can use a graphing calculator to analyze the shapes of curves and to explore zeroes of functions and systems of equations. Here are examples of two step-by-step investigations that students in an algebra course can perform to explore quadratic functions. Notice how each question builds upon the previous one and how mathematical understanding develops as a student works through this two-day exploration.

GRAPHING A PARABOLA, PART I

We have seen that the graph of the function $f(x) = x^2$ results in a U-shaped curve that we called a parabola. The purpose of this investigation is to use the graphing calculator to explore the effects of the values of a and c for the graph of the equation $f(x) = ax^2 + c$.

1. Turn on your calculator.
2. Press CLEAR.
3. Press WINDOW and set to:
   Xmin = −20
   Xmax = 20
   Xscl = 5
   Ymin = −50
   Ymax = 50
   Yscl = 5
   Xres = 1
4. Press Y= key and enter x^2
5. Press GRAPH to see your graph of $f(x) = x^2$
   Draw a picture of what you see to the right:

6. Press $Y =$, CLEAR, and change the equation to $f(x) = 3x^2$
   Draw a picture of what you see to the right:

7. Now, try $f(x) = 5x^2$ and $f(x) = 0.5x^2$
   Draw them on the same set of axes to the right:

8. Explain, below, what happens as the coefficient of x gets larger.
   What happens when it gets smaller?

9. What do you think will happen if the coefficient of x is a negative number?

10. Test your reasoning on the last question by comparing the following graphs on
    your calculator:

    $y = x^2$ and $y = -1x^2$
    $y = 0.3x^2$ and $y = -0.3x^2$
    $y = x^2$ and $y = -4x^2$

    Was your prediction correct?

11. Look at the picture you drew for 5. How would you predict that the graph
    from 5 would change if you changed the equation to $y = x^2 + 20$?

    Try it on your calculator. Were you correct?

12. Draw a sketch of your prediction of what $y = x^2 - 15$ would look like at the
    right.

    Try it on your calculator. Were you correct?

13. Now, let's put it together. Write a description of what you would expect this
    graph to look like: $y = -5x^2 + 12$.

    Use your calculator to draw the graph. Were you correct?

14. Draw a picture of what you would expect this graph to look like: $y = \frac{1}{5}x^2 - 7$

    Use your calculator to draw the graph. Were you correct?

15. Summarize what you have learned in this activity by completing the following statements:

When the coefficient of the x^2 term is positive, the graph . . .

When the coefficient of the x^2 term is negative, the graph . . .

When the coefficient of the x^2 term is a large number, it makes the graph . . .

When the coefficient of the x^2 term is a small number, it makes the graph . . .

When a constant is added, such as the +3 in the $y = 2x^2 + 3$, this number tells us . . .

GRAPHING A PARABOLA, PART II

In your first graphing exercise dealing with the parabola, you investigated the effects of the coefficient of the x^2 term and the constant. In this exercise, you explore some other features and uses for the graphs of parabolas.

1. Turn on your calculator.
2. Press CLEAR.
3. Press WINDOW and set to:
   Xmin = −20
   Xmax = 20
   Xscl = 5
   Ymin = −50
   Ymax = 50
   Yscl = 5
   Xres = 1
4. Solve the following equation for x below: $x^2 - 36 = 0$

5. Press $Y =$ and CLEAR any equations out that may be listed.
6. For your first equation, enter $Y_1 = x^2 - 36$
   Before drawing the graph, sketch what you think it will look like.

Press GRAPH and look at the parabola.
Was your prediction correct?

7. Use the TRACE key to approximate the x-values where the parabola intersects the x-axis.
What are the approximate x-values? _____ and _____
What does y equal when x equals these two values? _____

8. Solve this equation for x: $-x^2 + 9 = 0$

9. Press $Y =$
CLEAR the previous equation.
Enter $Y_1 = -x^2 + 9$
Before drawing the graph, sketch what you think it will look like.

Press GRAPH and look at the parabola.
Was your prediction correct?

10. Use the TRACE key to approximate the x-values where the parabola intersects the x-axis.
What are the approximate x-values? _____ and _____
Why are these values not exactly the same as you found by solving the equation by hand?

What does y equal when x equals these two values? _____

11. Let's review what you have just learned. One way to solve a quadratic equation is to factor it and set the factors equal to 0 to find the roots. The other way to solve a quadratic equation is to draw its graph.
COMPLETE THIS SENTENCE: When the graph is drawn, the solutions to the equation are . . .

12. Consider this problem: Find the roots of the equation $x^2 - 2x - 8 = 0$.
a) Solve the problem by factoring.
b) Graph the parabola $y = x^2 - 2x - 8$.

What makes this parabola different from the others we have looked at?

What about the equation makes it different?

Approximate the roots by using the TRACE key.
Roots are approximately: _____ and _____

13. Now, consider this equation: $x^2 - 5x + 1 = 0$
    Why is it not possible to factor the equation to solve it?

    Fortunately, although it cannot be factored, the equation can still be solved.
    Use your graphing calculator to approximate the roots to the nearest 100th.
    Roots are approximately: _____ and _____

14. Approximate the roots for each of the following:

    a) $-2x^2 - 3x + 14 = 0$

    Roots are approximately: _____ and _____

    b) $\frac{1}{2}x^2 - 7x - 9 = 0$

    Roots are approximately: _____ and _____

    c) $x^2 + x + 10 = 0$
    Why doesn't this quadratic equation have any roots? Explain.

    d) $-x^2 - 4x - 4 = 0$

    Roots are approximately: _____ and _____
    Why does this equation appear to only have one root?

    Solve the equation by factoring to verify that it only has one solution.

15. We would like to solve the system:

$$\begin{cases} y = 3x + 7 \\ y = x - 13 \end{cases}$$

    a) Solve the system by either elimination or substitution:
    The solution is the point (,   )
    b) Press $Y =$
    CLEAR any previous equations.
    Enter the equations $y = 3x + 7$ and $y = x - 13$
    Press GRAPH and use TRACE to approximate the intersection points.
    The solution is approximately the point (,   )
    How close are your answers for a) and b)?

    Which is the most accurate?

c) Solve the system using your graphing calculator:

$$\begin{cases} y = \frac{1}{2}x + 10 \\ y = -x^2 - x - 31 \end{cases}$$

(Note: you are finding the points where a line intersects a parabola.)
The approximate points of intersection are (rounded to the nearest 100th):
(,) and (,)

Notice how these activity pages take the students through an exploration of a variety of different mathematical concepts. How many can you name? You might notice quadratic functions, parabolas, zeroes of a function, parameter changes and their effects on graphs, reflections and translations, linear systems, quadratic systems, and estimating and approximating, to name a few. In fact, one could argue that these pages take a first- or second-year algebra student much deeper into the mathematics of quadratic functions than a student at this experience level has historically explored. However, with a graphing calculator, these types of explorations are very possible and allow for much more depth than can be accomplished by pencil-and-paper computations.

Again, the theme throughout our discussion of both computers and graphing calculators has been that students can now access and explore much richer problems because problems and pretty solutions do not have to be contrived. The exploration of functions, from linear to trigonometric and absolute value, can be exciting as students use guess-and-check approaches to make conjectures and formulate their own rules about how the functions behave. In addition, most graphing calculators are also programmable, and students can write and execute programs to solve a right triangle, find the area of a figure, and work on a host of other ideas. Some mathematics teachers build the programming of calculators into their classes; others allow students to develop and master these skills on their own. By using a *link*, two calculators can be connected so that data sets and programs can be readily shared by all of the class in a relatively short period of time. A Calculator-Based Laboratory (CBL) or Calculator-Based Ranger (CBR) system can also allow probes to be connected to graphing calculators. These probes can collect data on the change in temperature over time, the distance of an object from the calculator as it bounces from a spring, or the acceleration rate of a toy car on the floor.

Data are collected, entered into the calculator, plotted as a graph, and viewed in tabular form. Students can run best-fit regression programs to model the real-world data as part of their exploration of algebra and geometry. The possibilities are almost endless.

As is the case with computers, some teachers would like to use graphing calculators and their peripherals but do not have the funds for them. Even a classroom set often has to be shared among several teachers in a building, which requires advance planning and scheduling. Some schools now require students to purchase their own graphing calculators in the middle school, so that students will have them throughout their mathematics programs. But the technology changes rapidly, and a calculator that a student purchases for $85 today may be made obsolete by a much more powerful piece of technology at half the price in a year or two.

A recent example of the changes in graphing calculators is Texas Instruments's TI-92 hand-held computer. Complete with a full numeric keypad, the machine does symbol manipulation, including factoring a trinomial, simplifying expressions, and solving almost any equation. The mini-computer also graphs in three dimensions and contains a built-in Cabri Geometry dynamic software package. Figure 7–6 shows how the TI-92 can be used by a student to work through each step of solving the equation $3(x + 5) - 2x = 4x + 8$. Note that the mini-computer displays the root of the equation as a fraction unless instructed to convert it to a decimal.

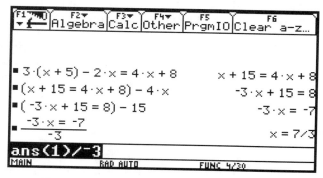

Figure 7–6 A TI-92 Used to Solve an Equation

A classroom set of 10 or 12 of these "calculators" can virtually replace computers for a mathematics class—and at the cost of less than one computer. Such changes in technology require a teacher to remain up to date by attending workshops and in-service programs as will be discussed in Chapter 10. We now turn our attention to the use of media in the classroom, including laser discs, CD-ROMs, and video.

■ LASER DISCS, CD-ROMS, AND VIDEOS

Today's students are the MTV generation. They watch television every day for a surprising number of hours. The TIMSS reports (Beaton et al., 1996) showed that one third of *fourth graders* in the United States watch three hours or more of television every day, and eighth graders watch an average of 2.6 hours of television per day.

More and more families are purchasing home computers; children are spending hours surfing the Internet, and the video-rental business has never been better. As a result, our students come to class having watched literally thousands of hours of television, movies, and videos and are expecting the same level of excitement and fast pace that they have experienced through these media. The teacher who uses hands-on, active lessons with an emphasis on student discourse and exploration is giving these students what they want and need, but teachers who use individual worksheets and insist on a silent classroom are likely to meet opposition and undesirable behavior. Along with graphing calculators and computers, a number of other effective technological teaching tools can also enhance the mathematics classroom.

A **laser disc,** which is larger than an audio compact disk, can be inserted into a player and viewed on a television or computer monitor. A number of mathematics laser disc presentations have been produced over the past several years for classroom use. For example, Vanderbilt University produced a series of laser disc programs entitled *The Adventures of Jasper Woodbury,* which include a number of short stories, followed by a list of mathematics problems that can be solved by using the information in each story. The characters count out money, make note of wind speeds, and look at clocks so that viewers can determine travel times, how much the characters can afford to spend, and so forth. Teachers are provided with a manual that contains reproducible masters, a list of content objectives, and extension questions with solutions. Students enjoy the pace and adventure of an on-screen story and find themselves caught up in a problem-solving situation.

The advantages of laser disc technology are numerous. First, each frame of the program is numbered, and the teacher or students can readily access a clip of the program to review a clue by either inputting a frame number (provided in the teacher's manual) or by using a bar code reader (bar codes are also provided). No rewinding or fast forwarding is required because the disc does not use tape. Second, because the programs are digital, a story can be stopped or shown in fast or slow motion with the press of a button. Students can slowly track through a scene to pick up more subtle clues and record the information. Finally, they can connect the laser disc player to a computer, allowing the computer to interface with the program. The student can point and click on a scene description on the computer screen to play the scene on the television. Computer software also includes additional maps and other information that the students can use in solving the problems.

Laser disc technology also has its drawbacks, however. A laser disc player and effective software can be very expensive. In some cases, teachers can borrow laser disc programs from a local lending library, but if they are not available, software can be a major purchase. Also, whenever we use television as a medium, we run the risk of provoking disgruntled parents and community members who think that children already spend too much time watching television. Direct communication with parents to explain why a laser disc program is being used and how it enhances mathematics education is critical to the acceptance of this strategy. Finally, because a laser disc program is on a single disc in a single player, the teacher must be adept at using a team approach to problem solving, in which each team of students is allotted a certain amount of time in which to access the discs for information. But the trade-offs can be well worth it as students so often get excited about solving problems posed on the television screen.

In a similar way, a CD-ROM allows students to access data and solve problems on the computer screen. The CD-ROM became a classroom tool when it became possible to put a great deal of data, including video, onto a small computer disc. Although early computer programs first came on cassette tapes, they later were stored on floppy disks, and most, today, are sold in the form of **CD-ROMs,** small software discs containing video or other information that can be played by a computer. In recent years, we have begun to see mathematics tutorials, explorations, and even teacher in-service programs released as CD-ROMs. A multivolume encyclopedia that would have taken up two shelves in a family room in the 1970s can be readily placed on a single CD-ROM, making it easier than ever for students to access the information that might help them solve a mathematics problem. CD-ROMs are also available that ask the student to select a career interest area, at which point the computer shows a short video clip that illustrates how a person in that job would use mathematics. The advantages and disadvantages of CD-ROM technology in the classroom are very similar to those discussed in the laser disc discussion. The cost of CD-ROMs and the availability of computers in schools are probably the most significant roadblocks to their use in the classroom.

One medium that has been available for quite some time in schools is videotape. Most schools have easy access to a videocassette recorder (VCR) and a television, and videos are relatively inexpensive. One of the popular video programs for secondary and middle school mathematics is *Futures,* a 12-part video series (and *Futures 2,* which contains another 12 segments) that focuses on real-life uses for mathematics. Starring Jamie Escalante, about whom the movie *Stand and Deliver* was developed, the series presents fifteen-minute segments about how mathematics is used in meteorology, fashion merchandising, music, and many other career areas. Each tape is designed to appeal to students from approximately grades 6 through 12, and the accompanying teacher's manual includes teaching tips, vocabulary words, and problems and discussion questions that can emanate from the viewing of each video segment.

Other videos on the market focus on problem solving, the use of geometry in the real world, discrete mathematics applications, computer-generated depictions of fractals, and a host of other mathematics topics. These videos can be the focal points of instruction or can supplement a unit or lesson with a clip that evokes student interest. One of the greatest benefits of video technology in the classroom is that videos are readily accessible and fairly inexpensive. Most libraries and public television stations have extensive collections from which teachers can borrow videos. Also, the video medium is practical because videotape use requires little or no technical training. And finally, because video technology has been available for quite some time, there are more programs available in this medium than in laser disc or CD-ROM format. The availability of tapes containing a wide range of topics and at varying mathematical levels makes it easy for teachers to select the tapes that are most appropriate for their classes. Videos, like laser discs, however, are prone to provoke parental reactions to the effect that they "don't want their children watching television in school." Again, community education is important. Remember, too, that videos take time to rewind and fast forward, and they are no match for the ease of using a laser disc or CD-ROM to access pictures or scenes. Just as it is easier to access Track 4 on a compact disc than to fast forward a cassette tape to a particular song, it is considerably easier to locate a program or clip on a laser disc or CD-ROM than on a video.

Laser discs, CD-ROMs, and videos are just examples, each with their own advantages and disadvantages, of the several ways to use media in classrooms. In the end, decisions on which forms of technology to choose are frequently made on the basis of availability of the hardware and software. Teachers who get excited about using CD-ROMs in the classroom but do not have access to computers or a budget to buy software will end up spinning their wheels. On the other hand, as you might expect, many schools have laser disc players and software that is just collecting dust on a shelf because teachers do not know how to use the technology or simply choose not to implement it.

■ THE INTERNET AND THE WORLD WIDE WEB

Probably the single most significant development in technology in the past 25 years has been the Internet, which includes the World Wide Web. The **Internet** is a worldwide network of computers that can talk to one another. Anyone who has a modem and an Internet Service Provider (ISP) such as America Online can readily access computers and information all over the world with a click of a mouse. It has become commonplace to send electronic mail (e-mail) around the world rather than write a traditional letter on paper and send it off in an envelope. And via e-mail, formatted documents can be sent as attachments to the other side of the world in seconds. The World Wide Web is a part or subset of the Internet that allows the user to access and send photos, videos, and audio messages. A person in New York can listen to a favorite radio station in Los Angeles over the World Wide Web, and a soldier stationed in Europe can view real-time images of her family back in Chicago. Never before has it been so easy to access information.

As a result of the Internet, mathematics teachers have a unique opportunity to take advantage of the technology. In this section, we discuss some ways that a mathematics teacher can do this. Specifically, we examine teacher resources and student research tools and conclude with an example of a mathematics project that utilizes the Internet.

Teacher Resources

As we discussed in Chapter 4, teachers frequently supplement textbooks with lessons and activities from outside sources. There are resource books devoted entirely to the use of a particular manipulative, such as pattern blocks, CD-ROMs containing high school mathematics lessons, and so forth. But now, literally thousands of teaching ideas are available at your fingertips through the World Wide Web. Teachers and curriculum designers have created entire websites dedicated to the teaching and learning of mathematics, and these sites can contain hundreds of teaching ideas. If you have access to the Internet, you have a significant resource available on your desktop.

Let's say, for example, that you are planning to teach a unit on polynomials, and you have decided to use algebra tiles to help students visualize and manipulate variable expressions (as discussed in Chapter 2). You can access ideas for your unit on the Internet. Generally, you start with a **search engine,** a computer program at various sites on the Internet that is used for searching the Web for sites related to the topic of interest. One such search engine is AltaVista, which can be found at <http://www.altavista.com> as mentioned in Chapter 4. You go to this address and type in the words "algebra tiles" and click on Search. The list of resources generated are all sites that have something about algebra, tiles, or both in the title. As with any selection of materials, the user needs to carefully review the possible resources and choose the one that will be most appropriate for the situation.

One of the helpful resources to emerge during an "algebra tiles" search is located at <http://plato.acadiau.ca/courses/educ/reid/tiles/tiles.html>. This location is "Learning About Algebra Tiles: Activities for Teachers." The site describes how a teacher can use algebra tiles to model polynomials and operations with polynomials, including addition, subtraction, multiplication, and factoring. This activity set is reprinted here both as an illustration of what is available on the Web and as a source of ideas on how to use algebra tiles effectively in your mathematics classroom:

LEARNING ABOUT ALGEBRA TILES: ACTIVITIES FOR TEACHERS

Algebra tiles provide a useful way to introduce operations on polynomials to students of all ages. The following can be used both as a self guided tour of teaching with algebra tiles, and as a set of activities for use with students. Examples of instructions to students are indented. The remainder of the text is addressed directly to the reader who is assumed to be a teacher.

Getting Started

Work with either the basic commercial set (small white & red squares, large white & green squares, and long white & green rectangles) or cutouts from one of the *attached sheets*. The commercial sets are nice and sturdy, but tempt students to negative numbers too quickly and cost too much to give away a set to every kid. The sheets are not as sturdy, but can be made available to kids to take home and delay the idea of negatives until the teacher is ready to cope with it. You may also have a commercial set with other colours for a second variable, and some more squarish rectangles. Hide them for the moment. The third sheet in the cutout set provided fulfills the same functions, so ignore it for the moment, too.

Naming

I call the small squares "nameless ones." This captures two important ideas: They aren't named when we talk about polynomials, and their value is 1. The reason for the name isn't something you'd tell kids on the first day, but having reasonable names for things makes the going easier later on.

Nameless ones behave like the bingo chips or whatever from learning integers, and like the bears the kids counted in kindergarten. One of them stands for 1, and five of them stands for 5. If you are using the cutout ones, they are one square centimeter, and you can make a connection to measurement if you want.

What do you want to call the other pieces? Settle on names within groups, and within the class. Naming conventions are important to mathematical communities. You might find you have pieces which look similar to another group's but not exactly the same (rectangles that are longer than yours for example). It's OK to give these the same names because they are used in the same way.

Some names which students have proposed in the past are: Longs & Big Squares, Rectangles & Rectangle squares, and X and X^2. The point to emphasize with names is not that there's a correct name for each piece, but that we need names to be able to talk about them. The mathematical concept here is that a variable is a *name* for something else (usually an unknown or variable quantity).

Collections, part 1

Make a collection of pieces, using all three kinds, and write down its name. Settle on a convention for writing collections which shows that all the pieces are added together in one collection. Abbreviations might help. You could call this collection:

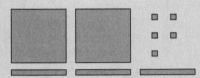

2BS + 3R + 5 (for two big squares, three rectangles and five nameless ones) or $2R^2$ + 3R + 5 (for two rectangle squares, three rectangles, and five nameless ones) or $2x^2$ + 3x + 5 (for two X^2, three X, and five ones)

Here you want to try to get the names sorted out, so that groups can describe their collections. Have the students draw their collections, and write the names of the collections with symbols.

Collections, part 2

Combine the collection you made with a collection another group member made. How would you name the resulting collection? How would you draw or write the action of combining them?

Now make a collection and take some pieces out of it. How would you name the resulting collection? How would you draw or write the action of taking out pieces from a collection?

This is introducing the idea of adding and subtracting polynomials. Not much attention needs to be paid to this right now. All we are doing is agreeing on some more notational conventions:

$(2R^2 + 3R + 5) + (R^2 + 2R + 6) = (3R^2 + 5R + 11)$ *means:*

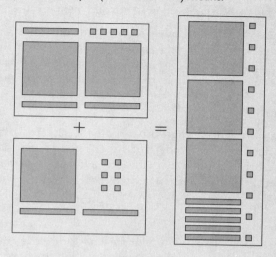

and

$(2R^2 + 3R + 5) - (R^2 + 2R + 3) = (R^2 + R + 2)$ *means:*

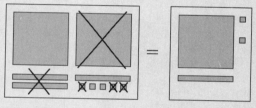

where crossing out the picture of a tile denotes removing it from the collection.

Again, have students perform the action on the tiles, and then draw the actions, and then write the symbols for the actions. If some of your lazier students want to stop drawing everything and just write symbols, that might be OK, but don't let them get the idea that drawing pictures and moving tiles is the "bad" way to do things.

Making rectangles

Make a collection with two big squares, seven rectangles, and six nameless ones. How would you name that collection? Now arrange the collection so it makes a rectangle.

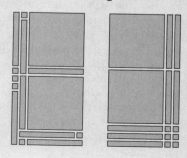

Both of these are rectangles made with the same pieces. I like the one on the right better. Why not introduce some aesthetic rules of Algebra tile rectangles? My first rule would be:

• Big squares can't touch little squares.

My second rule (which I am more lenient about) is:

• Little squares must all be together.

Measuring

Use rectangles and nameless ones to "measure" the length and width of your rectangles. For example:

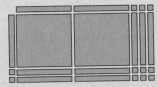

the length and width of this rectangle are 2R + 3 and R + 2. It is sometimes confusing to have the measuring tiles so close to the rectangle. To clarify we can use "crossed lines" to separate them. (The X in the corner is because they are "crossed")

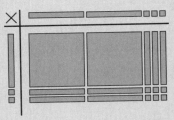

Spend some time on making rectangles, drawing them, measuring them, and writing down the collections and their measurements. For example, I could write $(2R^2 + 7R + 6) = (R + 2) \times (2R + 3)$ for the rectangle I made above.

If your students are getting tired of drawing you might introduce them to this notation:

X	2R	3
R	$2R^2$	3R
2	4R	6

This shows how the rectangle is made, and its measurements.

Now you have the idea of rectangles sorted you might give the students a break and do something easy for a while:

Given two measurements, what tiles are in the rectangle? Start by putting the tiles for the measurements along your crossed lines, and then fill in the rectangle. Draw your result (or use a symbol table).

A pause to get our bearings

You now know how to teach adding and subtracting polynomials (as long as there are no negatives involved), and factoring and multiplying polynomials with positive coefficients. Dividing is just factoring with one factor already known, so I skipped it. From here you can go a couple of directions.

You can introduce a new variable, and pull out those other tiles. If you are using the cutouts you need to get the kids to choose a new label for one set to distinguish it from the other one. We're going to use them differently now, so it's time for a new name. You also need those squarish rectangles. What do they stand for?

Another direction you can go introduces negative coefficients. This is a bit tricky, so I'll head that way now, and let you figure out extra variables by yourself.

Back to square ones

How would you take seven ones from three ones? Remember your work with integers. It's OK to turn the ones the other way up now. If you are using the commercial tiles they change colour, so you can use them for negative ones. If you are using the cutouts nothing happens at all, so this might be a good time to shade *one side* of each of your cut out tiles. Now, how do you find

$$(2R^2 - 3R - 7) - (R^2 - 5R - 3)?$$

Sorry about all those symbols, but by now you and your students can probably handle them. Did everyone get

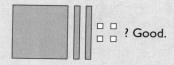 ? Good.

Crossed-lines with a flip

Set up your crossed-lines and figure out how these new negative pieces work there when you multiply. Draw some examples, using symbols if you want. This part is pretty easy after you've mastered integers and multiplying polynomials with positive coefficients.

If your students are a bit shaky on multiplying integers you might want to remind them that *positive* numbers are used to count, so 1 x 1 means one 1, which is 1; and 1x(-1) means one (-1) which is (-1). Once you have that sorted out, you can look at this multiplication:

Figuring out what to put in three of the four positions is easy. The fourth one is harder. But if we think about what we are multiplying (0x0) then we know what the answer is (0), so the fourth position must be occupied by (−1).

Now for the tricky part

Let's factor $(R^2 + R - 6)$. Put the pieces between your crossed lines. There aren't enough. Try anyway, and put things where you learned they belonged when you were working with positive coefficients:

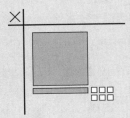

We know the R^2 and the nameless ones can't be in the same row or column because that violates one of our aesthetic rules. That leaves four spaces which look like they ought to have rectangles in them. Remember about adding zero? Try it. Now try some others.

Have students make up some by multiplying and give them to other people in their group.

You might have discovered already that it isn't always clear where to put the rectangles you add. It's easy in the above example to know you need to add two positive rectangles and two negative rectangles, but you can't put them just anywhere. For example, if you put them like this:

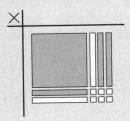

You'll find you can't measure your rectangle. We need a new aesthetic rule:

• The squares in a column or row must either all be the same colour as the rectangles, or all be the other colour.

Given this rule, we can see that we should put our four new rectangles in like this:

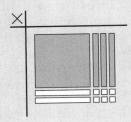

In conclusion

Polynomials are unlike the other "numbers" students learn how to add, subtract, multiply and divide. They are not "counting" numbers. Giving polynomials a concrete referent (tiles) makes them real.

Implicit in the treatment I have given above is an important educational principle:

- Learning, at any level, is easiest if it starts with concrete actions, then moves to iconic representations of those actions, then to symbolic representations of those actions, and finally to formal actions on symbols.

In the case of the tiles these four stages are:

1. Actions on the tiles themselves
2. Drawings of those actions
3. Using symbols in or instead of the drawings
4. Traditional algebraic manipulations of symbols.

(David A. Reid [1999], Acadia University. Reprinted with permission.)

As you can see, the author of these Web pages (Reid, 1999) presents the reader with a comprehensive overview of how to use algebra tiles in the classroom, with specific problems the students can explore and notes and hints for teachers. The reader can print out the pages and design a lesson or unit around the suggestions. You can find thousands of activities and ideas like this on the Internet by running a search and taking some time to scan through the options. Many of the activities online include reproducible activity pages, links to other related sites, and bibliographies.

A word of warning is in order, however: A search on the Internet can often turn up hundreds or thousands of "hits"—sites that match the query. Searching the Internet can be very time-consuming: you may have to leaf through many websites to find teaching ideas that fit your style and needs. You might also find many lessons that are poorly written, because anyone with an Internet account that allows Web pages to be created can post a lesson, and the quality is certainly not guaranteed. Just as you might rummage through books in a library, you often have to look at several resources before you find a credible source that you like and feel comfortable using. Do not assume that a resource is necessarily useful or well written just because it matches your query and addresses your topic. Be selective about the Web resources you use, and with a little discretion, you will find hundreds of good ideas just waiting for your implementation. Appendix E lists some suggested websites that carry teaching ideas and resources featuring the titles, addresses, and a short description of each site. It is designed to give you a start as you search the Web for teaching ideas in mathematics. Access to the Internet can also be very beneficial for students in your classes. If your school has even one computer that is online with the Internet, the possibilities for teacher and student use become almost endless. We now turn our attention to how students can use the Internet in their study of mathematics.

Student Research Tools and Projects

Suppose that a cereal company produces a special set of six commemorative cards containing pictures of wild animals. The cereal boxes have a message on the outside saying:

A special card is free inside. Collect all six!

This classic probability problem centers around students trying to determine how many boxes of cereal they should buy at the store to make it almost inevitable that they will actually collect all six cards. Of course, one could buy six boxes and get a different card in each, but this is *possible*, not *probable*. One could purchase 100 boxes of cereal and still only get five of the six cards, but if an equal number of the cards are randomly distributed, this isn't very likely either. So, how many boxes will maximize the chances? Probably the best way to approach the problem is to have students model the purchasing of boxes of cereal and record their results. Using a bag with six different-colored cubes in it, students can draw a cube, record the color, replace it in the bag, and continue this process until they have chosen all six colors at least once. Another way to model the problem is to roll a fair number cube until all six faces have shown at least once. In either case, students collect classroom data to refine their predictions about the optimal number of boxes of cereal to purchase.

Another way to have students model the problem is to visit the problem on the Internet. At <http://www.glenbrook.k12.il.us/gbsmat/NCTM/cereal2.html>, there is a simulation of the problem. Students select the total number of cards that a child would want to collect, and, by clicking on Run the Simulation, activate software that generates and logs the data so that students can use the Internet as their software source. The software runs a random selection process and tells the students how many boxes of cereal were needed to collect all of the cards. Thus, students can make use of the Internet to access available software. Websites contain software to sketch graphs, draw fractal designs, compute statistics, run simulations, and a host of other applications. Therefore, the school does not have to purchase the software; it is already available and able to be run from another site on the Web. Some sites also contain free software packages (sometimes called "shareware") that can be downloaded onto a computer and run locally by students in a school.

Another use of the Internet by students is to use e-mail to share results of problem solving with students in other schools. Take, for example, the case of the cereal-box problem. Students at a middle school in New Jersey could roll the dice 10 times each, pool their data, and e-mail their results to a secondary class in California that is following the same process. Students can compare data to determine if they have arrived at similar conclusions. At one website, students have pooled over 34,000 rolls of a number cube, and submitted the data via the Internet. The website administrator graphed the data to show which result occurs most frequently (see <http://lrs.ed.uiuc.edu/students/mcornell/cerealbox/results/results.html>). Similarly, students working on a project that requires two people on a team could be assigned a teammate in another state, with whom they would communicate by e-mail. This approach allows students to communicate mathematically with students whom they would not ordinarily be able to contact. Smaller, isolated school districts can easily connect with students in other parts of their state or country.

A popular trend in the mathematics classroom is to develop long- or short-term projects that include data gathering via the Internet. The Standards call for the use of real-world data, and the Internet contains a wealth of current information that can be helpful in problem solving. Here are just a few examples of projects in which a student can engage by using the Internet:

- Students explore the difference between predicted weather and actual weather for a particular city over a given period of time. *In this project, teams of students might select a city, locate the forecasted high and low temperatures for that city each day on the Web, and record the actual temperatures from the Web each day. Then, drawing line graphs, over time, the students can determine the accuracy of the forecasts and compare their results to those of students who selected other cities. Forecasts and databases of meteorological information can be readily located on the Internet.*

- Students research a mathematician or some historical topic, such as the history of π but are restricted to the Internet as their source of information. *A considerable amount of factual information about individuals and events is available on the Internet. Students learn about mathematicians and the history of mathematics while developing their searching and problem-solving skills on the Internet.*

- Students track the population growth rates in several cities, counties, or states and make predictions about future population sizes. *Databases of population information are plentiful on the Web, and students can look up information that can be used to draw graphs and determine the regression equations that allow them to make predictions.*

- Students plan a summer vacation for a family of four on a $1,500 budget. *Using the Internet, students can determine the travel distance between major cities, the cost of admission to various points of interest, and the cost of motels, food, and gasoline. They can estimate the travel time and costs and design a reasonable family vacation within the budget.*

- Students can design personal health-conscious diets and justify their content based on mathematics. *There are websites that allow individuals to input their age, height, and weight, and the software tells the user what is an optimal number of calories that they should consume in a day. By accessing sites with nutritional information, students can plan meals based upon their needs for caloric intake, maximum fat grams, and the like. This investigation could be a joint project for a health class and a mathematics class.*

- Students design their own Web pages focused on a problem of their choosing. *In collaboration with another teacher, such as an English, science, or social studies teacher, a team of students in a mathematics class can select a problem of interest, write it in an interactive manner, and create their own website that focuses on the topic. For example, a student might design a website that allows the user to explore various applications of the trigonometric functions.*

In all of these cases, access to the Internet is a necessity. The process of running and narrowing searches on the Web to gather data is, in and of itself, an interesting exercise in problem solving and reasoning. Most students are fascinated with the Internet and its wealth of information, so these projects are natural extensions of their interests and curiosity. Two of the most significant obstacles to the use of the Internet in mathematics, in general, are lack of availability and "clutter" on the Internet. Many schools have few computers; even more do not have Internet access. Some schools that do have access only have one computer—often located in the principal's office or in the library—that is wired to the Internet. Consequently, many teachers need to devise careful plans for small groups to use the computer while others work on a different project, or they will find themselves unable to do any Internet investigations at all. The other obstacle is the inappropriate material on the World Wide Web. Many sites contain objectionable content (from nudity to bigotry) and schools need to be careful about how students use the resource. Some schools have purchased software that blocks students from certain sites, and others ask students to sign contracts to the effect that if they are caught visiting an inappropriate website, they lose access to the Web for a year or more—with no exceptions. In general, the Internet provides an excellent opportunity for research and the study of mathematics, but some hurdles need to be overcome to make this practical.

■ CHOOSING BETWEEN PAPER AND PENCIL AND TECHNOLOGY

Probably one of a teacher's greatest fears is that students will become dependent upon the technological tools and won't be able to function without them. How many times have you heard that the workers at fast-food restaurants merely push a button containing a picture of french fries because they are likely to make mathematical errors otherwise? Or perhaps you've heard someone lament that clerks in stores don't even know how to count out change anymore. Many people believe that the use of technology means the reduction of brainpower; after all, who has to think if the calculator or computer already does the thinking? Still others ask, "If a hand-held computer can factor trinomials and solve equations, what is left to teach in an algebra class?" Actually, the answer to all of these concerns may not be as complex as it seems: No one, *including the NCTM Curriculum Standards,* is saying that we should allow technology to take over and do all the thinking. Instead, we should think of the technology as aiding our teaching and allowing us to solve problems and run projects that, without the new tools, would have been nearly impossible or, at least, very difficult to conduct.

Imagine sharing information among hundreds of schools while working on the cereal-box problem if you had to write your data on a piece of paper, stick it in an envelope, and mail it to all of the other schools. The fact is, most people simply wouldn't be interested in doing it at all. Then think about the activity sheets presented in this chapter that explore quadratics on a graphing calculator. Can you imagine doing that exploration with paper and pencil? Technology does not take the reasoning and thinking out of mathematics, but it certainly does ask us to teach differently than we did before the technology existed. In the *Curriculum and Evaluation Standards*

(1989), the NCTM stated that "access to technology is no guarantee that any student will become mathematically literate. Calculators and computers for users of mathematics, like word processors for writers, are tools that simplify, but do not accomplish, the work at hand. . . . The availability of calculators does not eliminate the need for students to learn algorithms" (p. 8). In *Principles and Standards for School Mathematics,* the authors stated that "like any tool, technological tools can be used well or poorly. They should not be used as replacements for basic understandings and intuitions; rather, they can and should be used to foster those understandings and intuitions" (NCTM, 1998, p. 40).

The authors of the *Curriculum and Evaluation Standards* presented the graphic of Figure 7–7 in their Introduction:

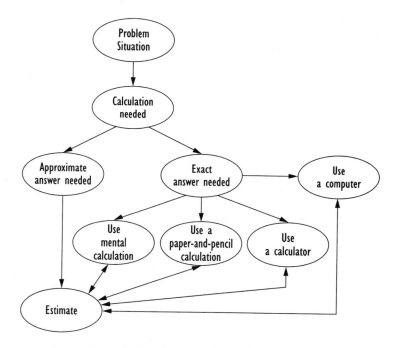

Figure 7–7 NCTM Problem-Solving Model

(NCTM, *Curriculum and Evaluation Standards for School Mathematics,* 1989, p. 9.)

This graphic reminds us that there are times when a calculator or a computer is appropriate in solving a problem and other times when mental or paper-and-pencil methods are best. For example, if you were multiplying the cost of a gallon of gas by the number of gallons to determine the total cost of a tank of gas, here are possible multiplication problems you might encounter:

A. 1.09×10
B. 1.10×2.2
C. 1.19×14.36

Most people would calculate (A) mentally by moving the decimal to get $10.90. Although some people might also prefer to do (B) mentally, a quick paper-and-pencil calculation shows a solution of $2.42. It would be rare to find someone who preferred to perform the calculation in (C) by hand and even more unusual to find someone who could do it mentally. So it makes sense to use a calculator for (C), keeping in mind that the answer should come out to somewhere between $15 and $20, because a number larger than 14 is being multiplied by a number slightly larger than 1. This last example also reminds us that it is extremely important to teach students to mentally estimate an answer before pressing calculator keys, so that they will know if their answer is at least in the ballpark. There has probably never been a period in history in which it was more important for students to develop number sense and be able to make mental approximations, because we need to ensure that answers coming from machines make sense. But to ask students to do calculations like (C) by hand tends to consume more time in the classroom than it is worth in the long run. So, allow technology to take over only when it is appropriate.

In the classroom, it is critical that we take the leadership role and help students to recognize when it is appropriate to use technology. If algebra students are asked to find (−9) + (−3) and reach for their calculators, it is our responsibility to remind them that they should be able to do this calculation mentally. Students learn how to use technology properly when their instructors demonstrate and model proper use of the tools. And as the NCTM stated, technology is merely a tool. A calculator may be able to draw a graph and solve an equation, but only its user knows when a graph is needed or how to set up the equation that needs to be solved in the first place. If our classrooms are dominated by real-life, application-oriented problems, our students will be able to spend more time reasoning and problem solving, thus allowing the technology to be the means that it was designed to be—not the end that many believe it has become.

■ CONCLUSION ■

Suppose that the first thing on your agenda today is to go grocery shopping, and you need to make a list. However, to make the list, you will be required to use a feather (quill) dipped in ink, and you will have to ride a horse to the grocery. You won't buy frozen foods at the grocery either, because you're not allowed to use your freezer. You probably wouldn't appreciate being told that you can't use a pencil or pen, that your car has to be left in the garage, and that you'll have to ignore the fact that you have a freezer in your kitchen. After all, these examples of modern technology are commonplace in our world. Similarly, television, calculators, computers, compact discs, and so forth, are also part of modern life, and to ask

you to solve problems and deal with current situations without the aid of these tools is unrealistic. The world has changed dramatically in the past 100 years, and we wouldn't dream of telling people that they had to ride horses to work, yet we still find educators who refuse to allow students to carry calculators into a mathematics classroom. They insist that students do all problems by hand prior to handing them a calculator. Using this same line of reasoning, perhaps we should expect all drivers to learn to ride a horse before getting behind the wheel of a car. The point is that, rather than using intimidation and fear, we need to approach the potential of technology with optimism and excitement. Our students have access to more current data and resources than ever in history; we have inexpensive machines that can do most of the problems in a 1970 algebra textbook with the press of a button.

In this chapter, we have outlined and described a number of technological tools that are available to teachers of mathematics and presented the advantages and disadvantages of each. We have also pointed out that finances and time will prevent teachers from using every form of technology available. Therefore, each teacher has to consider the needs of the students and decide what is appropriate and reasonable when selecting technology. Students should access mathematics that was not possible or reasonable before the introduction of the technology and should not only become better problem solvers but also gain confidence in using this technology in the process. In the *Curriculum and Evaluation Standards* (1989), the NCTM stated that "contrary to the fears of many, the availability of calculators and computers has expanded students' capability of performing calculations. There is no evidence to suggest that the availability of calculators makes students dependent on them for simple calculations" (p. 8). Furthermore, a review of calculator-use research by Dunham and Dick (1994) highlighted the fact that students who used graphing calculators demonstrated a better understanding of graphing items on an achievement test than their peers who were taught without calculators. Also, students taught with calculators tended to make stronger connections between the various ways of representing functions—graphically, numerically, and algebraically. They also cited research suggesting that students using graphing calculators were more likely to focus on the meaning of the problems themselves rather than the manipulation of symbols to solve the problems they were posed. In short, the technology is available, powerful, and paying dividends in terms of student achievement, so why not use it to its fullest extent?

It is difficult, of course, to determine what "the fullest extent" is. If you are planning to teach a unit on compound interest, where does the use of a calculator factor in, and what should students be able to do by hand? Of course, your district's curriculum will address some of these issues as was discussed in Chapter 4, but you still face the planning and decision making regarding the appropriate use of technology. Unfortunately, there are no easy answers to the question of how much technology is optimal, and the issue continues to be debated. What we do know is that students are generally motivated by and interested in lessons that involve the use of technology and manipulatives.

However, although a lesson may be active and fun for students, the experience is really only worthwhile if it results in some substantial student learning. After all, watching television can be fun, but it doesn't teach us important life skills. We have to be careful when evaluating the teaching and learning process because students' enjoyment of a lesson and their lack of questions on a related assignment do not necessarily imply that the lesson was worthwhile. And the fact that we used technology or manipulatives and actively involved our students does not necessarily mean that significant learning occurred. We need to look beyond student satisfaction and participation and assess whether students accomplished the goals and objectives set forth in the lesson. However, assessing student understanding of mathematics is not an easy task either.

Some students are good test takers, and others are not. Some students can perform well on a skill-based task but have difficulty explaining their thinking. Others are good problem solvers but lack such basic arithmetic skills as the quick recall of multiplication facts. If measuring the effectiveness of a lesson or unit depends on assessing student progress, then we need to look at how student understanding is measured and analyzed. The issue of assessment will be the primary subject of Unit IV. Chapter 8 will focus on the role of assessment in mathematics education, and Chapter 9 will describe issues related to assessment, such as equity, assigning and checking homework, and determining final grades.

■ GLOSSARY ■

CD-ROM: A CD-ROM is a small disc containing software easily loaded into a computer for use. CD-ROMs can contain video and still photographic images as well as audio tracks that can be easily accessed through a click of the computer's mouse.

Dynamic Software: Computer software is referred to as dynamic if it involves human interaction with what is viewed on the screen. For example, a geometry program would be considered dynamic if the user can draw a quadrilateral, grab one of the vertices, and view the effects on the shape of the polygon as the vertex is dragged around the page. This type of software is different from traditional drill-and-practice software that simply displays a question and requires the user to input an answer.

Hardware: Computer hardware includes the physical tools of technology, including a computer, monitor, printer, modem, calculator, and so forth.

Internet: The Internet is a worldwide network of computers that are capable of sharing information between them. The World Wide Web is a subset of the Internet that allows not only text but photographs, video, and sound to be easily transmitted between computers.

Laser Disc: A laser disc is larger than an audio compact disc and contains video and still photographic images. The laser disc can be used in the classroom to show video footage that can be easily searched for key scenes or pictures because each frame is numbered and can be accessed by either typing in a reference number or by using a bar code scanner. A laser disc player can also be interfaced with a computer so that a click of the computer's mouse can be used to access video footage or still images.

Search Engine: A search engine is a software program on the World Wide Web that can be used to find information on a particular topic. When the user types in key words, the search engine will indicate the locations of hits that match the user's query. One popular search engine, AltaVista, can be found at <www.altavista.digital.com>.

Software: The software includes the programs that are used to make the hardware achieve its purpose. So programs such as a spreadsheet or the Geometer's Sketchpad are examples of software that run on a computer. Cabri Geometry is an example of a software package made to run on a hand-held computer.

■ DISCUSSION QUESTIONS ■

1. When is it appropriate to use technology in the mathematics classroom? Consider the content of a unit on a topic such as equation solving, recursion, or exponential functions. Discuss how much of the content "should" be done by hand and what role technology can play in developing the concept.

2. Obtain two or more mathematics textbooks at the grade level of your choice. Examine the books and discuss the ways in which technology is used throughout the text. Is technology treated as an extra topic, with technology suggestions presented at the end of sections or chapters, or is technology integrated throughout the lessons?

3. Locate a lesson plan in a teacher's manual, resource book, or on the Internet that does not use technology at all. Rewrite the lesson by including experiences that make use of technol-

ogy while still addressing all of the stated objectives for the lesson.

4. Explore the functions of a graphing calculator or hand-held computer, such as the TI-83 or the TI-92. Discuss the advantages and potential disadvantages of making regular use of graphing calculator technology in the mathematics classroom. What does it mean to use this tool to fundamentally change the way that mathematics is taught rather than view it as a supplement to what is already being done?

5. Locate several examples of secondary or middle school mathematics computer software programs. Using the form presented in this chapter (or another that you may have available), critique the software and determine whether the purchase of this software would make a good investment.

6. Go to a local public television station or a library and identify several mathematics teaching videos, laser discs, or CD-ROM presentations. Preview the software and describe its strengths, weaknesses, and potential effectiveness in the classroom.

7. With a partner, surf the Web for useful mathematics education sites using the locations listed in Appendix E. By following links and running your own searches, identify several additional sites that might be useful to teachers of mathematics. What are the characteristics of the most helpful sites, and how can you tell if a site contains mostly "junk"?

8. In this chapter, several Internet-related projects were recommended. Develop an additional list of projects that students could pursue by searching for the relevant data on the Internet.

9. "Students should not be using technology in the classroom until they have first mastered all of the basic paper-and-pencil manipulations." This comment is frequently made by people who are skeptical about the use of technology in the teaching and learning process. List several statements in support of and several statements that counter the claim. What do you believe and why?

■ BIBLIOGRAPHIC REFERENCES AND RESOURCES ■

AltaVista. (1999). AltaVista search engine website. Retrieved August 20, 1999 from the World Wide Web: <http://www.altavista.com>

Beaton, A. E., Mullis, I. V., Martin, M. O., Gonzalez, E. J., Kelly, D. L., & Smith, T. A. (1996). *TIMSS: Mathematics achievement in the middle school years.* Chestnut Hill, MA: Center for the Study of Testing, Evaluation, and Educational Policy.

Becker, J. P. (1993). Current trends in mathematics education in the United States, with reference to computers and calculators. *Hiroshima Journal of Mathematics Education, 1,* 37–50.

Coes, L. (1995). Activities: What is the r for? *Mathematics Teacher, 88* (9) 758–762, 768–769.

Cornell, M. (1999). Fun with Probability: The Probable Pen in the Cereal Box. Retrieved August 20, 1999 from the World Wide Web: <http://lrs.ed.uiuc.edu/students/mcornell/cerealbox/results/results.html>

Day, R. (1996). Technology tips: Classroom technology: Tool for, or focus of, learning? *Mathematics Teacher, 89* (2), 134–137.

Dugdale, S. & Kibbey, D. (1999). *Green globs and graphing equations* (computer software). Pleasantville, NY: Sunburst.

Dunham, P. H. & Dick, T. P. (1994). Research on graphing calculators. *Mathematics Teacher, 87* (6), 440–445.

Fey, James. (Ed.). (1992). *1992 Yearbook of the NCTM: Calculators in mathematics education.* Reston, VA: National Council of Teachers of Mathematics.

Fragale, K. C. (1995). Power on the case of Jewels Jones. *Mathematics Teaching in the Middle School, 1* (7), 584–589.

Glasgow, B. (1998). The authority of the calculator in the minds of college students. *School Science and Mathematics, 98* (7), 383–388.

Gowland, D. (1998). Calculators: Help or hindrance? *Mathematics in School, 27* (1), 26–28.

Graham, A. (1996). Following form with a graphic calculator. *Teaching Statistics, 18* (2), 52–55.

Haney, J. & Brownell, N. (1999). *Software evaluation form.* Bowling Green, OH: Self-Published.

Heid, M. K. (1988). Calculators on tests: One giant step for mathematics education. *Mathematics Teacher, 81* (9), 710–713.

Heid, M. K. (1997). The technological revolution and the reform of school mathematics. *American Journal of Education, 106,* 5–61.

Joseph, L. C. (1998). Blue chip mathematics sites. *Multimedia Schools, 5* (1), 44–47.

Key Curriculum Press. (1999). *Geometer's sketchpad* (computer software). Emeryville, CA: Key Curriculum.

MECC. (1997). *Tesselmania* (computer software). Minneapolis, MN: The Learning Company.

Mercer, J. (1995). Teaching graphing concepts with graphing calculators. *Mathematics Teacher, 88* (4), 268–273.

National Council of Teachers of Mathematics. (1998). *Principles and standards for school mathematics* (working draft). Reston, VA: National Council of Teachers of Mathematics.

National Council of Teachers of Mathematics. (1997). *Standards blackline masters.* Reston, VA: National Council of Teachers of Mathematics.

National Council of Teachers of Mathematics. (1991). *Professional standards for teaching mathematics.* Reston, VA: National Council of Teachers of Mathematics.

National Council of Teachers of Mathematics. (1989). *Curriculum and evaluation standards for school mathematics.* Reston, VA: National Council of Teachers of Mathematics.

Reese, G. C. (1999). The cereal box problem. Retrieved August 20, 1999 from the World Wide Web: <http://www.glenbrook.k12.il.us/ gbsmat/NCTM/cereal2.html>

Reid, D. A. (1999). Learning about algebra tiles: Activities for teachers. Retrieved August 20, 1999 from the World Wide Web: <http://plato.acadiau.ca/ courses/educ/reid/tiles/tiles.html>

Rosner, M. A. (1998). *Teaching mathematics with the internet.* El Segundo, CA: Classroom Connect.

Scherer, M. M. (Ed.). (1999). Integrating technology into the curriculum (journal focus issue). *Educational Leadership, 56* (5).

Schoaff, E. K. (1993). How to develop a mathematics lesson using technology. *Journal of Computers in Mathematics and Science Teaching, 12* (1), 19–27.

Sharp, R. M. (1997). *The best math and science web sites for teachers.* Eugene, OR: International Society for Technology in Education.

Solomon, G. (1995). Planning for technology. *Learning and Leading with Technology, 23* (1), 66–67.

TERC, Inc. (1999). *The tabletop, senior edition* (computer software). Novato, CA: Broderbund Software, Inc.

Walsch, T. P. (1996). Exploring difference equations with spreadsheets. *Learning and Leading with Technology, 24* (1), 28–32.

Resource Book Sampler

Albrecht, M., Bennett, D., & Block, S. (1997). *Discovering geometry with the Geometer's Sketchpad.* Berkeley, CA: Key Curriculum.

Alexander, B. (1994). *What if . . . ? Investigations with the TI-82 graphics calculator.* Scarborough, Ontario: Bob Alexander Publishing.

Browning, C. & Channell, D. E. (1997). *Explorations: Graphing calculator activities for enriching middle school mathematics.* Austin, TX: Texas Instruments.

Dale Seymour Publications. (1995). *Graphing power: High school activities for the TI-81 and TI-82.* Palo Alto, CA: Dale Seymour.

Dale Seymour Publications. (1995). *Graphing power: Middle school activities for the TI-81 and TI-82.* Palo Alto, CA: Dale Seymour.

DeMarois, P. (1996). *TI-83 or TI-82 mini-labs: Algebraic investigations.* Urbana, IL: MathWare.

Embse, C. V. & Engebretsen, A. (1996). *Explorations: Geometric investigations for the classroom.* Austin, TX: Texas Instruments.

Kelly, B. (1997). *Investigating calculus with the TI-92.* Burlington, Ontario: Brendan Kelly.

Kelly, B. (1997). *Investigating statistics with the TI-92.* Burlington, Ontario: Brendan Kelly.

Kelly, B. (1996). *Investigating advanced algebra with the TI-92.* Burlington, Ontario: Brendan Kelly.

Kutzler, B. (1997). *Introduction to the TI-92: Handheld computer algebra.* Hagenberg, Austria: bk teachware Lehrmitttel GmbH&CoKG.

Lund, C. & Andersen, E. (1998). *Graphing calculator activities.* Menlo Park, CA: Dale Seymour.

Lund, C. & Andersen, E. (1996). *Introduction to the TI-92.* Urbana, IL: MathWare.

Masalski, W. J. (1990). *How to use the spreadsheet as a tool in the secondary school mathematics classroom.* Reston, VA: National Council of Teachers of Mathematics.

Morgan, L. (1997). *Explorations: Statistics handbook for the TI-83.* Austin, TX: Texas Instruments.

Osborne, A. & Foley, G. D. (1990). *Graphing calculator and computer graphing laboratory manual: Precalculus series.* Reading, MA: Addison-Wesley.

Vervoort, G. & Mason, D. J. (1995). *Calculator math Level D.* Parsippany, NJ: Fearon Teacher Aids.

Vervoort, G. & Mason, D. J. (1995). *Calculator math level E.* Parsippany, NJ: Fearon Teacher Aids.

Video/Laser Disc Presentations

Futures Videos

Public Broadcasting System. (1990). *Futures 1 with Jamie Escalante* (12 fifteen-minute videos).

Public Broadcasting System. (1992). *Futures 2 with Jamie Escalante* (12 fifteen-minute videos).

Laser Disc Program

Learning Technology Center. (1992). *The adventures of Jasper Woodbury* (12 laser disc programs). Nashville, TN: Vanderbilt University.

Videos Available through COMAP

Discrete mathematics: Cracking the code. (1993).

Hour 1: Geometry: New tools for new technologies. (1992).

Hour 1: Statistics: Basic data analysis. (1992).

Hour 2: Statistics: Data analysis for one variable. (1992).

Hour 3: Statistics: Data analysis for two variables. (1992).

Hour 4: Statistics: Planning data collection. (1992).

Hour 5: Statistics: Introduction to inference. (1992).

Math TV: Geometry. (1987).

Math TV: Management science. (1987).

Math TV: New horizons. (1987).

Math TV: Statistics. (1987).

Assessment in Mathematics

When making curricular and instructional decisions, the classroom teacher must constantly assess whether the students are learning what is stated in the objectives or outcomes. Many people use the terms "assessment" and "evaluation" synonymously, but the definitions of these words are very different. Evaluation involves making final decisions regarding how much a student has learned, but assessment is a broader term that includes any type of data gathering about student achievement. As such, assessment encompasses much more than making decisions about grades.

The process of assessment is also difficult. If, for example, paper-and-pencil examinations are used to measure student outcomes, there will inevitably be students who have a clearer understanding of the content than the test will show. Conversely, some students are good test-takers and can bluff their way to a good grade in a traditional testing situation. Somehow, the assessment strategy needs to capture the full range of student abilities and dispositions, and this entails much more than administering written tests. This unit focuses on assessment strategies and the uses of classroom assessment. Chapter 8, "The Role of Assessment," looks at classroom assessment, from its purposes to the variety of strategies available to teachers. Chapter 9, "Standards and Equity in Assessment," explores assessment further, through discussions of the NCTM assessment Standards, achieving equity in assessment, and the process of determining grades.

The Role of Assessment

Upon reading Chapter 8, you should be able to answer the following questions:

- How is assessment defined, and what are some of its major purposes?

- What are some of the issues associated with the construction of tests in mathematics?

- Why might a teacher need to develop other strategies for assessing student progress in mathematics than paper-and-pencil tests and quizzes?

- What are several alternative assessment strategies available to teachers beyond the traditional tests, quizzes, and homework assignments? Describe them.

- What are some advantages and disadvantages of various assessment alternatives such as journals, rubrics, interviews, and checklists?

How often have you been in the middle of a class and heard someone ask, "Is this going to be on the test?" Think about the ramifications of the teacher's response. If the teacher says "no," then the class has an excuse for shutting down and not participating because students know that they will not be held accountable for the information. On the other hand, a response of "yes" tells the students that they will need to know the material to succeed in the class, and the message is to stay alert and keep working. In other words, the teacher's response sends out a message about what is important—what is *valued*—in the classroom. And, after all, isn't that what the student is really asking? "Is this going to be on the test?" loosely translates to, "Is this important enough for me to have to worry about?" Ideally, virtually everything we do in the classroom should be "tested" because if students didn't need to know it, the material was probably not worth spending time on in the first place. As many experts on assessment have maintained, we should not be upset about students asking whether something is on the test; they are simply doing what is natural for human beings—determining whether mastering a particular skill should be a priority.

In mathematics education, not everything that is valued in the classroom can be measured or assessed by a written test. For example, suppose that, in keeping with the Standards, problem solving and oral communication are priorities in the classroom. One cannot measure oral communication skills and ability to work with others on an individual paper-and-pencil test. So, the teacher either must abandon communication as a goal or devise another method by which to assess student progress in this area. Alternatives to traditional tests include such strategies as interviews, observations, and portfolios. These nontraditional assessment techniques allow the teacher to gather more powerful data about student progress than can be measured by most paper-and-pencil tests. In this chapter, we explore the issue of assessment, from the definition and purposes for assessment to the construction of mathematics tests and the use of alternative strategies for measuring progress. We will begin by defining what we mean by "assessment."

■ WHAT IS ASSESSMENT?

If your instructor told you that you were going to be assessed on your understanding of this chapter at the end of the week, how would you interpret that statement? What does it mean to assess someone? In a workshop for inservice mathematics teachers, the word "assessment" generated the following list:

evaluation	test	high stakes	portfolio
measurement	grades	proficiency tests	homework
classroom behavior	pass/fail	observations	standardized tests
achievement	accountability	diagnosis	quizzes

Notice that the majority of these responses focus on the process of testing, quizzing, giving grades, and determining whether a student has passed or failed. These images surface because most people have a tendency to associate assessment with testing and giving grades. But assessment goes beyond tests and grades; it includes gathering and analyzing information along the way as teaching occurs rather than *doing* something to students *at the end* of a lesson or a unit.

Educators generally differentiate between two types of assessment—formative and summative. **Formative assessment** is used throughout the teaching and learning cycle to determine whether an individual is progressing at an acceptable rate. Often, formative assessment provides students with some useful feedback on how they are doing and how they can improve their performance. On the other hand, **summative assessment** is a final evaluation of a person's performance. After all of the data have been gathered over time, the student is given a final course grade, or the employee is rated to determine whether a promotion is warranted. Formative assessment is conducted *along the way,* whereas summative assessment is done *at the end* as a *summary* of previous collected data. So, in a broad sense, what does it mean to assess a student in mathematics?

In 1995, the National Council of Teachers of Mathematics released its third set of Standards—*Assessment Standards for School Mathematics*. In this document, assessment was defined as "the process of gathering evidence about a student's knowledge of, ability to use, and disposition toward, mathematics and of making inferences from that evidence for a variety of purposes" (p. 3). The authors noted that evaluation, a final judgment of progress, is only one of many uses for assessment. So, when we think of assessment, we need to frame it in a very broad sense as a data collection process. The nature of students' questions can be used to informally assess their understanding of the content. Assessment can take on many forms, from written tests to observations, interviews, and projects—anything that can be used to generate data that will be helpful to the teacher who is guiding the teaching and learning process. Let's explore some of the uses for data collected through the assessment process.

■ PURPOSES FOR ASSESSMENT

Consider the following assessments that were conducted in an Algebra II class studying a unit on probability over the past two weeks:

1. Students were given a pretest on their knowledge of probability before beginning the unit.
2. Students worked problems in teams as the teacher circulated around the room, listening to their conversations.
3. The teacher asked students to go to the board to explain their solutions to assigned homework problems.
4. The teacher collected homework assignments and checked them into the gradebook as having been completed.
5. The teacher walked around the room while students were individually attempting to solve a problem and selected three students to briefly question about their understanding of the problem.
6. Students were given a 100-point test at the end of the unit on probability.
7. Students wrote journal entries, summarizing the major points of the unit and discussing which lessons were most effective for them and why.

As you can see, a number of different assessments were used throughout the unit. Some were more formal, such as giving pre- and posttests and checking homework assignments, whereas others were more informal, observing students working in groups, briefly interviewing a sample of students, and asking students to write journal entries. Assessments may be formal or informal in nature, but the objective is always the same—*to gather information* about how students are performing. You may notice that the unit test is summative: It provides a final score that theoretically represents the degree to which students mastered the concepts (we deal with perception versus reality in testing later in this chapter). However, other assessments, such as students explaining problems at the board, correcting homework assignments, and being interviewed, provide the teacher with some ongoing or formative information about how the unit is progressing. Ideally, every teacher should use a combination of formative and summative assessments to monitor and validate student learning.

While all seven of the items on the list would be considered some form of assessment, only two of them—checking homework into the gradebook and giving a unit test—were used to evaluate student learning and ultimately affected the students' grades. The other five assessments were used to monitor progress and to help the teacher to more effectively guide the instruction. In fact, a journal entry about the relative strength of lessons in the unit is useful in two ways: (1) It helps the students reflect on their learning experiences, and (2) it helps the teacher plan by providing insight into how the students in the class regard the lessons.

Certainly, one of the major reasons why a teacher assesses student progress is to have enough data to eventually make a final evaluation of student achievement in the form of a grade. This grade shows both the students and their parents to what degree the goals and objectives of the course have been mastered. But assessment also monitors student progress over time. A special education student, for example, may be on an IEP (an Individualized Educational Plan), which consists of a number of mathematical and personal goals for the school year with strategies to accomplish them. The teacher, then, conducts regular assessments in a variety of ways to determine whether the student is on-track toward reaching those preset goals. Similarly, a student who is being assessed with a portfolio, which we discuss later in more depth, also frequently sets goals for the next unit, grading period, or semester, and those assessments can be used to track the student's progress toward those goals.

Another reason for assessing student progress is to evaluate the effectiveness of an entire mathematics program—within a building, school district, state, or country. In many states, students are required to take some form of proficiency tests, which are statewide exams at particular grade levels and keyed to objectives in a state's model curriculum or standards. In some cases, students can't graduate from high school until they pass some sort of exit exam between grades 8 and 12. Scores on these types of tests are often published in the newspaper, so that the community can have a snapshot of how effective the school is in teaching the state's recommended curriculum. Proficiency tests are an issue of heated debate, because a student's graduation—indeed, that student's entire future—often rests on a single examination. Perhaps you had to take a proficiency test or two in school and have a few opinions of your own. One of the purposes for proficiency tests is to ensure that teachers are actually addressing outcomes stated in the curriculum, so scores may reflect the effectiveness of instruction as much as the achievement of students. The debate on proficiency testing and its effects continues as school districts attempt to be accountable to the public that pays their bills.

Because proficiency exams are aligned with a set of standards and student scores are based on the degree to which they have mastered those objectives, the proficiency tests are **criterion-referenced tests**. The criterion is the set of standards for that state. Similarly, many school districts give their own **competency tests,** which are criterion-referenced tests based upon the outcomes stated in the local course of study. These tests measure whether the objectives in the local curriculum are being mastered by students, pushing educators to stick to the script and follow the adopted course of study as we discussed in Chapter 4. Another type of test used to measure the success of a program is a **norm-referenced test.** Students in a particular district are compared against the norm, a sample of other students at the same grade level and age from around the country. The PSAT, SAT, and ACT tests are norm-referenced tests that measure whether a student or group of students is scoring at, above, or below the average as compared to a sample of other students. Children in the elementary and middle grades often take the ITBS or Iowa Test of Basic Skills, yet another norm-referenced test that is given to determine whether a district's program is keeping up with other districts around the country. Standardized tests—both criterion referenced and norm referenced—are generally used to determine the effectiveness of an entire program for a school, district, or state.

Although it is frequently overlooked, probably the most important use of assessment data is to assist the teacher in making instructional decisions. If, for example, the teacher in the probability unit of an Algebra II or Second-Year Integrated class observes several students making significant errors when solving a problem at their seats, a decision might be made to adjust the lesson plan for the next day to meet the needs of those students. If a series of random interviews indicates that students understand the concepts and could be challenged at a higher level, the teacher might choose to accelerate the pace of the unit or to assign some different tasks than originally planned. In Chapter 5, we discussed the importance of flexibility in lesson planning. Assessment should provide clear information about what students are thinking in order that the teacher can fine tune the lesson or unit accordingly. When assessment depends entirely on an end-of-the-chapter test, the data regarding student progress come in too late—by the time the teacher realizes that the students are confused and need intervention, the unit has been finished. Formative assessments along the way put the teacher in a much better position to help students and, thereby, to enhance the teaching and learning process.

The diagram in Figure 8–1 is taken from the NCTM *Assessment Standards* and summarizes four major purposes for assessment—evaluating student achievement, monitoring student progress, evaluating programs, and making instructional decisions:

Figure 8–1 The Four Purposes for Assessment and Their Results
(NCTM, *Assessment Standards for School Mathematics*, 1995, p. 25.)

Because assessment is conducted for a variety of reasons, it makes sense that teachers would use several methods for gathering data about student learning. Some means of assessment are very formal, such as written exams, while others are more informal, such as observations or brief interviews. We examine some assessment strategies, beginning with the more traditional written tests and then exploring such alternatives as the use of journals and portfolios.

■ TEST CONSTRUCTION

After a two-week unit on perimeter and area of polygons, the eighth grade mathematics teacher has decided to give the students a written test on their understanding of the major concepts. How does the teacher decide what to include on the test? What types of questions should be asked? How long should the test be? How can one ensure that a reasonable number of questions have been asked and yet not make the test so long that students are overwhelmed? The answers to these questions are not easy because there is no set formula for designing a test; therefore, teachers frequently struggle with this issue. Here are some suggestions to consider when constructing a written test.

Preparing Items

First, remember the purpose of the test—to determine the degree to which students have mastered the objectives set forth in the unit and lesson-planning process. Each item on the test should flow directly from the stated objectives. If one of the objectives states that "given a polygon with the lengths of the sides labeled, the student will determine its perimeter," then the test needs to give the students an opportunity to demonstrate that they can do that. And, unless the objectives talked about circumference and area of a circle, it would also be unfair to place items on the test that involved circles, because the focus of the unit was on polygons. In Chapter 5, we noted that it is often useful, when sketching out a unit plan, to list some examples of the types of problems the student should be able to solve by the end of the unit. Doing this in the unit planning makes the test construction much easier because samples of problems students should be able to solve have already been written. The key element here is that every item on the test should match up with a stated objective for the unit.

Second, construct the test items in such a way that the chances of a student being able to guess a correct answer are minimized. The *Curriculum and Evaluation Standards* document (1989) provides the example in Figure 8–2:

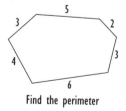

Find the perimeter

Figure 8–2 An Example of a Test Item on Perimeter

(NCTM, *Curriculum and Evaluation Standards for School Mathematics*, 1989.)

In a typical test on the topic of perimeter, students are asked to "Find the perimeter of this polygon." However, most students have learned enough about test taking to bluff their way through this type of an item. They realize that if the figure has six labeled sides, the only operation that makes sense is to add them all together, even if they have no idea what it means to find the perimeter! On the other hand, consider this problem: "Draw a six-sided figure that has a perimeter of 23 units." This alternate item makes it very difficult for students to bluff their way through the drawing without knowing anything about perimeter. Similarly, think of what happens when you give students a set of four polygons (see Figure 8–3) and ask them to find the area of each.

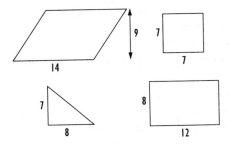

Figure 8–3 Find the Area of Each Polygon

Because students may be well aware that area involves multiplication, if they simply multiply the two given dimensions together in each case and write the answers on a blank, they are likely to get three out of the four correct, missing only the triangle question. On a hypothetical eight-item test containing four perimeter problems and the four area problems listed above, the student could get all of the perimeter problems and three out of four of the area problems—seven out of eight—correct without knowing anything about perimeter or area. Seven out of eight is the equivalent of 88 percent, which is a solid B on most grading scales. How do you feel about a student earning a B on a mathematics test without meeting any of the objectives of the unit? The point, of course, is that not only should the test items be carefully aligned with the stated goals and objectives of the unit, but they should also be written in a way that makes it as difficult as possible for students to bluff their way through the test. This is not to say that an entire test should be made up of questions like the alternative suggested for Figure 8–2; in fact, it is often desirable to place straightforward problems, such as the four diagrams and direction in Figure 8–3, on the test. But these items need to be balanced with enough nonroutine questions to help the teacher determine whether the student has mastered the concepts. This brings us to another important consideration when writing tests, the issue of length.

If you ask most secondary or middle school students about the ideal length for a test, they will often say that they would prefer that it be longer than shorter, because a longer test generally means that fewer points are deducted for each incorrect response. Yet, commonsense tells us that if a test is unreasonably long, many students are likely to look at it and give up, too overwhelmed to even attempt the tasks. The teacher should ask, "What kinds of things will the students need to be able to demonstrate to convince me that they have met the stated objectives?" Sometimes, this question may result in a test of no more than five items, and other times, because of the nature of the skills and competencies being developed, a test may require 20 items or more. Of course, the length of the class period also needs to be considered. If a mathematics class is forty-five minutes long, then the time factor will certainly drive the decisions about the nature and length of the test. Sometimes, teachers choose to spread a long test over two days, but this decision needs to be weighed against the loss of an additional forty-five minutes of instructional time.

After completing a unit involving the area and perimeter of squares, rectangles, parallelograms, and triangles, one way to test the class is to provide a series of 10 diagrams involving these figures, labeled with dimensions, and ask students to find the perimeter and area of each. By providing the class with 20 answer blanks (10 for area and 10 for perimeter), the students write their responses on the blanks, and the teacher counts the correct answers to determine a final score. If the student had 17 out of 20 items correct, the final grade would be an 85. But suppose, instead, that the teacher asked the following questions on the test:

1. Draw a rectangle whose perimeter is 20 and whose area is 24.
2. Draw a square whose perimeter is equal to its area.
3. Show, with diagrams and words, why the area of a triangle can be found by using the formula $A = \frac{1}{2}bh$.

How do you feel about this three-item test? The problems attempt to assess student understanding in a way that transcends the demonstration of a simple skill, and they often give us greater insight into a student's understanding of area and perimeter than traditional items typically provide. What would you think of a test that contained the four diagrams shown in Figure 8–3, coupled with these three questions? Perhaps a combination of skill-based and concept- or application-level items might be the best way to assess student understanding on a written test. Regardless of how the questions are asked, the test does not have to be lengthy to measure student understanding; it merely has to match the objectives and reduce the likelihood of students guessing most of the answers correctly.

A third issue to consider is how closely the assessment aligns with the day-to-day instructional practices that have been used. **Alignment** refers to the consistency of the type of questions raised and the tools required on an assessment as compared to the question formats and tools used in day-to-day instruction. Suppose, for example, that a high school mathematics teacher allows students to use a calculator to find trigonometric values when studying a unit on right triangles. If, on the unit test, students were given a table of trigonometric values and told that they are not allowed to use a calculator, this would be like training an employee on a computer but evaluating that person's job performance by requiring proficiency with a manual typewriter. The skills and tools required in the classroom should be mirrored in the assessment situation for two reasons: (1) Students should see a consistency between what is emphasized during classtime and what the teacher is expecting them to be able to do on a test. (2) The test items are a reflection of what the teacher sees as important, and these values should be consistent in both the classroom and the test. Otherwise, students may become confused and ask, "We used a calculator in class yesterday, so why can't we use one on the test today?" Widespread changes in the use of technology in the classroom, for example, spurred the creators of the SAT test to go from a rule of "calculators are prohibited" to "calculators are recommended." If a test is so computation driven that a student with a calculator can easily get most or all of the items correct, then the problem is not with the use of the calculator; it's probably with the design of the test. Alignment is all about consistency, and a teacher needs to be able to look at a test and ask, "Are the question formats and tools required for success on this test the same ones that I have emphasized in class during each day of the unit?"

Ensuring Validity and Reliability

Although this chapter will not discuss statistical measures in depth, it is important to note that any written assessment has a certain validity and reliability associated with it. **Validity** is a measure of the degree to which a test actually measures the content that the teacher intends it to measure. We often hear about students who do well in a class but then struggle on the written tests. This situation sometimes arises because the tests are not valid—they do not adequately measure the concepts emphasized in the class.

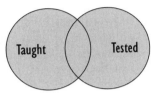

Figure 8–4 Relationship Between Outcomes Taught and Tested

Figure 8–4 illustrates the relationship between concepts that are *taught* and those that are *tested* on written assessments. Ideally, that which is taught is equivalent to that which is tested, and the two circles merge into one. However, much more is often taught in the classroom than is ever actually measured on a written assessment. On the other hand, a teacher preparing a test may inadvertently include items that do not align with instruction, so content is tested that was not directly taught. The overlap of the circles represents those concepts that were both emphasized in the class and assessed on the test. The more these circles overlap, the greater the validity of the test. In designing tests, teachers are trying to ensure that the assessment actually measures the content that was taught and emphasized in the classroom.

The **reliability** of a test refers to the likelihood that a student will obtain roughly the same score if given different versions of the test multiple times. A good test is one that the student could take twice (or, more realistically, take two similar versions of the same test, since taking the exact same test twice will inevitably raise the score due to familiarity with the questions) and score about the same each time. A reliable test score will serve as a fair representation of a student's knowledge level of the content. When students boast that they bluffed their way through a test and pulled an A, then it's likely that the test was not reliable, because the student could have just as easily bluffed and missed most of the items. Again, teachers should design tests so as to maximize the reliability of the instrument.

Scoring Student Work

Suppose that a student solved an equation on a written test in the following manner:

$$2x - 4(x - 3) = 10$$
$$2x - 4x - 12 = 10$$
$$-2x - 12 = 10$$
$$-2x = 22$$
$$x = -11$$

The correct solution to the equation, however, is +1. So, as a teacher, you have some choices to make in terms of scoring the item. Let's suppose the question is worth 10 points. You could insist on a perfect solution, put a line through the answer, and take off 10 points. In fact, some teachers tell their classes that the slightest error in calculation when designing a bridge can make the bridge tumble into the water; therefore, they do not accept even the most minor mistake. But let's analyze the error carefully. Notice that the only mistake the student made was on the first step, when −12, rather than +12, resulted from multiplying two negative numbers in applying the Distributive Property. From that point on, the rest of the steps and the solution are correct and consistent with one another. Consequently, you might say that the student was on the right track and understood the major concept and award the student half credit or 5 of the 10 points. Still another way to look at it is to consider each step of the equation as worth 2 points, and because one multiplication error was the only mistake made, you could award the student 8 of the 10 points. Of course, the choice that a teacher makes on scoring this type of an item will significantly impact test scores and final grades. If a student made a minor error in each of 10 equations on a short test or quiz, one teacher might assign a grade of 0 to that student, but a second teacher might assign a score of 50, and another would give the student an 80. In the first two cases, the student who makes a few minor computational errors will receive an F on the test, but the student in the third class will earn a C or low B. Which grade is the most reasonable? Is it fair to give a student who makes these kinds of mistakes an F? To which philosophy do you subscribe?

Deciding how to score student responses on a written test goes beyond gut feelings and opinion. Instead, think of the test as sending out a message to your students about what you value as a teacher. The first teacher values the student getting the right answers. We might wonder, for example, how that teacher would respond if the student simply wrote down +1 as an answer without showing any of the steps required to get to this answer. Would the first teacher award 10 points for the right answer or 0 points because no work was shown? Conversely, the second and third teachers emphasize and value the process involved in obtaining a correct solution. By scoring the item as 5 or 8 out of 10 points even though the final answer is incorrect, the teacher is essentially telling the student, "I value your thinking and because you know how to solve the equation, I will award some or most of the points to you." The emphasis, then, is not only on the correct answer but on whether the student understands the process of solving an equation. The second and third teachers are likely to award few, if any, points if the student writes down a correct answer but does not show what steps were taken in order to get the answer.

So, your decision about how to score items on a written test should be based on your philosophy of what is important in the classroom. If you value mathematical processes, including thinking and reasoning, then this position will be apparent by the way that you assign points to partial or incorrect answers. A teacher, on the other hand, who views mathematics as cut and dry and emphasizes only the "right answers" will grade accordingly. Of course, some questions such as definitions can only have one right answer. If a student who is asked for the name of a triangle in which each angle measures 60° answers, "right triangle," no teacher is likely to assign any partial credit to the answer. However, a written test should give students the opportunity to not only identify terms but to demonstrate mathematical thinking. Making reasonable judgments about how to award points for mathematical thinking is up to each teacher and is not as easy as it sounds.

Including Review Items

Some mathematics teachers include review items on a written test to ensure that students continue to review and study skills and concepts from earlier units. If a middle school class has progressed from studying the metric system to exploring graphing, the teacher may choose to include a few items on the graphing test that review the metric system. Of course, these review items are not a surprise; the class should be told, in advance, what type of review items to expect. In this way, the review items motivate students to go back and review prior concepts, and class performance on these items can provide the teacher with evidence as to whether students are progressing or whether they have forgotten prior topics.

The idea of including review items on tests has surfaced in some major textbooks and their test booklets. These authors see each test as a measure of everything that has been discussed since the first day of class. Although this might seem overwhelming to students at first, this point of view can actually assist them in keeping up with the concepts and making connections along the way. If teachers believe that the practice of placing review items on tests is worthwhile, then they have to decide how much of the test to devote to review. Again, there is no formula or typical way for teachers to make this decision. A rule of thumb might be to allow no more than one third of the test for review and let the other two thirds measure students on new concepts that have been developed since the last test.

Unfortunately, no matter how valid or reliable the test is and no matter how the teacher scores the individual items, no individual test can accurately measure a student's achievement. A written test has a number of limitations. First, a test is a snapshot—a forty-five-minute glimpse of student performance on a particular day on a set of items written by the teacher or a textbook publisher. It cannot possibly capture all of the dimensions of learning and usually provides no opportunity for the student to react, ask a question, or follow up a response with a question or an explanation. Second, some students are simply not good test takers. As we noted in Chapter 2, many students have mathematics anxiety and freeze up when they are given a written test. They may understand the concepts but are unable to effectively demonstrate their comprehension in a written testing situation. Third, as we have seen, the score on a written test often has little meaning because two teachers will grade the same test differently. Teacher A may give the student 71%, and Teacher B may give the student 93% on the same paper because they employ different grading practices. In turn, the scores might cause a person to ask, "93% of what?" In a sense, the numerical scores are almost arbitrary as they depend not only on student performance but on teacher opinion about how the tests should be graded.

Limitations on the value of written tests have sent educators in search of other methods to assess student understanding. In order to capture the diversity of thinking and the depth of comprehension, a number of other assessment strategies are available to teachers of mathematics. The next section describes a few of the more common assessment alternatives that a mathematics teacher can use in conjunction with or in place of more traditional test scores to paint a picture of student progress.

■ ALTERNATE STRATEGIES FOR ASSESSING STUDENT PROGRESS

Journals

Students in an introductory algebra course have been given the following task as illustrated in Figure 8–5:

> *Toothpicks are arranged on a table to create a string of squares as shown in Figure 8–5. Determine the total number of toothpicks required to build the structure 10 squares long. Also, find a formula for determining the number of toothpicks required if you know the number of squares, x. Explain your reasoning.*

Figure 8–5 Forming Squares with Toothpicks

Within a few minutes, one student raises a hand and says, "It would take 31 toothpicks to make ten squares, and the formula is $3x + 1$." Other students nod their heads in agreement, and the bell signals the end of the period. As students leave the classroom, the teacher wonders whether every student in the class really understood how to solve the problem. Also, it is not clear how the student who answered the question found either the answer or the formula, and the teacher can't even be certain that other students used the same formula to solve the problem.

As an alternative, the teacher could have posed the problem near the end of the period and asked students to write their responses in a **mathematics journal,** a binder or spiral notebook containing student writing that reflects their thinking, problem-solving approaches, and opinions. The math journal is considered an assessment tool because each student can write about a problem or classroom issue and know that these reflections are being "heard" by the teacher. The teacher can use the journal entries to determine the progress of the class and to make instructional decisions for the future. The following journal entries, for example, were generated in response to the toothpick-square problem.

Student I:

I made a list of values like this:

x	1	2	3	4	x
y	4	7	10	13	$4 + 3(x - 1)$

I saw that each one of the squares was the original square containing 4 toothpicks added to 3 toothpicks for each extra square. So, I took 3 times one less than the number of squares and added that to the first square with 4 toothpicks. From that formula, I could find the total toothpicks for 10 squares to be 31.

Student 2:

For my formula, I found $4x - (x - 1)$. I pretended like each square took 4 toothpicks, and that's how I got my $4x$. Then, I figured that the left side of the square was missing a toothpick for every one of them except for the first, so I took away $x - 1$ toothpicks from the $4x$. If you put 10 into the formula, you get 31 toothpicks to form 10 squares.

Student 3:

If you take off the last toothpick on the left, each square is really only made of 3 toothpicks, not 4. So, if you multiply 3 times x, that will leave you 1 toothpick short of the total. So, for my formula, I used $3x + 1$. If you put 10 in for x, you find that 10 squares will need 31 toothpicks.

Student 4:

I looked at how many toothpicks it took across the top, along the bottom, and vertically. For x squares, you use x toothpicks across the top, x toothpicks across the bottom, and 1 more than x toothpicks vertically (you have to add 1 because of the toothpick on the left that starts the chain). So, for my formula, I used $x + x + x + 1$. Using 10 for x, you find that 10 squares will need 31 toothpicks.

Interestingly, all four of these students obtained the correct answer of 31 toothpicks and generated an acceptable formula. However, you may also notice that the mathematical thinking and what the students were visualizing were very different in each case. If we look beyond the answers, we discover individual differences that would not have been readily apparent if we had simply asked the class for a solution. Also, students can be creative in journal entries because they are not restricted by the thinking of others. We often find that one student's explanation of a solution can hinder others from thinking divergently because others feel that if the person who contributed was "right," then their answer is either wrong or irrelevant. If students think that one particular student is always right, then they have little incentive to contribute a solution or process that differs from the answer of that individual. When students first address the problem in a journal, they are more inclined to share and express their approaches in class that day or in the future. Writing in the journal thus actually promotes rich classroom discourse.

Of course, the teacher gains valuable information from the students' journals as well. For example, the teacher of the class just described had not yet talked about similar terms in the course. But the four stated formulas, $4 + 3(x - 1)$, $4x - (x - 1)$, $3x + 1$, and $x + x + x + 1$, provide an excellent opportunity to distribute algebra tiles to the class and explore why these four expressions are equivalent to one another—a teachable moment. In this way, the discussion of similar terms flows naturally from the toothpick-square problem rather than being viewed as a disconnected, new topic in a textbook chapter. If we read journal entries carefully, they can give us insights into student thinking that suggest patterns for intervening when misconceptions arise as well as determining teaching strategies for the future.

Mathematics journals can be written at virtually any grade level. Some teachers have students write in journals on a daily basis, and others require their students to do so once or twice a week. Often, students are given a **prompt**—a question or problem posed to a class, which is either to be addressed in class or for an assignment in the journal. Some generic journal prompts that can be useful to both the teacher and the student are:

- *What was the most difficult topic we studied this week? What made it difficult for you?*
- *How do you think that you performed on today's test? What was the easiest part of the test and why?*
- *Complete this thought: Compared to the past ten weeks, my recent performance in mathematics has been . . . .*
- *Which homework problem gave you the most trouble last night? What did you learn about this problem in class today?*
- *How much time did you spend on your homework last night? Describe how and where you did your work (e.g., at the table, in your room, working alone, working with a friend on the phone, with help from a parent, etc.).*
- *Comment on the teaching strategies used this week. Were the classes effective? Why or why not?*

Many secondary and middle school teachers have multiple classes and may teach 150 or more students. So, daily writing in and regular collection of the journals may be unrealistic. Each teacher needs to decide what is a possible and helpful schedule for collecting data about student progress and the effectiveness of lessons. Journal entries might be made once or twice a week and collected in rotating classes (e.g., Period 1 this week, Periods 2 and 3 next week, etc.) to make the task more manageable. Remember that the information gained by reading individual insights often allows the teacher to get to know each student far better than would be possible without this tool. Another example of a nontraditional assessment in mathematics is the use of open-ended questions and rubrics on which to score student responses. We explore this strategy in the next section.

Open-Ended Questions and Rubrics

An **open-ended question** is one in which there are either multiple acceptable answers or one right answer with multiple means of arriving at the solution. Teachers use open-ended questions to gather information about how students are thinking about a problem and to send out the message that student thinking processes are valued. So, instead of asking a student to find the probability of pulling the ace of hearts from a deck of ordinary playing cards, a teacher might challenge the student to describe a situation in which one would have a one-in-four chance of winning when pulling one card from a deck. The student is not being required to simply recall a fact or solve a simple problem. Instead, the student is expected to produce a game or situation. Sometimes this type of question is referred to as a **performance task** because the student has to make, display, create, or explain something—to perform.

In California in 1988, twelfth graders were asked to respond to the following question (California Assessment Program, 1989):

Imagine you are talking to a student in your class on the telephone and want the student to draw some figures. The other student cannot see the figures. Write a set of directions so that the other student can draw the figures exactly as shown in Figure 8–6.

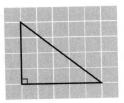 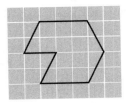

Figure 8–6 Describing a Polygon on a Standardized Test
(Reprinted by permission of the California Department of Education.)

This item tested students' ability to use proper geometric language to describe a polygon. A number of misconceptions surfaced, and less than 15% of approximately 500 twelfth-grade papers demonstrated an acceptable response. Most teachers would agree that even a middle school child should be able to effectively describe a right triangle, but relatively few of these high school seniors were able to do this. This information gives us a clearer picture of the type of communication that needs to occur on a regular basis in the classroom if students are to become more adept at using proper mathematical terminology.

Recognizing the difficulty that students may have in using proper terminology to describe polygons, the teacher could intervene by providing the class with a task using a **geoboard**, a square board, made of plastic or wood, that contains pegs that are generally arranged in a square. Many geoboards contain 25 pegs (5 × 5), but some are as large as 12 × 12 (144 pegs) or have pegs arranged in a circular pattern. By placing rubber bands (geobands) on the geoboard, students can produce images of such geometric figures as the polygon in Figure 8–7.

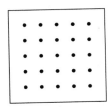 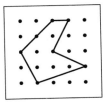

Figure 8–7 A Geoboard and a Concave Hexagon Created on a Geoboard

Geoboards can be used to study the properties of triangles, angle measurement, area, perimeter, the Pythagorean Theorem, and a host of other mathematical concepts.

Suppose that the teacher arranges the class in pairs, gives each student a geoboard and a geoband, and asks each person to sit back to back with a partner. One person from each pair is asked to create any polygon on the geoboard. Then, that student has to describe it to the partner so completely that the partner eventually can create exactly the same polygon without ever having seen it. This exercise can be very powerful and requires students to use accurate terminology as they provide directions to their partners. We might expect that the activity would improve the performance of students on an item such as the one in Figure 8–6. The open-ended question then can provide data indicating that students need more practice in communicating mathematically and sends the teacher in search of an activity through which to provide the practice.

Considerably more is learned from the open-ended item in Figure 8–6 than would have been gained by asking a list of such fill-in questions as, "The triangle is an example of a(n) _____ triangle" that emphasize recall over understanding. Generally speaking, open-ended or free-response questions, as they are often called, allow the teacher to ask richer questions that tell us a great deal about how students think.

Because students may often be able to respond in a variety of ways to an open-ended question, a simple right-or-wrong scoring strategy or even a partial-credit approach may not be appropriate. Instead, teachers often use a rubric, a generalized scoring standard that can be applied to an open-ended question as discussed in Chapter 1. A student's rubric score indicates the level at which a response can be placed. Some rubrics are simple, containing only three levels—high, middle, and low—whereas, others may have seven to ten levels. The 1992 National Assessment of Education Progress (NAEP) exam used a six-level rubric, with scoring levels spanning from a 0 to a 5. The descriptors of student's response categories are presented in Table 8–1.

Table 8–1 Six-Level NAEP Scoring Rubric

Score	Level	Descriptor
0	No Response	There is no response.
1	Incorrect Response	The work is completely incorrect or irrelevant. Or the response states, "I don't know."
2	Minimal	The response demonstrates a minimal understanding of the problem posed but does not suggest a reasonable approach. Although there may or may not be some correct mathematical work, the response is incomplete, contains major mathematical errors, or reveals serious flaws in reasoning. Examples are absent.
3	Partial	The response contains evidence of a conceptual understanding of the problem in that a reasonable approach is indicated. However, on the whole, the response is not well developed. Although there may be serious mathematical errors or flaws in the reasoning, the response does contain some correct mathematics. Examples provided are inappropriate.
4	Satisfactory	The response demonstrates a clear understanding of the problem and provides an acceptable approach. The response also is generally well developed and coherent but contains minor weaknesses in the development. Examples provided are not fully developed.

Score	Level	Descriptor
5	*Extended*	The response demonstrates a complete understanding of the problem, is correct, and the methods of solution are appropriate and fully developed. Responses scored 5 are logically sound, clearly written, and do not contain any significant mathematical errors. Examples are well chosen and fully developed.

(Dossey et al., 1993, p. 89.)

Using the framework in Table 8–1, teachers can ask students an open-ended (free-response) question and score or place them at a particular level based on the categories listed. In this sense, the numbers actually mean something. In other words, a score of a 4 indicates a performance level that is clearly described in the rubric. Contrast this score with an 86% on a test, which does not tell us anything specific in terms of content mastery. It is important to remember that rubric scores generally have nothing to do with percentages. A score of 4 on an open-ended question does *not* imply 4 out of 5 or 80% of the points. Instead, the number merely places the response into a category, and by recording the response levels over time, the teacher can track a student's growth in answering these types of questions.

Notice also that this rubric can be used to score anything from an equation-solving task to a problem in which a student is to find the area of some irregular shape. Rubrics provide a *holistic* alternative to scoring a student's response because, instead of looking at each step of the process and assigning credit based on pieces of a solution (often referred to as an analytic grading scale), the teacher looks at the whole and places the response into a category. Scoring papers on a rubric can be time consuming, particularly for the novice teacher. It can also be a shock to the student who has never been assessed in this manner. However, as the teacher becomes more adept at using a particular rubric, it can actually save time in the long run, because it takes the guesswork out of assigning performance levels. After all, the rubric states what the student needed to do, and all the teacher is doing is determining whether the student met particular criteria. Then, the score on the paper has meaning to the student because the rubric category of the paper provides feedback on what is needed for a better performance. Most importantly, the use of scoring rubrics allows student papers to be graded according to established and well-communicated criteria rather than by comparing one student's paper to another. The rubric communicates the expectations to students, and the subjectivity in scoring responses is minimized.

Individual and Team Projects

As another alternative to more traditional written tests, the teacher has the option of assigning individual or team projects. Students in a high school geometry class, after completing an introductory unit on fractals, were asked to design their own fractal picture, draw the image to show five iterations, and generate and solve a mathematical problem using the algorithm, such as exploring what happens to the area or perimeter after *n* iterations. A scoring rubric was then developed that included mathematical rigor, creativity, and neatness of the work. The teacher employed this project instead of a test to obtain a more *authentic* look at student understanding of fractals than could be gained by asking students to answer a list of questions.

A middle school mathematics teacher who had just completed a unit on ratio and proportion, including unit pricing, assigned a project in which students were required to visit a local grocery store sometime within a one-week time frame and collect price information on large and small containers of twenty foods. Then, students had to determine and compare unit prices, providing the data in a table and writing their findings and observations into a short paper. Finally, each student was required to make a five-minute presentation to the class on the results of the study. The scoring rubric included accuracy of the calculations, depth of the data analysis, clarity of writing, and organization of the presentation. Not only did this project assess student understanding of unit pricing, but it also emphasized communication in written and oral forms and went beyond just having students find the unit price for several items on a written exam.

The following problem-posing project was assigned by the teacher of a First-Year Integrated course during the last two months of the academic year to determine whether students could apply algebraic reasoning skills to some real-life problem solving context. Students worked alone on the task and made presentations to the class. The characteristics of a good problem as well as the rubric used for scoring the project were developed by the students themselves as a class activity. Many teachers find that when students are actively involved in developing the task and its scoring rubric, they are more likely to assume ownership of the project. This ownership, in turn, results in a higher level of student performance because they helped to determine the criteria for grading the project.

PROBLEM-POSING PROJECT: INTEGRATED MATHEMATICS, YEAR ONE

Rationale:
Throughout the school year, you have solved a wide variety of problems, dealing with issues from predicting the death rate in a group of smokers to determining which of two local Internet services is the most economically feasible. But all of these problems had one thing in common: They were posed by an instructor for you to solve. The purpose of this assignment is to get you to identify and pose an interesting problem that someone else could solve by using the algebra skills we have developed this year.

Task:
Your assignment is to do the following:

• Identify/create and pose an interesting mathematics problem that can be solved by using the algebraic knowledge we have developed this year.
• Explain *why* you think this a worthwhile and interesting problem.
• Outline a process by which the problem can be solved (although you need not actually solve the problem in its entirety, partly because it may not be possible to do that—for example, some problems we posed this year could only be explored by collecting classroom data over time) and/or solve the problem.

A *typewritten* paper is to be turned in on the due date, and the paper must include all of the three parts listed above.

A *classroom presentation* of your problem will be given to a small group of students on the due date. You will have 10 minutes to present your problem, reasons why you saw it as interesting, and its solution to the rest of the group.

Timeline:

5/14	(Tuesday)	Explanation of rationale and task
		• Journal entry to consider scoring process
5/21	(Tuesday)	Development of scoring rubric
5/28	(Tuesday)	Problems are due

A Good Problem

The class has defined a good, worthwhile problem as one that

- makes you think
- is realistic (real life)
- requires algebraic thinking skills
- is interesting
- evokes curiosity
- is one that we can relate to
- does not necessarily have just one or any solutions
- lends itself to having different ways to solve it
- has enough data presented and is worded well enough to be solvable
- is unique and not merely a copy of another problem we have solved

Assessment Criteria:

The project will be worth 50 points—½ of a regular test score. You also have the option of doubling your project to be worth 100 points, but this choice must be made when you hand in the project. Your final grade on the assignment will be determined as follows: 40 points = written paper; 10 points = class presentation

Written Paper
Your written paper will be scored on a 5-level rubric as follows (it is possible for your project to fall between two categories as well):

40 Points (A)
- Must include all three sections (problem, explanation of why it is a worthwhile problem, and solution)
- Not only are all three sections included, but they are all carefully written and clearly communicated
- Problem meets a majority of the good-problem criteria
- Contains a solution that makes sense to the reader
- If there are multiple solutions possible, this must be pointed out and discussed in the paper
- The problem and related writing is interesting to read
- Paper is neatly prepared and on time

35 Points (B)	• Must include all three sections
	• Problem meets a majority of the good-problem criteria *or* the problem is not great, but the supporting writing is excellent
	• The discussion about the value of the problem may be somewhat weak *or* the solution to the problem may be sketchy and unclear
	• Multiple solutions may not have been discussed or recognized by the writer
	• The problem and related writing is fairly interesting to read
	• Paper is neatly prepared and on time
32 Points (C)	• Must include all three sections
	• Problem may not meet most good-problem criteria and be just a fair problem
	• The paper, overall, presents both a weak discussion about the value of the problem and a sketchy discussion of its solution
	• The problem and writing are not particularly interesting
	• Bare minimum requirements are covered, but the problem and its related discussion and solution could have been considerably strengthened
	• Paper is fairly neat and on time
28 Points (D)	• May not include a significant discussion or solution at all
	• Problem does not meet most of the good-problem criteria and is weak
	• Discussion and solution are both sketchy and unclear
	• Paper is not interesting to read overall
	• It is evident that the point about what makes a good problem has been missed
0 Points (F)	• Assignment is not completed on time or at all

Class Presentation
This part of the grade will come from the peers in your small group who observe your presentation. Each member of your group will rate you on each of the following: (1) value of the problem, (2) discussion of its value, (3) presentation of the solution, (4) your overall attitude and presentation style.

One student in this class decided that, for her project, she would investigate whether it was better for her to count the project as being worth 50 or 100 points. She wrote equations based on her current grade in the class, graphed them, and found a break-even point in terms of the minimum score she needed to attain, above which making the project worth 100 points would be to her advantage. The intent of this project is clear: It challenges the students to think about real-life applications of the algebra that they have studied and to explore a problem of interest to them. As such, the project gives the teacher a unique window into the thinking of students.

More recent textbooks, particularly the NSF-funded curriculum project materials described in Chapter 4, tend to include assessment packages that provide teachers with performance tasks and projects that students can complete as alternatives to testing. In fact, many of the more recent resource books include the tasks, solutions, and suggestions for how to score the tasks on a rubric. Several resources that can be used as sources of these tasks and that provide further direction on how to design projects have been included in the resource listing at the end of this chapter. Sometimes, identifying worthwhile projects and organizing them can be time consuming for the classroom teacher. But, again, the key question that a mathematics teacher needs to ask is, "Can I learn more about my students by assigning a short-term or long-term project than from giving a written test?" This decision, in part, will depend on what kind of a message the teacher wants to send regarding the nature of mathematics. By assigning projects, the students not only engage in an alternative assessment task, but they also gain a first-hand experience with "doing" mathematics, rather than simply solving a few routine exercises for the teacher.

Observations and Checklists

Perhaps the most powerful way to assess student understanding is to watch what the student is doing in class—to observe. In the 1993 NCTM *Yearbook*, which focused on the topic of assessment, the author quoted the following five recommendations about classroom assessment that have been offered by others over time:

1. In general, observation, discussion, and interview serve better than paper and pencil tests in evaluating a pupil's ability to understand the principles and procedures he [sic] uses.
2. Information is best collected through informal observation of students as they participate in class discussions, attempt to solve problems, and work on various assignments individually or in groups.
3. Evaluation of the thinking and procedures employed by students is usually better done by careful observation and interview than by objective testing.
4. From the standpoint of the classroom teacher in particular, frequent *informal* observations of student behavior have a vital role to play in the evaluation process. They neither replace nor are replaced by the more formal observations of student behavior that are made on the basis of tests and the like.
5. Observation of the pupil's oral and written work . . . [is] a very important testing procedure and should be encouraged. Closely associated with the observation technique is the interview with the pupil regarding his daily work or his solution or attempted solution of items of a test (Lambdin, 1993, p. 8).

Interestingly, these quotes come from 1946 (Sueltz, Boyton, & Sauble), 1989 (*Curriculum and Evaluation Standards*), 1961 (Sueltz), 1970 (Weaver), and 1951

(Spitzer), respectively. In other words, for more than 50 years, educators have argued that observations and interviews with students are the best ways to determine whether they are making progress in a mathematics class. Although written tests, journals, and projects certainly also provide a great deal of insight, there is no substitute for watching students work and asking them questions about a particular problem or task as they solve it. But observing students as they work is a skill and, as is true for any other assessment strategy, there are specific techniques for conducting effective observations in the classroom. There are several informal observation opportunities, such as watching students work at the chalkboard or asking for a show of hands, but other more detailed techniques are available as well. We will discuss a few of them here.

Suppose that students are working on a problem in teams, and the teacher wants to make notes about how the individuals or teams are performing. If the teacher circulates about the room and takes notes onto a sheet of paper, this will necessitate recopying the notes onto some other form or page later on and is not time-efficient. Instead, one popular observational strategy is for the teacher to carry a set of mailing labels on a clipboard. If, as students work, the teacher notices that Susan has observed that a pattern of numbers involves perfect squares, the teacher can write Susan's name, the date, and the following statement on the label:

noticed a pattern of perfect squares when others in the team did not

At the end of the period, the teacher simply pulls the label from the sheet and sticks it on a premade page with Susan's name on it for future reference. If this strategy is used regularly, over time, the teacher will amass a number of mailing label observations for each student. These labels provide the teacher with a picture of that particular student's participation and insights over the grading period. When it comes time for parent-teacher conferences, instead of having to describe Susan by reading off lists of numbers, the teacher has rich observational data and can report specifically what Susan did or did not do on particular days in class. Parents appreciate these details much more than numerical averages. As we have discussed, a number really doesn't convey how a student is performing on a day-to-day basis in the classroom. Similarly, some teachers make observations on Post-it notes and stick them directly on the students' desks so that they are aware of what the teacher saw when passing by their work stations. Then, at the end of the period, the Post-its are collected and placed on the student page in an assessment binder. Again, this process formalizes the observations so that teachers are not only watching how students are performing but are also recording and compiling the data to look for changes over time.

It is sometimes helpful to have a checklist of anticipated behaviors or skills during the class period. Then, instead of writing anecdotal comments on labels or pages, the teacher assesses by determining whether a student meets the criteria spelled out on the checklist. For example, one teacher decided that she would try to observe process skills and told the students that she would be listening to their team conversations for evidence of problem solving, reasoning, communication, connections, and representation skills. She sat down ahead of time and made a list of a few behaviors that she might observe which would provide evidence of these processes being developed in the classroom. Table 8–2 presents some criteria from her list:

Table 8–2 Sample Checklist of Mathematical Process Skills

Problem Solving	• uses a variety of strategies • demonstrates high level of thinking • shows persistence in problem solving • is able to analyze and understand a problem
Reasoning	• is able to justify thinking • recognizes a reasonable solution • asks questions such as Why? What if? What would happen? Couldn't we?
Communication	• is effective listener • is willing to help others • presents thinking and results in an understandable manner • produces clearly written work
Connections	• recognizes usefulness of concepts • recalls related tasks • uses prior knowledge effectively • asks "How is this different from . . . " • sees the connection between today's lesson and the past (or with other subject areas)
Representation	• uses representations to model real-life data • is able to use multiple representations of the same problem • demonstrates effective mathematical communication with teammates by utilizing proper representations

Another teacher was more interested in how well students were working together as a team in a problem-solving task and created the form in Table 8–3.

Table 8–3 Observation Checklist for Cooperative Learning Team Behaviors

Student Name	Behavior	Rating (−, ✓, +) and Comments
	Assists others who are having difficulty	
	Remains on-task when problem solving	
	Open to hearing suggestions from team members	
	Discusses, rather than argues, with other team members	
	Works with others and does not move ahead of the team	

After placing the student's name in the box on the left, the teacher can record up to five characteristics of the individual's performance in teamwork. Making ratings or writing brief comments gives the teacher a framework with which to assess student performance in a cooperative learning environment. The observation checklist serves as a reflection of what the teacher values during classroom teamwork. Students should be given a copy of the form in advance so that they know what the teacher is planning to record and they can reflect on what the teacher believes is important. As we know, the checklist can be particularly powerful when students become involved in designing the criteria. The teacher can ask, "I am about to observe you working in teams and want to make some notes about what I see. Can you help me to make a list of the types of behaviors that I would hope to see at your tables?" Students then make suggestions; the teacher writes them on the board or on poster paper, and the list is narrowed to a Final Form that is used for an observation sheet. Students who help develop their own checksheets will most certainly know what is expected of them, because they wrote the criteria for participation themselves. The teacher, however, needs to keep in mind that any kind of observation is a glimpse of student performance, as students will often point out that "you came by my desk at a bad time; I figured out the next problem by myself, and you weren't there to see it." Consequently, observation data need to be placed in context with other assessment data. Another way to gather data on performance is through formal and informal student interviews.

Interviews

As the teacher observes students at work on a problem alone or in a team, it is almost inevitable that the teacher will want to ask, "Why are you solving the problem that way?" or "Can you explain the table that you just constructed?" to gain additional insight into student thinking. As soon as these questions surface, the teacher moves into interview mode. Interviewing students is one of the best ways to find out what they are thinking because the technique involves a one-on-one discussion, and, unlike a written test, the interview allows the teacher to pursue particular points with follow-up questions.

Thomas has been exploring the graphs of quadratic equations on his graphing calculator, and Ms. Breckenridge approaches his desk:

Ms. Breckenridge: Can you tell me about what you're doing, Thomas?

Thomas: Yes, I'm trying to find a pattern, but I'm not seeing it.

Ms. Breckenridge: What have you tried so far?

Thomas: Well, we were supposed to graph $y = x^2$ and then compare that to the graph of $y = 2x^2 + 3$. I did that, but they pretty much look the same to me.

Ms. Breckenridge: Pretty much? What does that mean?

Thomas: I mean, they're basically the same shape, so I don't know where to go from there.

Ms. Breckenridge: You said they're basically the same, so you must not think the two graphs are exactly the same, right?

Thomas: No, they aren't exactly the same . . . one is . . . I don't know . . . .

Ms. Breckenridge: One is . . . ?

Interviewing is a powerful assessment technique that allows the teacher to probe individual student responses.

Thomas: Well, one is, like, skinnier than the other one. When you graph the x^2 one and compare it to the $2x^2$ one, the second one is skinnier.

Ms. Breckenridge: Oh, so you *did* notice *something*. Do you have any predictions about what other graphs like this might look like?

Thomas: I guess I would predict that if you graph, say $y = 3x^2$, it would even be skinnier. (Thomas proceeds to draw the graph of the new function.) Yep, I was right. It's almost like that number that multiplies the squared term determines how skinny or steep it is.

At this point, Ms. Breckenridge can pursue the issue of how the y-intercepts change or make a note about how Thomas never brought it up and then move on to another student. The important point here is that Thomas started off the interview by saying that he couldn't find any pattern and that the two graphs were basically the same. If he had been given a written test over this exploration, he probably would have left the question blank, claiming that he never found a pattern. But, in reality, he *did* find the pattern and just needed an external catalyst—the teacher—to prompt him and challenge him to communicate his thinking. The interview technique allows the teacher to pursue student thinking and to probe more deeply than a written instrument can often do. The interview is particularly useful when assessing students with learning disabilities, who may be unable to express their thoughts accurately in writing but can explain the thinking process and demonstrate understanding of the concept.

Interviews are also effective follow-ups of observations or written journal entries. For example, if a student's misconception appears in a journal entry, the teacher can conduct a brief interview the next day to see if the student has overcome the initial misunderstanding. Not all classroom interviews are formal; in fact, most are informal and consist of no more than a question or two asked by the teacher during a problem-solving situation. It would be unrealistic for a teacher to conduct weekly in-depth interviews with students; after all, an interview may take 5 to 10 minutes, and many secondary and middle school teachers have 100 or more students. But interview questions asked of even a small sample of students each week can provide a cross-sectional glimpse of how a class is thinking or in-depth information about how one student is developing.

Portfolios

As a student progresses through an academic year, evidence of academic growth can be collected and assembled in a folder or a binder. A **portfolio** is a purposeful collection of work, produced by a student over time, that provides a glimpse of what the student is able to do and believes about mathematics. A portfolio might contain some or all of the following:

- written tests, with errors corrected
- sample homework papers demonstrating problem-solving, reasoning, communication, connections, or representation skills
- a paper or project designed for the class
- a solution to an open-ended question or problem that illustrates a high level of mathematical thinking
- sample journal entries that illustrate attitudes and skills
- interview notes from a teacher
- video or audiotapes of teamwork or individual presentations
- observation checklist completed by the teacher
- self-assessment writing in which the student discusses growth over time

Generally, the student writes a short introduction to each section of a portfolio, explaining what can be found in that section and why it was selected. For example, one student wrote the following introduction to a sample test included in a portfolio:

> I chose to include this test because I made a number of careless mistakes when I took it. But I went back and corrected my errors, and for each correction, I gave a short explanation of why I missed the item in the first place and what I need to remember for the next time. I believe that carefully correcting my mistakes on early tests helped me to achieve much better later on in the year. I still look at every wrong answer on tests and homework papers and ask myself, "Why did I miss that?" and "What can I do next time to make sure I don't do the same thing again?"

Finally, the student writes an introduction to the portfolio and creates a table of contents. The portfolio generally is put into either a file box or a three-ring binder and can be used by students to demonstrate their abilities to other teachers or at parent-teacher conferences. The portfolio represents students' growth over time and illustrates the way that they solve problems and what they believe about the nature of mathematics. A portfolio is a much more concrete illustration of mathematical abilities than a percent average in a course. Consequently, some teachers have begun to use portfolio assessment as a complement to current assessment procedures or as *the* determining factor in assigning grades. Some states have already mandated that a mathematics portfolio be created for every student beginning in kindergarten and that it be passed along from one grade level to the next so that teachers have an overview of student competencies prior to starting a new school year.

Stenmark (1991) suggested that portfolios themselves should be assessed on a rubric for their effectiveness. Such a rubric would have the following categories and descriptions:

RUBRIC FOR SCORING A MATHEMATICS PORTFOLIO

Level 4 (top level)
The Level 4 portfolio is exciting to look through. It includes a variety of written and graphic mathematical work, indicating both individual and group work. Projects, investigations, diagrams, graphs, charts, photographs, audiotapes or videotapes, and other work indicate a broad and creative curriculum that leads students to think for themselves. There is evidence of student use of many resources: calculators, computers, reference libraries, and conversations with adults and students. Papers display student organization and analysis of information. Although neatness may not be a primary requisite, clarity of communication is important. Student self-assessment is shown by revisions of drafts, letters that explain why the student chose certain papers, or student-generated assessment lists or reports. Improvement in communication over time is reflected in samples from the beginning, middle, and end of the term. Student work reflects enthusiasm for mathematics.

Level 3
The Level 3 portfolio indicates a solid mathematics program. There is a variety of types of work presented, as in the top level. Students are able to explain fairly well their strategies and problem solving processes. Some use of resources and group work may be evident, and students indicate good understanding, especially of basic mathematics concepts. Work over a period of time is included. The factors most likely to be missing are indications of student enthusiasm, self-assessment, extensive investigations, and student analysis of information.

Level 2
The Level 2 portfolio indicates an adequate mathematics program, somewhat bound by textbook requirements. There is little evidence of student original thinking as shown by projects, investigation, diagrams, and so on. Student explanations of the process by which they solved problems are minimal. There may be an overconcentration on arithmetic or similar algorithmic topics and a resulting lack of work from other content areas.

Continued

Level I

The Level I portfolio includes almost no creative work and may consist mainly of ditto sheets or pages copied from a textbook. There is almost no evidence of student thinking. Papers are likely to be multiple choice and short answer and show no evidence that students are discussing mathematical ideas in class. Students do not explain their thinking about mathematical ideas.

(Stenmark, 1991, p. 44. Reprinted with permission.)

As with the use of rubrics to score open-ended questions, it is important that the students help to develop a portfolio-scoring rubric or at least that they are given the rubric well in advance so that they are aware of the teacher's expectations. Although some students resist the first time they are asked to assemble a portfolio, the benefit of being able to display growth ultimately makes the use of this assessment strategy very appealing to them. Many teachers also resist implementing portfolios in the classroom because of the perceived difficulty in organizing the assignment and in scoring the portfolios. However, the effort is certainly worthwhile when students are able to display their mathematics portfolio with pride and reflect upon their accomplishments over a term or an entire year.

The use of multiple techniques of collecting assessment data provides the teacher with a broad, diverse methodology for determining the level of development for each student. As a filmmaker shows a scene from several angles in order to get the viewer involved in the action, a variety of assessment strategies can illuminate the many dimensions of mathematical development. If the primary aim of assessment is to determine student progress, there are certainly more ways to measure that progress than paper-and-pencil testing means.

■ CONCLUSION ■

It has been said that the ultimate goal of the assessment process is to make students effective self-assessors who recognize quality work when they produce it. By asking students to create rubrics and to reflect on their performances in journals and portfolios, we are helping them to think about what it means to do mathematics and to monitor their own academic and attitudinal growth over time. When an external person, such as the teacher, does all of the assessment and tells you how you performed, you will naturally begin to expect someone else to monitor your growth, and that external assessment ultimately shifts the responsibility for reflection on work from you to the teacher. Self-assessment, on the other hand, places the students in an active role as they think about their own development and set goals for improvement. Similarly, we see a recent trend in business and industry toward employees setting their own goals for professional development based on their perceived weaknesses and planning a process for meeting those goals. In a sense, the use of alternative assessment strategies in the classroom not only provides the teacher with a richer view of the development of each student, but it also helps students to prepare for careers in which they may need to track their own professional growth over time.

In this chapter, we have discussed why, if inferences about student achievement are to be valid, a variety of data sources are necessary. Simply put, the Friday afternoon or weekly test or quiz does not provide enough information for a teacher to really gain a complete picture of each student's mathematical understanding. Consequently, we have seen the advent of a variety of nontraditional assessment strategies in mathematics, including techniques such as the use of journals, open-ended questions and scoring rubrics, individual and team projects, checklists and observations, interviews, and portfolios. Each of these strategies has been described at some length in this chapter. We must also realize that it may not be physically possible nor desirable for a teacher to use all of these strategies to assess student achievement and attitudes. Instead, each classroom teacher must design a coherent assessment system that effectively monitors student progress.

The use of strategies such as writing and employing rubrics are not new in education. In fact, journals and rubrics have been standard assessment procedures in English and in the arts for decades. However, many of these strategies are in their infancy in mathematics, and this has led to some controversy. A local mathematics teachers' organization, for example, sponsors an annual mathematics contest for grades 6–12. Two open-ended items were added to the test after many years of administering a straightforward multiple-choice exam. Parents immediately complained that the decision as to who won the contest would be the result of a subjective score based on a rubric and that this process was not fair. Thinking quickly, the president of the organization asked the parents if their children had ever entered a writing contest, such as an essay competition for the Daughters of the American Revolution, or an art contest. After their affirmative replies, the president reminded them that scores for such contests are almost always based on rubrics, which are no more than predetermined performance standards—after all, you can't run a painting or an essay through a grading machine. In a similar way, a rubric for an open-ended mathematics question is predetermined and takes most of the guesswork out of assigning scores to papers. Once parents realized that the mathematics educators were doing what English and teachers in the arts have done for generations, the complaints almost immediately ceased. The problem, of course, is that these nontraditional assessment strategies are just that—nontraditional, and, therefore, they are not within many people's comfort zones. Changing assessment practices, for many, involves, first, realizing that assessment has other purposes than assigning grades and that traditional methods don't provide the total picture of student achievement and attitudes.

In the next chapter, we continue our discussion of assessment by exploring the *Assessment Standards for School Mathematics,* released by the NCTM in 1995. When we think about assessment strategies that teachers are now employing in an attempt to meet those Standards, a number of other issues begin to surface. For example, how do we use assessment data to try to meet the needs of all students? And, on a practical matter, how should teachers make day-to-day decisions about selecting homework problems and determining final grades? These questions are pursued in Chapter 9.

■ GLOSSARY ■

Alignment: Alignment refers to the consistency between the type of questions raised and the tools required for an assessment, compared to the question types and tools used in day-to-day instruction. In other words, if the teacher regularly emphasizes problem solving and the use of technology in class, then a test with a high degree of alignment would also contain problem-solving items and expect students to use technology to answer some or all of the questions.

Assessment: The National Council of Teachers of Mathematics defines assessment as "the process of gathering evidence about a student's knowledge of, ability to use, and disposition toward, mathematics and of making inferences from that evidence for a variety of purposes" (1995, p. 3). Assessment is the process by which a teacher tracks student progress; it is a broad term that is often confused with *evaluation,* which refers to a final judgment of student performance.

Competency Tests: Competency tests are criterion-referenced tests that are generally given at the local level (such as an individual school district or county). They measure the degree to which objectives in the local curriculum are being mastered by students as a means of encouraging educators to stick to the script and follow the adopted course of study.

Criterion-Referenced Tests: Criterion-referenced tests are aligned with a set of standards, such as a local curriculum or a state curricular model. Scores on criterion-referenced tests are, then, based on the degree to which students have mastered the stated outcomes. Proficiency tests at the state level are examples of criterion-referenced tests.

Formative Assessment: Formative assessment is used during the teaching and learning process to determine whether an individual is progressing at an acceptable rate. Often, formative assessment provides the individual with feedback.

Geoboard: A geoboard is a square board made of plastic or wood on which pegs are arranged in square or circular patterns. The square on a geoboard varies from 25 to 144 pegs.

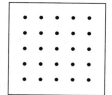 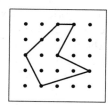

Geoboards can be used to study the properties of triangles, angle measurement, area, perimeter, the Pythagorean Theorem, and a host of other mathematical concepts.

Mathematics Journal: A Mathematics journal is a notebook or binder in which a student reflects on learning experiences in the classroom. The journal generally contains some problem solving, reactions to problems and projects, reflections on the value of a team activity, and other self-assessments. By regularly collecting mathematics journals, the teacher can gain insights into how individual students are

learning and viewing the class that are difficult, if not impossible, to obtain by observation of student work in the classroom.

Norm-Referenced Tests: Norm-referenced tests compare the performance of students in a particular district or county to the norm, a sample of other students at the same grade level and age from around the country. The PSAT, SAT, and ACT tests are norm-referenced tests and measure whether a student or group of students is scoring at, above, or below the average when compared to a sample of other students.

Open-Ended Question: An open-ended question is one on which there are either multiple acceptable answers or one "right" answer but multiple means of arriving at the solution. The most common reasons for using open-ended questions are (1) to gather information about how students are thinking about a problem and (2) to send a message that student thinking processes are valued. Open-ended questions are often referred to as free-response items.

Performance Task: A Performance task requires the student to make, display, create, or explain a mathematical situation. An open-ended question constitutes a performance task as does the completion of a project in mathematics.

Portfolio: A portfolio is a purposeful collection of work produced by a student over time that provides a glimpse of what the student is able to do and believes about mathematics. Assembled into a folder or binder, a portfolio often contains samples of written tests (with errors corrected), homework papers, a paper or project, a solution to an open-ended question, sample journal entries, interview notes from the teacher, observation forms filled out by the teacher, and student self-assessments.

Prompt: A journal prompt is a question or problem posed to a class, which is to be addressed in class or for an assignment. Sometimes, prompts are very specific problems or questions, and other times, they are open ended and allow students to choose their own directions for responses.

Reliability: The reliability of a test refers to the likelihood that a student would obtain roughly the same score if given different versions of the test multiple times. Often, standardized test makers report a reliability measure, which indicates the likelihood that a student would score about the same if taking two equivalent tests on two different days.

Summative Assessment: Summative assessment is a final evaluation of performance. After all of the data have been gathered over time, the student is given a final course grade, or the employee is given a rating used to determine whether a promotion is warranted.

Validity: Validity is a measure of the degree to which a test actually measures the content that the teacher intends it to measure. A test is said to be valid when its content is consistent with the stated objectives for the unit that the test is assessing.

■ DISCUSSION QUESTIONS ■

1. Discuss the teachers' assessment strategies in several of your own recent courses. What did you learn about the values of your instructors from the way that your grades were determined?

2. Proficiency testing is the topic of continual heated debates across the United States. In this chapter, several arguments in favor of and opposed to proficiency testing were presented. Take a stand for or against the notion that all students should pass a standardized proficiency test to graduate from high school and defend your position.

3. Obtain a copy of a test from the teacher's manual of a textbook series or from a mathematics teacher in the field. Critique the test by considering some of the issues described in this chapter, such as validity and reliability, length of the test, inclusion of review items, alignment with stated outcomes, and likelihood of students bluffing correct answers.

4. Earlier in this chapter, a student response to an equation-solving question was discussed. The student did the following steps: $2x - 4(x - 3) = 10$, $2x - 4x - 12 = 10$, $-2x - 12 = 10$, $-2x = 22$, $x = 11$. If the problem was worth 10 points on a 100-point test, how would you score it? What is a fair grade for this student, and what needs to be considered when making this decision?

5. Sketch out a conceptual map for a unit on the topic of your choice. Then, design two different assessments for the unit. One of the assessments should be a more traditional but well-written test, and the other assessment should be a performance task such as a project or interview. Discuss the benefits and potential drawbacks of each method of assessment.

6. Interview a secondary or middle school student in depth about one particular mathematical concept or view a videotape of a student interview. You could begin by looking at some problem that the student's class may have done for homework and ask a series of questions to find out how much the student actually knows about that topic. In a small group, discuss the interview and what you learned about the student's understandings and misconceptions.

7. Create an open-ended question (or borrow one from another source) and administer it to a class of secondary or middle school students. Using the sample rubric from this chapter or some other similar rubric, grade the student papers by placing them into categories. Describe the difficulties you encountered while attempting to use the rubric for scoring the student papers. What are the benefits of this assessment strategy?

8. Select an alternative assessment strategy and generate a list of its advantages and disadvantages. In a team with three others who explored different strategies, compare notes and discuss which of the techniques described in this chapter are potentially the most useful and practical.

9. Interview an English, social studies, or art teacher and ask them how essays and artwork are assessed in their classes. What type of rubrics do they use, and what can we learn, as teachers of mathematics, from assessment in the other content areas?

10. "Is this going to be on the test?" Recognizing that it is essentially impossible to assess every single mathematical point that is raised in the classroom, how do you react to the comment that "if it's not going to be on the test, there's really no point in my paying attention and taking notes on it in class"? How do you motivate students to engage in a mathematical discussion when they know that the conversation has strayed from the teacher's objective for the day and is not likely to be included on an assessment?

■ BIBLIOGRAPHIC REFERENCES AND RESOURCES ■

Barton, J. & Collins, A. (1997). *Portfolio assessment: A handbook for educators.* Menlo Park, CA: Addison-Wesley.

Becker, J. P. & Shimada, S. (1997). *The open-ended approach: A new proposal for teaching mathematics.* Reston, VA: National Council of Teachers of Mathematics.

Brahier, D. J. (1999). Assessment Project Extended to the Northwest. Retrieved August 20, 1999 from the World Wide Web: <http://www.bgsu.edu/colleges/edhd/programs/ASPEN>

Brahier, D. J. (1999). Assessment Project for Erie County Teachers. Retrieved August 20, 1999 from the World Wide Web: <http://www.bgsu.edu/colleges/edhd/programs/ASPECT>

Bryant, D. & Driscoll, M. (1998). *Exploring classroom assessment in mathematics.* Reston, VA: National Council of Teachers of Mathematics.

California Assessment Program. (1989). *A question of thinking: A first look at students' performance on open-ended questions in mathematics.* Sacramento, CA: California State Department of Education.

Clarke, D. (1997). *Constructive assessment in mathematics.* Berkeley, CA: Key Curriculum.

Cross, M. (1995). *How to's in getting started with assessment & evaluation using portfolios.* Barrie, Ontario: Exclusive Educational Products.

Crowley, Mary L. (1997). Aligning assessment with classroom practices: A promising testing format. *Mathematics Teacher, 90* (9), 706–711.

Danielson, C. (1997). *A collection of performance tasks and rubrics: Middle school mathematics.* Larchmont, NY: Eye on Education.

De Fina, A. A. (1992). *Portfolio assessment: Getting started.* New York, NY: Scholastic.

Dossey, J. A., Mullis, I. V., & Jones, C. O. (1993). *Can students do mathematical problem solving?* Washington, DC: U.S. Department of Education.

Driscoll, M. (1995). Implementing the professional standards for teaching mathematics: "The farther out you go . . . ": Assessment in the classroom. *Mathematics Teacher, 88* (5), 420–425.

Educational Testing Service. (1993). *Performance Assessment Sampler.* Princeton, NJ: Educational Testing Service.

Freedman, R. L. (1994). *Open-ended questioning: A handbook for educators.* Menlo Park, CA: Addison-Wesley.

Graue, M. E. & Smith, S. Z. (1996). Shaping assessment through instructional innovation. *Journal of Mathematical Behavior, 15* (2), 113–136.

Haines, C. & Izard, J. (1994). Assessing mathematical communications about projects and investigations. *Educational Studies in Mathematics, 27* (4), 373–386.

Hart, D. (1994). *Authentic assessment: A handbook for educators.* Menlo Park, CA: Addison-Wesley.

Hunting, R. P. & Doig, B. A. (1997). Clinical assessment in mathematics: Learning the craft. *Focus on Learning Problems in Mathematics, 19* (3), 29–48.

Jasmine, J. (1994). *Middle School Assessment.* Huntington Beach, CA: Teacher Created Materials.

Kuhs, T. (1992). *Mathematics assessment: Alternative approaches* (video program). Reston, VA: National Council of Teachers of Mathematics.

Kulm, G. (1990). *Assessing higher order thinking in mathematics.* Washington, DC: American Association for the Advancement of Science.

Lambdin, D. V. (1993). The NCTM's 1989 evaluation standards: Recycled ideas whose time has come? In N. L. Webb (Ed.), *1993 Yearbook of the NCTM: Assessment in the mathematics classroom,* pp. 7–16. Reston, VA: National Council of Teachers of Mathematics.

Lesh, R. & Lamon, S. J. (1992). *Assessment of authentic performance in school mathematics.* Washington, DC: American Association for the Advancement of Science.

Mathematical Sciences Education Board National Research Council. (1993). *Measuring counts: A conceptual guide for mathematics assessment.* Washington, DC: National Academy.

Mathematical Sciences Education Board National Research Council. (1993). *Measuring up: Prototypes for mathematics assessment.* Washington, DC: National Academy.

McIntosh, M. E. (1997). Formative assessment in mathematics. *The Clearing House, 71,* 92–96.

National Council of Teachers of Mathematics. (1998). *Principles and standards for school mathematics* (working draft). Reston, VA: National Council of Teachers of Mathematics.

National Council of Teachers of Mathematics. (1996). *Emphasis on assessment: Readings from NCTM's school-based journals.* Reston, VA: National Council of Teachers of Mathematics.

National Council of Teachers of Mathematics. (1995). *Assessment standards for school mathematics.* Reston, VA: National Council of Teachers of Mathematics.

Romberg, T. A. (1992). *Mathematics assessment and evaluation.* Albany, NY: SUNY UP.

Ryan, C. D. (1994). *Authentic assessment.* Westminster, CA: Teacher Created Materials.

Seeley, A. E. (1994). *Portfolio assessment.* Westminster, CA: Teacher Created Materials.

Sharma, M. C. (1996). Assessment of mathematics learning. *Math Notebook, 10* (1–2), 1–52.

Spitzer, H. S. (1951). Testing instruments and practices in relation to present concepts of teaching arithmetic. In N. B. Henry (Ed.), *The teaching of arithmetic,* 50th Yearbook for the National Society for the Study of Education, Pt. 2, pp. 186–202. Chicago, IL: University of Chicago Press.

Stenmark, J. K. (1991). *Mathematics assessment: Myths, models, good questions, and practical suggestions.* Reston, VA: National Council of Teachers of Mathematics.

Stenmark, J. K. (Ed.). (1989). *Assessment alternatives in mathematics.* Berkley, CA: Regents, University of California.

Stewart, C. & Chance, L. (1995). Making connections: Journal writing and the professional teaching standards. *Mathematics Teacher, 88* (2), 92–95.

Sueltz, A. (1961). The role of evaluation in the classroom. In D. A. Johnson (Ed.), *Evaluation in mathematics,* 26th Yearbook of the National Council of Teachers of Mathematics, pp. 7–20. Washington, DC: National Council of Teachers of Mathematics.

Sueltz, A., Boyton, H., & Sauble, I. (1946). The measurement of understanding in elementary school mathematics. In *The measurement of understanding,* 45th Yearbook of the National Society for the Study of Education, Pt. 1. Chicago, IL: University of Chicago Press.

Weaver, J. F. (1970). Evaluation and the classroom teachers. In E. C. Begle (Ed.), *Mathematics education,* 69th Yearbook of the National Society for the Study of Education, Pt. 1. Chicago, IL: University of Chicago Press.

Webb, N. (Ed.). (1993). *1993 Yearbook of the NCTM: Assessment in the mathematics classroom.* Reston, VA: National Council of Teachers of Mathematics.

Standards
and Equity in
Assessment

Upon reading Chapter 9, you should be able to answer the following questions:

■ What are the six NCTM assessment Standards and the assessment Principle? Discuss the criteria that they establish as benchmarks for the effective implementation of an assessment system.

■ What does it mean to achieve equity, and how can this issue be addressed through assessment?

■ In what ways are the needs of individual students met through a variety of assessment strategies?

■ What role do homework assignments play in the mathematics teaching and learning process, and how can they be used as an assessment tool?

■ What factors should be taken into account when determining a student's final grade?

Colleen was a student in Mr. McAlister's Calculus course in her senior year of high school. The students' "senior privilege" exempted them from their final exam if they were averaging an A or a B in the second semester. In the last week of class, Mr. McAlister read off a list of students who were exempted and called Colleen's name. Elated, she walked out of the room knowing that she would not have to take the Calculus exam. The following week, when grades were posted, she discovered that she had received a B in the class. She was upset because she thought that Mr. McAlister had read a list of students who were exempted with an A, and if she had known that she had a B average, she would have elected to take the final exam to attempt to raise her score. She went home that night and told her parents about the situation. Her father called the teacher to ask what had happened. In his response, the teacher explained that Colleen had been averaging a B for the fourth quarter, and that with the level of material being studied, she should be proud of her performance. In response, her father said, "But if only she had known that you were going to give her a B. . . ." Mr. McAlister responded, "I didn't *give* her anything; she earned the grade that she received!" Upset and realizing that they had reached an impasse, they both hung up the phone, and Colleen graduated with the only B she had received in four years of high school mathematics.

Have you ever expected one grade in a class but were given another? Have you ever been in a class in which someone asked you, "What grade do you think you're getting in this course," and your response was something like, "I have no idea. I don't know how the number of points we get on tests and assignments relate to the final grade"? Colleen's situation is not unusual, as there is often much confusion over how a student is being assessed and where that student stands in terms of a final evaluation in the course. Mr. McAlister was absolutely correct when he stated that students are not *given* grades; instead, grades are *earned*. On the other hand, students have a right to know how their grades are being determined and where they stand at any particular time in a class. Final grades should never be a surprise to the student; they should be a natural reflection of how the student has performed and be very predictable based upon evidence collected throughout the grading period. In this chapter, we turn our attention to some of the ramifications of developing a coherent system for assessing student progress. We begin with a discussion of the assessment Standards (NCTM, 1995) and the assessment principle (NCTM, 1998), put forth by the National Council of Teachers of Mathematics. Then, we explore a few of the practical issues, including the use of assessment to meet the needs of individual students, assigning and checking homework as an assessment tool, and the process of determining final evaluative grades in a course.

■ NCTM RECOMMENDATIONS ON ASSESSMENT

The Assessment Standards

After providing educators with suggestions for both curriculum and teaching in 1989 and 1991, respectively, it made sense that the next NCTM document would focus on the issue of student assessment. *Assessment Standards for School Mathematics* was released in 1995. The book is divided into two major sections—the mathematics assessment Standards and the use of the assessment Standards for different purposes. In Chapter 8, we discussed the various uses for assessment data. Now, we visit the six assessment Standards themselves and their implications. It is important to remember that these six Standards are guidelines or benchmarks that can be used by a state, county, district, building, or even an individual teacher to determine the effectiveness of an assessment system.

The Mathematics Standard—Assessment should reflect the mathematics that all students need to know and be able to do.

Key questions that follow from this Standard are:

- What mathematics is reflected in the assessment?
- What efforts are made to ensure that the mathematics is significant and correct?
- How does the assessment engage students in realistic and worthwhile mathematical activities?

- How does the assessment elicit the use of mathematics that it is important to know and be able to do?
- How does the assessment fit within a framework of mathematics to be assessed?
- What inferences about students' mathematical knowledge, understanding, thinking processes, and dispositions can be made from the assessment?

(NCTM, *Assessment Standards for School Mathematics*, 1995, pp. 11–12.)

The first Standard relates to the idea that assessment should focus on what we value in the classroom. If the process skills such as problem solving and reasoning are emphasized in the classroom, then the assessment program used by a teacher, district, or state should emphasize the same goals and objectives. The mathematical content in an assessment should provide a window into the content that a state, district, or teacher believes is important.

The Learning Standard—Assessment should enhance mathematics learning.

Key questions that follow from this Standard are:

- How does the assessment contribute to each student's learning of mathematics?
- How does the assessment relate to instruction?
- How does the assessment allow students to demonstrate what they know and what they can do in novel situations?
- How does the assessment engage students in relevant, purposeful work on worthwhile mathematical activities?
- How does the assessment build on each student's understanding, interests, and experiences?
- How does the assessment involve students in selecting activities, applying performance criteria, and using results?
- How does the assessment provide opportunities for students to evaluate, reflect on, and improve their own work—that is, to become independent learners?

(NCTM, *Assessment Standards for School Mathematics*, 1995, pp. 13–14.)

Assessment is a data-collection process that goes well beyond simply assigning grades. Teachers should use assessment data to make instructional decisions, as students use the information to determine their weaknesses and target those areas for intervention. This Standard is a reminder to teachers that assessment should help them to assist their students by providing feedback that is critical in the teaching-and-learning cycle.

The Equity Standard—Assessment should promote equity.

Key questions that follow from this Standard are:

- What opportunities has each student had to learn the mathematics being assessed?
- How does the assessment provide alternative activities or modes of response that invite each student to engage in the mathematics being assessed?

- How does the design of the assessment enable all students to exhibit what they know and can do?
- How do the conditions under which the assessment is administered enable all students to exhibit what they know and can do?
- How does the assessment help students demonstrate their best work?
- How is the role of students' backgrounds and experiences recognized in judging their responses to the assessment?
- How do scoring guides accommodate unanticipated but reasonable responses?
- How have the effects of bias been minimized throughout the assessment?
- To what sources can differences in performance be attributed?

(NCTM, *Assessment Standards for School Mathematics,* 1995, pp. 15–16.)

Some students are good test takers, and others are not. Some enjoy getting up in front of a class and explaining their thinking; others would rather write their thoughts in a journal. The equity Standard is a reminder that when students score low in a mathematics class, it doesn't necessarily mean that they don't understand the concepts, nor is the highest-performing student in the class necessarily the one with the highest level of understanding. One of the major reasons why we use a variety of assessment strategies is to give every student an opportunity to demonstrate an understanding of the content and processes. As we discussed in Chapter 8, a teacher who relies on written tests and quizzes as the sole tools for determining student progress is most certainly missing major dimensions of student learning, and, thus, an equal opportunity to demonstrate learning is denied to some students. We discuss the issue of how assessment can be used to promote equity later in this chapter.

The Openness Standard—Assessment should be an open process.

Key questions that follow from this Standard are:

- How do students become familiar with the assessment process and with the purposes, performance criteria, and consequences of the assessment?
- How are teachers and students involved in choosing tasks, setting criteria, and interpreting results?
- How is the public involved in the assessment process?
- What access do those affected by the assessment have to tasks, scoring goals, performance criteria, and samples of students' work that have been scored and discussed?
- How is the assessment process itself open to evaluation and modification?

(NCTM, *Assessment Standards for School Mathematics,* 1995, pp. 17–18.)

In the short scenario at the beginning of this chapter, we saw a high school student—Colleen—who was earning a B in Calculus but thought that she was earning an A because the teacher's grading process was so confusing and unclear. The openness Standard emphasizes that when students are being assessed, they (and their parents) deserve to know the criteria on which they are being assessed and the consequences of performing well or poorly. In the case of statewide proficiency testing, many states make it mandatory for students to pass some type of exit exam in mathematics in order to graduate from high school. With the stakes so high, students and their teachers have the right to be provided with a detailed set of outcomes if not a list of sample test items, so that they know exactly what is expected of them. Similarly, if a teacher plans to use a rubric to score an open-ended question or a portfolio, students should at least be given a copy of the rubric in advance, if they do not assist in creating it themselves.

The Inferences Standard—Assessment should promote valid inference about mathematics learning.

Key questions that follow from this Standard are:

- What evidence about learning does the assessment provide?
- How is professional judgment used in making inferences about learning?
- How sensitive is the assessor to the demands the assessment makes and to un-expected responses?
- How is bias minimized in making inferences about learning?
- What efforts are made to ensure that scoring is consistent across students, scorers, and activities?
- What multiple sources of evidence are used for making inferences, and how is that evidence used?
- What is the value of the evidence for each use?

(NCTM, *Assessment Standards for School Mathematics*, 1995, pp. 19–20.)

The teacher has to eventually decide whether the student is doing A work, B work, and so forth. To make a reasonable judgment about a student's learning, a variety of data needs to be collected. This Standard emphasizes that generalizations or inferences can only be made if the assessment data provide a broad enough spectrum of information on which to make instructional and evaluative decisions. Again, we discussed in Chapter 8 how a variety of assessment strategies can be used together to generate a holistic sense of a student's progress over time.

The Coherence Standard—Assessment should be a coherent process.

Key questions that follow from this Standard are:

- How is professional judgment used to ensure that the various parts of the assessment process form a coherent whole?
- How do students view the connection between instruction and assessment?
- How does the assessment match its purposes with its uses?
- How does the assessment match the curriculum and instructional practice?
- How can assessment practice inform teachers as they make curriculum decisions and determine their instructional practices?

(NCTM, *Assessment Standards for School Mathematics*, 1995, pp. 21–22.)

The last of the six assessment Standards is designed to pull together the other five. It serves as a reminder that a state, district, or teacher's assessment system has to fit together and make sense. The assessment strategies employed should align with instruction and accomplish what they set out to do—evaluating students, charting progress, making instructional decisions, or serving as an accountability tool.

Using the Standards as benchmarks, teachers can evaluate their own systems of assessing student work and determine the degree to which the system meets the criteria set forth in each of the Standards. For example, if a teacher decides to use written journals as a major part of the assessment program, this may help in making more reasonable inferences but might also make the system less equitable, because not all students are adept at expressing their thinking in writing. A teacher who uses only tests to assign grades may be very clear about expectations and be meeting the openness Standard, but because the tests do not measure student ability to solve problems in teams or make oral presentations—which may be a major focus of the program—we might question whether the important mathematics Standard is being addressed. Ideally, an assessment system designed by a mathematics teacher at the secondary or middle school level should meet, to the highest degree possible, each of the six assessment Standards.

The Assessment Principle

In late 1998, the NCTM published *Principles and Standards for School Mathematics,* which included the assessment Principle as one of the six Guiding Principles in the teaching and learning of mathematics. The assessment Principle stated that "mathematics instructional programs should include assessment to monitor, enhance, and evaluate the mathematics learning of all students and to inform teaching" (NCTM, 1998, p. 36). The Principle described an **assessment cycle** that includes setting goals for learning, gathering evidence of student progress, interpreting the evidence and then making instructional decisions based on the interpretations or inferences as shown in Figure 9–1.

Figure 9–1 The Classroom Assessment Cycle from *Principles and Standards for School Mathematics*

Clearly, this more recent document continued to describe assessment as a process over time, recognizing that determining final grades in a class is only one of many possible purposes for conducting assessments. The authors concluded the section on the assessment Principle by stating that, "The purpose of classroom assessment is to help students learn and achieve high standards, not to sort and compare them. The quality and depth of learning is determined by the decisions teachers make. Therefore, assessment should inform the teacher about students' understanding and help in choosing interventions with individual students and next steps for a whole class" (NCTM, *Principles and Standards for School Mathematics,* 1998, p. 40). In the next section of this chapter, we explore the issue of helping individual students to address the issue of equity through the assessment process.

■ EQUITY THROUGH ASSESSMENT

Throughout this book, from the discussion of learning theories to curricular and instructional models, we have operated under the assumption that *all* students have the capacity to learn mathematics. We have argued that no one is born with a mathematics gene; each of us has the potential to develop our mathematical reasoning skills. Whether or not we accomplish this is largely a function of our environment, including the home environment and the efforts of classroom teachers. The assumption that all students have a right to equal access to the study of mathematics is referred to as **equity.** According to Croom (1997), "equity in mathematics education implies fairness, justice, and equality for all students so that they may achieve their full potential, regardless of race, ethnicity, gender, or socioeconomic status" (p. 2).

If all students were truly gaining equal access to the mathematics curriculum, to adequate instructional materials, and to quality classrooms and teaching, we might expect the research on student achievement and career trends to reflect consistency across gender, race, and ethnicity. But this has not historically been the case. Research has shown males outperform females in mathematics achievement and that this might be explained, in part, because males are more likely to take upper-level secondary mathematics courses, such as probability and statistics, than their female peers (see Leder, 1992, for details). Although more recent research indicates that females are taking more mathematics courses, career statistics show, for example, that only 9 percent of all engineers are females (National Science Foundation, 1994). Similarly, white students tend to outperform their Hispanic and African-American peers. Malloy (1997) argued that African-American students may learn differently than their white counterparts and that mathematics educators have not historically addressed these learning differences. She asserted that "mathematics educators have little knowledge of how African American students perceive themselves as mathematics students, how they approach mathematics, or the role of culture in their perception and mathematics performance" (p. 23). These learning differences, in turn, may account for some of the differences in performance. Certainly, the lack of financial resources in the inner-city settings has contributed to a lack of equal access of all students to quality mathematics education as well. (For an extensive treatment of the issue of equity in mathematics education, see the 1997 *Yearbook of the NCTM* edited by Janet Trentacosta.)

One of the issues, of course, is that not only do all students deserve equal access to the curriculum and to quality instruction, but also they should have an opportunity to demonstrate an understanding of mathematical concepts in a way that is consistent with their learning styles. As we discussed in Chapter 8, some students prefer to make a presentation, and others would rather write a paper. Some students are better at taking tests, and others perform better on teams or by conducting individual projects. The equity Standard stated that "because different students show what they know and can do in different ways, assessments should allow for multiple approaches" (NCTM, 1995, p. 15). Furthermore, in a discussion of the equity Principle in the *Principles and Standards for School Mathematics* document (NCTM, 1998), the authors noted that, "All students need access to a coherent and challenging mathematics curriculum that is taught each year by a competent and well-supported mathematics teacher. Moreover, students' learning and achievement need to be assessed and reported in ways that attend to a reasonable range of important dimensions of mathematics and mathematical performance" (p. 26).

Addressing the issue of the promotion of equity through assessment practices, Belcher, Coates, Franco, and Mayfield-Ingram (1997) presented five suggestions for teachers to consider. They recommended that (1) assessment goals need to be made clear to students (which, of course, is an underlying principle of the openness Standard), that (2) students should be assessed on the same principles that guide classroom instruction (e.g., if problem solving is emphasized on a day-to-day basis, then it should be a cornerstone of the assessment), that (3) equitable assessment tools should be used, in terms of their format and design, that (4) instruction should be connected to assessment, and that (5) self-assessment should be part of the information-gathering process. A classroom teacher who uses a variety of assessment strategies does so out of a desire to get to know each student in the classroom and see how well that student is progressing. If we look at the total person and give students the opportunity to demonstrate their mathematical knowledge in a variety of ways, we open new doors to students who might have opted not to take a course or might have been unsuccessful in a more traditional classroom and, thereby, promote equity.

Practically speaking, addressing equity might mean that a teacher includes several assessment strategies in the information-gathering process as was described in the previous chapter. So, a teacher might use journal writing, interviews, and a portfolio in determining grades along with tests and homework. In this way, students who have difficulty with written tests might have the opportunity to demonstrate their understanding through writing. Students who are poor writers still have an opportunity to show progress in oral interviews, and so forth. Moreover, a teacher might attempt to make a class more equitable by giving students a choice of assessment type. For example, suppose that a middle school mathematics class was completing a unit on angle measurement and triangles. The teacher might pose the following options to the students:

> *As an assessment of your understanding of angles and triangles, you may select one of the following:*
>
> 1. *Take a traditional twenty-five-item test issued on Friday.*
> 2. *Interview an architect or carpenter and ask that individual how angles are used in the profession. Write a three to five page paper about the interview, including diagrams that show examples of how triangles and angles are involved in that job.*
> 3. *Come in during a study hall or before or after school for a ten- to fifteen-minute interview with the teacher. In the interview, you will be asked three questions*

involving angles and triangles. Each question will also have a follow-up question, based on your response.

In each of these cases, the student is being asked to demonstrate an understanding of angles and triangles, and the assessment is worth 100 points. But the student can choose whether to be assessed in a traditional testing format, by way of a written paper, or orally, through an interview. Some students simply don't want to hassle with interviewing a professional and writing a paper and may feel content with taking a written test. However, if students feel that they can explain their thinking more readily in an interview than on a twenty-five-item test, they may select the option of an interview. Then, on the day of the written test, the students who chose one of the alternative assessments might spend the test time preparing for their assessment, completing an assignment, or studying for another class.

Is giving a choice of assessment methods realistic for the teacher? The answer to this question depends on the teacher's class schedule and the experience that instructor may have had with various assessment strategies in the past. For example, after giving students this type of choice a number of times, a teacher might discover that only two or three students in each class consistently ask to use an alternative assessment; thus, the projects and interviews can be very manageable. The teacher may even wonder if it is worth it to offer alternative assessments, but for those few students, it could make the difference between failing and demonstrating competency. Also, the teacher may require some written tests or some projects for all students to complete, so it's not necessary to provide these options on every assessment.

Teachers must decide what is workable in their own particular cases and remember that any attempt to adjust for various learning styles promotes equity and can serve as a major improvement over what has historically been offered to students in the mathematics classroom. One of the more traditional ways to assess the formative progress of each student is to assign and collect homework. Individual assignments can provide the teacher with data on how students are progressing in their problem-solving performances. This data may, in turn, help the teacher determine whether females and males are thinking mathematically in similar ways and the degree to which problems that have been posed are appealing and understandable to all students in the classroom, regardless of their backgrounds. We now turn our attention to some of the practical issues associated with homework assignments in mathematics.

■ HOMEWORK ASSIGNMENTS

In the Third International Mathematics and Science Study (Beaton et al., 1996), research on middle school achievement showed that although 22 percent of Japanese students have mathematics homework three times or more per week, 87 percent of eighth graders in the United States have homework at least three times per week. In addition, U.S. students' homework assignments affect their grades in 95 percent of the cases; whereas only 31 percent of the Japanese students' grades are impacted by homework. Simply put, teachers in the United States place a higher value on homework assignments and assign homework more frequently than do teachers from most other countries in the world. Yet, achievement test scores, as we discussed in Chapter 1, were well below the international average at the eighth-grade level and even worse at the twelfth-grade level in the United States, and the scores were near the top in Japan. Interestingly, eighth graders from both Japan and the United States reported an average of about forty-five minutes spent on mathematics studying per night. Does that sound like a contradiction to the last statistic? Not really. Consider the following: Students in the United States are studying mathematics because the teacher gives a particular assignment; Japanese students choose to spend about the same amount of time working on mathematics, studying and reviewing class notes, but not because teachers require it. As much as anything, this might reflect a cultural difference in which Japanese parents encourage children to study mathematics every day, regardless of whether or not they have a formal homework assignment to complete for the next day. So, how much homework is reasonable, and how should it be checked?

Homework Amount and Frequency

Of course, there are no clear-cut answers to the questions of frequency and quantity of homework assignments. Teachers should assign as much homework as they feel is necessary to lay the groundwork for a new lesson, to allow students to complete a problem or project begun in class, or to provide practice on some type of exercise that was explored during class time. If a teacher brings a topic to closure during class, has no particular skill for students to practice, and intends to introduce the class to a new concept the following day, there is probably no reason to assign any homework problems at all. But students need to be reminded that even though a teacher did not assign a written homework lesson to be collected the next day, it is always wise to go back and review the day's lesson, brush up on previous topics, or review one test to begin to prepare for another. The following are examples of homework assignments that complement the classroom routine:

Laying the Groundwork for the Next Day

Suppose that Mr. Vail decides to have students conduct an investigation to approximate the value of π and to discover the formula for circumference, $C = \pi d$. To carry out the investigation, students will use a piece of string and determine the circumference and diameter of each of three different circles. After placing the values in the form of Table 9–1, the students will calculate and average the ratio as shown:

Table 9–1 Data Collection Table for Approximating the Value of π

Item Used	Circumference	Diameter	C ÷ D
#1			
#2			
#3			
Average	XXXXXXXXXXXX	XXXXXXXXXXXX	

After all of the classroom data have been collected, the students will discuss the values they found when dividing circumference by diameter and will average the averages to find a classwide value, which will serve as an approximation for the value of π.

The day before this discussion, as a homework assignment, Mr. Vail gives each student a piece of string. Each student is to take the string home and, along with a ruler or yardstick, select three circular objects in the house—a plate, a glass, a bowl, a wheel, a table, and so forth—and find each object's circumference and diameter, recording the measurements in the table (see Table 9–1) provided. Then, the next day in class, the students will be given calculators and asked to find the ratio of circumference to diameter, rounded to the nearest thousandth. After this, the class will discuss the numbers found, discover an approximation for the value of π, and develop a formula for determining the circumference of a circle, given the diameter or radius.

In this case, Mr. Vail has used the homework assignment to get students involved in the investigation by using objects familiar to them in their own home environment. It is also a clever time-saving device, as he could save as much as twenty minutes of classtime, during which students would be roaming about the room, measuring predetermined circular objects. Of course, if the students do the measuring in class, he can also assess their ability to properly use a ruler and record the results, but he has decided that using objects at home is more advantageous.

Completing a Classroom Problem

Ms. Aspen's geometry class is discussing the concept of a midpoint. She poses the following problem to the class:

If the endpoints of a line segment are located at (5,9) and at (1,3), find the coordinates of the midpoint joining the segment.

Having had no previous instruction on the midpoint formula, the students in the class begin to explore the problem. After about ten minutes, several students are ready to share their solutions and explanations.

Ms. Aspen: Joseph, can you tell us what you found?

Joseph: Well, I got the point (3, 6) as the midpoint. I used a piece of graph paper and plotted the two points you gave us. I noticed that you eventually have to go 4 up and 6 over to get from (1, 3) to (5, 9). So, if you only go 2 up and 3 over, you'll be at the midpoint. I took the coordinates of (1, 3) and added 2 and 3, and I got (3, 6) as my answer.

Ms. Aspen: Did anyone else do anything different? Krissy?

Krissy: I think Joseph's right because it's just about like finding a slope. I did about the same thing except I figured that to get from 1 to 5, you have to go 4 units, and to get from 3 to 9 takes 6 units. So, I took half of each and subtracted those numbers from (5, 9), and that brought me down to (3, 6). That was my answer too.

Ms. Aspen: Thanks, Krissy. (seeing Angelia raise her hand) What did you get, Angelia?

Angelia: I got the same answer, but I used my graphing calculator. I had it draw a segment with those two endpoints and used the TRACE function to estimate the midpoint. Then, I figured it was common sense . . . it has to be sort of halfway between the points, so (3, 6) made sense to me.

Ms. Aspen: The answer was common sense to you. Good. Did anyone do anything else? Any different answers? (No one raises a hand.) Can you find the midpoint of the segment with its endpoints at (–13, 25) and (7, –84)? (Students look puzzled.) What's the problem?

Joseph: There's no way I'm going to use graph paper on this one!

Teachers often pose rich problems during class that students can investigate as a homework assignment.

Angelia: (laughing) I don't think my graphing calculator will do much good either.

Ms. Aspen: Well, the old methods may not be the best here, right? Unfortunately, time is running out . . . Here is your homework for tomorrow: First, I want you to find the midpoint for the segment joining (-13, 25) and (7, –84) by using any method that you choose. Second, analyze that question and the one we did today and see if you can write down a quick, easy shortcut that will allow us to do these problems without using graph paper or calculators, because I think we just found out that those methods aren't always going to be the best. (The bell rings.)

The intent of Ms. Aspen's lesson was for the students to discover and develop the midpoint formula. Acting in a constructivist mode, she does not want to simply tell her students the formula; instead, she values the process of students developing or inventing their own formula. But with time running out, she leaves one specific problem and an attempt to generalize a formula up to the students for homework. The homework assignment should put closure on a problem that was posed and partially investigated in class. Although she could have opted to tell students to close their books and come back tomorrow to finish the exploration, she decided that it would be valuable for students to explore on their own and allow the homework results to serve as tools for the development of the formula the following day. In the end, she wants students to recognize that for any two points, (x_1, y_1) and (x_2, y_2), the midpoint can be represented by the formula $\left(\dfrac{x_1 + x_2}{2}, \dfrac{y_1 + y_2}{2}\right)$. The homework assignment serves as the bridge between today's classroom discussion and the closure to the formula development planned for tomorrow. She fully expects that several, although not all, of the students will discover that the midpoint coordinates are merely the arithmetic mean of the coordinates of the two given points. From that point, the class can generalize the formula and move forward.

Practicing a Skill Developed in Class

Ms. Estes-Park has completed a two-day discussion of right triangle trigonometry, and students have determined the three trigonometric ratios—sine, cosine, and tangent—and their inverses. One of the objectives in her course of study is for students to be able to solve a right triangle; that is, given the length of any two sides, the student should be able to find the length of the third side and determine the approximate measures of the three angles by using the Pythagorean Theorem and the trigonometric ratios. As a homework assignment, Ms. Estes-Park gives the students the following information about five triangles:

Triangle 1: The lengths of the legs are 5 and 7.
Triangle 2: The lengths of the legs are 6 and 8.
Triangle 3: The length of one leg is 7, and the length of the hypotenuse is 10.
Triangle 4: The length of one leg is $5\sqrt{3}$, and the length of the hypotenuse is 12.
Triangle 5: The length of the hypotenuse is $15\sqrt{2}$, and the triangle is isosceles.

For homework, students are asked to draw a rough sketch of each of the five triangles and to use the Pythagorean Theorem along with the trigonometric ratios to solve each triangle. The students are to bring the lengths of the three sides and the measures of the three angles for each of the five triangles to class the next day. Ms. Estes-Park wants students to practice a skill that was developed in class over the past two days. She recognizes that there is a place for skill-building and practice, as long as it does not dominate what goes on in the classroom and homework on a daily basis. In addition, through her selection of homework problems, she sets the stage for another discussion the next day.

In problem 2, notice how the lengths of the sides are 6 and 8; therefore, the hypotenuse must have a length of 10, and students will discover a Pythagorean Triple. The next day, she would like to engage her class in a discussion of Triples, so she purposely assigned that problem so that students would notice that, sometimes, the lengths of all three sides of a right triangle are integral values. Also, she assigned 4 and 5 to give students some practice in working with radicals, since they recently completed a chapter on irrational numbers, including simplifying radicals. Finally, problem 5 was assigned so that students would recognize that the relationship of the lengths of sides in a right isosceles triangle has a ratio of $1:1:\sqrt{2}$. Later, she will explore the lengths of sides in a 30–60–90 triangle so that students can discover a ratio of $1:\sqrt{3}:2$. In other words, even though the homework assignment appeared to be nothing more than a set of five practice problems to sharpen skills, the careful selection of homework items also set the stage for discussions in class over the next couple of days.

A mathematics teacher must purposefully and carefully select the homework problems. An easy way to create an assignment is to ask students to do the even-numbered problems at the end of a section of the book. But do the even-numbered problems ask students to practice what you think is important? Will those particular problems lead students to the discourse you intend to pursue on the following day? Is it necessary to do all of the even-numbered questions, or would a few of them be sufficient? Ms. Estes-Park could have given the students ten or more triangles to solve for homework, but she realized that if a student already understood the concepts of the Pythagorean Theorem and the trigonometric ratios, five problems would provide sufficient practice, and that anything more than five problems may be busywork that is wasting the students' time. On the other hand, if a student is confused and does not know how to find the angle measures, the student is likely to miss all of the problems and will need to redo the assignment anyway whether it consists of five or twenty triangles to solve. Students who need additional help do not have to struggle through twenty problems when five examples would be sufficient to make them realize that help is needed.

Therefore, teachers need to consider length of homework assignments in terms of what it is really necessary for students to do on their own. A textbook publisher may provide twenty-five-problem practice worksheets for sections on synthetic division, total surface area, or solving proportions, but it may only be necessary and reasonable for the teacher to assign ten of the problems on the sheets if the pages need to be used at all. Remember that in Chapter 6, we discussed how effective mathematics teachers tend to assign worthwhile tasks: Each time we plan a homework assignment, we have to ask ourselves, "What is my purpose for giving this assignment?" and "Which problems are worthwhile for my students to solve?" If a teacher concludes that the assignment is essentially busywork that will not significantly advance the classroom discourse into the next day, there may be no need to assign homework at all for that day. If a teacher chooses to give the class a homework assignment, then the following day, a decision is needed on how to check the work and use it to promote classroom discourse.

Checking Homework Assignments

There are a multitude of ways in which mathematics teachers typically handle student homework assignments. The following is a list of possible options for checking homework and the advantages and disadvantages of each strategy:

1. Students put all of the problems on the chalkboard, discuss the solutions, and correct errors on their papers. Papers are handed in for the teacher to check and record.

   ADVANTAGE: Every problem assigned is discussed, and students have an opportunity to compare each problem on the chalkboard to the work on their papers.

   DISADVANTAGE: If every student in the class got a particular problem correct on the homework assignment, classtime may be misused on discussions of common knowledge. If three students missed a problem, and twenty others got it correct, one has to question whether it's an effective use of classtime for all twenty-three students to discuss that particular problem.

2. The teacher asks the students which problems were the most difficult for them, and those problems are put on the board by volunteers and discussed so that students can correct their own homework papers. Papers are handed in for the teacher to check and record.

ADVANTAGE: Only those problems on which students had difficulty need to be discussed; relatively easy problems are not given classtime. Students are actively involved in placing solutions on the chalkboard and defending their methods of solving the problems.

DISADVANTAGE: Suppose that in a class of twenty-five students, one student does not understand problem 4. If that student asks for the problem to be worked through at the chalkboard, the other twenty-four students spend several minutes of classtime sitting through the explanation of a problem that only that one person missed. Also, if a student lacking confidence (or, for example, a female student in a classroom dominated by male peers) misses a problem and is aware that most other students understand it, the problem may be avoided when it really deserved a full class discussion.

3. The teacher reads correct solutions from an answer book, and students check their papers, asking questions where necessary. Papers are handed in for the teacher to check and record.

ADVANTAGE: By providing the students with solutions, the teacher allows them to check their own work so that they know what questions to ask later. This is a relatively time-efficient method, and minor questions can be dealt with as the teacher reads the solutions.

DISADVANTAGE: Remember our discussion of the role of the teacher in Chapter 6? We once again see the teacher in the role of a dispenser of knowledge here. Giving students solutions to homework assignments tends to promote the notion that mathematics problems always have single solutions, that the authority in the classroom is the teacher, and that the students' job is to try to get the same answers the teacher was seeking. The method may appear to be efficient, but it may also send out the wrong message about the nature of mathematics and the role of the teacher in the classroom.

4. Students work homework problems in a notebook, ask the teacher to help them through the most difficult problems each day, and turn in the notebook with solutions corrected at the end of the week.

ADVANTAGE: With this technique, students can update and revise homework answers throughout the week. If they were confused about a skill on Monday, they can ask questions on Tuesday, knowing that they have until Friday to revise Monday's homework and submit their answers.

DISADVANTAGE: Teachers helping students through the homework again places teachers at the focal point of the classroom. Also, some teachers prefer to obtain daily written feedback on student progress, and a weekly notebook collection may not be sufficient to track student understanding of concepts. Finally, many students need daily feedback and reinforcement to keep them on schedule for completing required assignments.

5. Students compare solutions to homework problems in small groups, correct their own papers, and ask the teacher for help, as needed. Papers are handed in for the teacher to check and record.

ADVANTAGE: Students are responsible for their own learning in this model. If all four members of a learning team agree on a homework solution, they can be reasonably certain that they understand the concept and can move on at their own pace, checking their own work. Conversely, whenever a question arises on which all of the team members need assistance, they can raise their hands and obtain the help they need as a group.

DISADVANTAGE: It is possible for a student to simply copy another team member's solution to a problem without understanding the concept. Of course, whether students are able to do this depends on how the cooperative learning tasks are structured as discussed in Chapter 6. Therefore, the teacher should actively monitor the homework checking process by moving from group to group using observation techniques (see Chapter 8 for details). Also, some groups will always finish checking homework assignments more quickly than others, so the teacher needs a plan to keep those students on task while others finish checking their assignments. Sometimes, for example, the teacher may ask a student from an early-finishing table to put a problem on the board or to move to a different group to assist other students who are experiencing difficulty.

The decisions on how to handle homework assignments are largely a reflection of the values and philosophies held by the classroom teacher. For example, a teacher with a belief system rooted in the constructivist or student-centered model would not work through the problems for the students on the chalkboard because that teacher values the classroom discourse in which students argue and use mathematical reasoning to confirm their own solutions. A teacher who believes that it is important to view student work every day is not likely to allow students to hand in a notebook once a week because the teacher fears losing contact with the day-to-day development of the students. Finally, a teacher who places a high value on communication and teamwork might choose to have students compare solutions in small groups and spend that time monitoring, assessing teamwork, and tuning in to misconceptions. Because these decisions are based on values and beliefs, we see teachers using a variety of techniques to check homework. As with any decision regarding how to manage the classroom, you have to select the method that appears to be the most appropriate and is the closest fit for your belief system. And just as options exist for checking homework assignments, there are also several ways to count the homework toward a student's summative evaluation or final grade.

Using Homework Assignments in Assessment

Once a homework assignment has been collected, a teacher has several decisions to make, such as: (1) How will I count this assignment toward the student's grade in the class, if at all? (2) Should I count it as complete or incomplete, or should I score the paper for correct answers? (3) Should I attempt to hand back homework papers daily or collect and hand them back every other day or weekly? Again, the manner in which a teacher handles homework assignment grading will vary, depending on the style and beliefs of the teacher. Here are examples of a few methods of scoring homework assignments and the advantages and disadvantages of each:

1. The teacher collects homework daily and scores the assignment as complete or incomplete/missing, based upon whether or not the student has finished the entire assignment. At the end of the grading period, the student receives a homework percentage based on the number of complete assignments out of the total number collected. For example, if twenty assignments were given, and the student completed eighteen of them on time, the student would receive a 90% (18/20) as a homework score.

    ADVANTAGE: This is a relatively simple method in terms of teacher work time. The teacher just has to make sure that the student completed the assignment and to record it, not to score the paper in any detail.

    DISADVANTAGE: If a student has completed thirteen out of fifteen homework papers and simply skipped two assignments, the student would receive two incomplete/missing marks, as would a student who fails to complete two assignments during the grading period. Therefore, there is no way to numerically distinguish between a student who regularly almost completes assignments and one who rarely attempts the assignments at all.

2. Homework papers are collected daily and scored on a rubric. For example, the teacher might use a simple, four-level rubric such as:

    3 = Complete with all mistakes corrected

    2 = Complete with minor errors on problems not having been corrected

    1 = Incomplete paper but a majority of the problems have been attempted

    0 = Incomplete paper in that less than half of the problems have been attempted, or the student has turned in no paper at all.

    Then, the teacher who has required 20 homework assignments for the grading period can use a scale for accumulated points—for example, a student earning a total of 50–60 rubric points earns an A for homework performance; 40–50 points is a B, and so forth.

    ADVANTAGE: This grading method differentiates between levels of student performance, and the rubric scores *tell* the students and their parents something about the type of work that has been submitted. Rubric scores have the advantage of providing valuable information about a student's performance beyond the fact that the student completed or did not complete an assignment.

    DISADVANTAGE: The rubric-scoring method can be more time consuming than simply determining whether a student has completed an assignment, and it also requires the teacher to develop a workable rubric and final grading scale.

3. Homework assignments are rarely checked in class, and the teacher uses answers on them to determine whether the students have mastered a concept. Assignments are graded in that students receive a percentage score based on how many problems were solved correctly. These percentages are averaged to determine the student's homework grade.

ADVANTAGE: By scoring homework problems, the teacher can save a great deal of classroom time that might otherwise be spent discussing problems the students already know how to do. The teacher can gather information about what students know and can do outside of classtime and keep homework checking time to a minimum.

DISADVANTAGE: The purpose of many homework assignments is to practice a skill that has been taught. If students misunderstand and miss several or most problems on a homework assignment, they are essentially punished in a final grade for making mistakes in the practice exercises. This would be akin to an athlete having deductions taken from an Olympic performance for mistakes in a practice session two weeks before the competition.

There are other homework scoring strategies as well. For example, some teachers assign and collect homework but do not count it toward final grades. In one of the TIMSS reports (Beaton et al., 1996), for example, it was reported that although 46% of Japanese teachers sometimes or always collect, correct, and return assignments to their students, 32% of those teachers never use the homework as a factor in determining final grades. On the other hand, 80% of teachers of eighth graders in the United States sometimes or always assign homework, and 95% of those teachers use the homework in some way to determine final grades. Some teachers collect a weekly homework notebook from students and score it as complete or incomplete or on a rubric but only record a weekly mark, as opposed to scoring each day individually. Still other teachers occasionally assign homework but do not require or collect it—a practice not recommended here because students have little, if any, motivation to do uncollected homework assignments. Also, if the teacher does not collect homework, valuable feedback about student progress is lost.

As we have seen, there are a variety of reasons why a teacher might assign homework, and, once it has been collected, there are also several ways to score and record the assignment before handing it back to students. When making a decision about what homework to assign and what to do with it when students hand in the assignment, keep the six assessment Standards and the assessment Principle in mind and ask yourself questions such as the following:

- Are the homework tasks worthwhile?
- Will the assignment enhance the mathematics teaching and learning process?
- Does the assignment promote equity?
- Have I been open with my students about the purpose for homework and how it will be assessed?
- Will this homework assist me in making reasonable inferences about each student's progress?
- Does this assignment "fit" in the grand scheme of how I teach and assess my students?

In the next section, we explore how a teacher combines all of the assessment data, from test scores to homework averages and portfolio rubric levels, and devises a system for determining final evaluative grades for students.

■ EVALUATION: DETERMINING FINAL GRADES

Although some school districts, counties, and even states use portfolio and checklist assessments without letter grades, most mathematics teachers at the secondary and middle school levels will ultimately be responsible for reporting a letter (or numerical) grade for each student at the end of each grading period. After our discussions about assessment in this chapter and in Chapter 8, we need to think about how all of the pieces of assessment data might come together to determine a student's final grade. Consider the following vignette:

Julio is a student in Mr. Lieb's second period Grade 7 mathematics class. He is an intelligent student who catches on to mathematical concepts quite easily. In the first quarter of the school year, Julio earned a solid B average (89%) on his tests and quizzes. However, because the mathematics comes easily to him, and he spends a great deal of time watching television, Julio only turned in half of his homework (50%) for the quarter. Mr. Lieb firmly believes that tests, quizzes, and homework alone should determine a student's grade, but he has been quoted as saying, "The most important parts are the tests and quizzes; if they can't show me how to do it on a test, they don't understand the material." Consequently, he weighs tests and quizzes as 90% of the grade and homework as 10% of the final grade. At the end of the quarter, he determines Julio's grade as follows:

$$90\%(89\%) + 10\%(50\%) \approx 85\%$$

In the school district, there is a prescribed grading scale, a common occurrence in many districts in the United States:

100%–93%	A
92%–85%	B
84%–77%	C
76%–70%	D
<69%	F

Because of the result of the calculation (85%) and the required grading scale, Mr. Lieb gives Julio a B for the first quarter.

Across the hall, Ms. Ward is teaching a seventh grader by the name of Ashleigh. Like Julio, Ashleigh does well on tests but generally forgets to do her homework assignments and rushes to finish them on the bus in the morning when she can. Coincidentally, she also averages 89% for tests and quizzes and has done 50% of her homework in the first quarter. However, Ms. Ward believes that homework is a sign of motivation, character, and disposition, and she weighs it as one third of a student's final grade, whereas tests and quizzes account for the other two thirds. At the end of the quarter, Ms. Ward does the following calculation:

$$\tfrac{2}{3}(89\%) + \tfrac{1}{3}(50\%) = 76\%$$

Using the scale required by the district, Ms. Ward gives Ashleigh a D for the first quarter because her average fell in the range of 70% to 76%.

Imagine how Julio and Ashleigh will feel at lunch when they discover that they both had an 89% test and quiz average and did half of their homework in mathematics, but Julio received a final grade of a B, and Ashleigh got a D in the same course. Because schools often use a generalized grading scale but seldom require a particular system of arriving at the numerical averages, these differences occur all the time. Which final grade do *you* believe is the most reasonable? The answer probably lies in what you value as a teacher. If you, like Mr. Lieb, believe that competencies measured by tests and quizzes tell most of the story, then you might be inclined to give the student a B. If, on the other hand, you want to reward students for doing homework and punish those who don't, you might find Ms. Ward's grade of a D more reasonable. But think about it—without knowing the students or their teachers, how do you feel about a student who maintains a high B average on tests and quizzes but only does homework half of the time? Is it reasonable to assume that this student should, at least, receive a C in the course? Or is Ms. Ward's grade of a D acceptable? This scenario paints a very realistic picture in terms of how students are assessed in school mathematics: Final grades are essentially arbitrary. The grades often depend more upon the values and beliefs of the teacher than on the performance of the student.

This story also holds another moral for us as we look at ways of determining student grades: Perhaps the example serves as a case for why more diverse assessment tools than tests, quizzes, and homework are necessary in determining a student's final grade. For example, if these students were required to write in journals twice a week and keep a portfolio, we might discover that Ashleigh eloquently expresses herself in journal writing and portfolio reflections, but Julio does not, and we would obtain a further window into student thinking that allows us to more adequately evaluate their performance in a final grade.

Let's imagine, for example, that Ms. Ward agrees that her current system of determining grades is inadequate; all dimensions of student learning are not accounted for when only tests, quizzes, and homework are utilized. She has decided to have students write in mathematics journals twice a week and to collect, read, and react to the journal entries every two weeks. She has also decided to assign a team project each grading period. Finally, she will ask an open-ended question every Wednesday and score it on a holistic rubric to give students experiences with solving problems and defending their thinking. She has added these three assessment tools to gain a deeper understanding of how her students develop. The journal entries will allow students to express their thinking in writing and bring Ms. Ward more in touch with their opinions and learning styles. The projects will promote interpersonal communication and demonstrate for students that real mathematics problems are not always clearly defined or easily solved. The open-ended questions will give students practice in defending answers and communicating clearly and will serve as practice for state proficiency testing that includes open-ended questions.

The journal entries can be scored as complete or incomplete or can be placed on a simple rubric. For example, a rubric from 0 to 2 could be used as follows:

2 = a journal entry has been completed, contains clear written communication, and illustrates depth and insight

1 = a journal entry has been completed but may be vague or entail surface-level thinking without the depth that was expected

0 = the journal entry was incomplete or not turned in at all

Since a grading period is ten weeks, Ms. Ward will have collected the journals five times over that time period. A student earning 8 to 10 total rubric points receives an A for journal writing; a total of 6 or 7 points earns a B; 4 or 5 points earns a C; 2 or 3 points is a D, and 0 through 2 points is an F. By using this type of conversion scale, the rubric points can be translated into more traditional percentage-type scores used in a final grade. Keep in mind, as was pointed out in Chapter 8, that rubric points should not be thought of as percentages. A score of a 1 on a journal does not indicate 1 out of 2 or 50%. A 1 simply places a journal entry in a category so that the teacher and student have an indicator of the quality of that particular journal entry.

Similarly, the open-ended questions could be scored on a five-point rubric. Because a weekly question is to be given for ten weeks, the students could earn up to 50 rubric points. Through experience, Ms. Ward can determine how many points out of 50 the student needs to accumulate to earn an A, a B, and so forth. The project grades can be based on a 100-point scale that includes data collection, a written report, and a classroom presentation. In this way, each of the areas in which she is assessing her students' progress can be quantified so that a letter or percentage grade—which is required by her district—can be determined.

The final grading scheme in terms of weight for each of the grade's components depends on what the teacher values. For example, the final grade could be determined as follows:

30%	Tests
15%	Quizzes
15%	Project
10%	Open-Ended questions
10%	Journals
20%	Homework

Utilizing this grading scale, Ms. Ward preserves a relatively heavy weighting for homework but builds in several other "pieces" that show the total progress of the student. With the new assessment system containing all of these additional assessments, Ashleigh's first quarter grade may be more likely to reflect her total performance in the class. Let's take a closer look at how her grade might be determined.

Suppose that Ashleigh's test average was 85%, and her quiz average was 95% for the first quarter. She also conducted a project on which she earned 80 points out of 100—an 80%. We already know that she completed 50% of her homework assignments for the grading period. The class was given ten open-ended questions during the term, and each question was scored on a five-point rubric. Based on previous experience with using rubrics to assess student work, Ms. Ward converted rubric scores into percentages by applying the following scale:

50–45 rubric points	→	A work	→	use 95% as the numerical score
44–35 rubric points	→	B work	→	use 88% as the numerical score
34–25 rubric points	→	C work	→	use 81% as the numerical score
24–15 rubric points	→	D work	→	use 73% as the numerical score
14–5 rubric points	→	F work	→	use 60% as the numerical score

She has never had a student earn fewer than 10 total rubric points for the quarter.

Suppose that Ashleigh accumulated a total of 32 rubric points. Using Ms. Ward's scale, she would receive a grade of a C or 81% for open-ended questions. Finally, student journals were collected five times, and Ms. Ward used the following conversion scale for journal grades:

10–8 total journal rubric points $\rightarrow$ A work $\rightarrow$ assign a score of 95%
7–6 total journal rubric points $\rightarrow$ B work $\rightarrow$ assign a score of 88%
5–4 total journal rubric points $\rightarrow$ C work $\rightarrow$ assign a score of 81%
3–2 total journal rubric points $\rightarrow$ D work $\rightarrow$ assign a score of 73%

Ms. Ward has never had a student earn less than 3 journal rubric points in a quarter.

For the first quarter, Ashleigh earned 6 total rubric points, so she is assigned a grade of 88% for journals. Therefore, all of the collected data can be used to determine her grade.

Tests:	30%(85%) = .255
Quizzes:	15%(95%) = .1425
Project:	15%(80%) = .12
Open-ended questions:	10%(81%) = .081
Journals:	10%(88%) = .088
Homework:	20%(50%) = .10

So, her grade can be calculated by finding $0.255 + 0.1425 + 0.12 + 0.081 + 0.088 + 0.10 = 0.7865$, which rounds to 79% and is a C on the school's grading scale. Contrast this grade to the original situation in which Julio received a B and Ashleigh earned a D when only test and quiz scores, along with homework assignments, were used in the assessment process. We might claim that Ms. Ward's revised grading system results in a fair and realistic assessment of Ashleigh's performance for the first quarter.

However, we need to be careful about assuming that this grading practice will water down grades. Some people automatically assume that if tests and quizzes count for a smaller fraction of the grade, the students will earn higher percentages in the class, and this will cause an inflation of grades. But some students are good test takers and would much rather have grades based on exam performance than have to complete projects and write in journals. In fact, many students who have been historically successful with tests and quizzes as performance indicators may earn considerably lower grades on this scale because they may not be as proficient at expressing their thoughts in writing and defending solutions. On the other hand, students who perform well in a team setting and appreciate the forum in which to discuss thoughts about the class may see their grades enhanced by the same system.

In the end, no grading system, per se, is perfect. In an attempt to meet the six criteria set forth in the assessment Standards and the assessment Principle, it is important to vary the assessment strategies. But how many strategies are ideal? Is it reasonable to assume that if observations are being used, formal interviews may not be necessary? If students are regularly answering open-ended questions, are quizzes necessary at all? These are decisions that each teacher has to make: No answers universally apply to all classrooms. The most important issue to consider is that once a grading system has been devised, the teacher needs to ask, "How well will I get to know the development of each of my students by using this approach?" If the system appears to maximize the teacher's window into each student's thinking, then it's probably on the right track. Julio and Ashleigh may earn final grades that are a letter grade or two higher or lower than they have earned under their current systems because of the use of other strategies for assessing their progress.

■ CONCLUSION ■

Equity has become a focal point in mathematics education reform over the past decade. The notions that every student should have equal access to important mathematics and that teachers need to provide a variety of assessment opportunities so that each student can demonstrate an understanding of the mathematics have become critical in the reform process. However, recent research (Senk, Beckmann, & Thompson, 1997) showed that secondary teachers still rely heavily upon tests, quizzes, and homework to assess student progress and that most test items tend to be low level and are not open ended. A previous study by Garet and Mills (1995) suggested that assessment practices are still dominated by short-answer and multiple-choice tests and that there has been little change in the use of these techniques over time despite the recommendations of professional organizations and the availability of assessment ideas in mathematics education literature. So, although standards have been set to suggest changes in assessment strategies, many are still comfortable with the old ways of collecting data on student progress and assigning grades. But why has it been so difficult to get mathematics teachers to alter their practices?

Research by Cooney, Badger, and Wilson (1993) suggests that teachers will only use a variety of strategies to determine student progress under three conditions: (1) The assessment tasks must be consistent with the teacher's own understanding of what it means to do mathematics; (2) the teachers must see the value of the tasks in determining student understandings of mathematics, and (3) teachers must believe that the outcomes these alternative assessment strategies measure are important. If one views mathematics

as nothing more than a list of discrete, measurable skills to be learned over time, it is difficult to convince that individual of the value of students writing in a journal or keeping a portfolio. If a teacher does not appreciate the value of communication in the mathematics classroom, then that individual will probably not use team projects in a class. So, as we have previously stated, the assessment strategies that you choose will reflect what you believe about the nature of mathematics and what you think is important in your classroom. And students will pick up on your values and often make them their own. In the end, the assessment system we choose in our mathematics classroom and the way that we determine grades will teach students important lessons about the very nature of the subject area.

In this chapter, we have extended the ideas about assessment presented in Chapter 8 into a discussion of how authentic assessment strategies can promote equity and visited the very practical issues of assigning and scoring homework and determining final grades in a class. As you conduct your classes, over time, you will find some strategies to work better for you than others and are likely to change your thinking and refine your teaching practices. Just because you used a particular system last year doesn't mean that you have to feel committed to use it the following year. In fact, many teachers modify their assessment practices by trying one new technique each year and reflecting on whether they will adopt it and use it on a continuing basis. In order to explore ideas for change, effective teachers of mathematics regularly go back to school, attend conferences, and take part in a variety of other professional development opportunities so that their education is ongoing. In the final chapter, Chapter 10, we explore the role of the teacher in the school context. We discuss how teachers work with parents, administrators, and within a department and the importance of participating in ongoing professional activities.

■ GLOSSARY ■

Assessment Cycle: In *Principles and Standards for School Mathematics,* the NCTM describes assessment as an ongoing cycle that includes goal setting, evidence gathering, the interpretation of evidence, and taking action based on the interpretations. Teachers are constantly in the process of gathering data on student progress and analyzing it for a variety of purposes.

Equity: Equity is the assumption that all students have a right to equal access to the study of mathematics. The term "all students" refers to students of various ethnocultural and socioeconomic backgrounds as well as students who are female and male. Equity is a key issue in the assessment process, as teachers look for ways to provide each student with an opportunity to demonstrate understanding of mathematical concepts.

Inference: An inference is a conclusion that is based on the collection and analysis of evidence or data. For example, in statistics, we might look at the value of a correlation coefficient and infer that two variables are related, such as the performance of a student on the SAT and that student's eventual college grade-point average. Similarly, when teachers collect assessment data, they make inferences about the progress that their students are making in terms of academic achievement and attitude development.

■ DISCUSSION QUESTIONS ■

1. Obtain a syllabus from a secondary or middle school mathematics class that includes a description of how students are assessed. Using the six assessment Standards as the criteria, critique the strengths and weaknesses of the assessment system for the course.

2. In a small group, brainstorm some specific strategies that a teacher might employ to promote equity in the mathematics classroom. What type of activities and classroom environment characteristics can promote equal access to mathematics for females, minorities, and socioeconomically disadvantaged students?

3. Discuss reasons why female students tend to take fewer mathematics courses and select careers that use less mathematics than their male peers. What specific steps can teachers at the secondary and middle school levels take to increase female participation in mathematically oriented career areas?

4. Select a mathematical topic, such as constructing and interpreting circle graphs, and devise three assessment alternatives from which students could choose to demonstrate their understanding of the concept.

5. What is a reasonable amount of time for a secondary or middle school student to spend on a homework assignment each evening? How can you determine whether you are assigning too much or not enough homework and whether the assignments are actually beneficial for the students in your class?

6. In the chapter, five methods of checking homework assignments were described and critiqued. Which methods appear to be the most desirable for you, and why would you select them over the others? Small groups could each select a favorite and then compare their thinking with other groups.

7. Three methods of using homework assignments to contribute to final grades were discussed, and two other methods were mentioned in this chapter. In small groups, discuss which methods appear to be the most desirable, and why you would select them over the others.

8. The cases of Julio and Ashleigh were described in this chapter. Julio and Ashleigh are seventh grade students who are both carrying an 89% test and quiz average but have only completed half of their homework assignments for the

grading period. What final grade do you believe that they deserve in mathematics? Be prepared to defend your answer in terms of fairness to these students and the rest of the class.

9. Design a system for determining final grades in your class by including any categories of evidence that you wish and their weighing as percentages. Explain how the system is fair, equitable, and meets the criteria in the assessment Standards and the assessment Principle.

10. Teachers devise their assessment systems based on their beliefs about the nature of mathematics and what they value in the classroom. What do you value in the teaching and learning of mathematics, and how are your values demonstrated in your plan for determining final grades for students in your classes?

■ BIBLIOGRAPHIC REFERENCES AND RESOURCES ■

Beaton, A. E., Mullis, I. V., Martin, M. O., Gonzalez, E. J., Kelly, D. L., & Smith, T. A. (1996). *TIMSS: Mathematics Achievement in the Middle School Years.* Chestnut Hill, MA: Center for the Study of Testing, Evaluation, and Educational Policy.

Belcher, T., Coates, G. D., Franco, J., & Mayfield-Ingram, K. (1997). Assessment and equity. In J. Trentacosta (Ed.), *1997 Yearbook of the NCTM: Multicultural and gender equity in the mathematics classroom: The gift of diversity*, pp. 195–200. Reston, VA: National Council of Teachers of Mathematics.

Bolte, L. A. (1999). Using concept maps and interpretive essays for assessment in mathematics. *School Science and Mathematics, 99* (1), pp. 19–30.

Cooney, T. J., Badger, E., & Wilson, M. R. (1993). Assessment, understanding mathematics, and distinguishing visions from mirages. In N. L. Webb (Ed.), *1993 Yearbook of the NCTM: Assessment in the mathematics classroom,* pp. 239–247. Reston, VA: National Council of Teachers of Mathematics.

Croom, L. (1997). Mathematics for all students: Access, excellence, and equity. In J. Trentacosta (Ed.), *1997 NCTM Yearbook: Multicultural and gender equity in the mathematics classroom: The gift of diversity*, pp. 1–9. Reston, VA: National Council of Teachers of Mathematics.

Eisenhower National Clearinghouse. (1998). *Making schools work for every child CD-ROM.* Columbus, OH: Eisenhower National Clearinghouse.

Eisenhower National Clearinghouse. (1998). Multicultural approaches in math and science. *ENC Focus, 5* (1).

Fennema, E. (1994). Gender and mathematics education research. *NCRMSE Research Review: The Teaching and Learning of Mathematics, 3,* 6–7.

Frankenstein, M. (1997). In addition to the mathematics: Including equity issues in the curriculum. In J. Trentacosta (Ed.), *1997 Yearbook of the NCTM: Multicultural and gender equity in the mathematics classroom: The gift of diversity.* Reston, VA: National Council of Teachers of Mathematics.

Garet, M. S. & Mills, V. L. (1995). Changes in teaching practices: The effects of the curriculum and evaluation standards. *Mathematics Teacher, 88,* 380–389.

Lambdin, D. V. (1995). Implementing the assessment standards for school mathematics: An open-and-shut case? Openness in the assessment process. *Mathematics Teacher, 88* (8), 680–684.

Leder, G. C. (1992). Mathematics and gender: Changing perspectives. In D. A. Grouws (Ed.), *Handbook of research on mathematics teaching and learning,* pp. 597–622. Reston, VA: National Council of Teachers of Mathematics.

Malloy, C. E. & Brader-Araje, L. (1998). *Challenges in the mathematics education of African American children: Proceedings of the Benjamin Banneker association leadership conference.* Reston, VA: National Council of Teachers of Mathematics.

Malloy, C. E. (1997). Including African American students in the mathematics community. In J. Trentacosta (Ed.), *1997 Yearbook of the NCTM: Multicultural and gender equity in the mathematics classroom: The gift of diversity*, pp. 23–33. Reston, VA: National Council of Teachers of Mathematics.

Mayer, J. & Hillman, S. (1996). Implementing the assessment standards for school mathematics: Assessing students' thinking through writing. *Mathematics Teacher, 89* (5), 428–432.

McLean, E. (1993). Tips for beginners: Steps for better homework. *Mathematics Teacher, 86* (3), 212.

Michigan Department of Education and the NCREL. (1999). *Connecting with the learner: An equity toolkit.* Oak Brook, IL: North Central Regional Educational Laboratory.

National Council of Teachers of Mathematics. (1998). *Principles and standards for school mathematics* (working draft). Reston, VA: National Council of Teachers of Mathematics.

National Council of Teachers of Mathematics. (1995). *Assessment standards for school mathematics.* Reston, VA: National Council of Teachers of Mathematics.

National Science Foundation. (1994). *Women, minorities, and persons with disabilities in science and engineering.* Arlington, VA: National Science Foundation.

Nelson, D., Joseph, G. C., & Williams, J. (1993). *Multicultural mathematics: Teaching mathematics from a global perspective.* New York, NY: Oxford UP.

Ortiz-Franco, L., Hernandez, N. G., & De La Cruz, Y. (Eds.). (1999). *Changing the faces of mathematics: Perspectives on Latinos.* Reston, VA: National Council of Teachers of Mathematics.

Secada, W. G., Fennema, E., & Adajian, L. B. (1994). *New directions for equity in mathematics education.* Reston, VA: National Council of Teachers of Mathematics.

Senk, S. L., Beckmann, C. E., & Thompson, D. R. (1997). Assessment and grading in high school mathematics classes. *Journal for Research in Mathematics Education, 28,* 187–215.

Trentacosta, J. (Ed.). (1997). *1997 Yearbook of the NCTM: Multicultural and gender equity in the mathematics classroom: The gift of diversity.* Reston, VA: National Council of Teachers of Mathematics.

Vincent, M. L. & Wilson, L. (1996). Implementing the assessment standards for school mathematics: Informal assessment: A story from the classroom. *Mathematics Teacher, 89* (3), 248–250.

The Teaching Profession and Appendices

Curricular issues, including content and sequencing, together with instructional issues, such as the teaching strategies used in the classroom, and assessment (discussed in Unit IV) are the three major issues in the field of mathematics education. In this final unit, we discuss the context in which mathematics teaching and learning occurs. Teachers are professionals who work in conjunction with colleagues toward a common purpose—preparing young minds for successful integration into our society. The school environment includes interactions with peers, administrators, parents, and the community at large. As trends in curriculum, teaching, and assessment change, it is critical for teachers to create a professional development plan and to use coursework and other inservice opportunities to update their skills and continue their lifelong education. In Chapter 10, "The Teacher of Mathematics in the School Community," we discuss what it means to teach mathematics in the school context. Following Chapter 10, several appendices serve as a resource for additional information, discussion topics, and teaching ideas.

The Teacher of Mathematics in the School Community

After reading Chapter 10, you should be able to answer the following questions:

■ What can the teacher do to enhance communication between the parents of students and school personnel?

■ What are the criteria by which the performance of teachers of mathematics can be supervised and evaluated?

■ How do departments of mathematics function in a secondary or middle school? What is the role of the classroom teacher within the department?

■ What psychological factors interact and affect the decisions that a teacher makes during class? Discuss these factors. Why is participation in staff development activities critical?

■ What are some opportunities that teachers of mathematics have for professional development? Why is it important for teachers to write a professional development plan?

A teacher once said that he had 100 reasons to get out of bed and teach every day and that his greatest joy was greeting those 100 "reasons" and calling them by name five days a week in his classroom. In addition to being excited about mathematics, successful teachers who enjoy their jobs need to be equally excited about kids—after all, the development of thinking skills in students is the ultimate product of our efforts. It is very rewarding for a teacher to see a student volunteer a nonroutine approach to a problem, make an effective presentation to the class, or suddenly gain a profound insight on a task. Indeed, the teaching profession carries with it a great deal of interaction with children and young adults, which can be exciting and gratifying.

In the midst of that enjoyment in the classroom, however, many teachers still feel isolated and disconnected in their workplace. After the teacher greets the students and closes the classroom door, what occurs during the next 40 to 120 minutes is up to that teacher. There is generally not another colleague or adult in the classroom during the entire time period. Consequently, teaching is, for some, a lonely profession. But teaching also has the potential to be very connected as all the teachers in a school have a common purpose—educating young minds.

Although teachers may feel alone at times, they are part of a much larger education community that includes colleagues, parents, administrators, members of the community, and other mathematics teachers around the city, county, state, country, and the world. None of us acts entirely alone, and everything we do in the classroom ultimately impacts a host of other people. In this chapter, we discuss the context in which the teaching and learning of mathematics occurs and the role of the teacher in that greater context. We begin by exploring the role of parents in the educational process.

■ WORKING WITH PARENTS

The following is a list of actual contacts that parents of secondary and middle school students have made with their children's mathematics teachers:

- A parent called a teacher to express displeasure with perceived classroom instructional practices. The teacher frequently assigned homework problems and encouraged students to explain their approaches to others in the class. During the phone call, the parent was clearly upset and said, "It is apparent that you don't understand the mathematics yourself and are hoping that students will bail you out by having them explain the problems to one another."
- A parent sent a note to the mathematics teacher that called the teacher "the most significant positive influence on my daughter's life in her educational career."
- A parent called the principal to complain that the teacher had used a laser disc problem-solving program in class that day. He claimed that "the teacher is forcing students to watch television in class and calling it mathematics education." Later in the conversation, the parent stated that "kids watch too much TV at home these days, and they certainly don't need another hour of it in your classroom!"
- A parent shook a mathematics teacher's hand at parent-teacher conferences and said, "I don't know what you're doing in that classroom, but my son literally can't wait to get out of bed in the morning to get to your class. It's just surprising because he has never really liked math that much in the past. Thank you!"
- A parent called the teacher because students had been using graphing calculators in class. He argued that "when students are using calculators, they're not learning math; the machine is doing all the thinking in that classroom" and asked the teacher, "Why are you allowing your students to cheat with those things?"
- A parent showed up at a mathematics teacher's house on the last day of school with a bouquet of flowers just to say "thank you" to the teacher and his spouse for their support of the students in the class.

- A parent approached a teacher before school one morning and explained how her son had "always been good at mathematics until he got to your class" and that "his uncle is a math teacher, and whenever he works with my son, he says that he can't imagine why my son isn't getting an A." Although she didn't actually say so, the parent believed it was the teacher's fault that her son's performance had declined over the past year.
- A parent approached her daughter's middle school mathematics teacher after her daughter had graduated from college with a degree in mathematics education and said, "It all started with you. . . . Your class inspired her to become a mathematics teacher."

Clearly, parents can be our hardest critics, but they can also be our strongest allies. One thing that all of the scenarios above have in common is that the parents are interested in the development of their children and care enough to speak to the teacher about it, whether they are critical or complimentary. Teachers cannot begin to spend the same amount of time with a student that a parent or guardian does, and no one has invested as much time and energy into the students' lives as their parents. Whereas parents watch their children grow and change throughout their entire lives, the teacher only gets a glimpse of the students' total development. No one knows the students better than the people who live with them, and this puts parents in a position to help teachers understand the development of each child. But how can we solicit the help of parents and keep them supportive of our efforts? Here are some practical suggestions for working with them.

- Communication with parents is extremely important. The more frequently and clearly that a teacher communicates with parents, the more likely they are to understand the focus in the classroom. In fact, in the NCTM *Curriculum and Evaluation Standards* (1989), the authors stated that "parents who expect students to do mathematics homework on paper at a desk rather than by gathering real data to solve a problem will be surprised. The best way to bring about reform is to challenge directly the perceptions held by many about the content of mathematics" (p. 255). There are a variety of ways to open these doors with parents and help them examine their perceptions. Some teachers send an informal newsletter out to parents biweekly, monthly, or once in a grading period. In the newsletter, the teacher describes the topics the class has been studying and provides examples of the type of activities and problems the students have been encountering. The newsletter often contains an article encouraging parents to call if they have questions. Other teachers put on a "family math night," in which parents can come to the classroom and engage in hands-on activities themselves to model what their children are doing in school. Sometimes, parents believe that "manipulatives are toys" or that "calculators are cheating devices" until they personally experience a lesson that involves the use of these tools. The family math night also gives the teacher an opportunity to explain and to model the philosophy of the classroom. Finally, some teachers make regular phone calls to parents just to touch base and talk to them about student progress. A five-minute phone call to each parent, once per grading period, is usually time extremely well spent.

- When parents do call or send a note, be sure to respond to their concerns immediately, and when you have a concern about a particular student, do not hesitate to call the parents. Many teachers believe that a phone call to parents is a last resort, used only when all else fails. In reality, however, most parents appreciate a phone call sooner rather than later. It is much easier to head off a problem at the start (for example, if a student is not attempting homework assignments) than to wait until it is too late and grades suffer. A conversation with a parent may result in changing the way the student's time is organized or securing a tutor to assist the student with the content of a particularly difficult unit.

- Consider having each student keep a portfolio as an assessment strategy as was described in Chapters 8 and 9. Portfolios can be used to track student progress over time, and they provide an excellent tool with which to review a student's work with parents during scheduled meetings, parent-teacher conferences, and so forth. When a parent comes in to discuss a child's performance, it is much more effective and desirable to walk the parent through a portfolio that highlights the student's work than to quote numbers representing test and quiz scores. Parents appreciate the fact that the teacher can show concrete evidence of what the student believes and is able to do rather than simply telling them that "your daughter has an 84% average in my class and is doing okay."

- Whenever possible, involve parents in the process of problem solving and doing homework assignments. Suppose, for example, that you developed the concept of why the area of a circle can be found by taking πr^2 with your students. The homework assignment for the evening could be for the students to go home and re-explain this concept to their parents and bring a note back from them the next day indicating that the task was completed. Sometimes parents can be used to assist in the collection of data for a long-term project: Students might, for example, ask their parents how much electricity their family uses on a monthly basis according to old electric bills. Not only do these types of projects and assignments get the parents involved in the child's education, but they also serve as a means of communicating to parents the mathematical content and processes the students are developing in school and bringing them on board.

- Whenever possible, involve parents directly in the teaching and learning process. For example, some parents like to come into the classroom and observe a lesson now and then. With the principal's permission, parents should feel welcome to do this so that they can experience the classroom for themselves. Also, if you know the career areas of parents and guardians of your students, you might invite them to give presentations on particular topics. The class may be interested in hearing from Marge's father who works for the Water Department and can explain how mathematics is used in the water-treatment process or from Bill's mother who is a surgeon and can describe the use of problem-solving and reasoning skills during an operation.

Parents and guardians play a pivotal role in the success of a mathematics class, so whatever you can do to involve them and communicate with them is likely to work to your advantage. Similarly, parents want to help their children in your class. So, a frequently asked question is, "How can I best help my student to learn mathematics in your class?" At the beginning of the school year, you may want to consider distributing a handout with tips for parents on how to help their children at home. Here is an example of a such handout that was provided to parents of algebra students at a beginning-of-the-year Parent Night:

HINTS FOR HELPING YOUR CHILD IN ALGEBRA

- When assisting your child with a homework assignment, it is generally *not* helpful to show him/her how to do an individual problem. This is particularly true in a class like this, in which hands-on materials and technology are emphasized. There is often a shortcut to an answer, but when the student is shown the trick, the underlying reasons why it is done a certain way are lost.
- When your child is struggling with a problem or concept, sympathize with him/her by saying, "That problem/concept is difficult for me to understand too" but *never* remark, "I don't know . . . I never was very good in math either." The latter statement sends a message that if algebra was not important and useful to you—and you got where you are today—then there's no real need for your child to know it either.
- You do *not* need to be an expert at algebra to help your child with homework or studying. The best way to do this is to ask leading questions. Ask such questions as: "What is the problem asking you to figure out?" "How might you start the problem?" "Did you do an example similar to that in class today or this week? What did you do in that problem?" "Can you show me your notes from today and explain what you discussed in class?" Research shows that those parents in other countries who are excellent helpers tend to *motivate* and *monitor* the efforts of their children, but they also tend to be scared of the math content of their children's classes.
- If you and your child are both stuck on a problem, make sure that he/she knows where the difficulty began and encourage him/her to ask about it in class the next day. Say to your child, "When you come home tomorrow, I want *you* to explain to *me* how to do that problem. I'll be curious to know how other people attacked it. . . ." In this way, you become part of the learning team at home, and your child knows you're concerned about his/her frustration and that you want to know how to solve the math problem, too.
- Encourage your child to work with other students in the class. Often, a short phone call to a classmate/friend can help a student to realize that he/she is not the only one who has a certain question. A conversation with another person in the class may help to clear up the problem. It's not unusual for students to get together after school, in the evening, or on the weekend to work through a set of problems or study together. Mathematics can be a social activity— research shows that students learn math concepts best when they talk to other students about what they're doing. On the first day of class, each student was

asked to write down the name and phone number of one other person in their notebooks so that they could contact that person if needed.

- Completion of homework assignments and writing of journal entries are essential for success in the course. Students have been told that if they establish any kind of pattern of missing assignments or not completing them, you will be contacted.

- Ask and expect your child to bring tests, quizzes, projects, etc., home and show you his/her progress with some regularity. As parents of an adolescent, you want your child to have some autonomy and personal responsibility. However, he/she is still in a stage in which parents watching over the shoulder now and then continues to be very helpful. You would be surprised how many students go through an entire quarter (or even semester) without showing a parent a single paper from class. When you look at a test, focus questions and comments on, "What have you been learning to do lately? Can you show me?" rather than focusing on the grade and questions that he/she missed on the test.

- Encourage your child to participate actively in class and not to be afraid to ask and answer questions. There is no such thing as a wrong answer in a mathematics class. Every incorrect response is simply a door that leads the class into another discussion, and students can learn more from a mistake than a correct answer. Generally, the students who have a positive attitude and take an active role in class discussions are the ones who excel in this course.

- No textbook is used for this course because the class is student centered. The direction in which we move depends on questions raised and the needs of the class. Before the year is over, we will have explored every algebra concept required by the Course of Study (and then some). If, however, your child wants or needs additional skill practice, algebra textbooks are available that can be checked out for a short time or the entire year. *Because of the student-centered nature of the class, assignments for upcoming days can generally not be given in advance (for vacations, etc.).*

- It is important that students in this course feel successful, challenged, and confident in their study of mathematics. Often, students are very active in organizations, playing on athletic teams, helping with activities at church, etc. Watch for signs that may indicate that your child is overloaded (e.g., a great deal of stress, work not getting completed, late bedtimes, grades falling in other classes), so that we can work out a strategy to help.

- If, at any time, you have questions about your child's progress, please call me. I can be most easily reached by calling the office at (419) 555-8662. If I am not available, leave a voice-mail message, and I will return the call as soon as possible.

As you read over this handout, you might have noticed that openness with parents is paramount. The teacher has explained how the classroom will be student centered and why homework assignments are generally not given in advance. Likewise, the teacher has explained why a textbook is not being used but offers to allow the students to check out a book if the parents or student would like one. Clear com-

Parents and siblings participate in a Family Math Night to promote active parental involvement in the educational process.

munication about rules, as well as suggestions for parents, are essential elements of a successful school year. As the teacher noted in the handout, parents help their students the most when they monitor what the students are doing and motivate them to do their best.

In *Family Math* by Stenmark, Thompson, and Cossey (1986), the authors make a number of recommendations as to how parents can help their students to be successful in class. In addition to those listed in the sample handout above, they also suggest that parents should communicate to their children that they have confidence in their ability to succeed. They encourage parents to provide a specific location for study, depending upon the learning style of the student. A particular room or a special table in a well-lit room can help to make the process of studying more of a regular routine. Finally, they ask parents to be models of persistence and enjoyment of doing mathematics. As we have seen in Chapters 2 and 6, students become persistent, confident, and interested in mathematics by working with people—such as parents and teachers—who espouse those same dispositions. Becoming a positive person generally results from associating ourselves with other positive people.

The success of a teacher in working with students and their parents may be measured and reported in a variety of ways. Generally, the principal is responsible for assessing the performance of teachers, although department chairs, assistant principals, or even central office supervisors are also often involved in the process. In the next section, we will take a look at the process of assessing and evaluating teaching performance.

■ THE SUPERVISION AND EVALUATION OF TEACHERS

It is Thursday morning, and you have just prepared the most exciting mathematics lesson of the year. Students will be rotating among learning centers, spinning spinners, dealing cards, and pulling marbles from bags to examine counting rules and probability. Even better, today is the day that the principal has decided to visit your classroom to observe and read through your lesson planning book. The students come to class and are oriented to the learning centers, but as they begin to circulate about the room, everything goes wrong. It's rapidly approaching Prom Weekend, and at the tables, students are more interested in talking about the band, tuxedos, and dresses than the chances of pulling a red marble from the bag. The spinner falls apart at one table, and a student drops a bag of marbles, spilling them all over the classroom floor. In your frustration, you try to stop the class and reorganize the activity, but it's too late—the students are laughing about the marbles on the floor and do not understand the point of what they are doing at the stations. As the bell signals the end of the period, you take a deep breath and watch the principal walk out the classroom door with a frown on her face. It's not that you haven't had a lesson bomb before, but the principal hasn't been there to witness it. You realize that your evaluation for the semester depended on her observation of this lesson, and you fear that your file will be adversely affected by this disaster. You think back to the day that Francine, one of your students, said to you, "It's too bad that one third of our semester grade is based on this exam; I know so much more than the test measured, and I just had a bad day." Similarly, you are aware that you are a much better teacher than the one that the principal just observed, but you also had a bad day.

If you are fortunate enough to have an administrator who acknowledges that assessments are merely snapshots of the whole, then that person is probably going to use more data in an evaluation than observation notes from one classroom visit. Just as we emphasized throughout Unit IV that it is important to use a diverse array of assessment strategies to determine student progress in mathematics, administrators should use several pieces of evidence to determine your effectiveness as a teacher. The ways in which teachers are assessed and evaluated often varies greatly from one school or district to another. The following is a list of some of the pieces of evidence that can be collected to determine your effectiveness as a teacher:

- classroom observation notes from announced visits
- classroom observation notes from unannounced visits
- an examination of your lesson plan and grade books
- preobservation and postobservation interview notes
- degree to which you have addressed your self-stated goals on your annual professional development plan (which we will discuss later in the chapter)
- formal or informal input from peers, including colleagues and a department chair regarding your classroom performance, adherence to standards, use of

technology or manipulatives, understanding of mathematics content, and so forth
- letters written by parents or students in support of your teaching performance
- scores earned by students on standardized district- or statewide tests of achievement
- professional activity within local, state, or national mathematics organizations
- evidence of the establishment of positive classroom environments, including photographs of bulletin boards and student projects
- other samples of student accomplishments, including project posters, videotapes of classroom presentations, and models (such as three-dimensional solids) constructed by students

While few districts would use *all* of the pieces of evidence listed here, many use a combination of *some* of them to serve as a sample of your work in the process of evaluating teaching performance. Consequently (and luckily) a teaching evaluation for the file does not generally hinge on one classroom observation alone. As a result, if the principal saw your probability lesson going awry, she would also have a file that included a host of evidence to support that, despite the lack of success on that particular day, you are still an excellent teacher. In fact, many administrators would look at the probability lesson through a positive lens and compliment the teacher for at least attempting a hands-on activity that involved groups of students working in centers. They would also recognize the difficulty with teaching the week of the Prom and take that into consideration when reporting on your teaching performance. In the end, the analogy of assessing teaching performance to that of assessing student progress in mathematics is powerful. Any one of the assessment items on its own would be an insufficient base for an entire report on your teaching performance just as test scores are not the only components of a grade when both teachers and students have other dimensions that are worth measuring and including in a final evaluation.

In the *Professional Standards for Teaching Mathematics* (1991), the authors addressed the issue of teacher evaluation by putting forth eight Standards for evaluation. The first three Standards deal with the process of evaluating a mathematics teacher, whereas, the other five list characteristics that should be observed and measured when a teacher is evaluated.

Standard 1: The Evaluation Cycle

The evaluation of the teaching of mathematics should be a cyclical process involving

- the periodic collection and analysis of information about an individual's teaching of mathematics;
- professional development based on the analysis of teaching;
- the improvement of teaching as a consequence of the professional development.

(NCTM, *Professional Standards for Teaching Mathematics*, 1991, p. 75.)

Like the assessment cycle for student progress described in Chapter 9, teacher evaluation should follow a sequential process of collecting data, analyzing it, and attempting to improve performance based on the analysis. Throughout the book, we have emphasized the importance of reflection in the teaching and learning process and made the point that teaching improves when we think about what we attempted to do in the classroom, how our plan actually played out, and what we might do to improve our lesson the next time. In *Principles and Standards for School Mathematics,* the authors stated that "planning, teaching, and assessing should be linked through teachers' ongoing analysis about what is working, what they know about the students, and what constitutes learning of important mathematics" (p. 31).

Standard 2: Teachers as Participants in Evaluation

The evaluation of the teaching of mathematics should provide ongoing opportunities for teachers to

- analyze their own teaching;
- deliberate with colleagues about their teaching;
- confer with supervisors about their teaching.

(NCTM, *Professional Standards for Teaching Mathematics,* 1991, p. 80.)

The evaluation of teaching performances should not be *done to* the teacher; instead, it should be a cooperative venture involving the local administrator working *with* the teacher on long-term improvement of practice. Using the constructivist model, for example, the principal might ask the teacher to describe the observed lesson and how the students reacted and then to suggest three ways the lesson could have been improved—a very different approach from having the principal observe a lesson and then sit down and tell the teacher what should have happened and how the lesson could have been taught more effectively. As both the teacher and the student have a role in classroom discourse, the teacher and the supervisor have a role in the teaching evaluation process.

Standard 3: Sources of Information

Evaluation of the teaching of mathematics should be based on information from a variety of sources including

- the teacher's goals and expectations for student learning;
- the teacher's plans for achieving these goals;
- the teacher's portfolio, consisting of a sample of lesson plans, student activities and materials, and means of assessing students' understanding of mathematics;
- analyses of multiple episodes of classroom teaching;
- the teacher's analysis of classroom teaching;
- evidence of students' understanding of, and disposition to do, mathematics.

(NCTM, *Professional Standards for Teaching Mathematics,* 1991, p. 84.)

Does this sound familiar? In Unit IV, we argued in favor of using several assessment strategies to determine student progress and pointed out that test scores may not present a total picture of student achievement. Likewise, the assessment of teaching performances demands a variety of sources of information, more than a classroom observation or two.

Standard 4: Mathematical Concepts, Procedures, and Connections

Assessment of the teaching of mathematical concepts, procedures, and connections should provide evidence that the teacher

- demonstrates a sound knowledge of mathematical concepts and procedures;
- represents mathematics as a network of interconnected concepts and procedures;
- emphasizes connections between mathematics and other disciplines and connections to daily living;
- engages students in tasks that promote the understanding of mathematical concepts, procedures, and connections;
- engages students in mathematical discourse that extends their understanding of mathematical concepts, procedures, and connections.

(NCTM, *Professional Standards for Teaching Mathematics*, 1991, p. 89.)

Teachers who possess a firm grasp of their content areas and their course of study tend to be the best at pursuing student questions, recognizing teachable moments, and helping students to make connections. Although it is important for a teacher to have a strong background in education and psychology, a solid understanding of the mathematical concepts being taught is also an important component of effective teaching. Knowledge of the content area can help teachers to select tasks and mathematical topics that are important for students to explore—an important consideration in the implementation of the mathematics curriculum Principle in *Principles and Standards for School Mathematics* (1998). Examining several related pieces of research on teachers' understandings of mathematical concepts, Fennema and Franke (1992) concluded that "[mathematical] content knowledge does influence the decisions teachers make about classroom instruction" (p. 149). Therefore, it is important for supervisors of teachers of mathematics to consider the subject-area knowledge of the teacher.

Standard 5: Mathematics as Problem Solving, Reasoning, and Communication

Assessment of teaching mathematics as a process involving problem solving, reasoning, and communication should provide evidence that the teacher

- models and emphasizes aspects of problem solving, including formulating and posing problems, solving problems using different strategies, verifying and interpreting results, and generalizing solutions;
- demonstrates and emphasizes the role of mathematical reasoning;
- models and emphasizes mathematical communication using written, oral, and visual forms;
- engages students in tasks that involve problem solving, reasoning, and communication;
- engages students in mathematical discourse that extends their understanding of problem solving and their capacity to reason and communicate mathematically.

(NCTM, *Professional Standards for Teaching Mathematics*, 1991, p. 95.)

In Chapter 1, we described mathematics as a combination of content and processes—something that one does as well as what someone knows. This Standard emphasizes that, as teachers of mathematics, it is important that we recognize and value the role of the five process skills (problem solving, reasoning, connections, communication, and representation) in our day-to-day teaching routine. Ideally, a supervisor should be able to record evidence of all five mathematical processes in every lesson that is observed. This makes an interesting criterion for reflection on one's own lesson: Watch a videotape of the lesson and ask yourself, "At which point in the lesson did I promote each of the five process skills?"

Standard 6: Promoting Mathematical Disposition

Assessment of a teacher's fostering of students' mathematical dispositions should provide evidence that the teacher

- models a disposition to do mathematics;
- demonstrates the value of mathematics as a way of thinking and its application in other disciplines and in society;
- promotes students' confidence, flexibility, perseverance, curiosity, and inventiveness in doing mathematics through the use of appropriate tasks and by engaging students in mathematical discourse.

(NCTM, *Professional Standards for Teaching Mathematics*, 1991, p. 104.)

The presence of mathematics anxiety and a general perception that "I was never very good in mathematics, and I'm a successful person" in our society have made it essential that the development of positive dispositions be one of the major goals of teachers. In Chapter 2, we described the various dispositions and noted how research supports the theory that students will develop a positive outlook toward mathematics and persistence in problem solving if they view these characteristics on a regular basis in their teachers. In the teacher evaluation process, administrators should be able to collect evidence that a teacher is demonstrating an ability to cultivate positive attitudes and dispositions in the students.

Standard 7: Assessing Students' Understanding of Mathematics

Assessing the means by which a teacher assesses students' understanding of mathematics should provide evidence that the teacher

- uses a variety of assessment methods to determine students' understanding of mathematics;
- matches assessment methods with the developmental level, the mathematical maturity, and the cultural background of the student;
- aligns assessment methods with what is taught and how it is taught;
- analyzes individual students' understanding of, and disposition to do, mathematics so that information about their mathematical development can be provided to the students, their parents, and pertinent school personnel;
- bases instruction on information obtained from assessing students' understanding of, and disposition to do, mathematics.

(NCTM, *Professional Standards for Teaching Mathematics*, 1991, p. 110.)

If the building principal walks into your classroom and asks to see your syllabus, including a description of how you assess your students and determine final grades, it is important to be able to show how you are using multiple sources of data to fairly and accurately assess student progress. An important consideration in the supervision of mathematics teachers is to determine whether they are valuing performance data beyond paper-and-pencil tests and homework assignments as we discussed in Unit IV.

Standard 8: Learning Environments

Assessment of the teacher's ability to create a learning environment that fosters the development of each student's mathematical power should provide evidence that the teacher

- conveys the notion that mathematics is a subject to be explored and created both individually and in collaboration with others;
- respects students and their ideas and encourages curiosity and spontaneity;
- encourages students to draw and validate their own conclusions;
- selects tasks that allow students to construct new meaning by building on and extending their prior knowledge;
- makes appropriate use of available resources;
- respects and responds to students' diverse interests and linguistic, cultural, and socioeconomic backgrounds in designing mathematical tasks;
- affirms and encourages full participation and continued study of mathematics by all students.

(NCTM, *Professional Standards for Teaching Mathematics*, 1991, p. 115.)

In Chapter 6, we discussed how "good" teachers are adept at organizing the physical and psychological environment in the classroom so that students feel comfortable with being part of the mathematical community and know that their opinions and thinking processes are valued. Recognizing that most classrooms contain students with different socioeconomic backgrounds, minority students, and, usually, both genders, the teacher needs to establish an environment that is open and inviting and that promotes the learning of mathematics for all students. The assessment of this atmosphere or environment, then, becomes a major factor in the evaluation of the professional teacher.

Keep in mind that the eight teacher evaluation Standards represent the ideal process of assessing teaching performance in mathematics. The model recommends an ongoing cycle that includes active involvement by the teacher and the collection of multiple pieces of evidence. The focus of observation and data collection is on those issues that we have identified throughout this text as important in the mathematics classroom—important mathematical content, mathematical processes, the development of disposition, the use of multiple means of assessment, and the development of a healthy classroom environment. Just as student assessment should be aligned with what goes on in the classroom and be communicated to the student, the evaluation of teachers should also be an open process with an emphasis on the multiple components of what it takes to be an effective teacher.

If school districts used these eight Standards to develop their teacher evaluation process, you could be confident that your success was being measured by the degree to which you implement the ideas expressed throughout this text. However, many districts have a "one-size-fits-all" teacher supervision and evaluation process that is used at the elementary, middle, and secondary levels and cuts across content areas. The evaluation tools often include the major components of effective teaching, such as effective lesson planning and teaching, classroom management, and professionalism, but they may not be specific to the mathematics content area. As a result, some of the components mentioned here may not be a part of the assessment process at all. And, in fact, some school districts actually do use one or two classroom observations as the basis of an entire evaluation of the teacher. A sound knowledge of the teacher evaluation Standards, however, at least gives you a picture of what the National Council of Teachers of Mathematics holds up as an *ideal* in terms of what mathematics teachers should be doing in the classroom and may help you to focus your efforts in your professional development. And if your department has more than one teacher, you can also compare notes with peers (as teacher evaluation Standard 2 suggests) to improve your performance in any of the listed areas. In the next section, we discuss how the mathematics teacher can work with others in a department.

■ FUNCTIONING IN A DEPARTMENT

In virtually every school or district, secondary and middle school teachers are organized into mathematics departments that are responsible for the teaching and coordination of the mathematics program at that level, which might include some or all of the following activities:

- organizing and serving on a curriculum-writing team
- proposing major changes in the curriculum, such as adding or deleting entire courses or changing from a traditional to an integrated sequence of classes
- selecting textbooks and materials
- managing a departmental budget for classroom supplies, such as calculators, computer software, or hands-on manipulatives
- supervising or peer coaching members of the department
- preparing reports and analyzing results of external assessments such as proficiency test scores

Generally, the mathematics department has a chair, who is responsible for leading the process, running meetings, and overseeing the implementation of programs. It is extremely important that each member of a department actively contribute to the improvement of the program. You have probably heard the expression "if you're not part of the solution, you're part of the problem," and that is certainly true when it comes to working with other teachers in your school. Part of the responsibility of the professional mathematics teacher is to identify problems with the program—weaknesses of the curriculum, content of the texts, or the lack of classroom materials—and work toward the improvement of that area. Complaining about the system does not help anyone and, in fact, can spread negativism about the department. Developing a plan of action to improve the program can make a major difference in a school district. It is important to remember that although teachers are responsible for students and accountable to parents and the community, they are also responsible for helping one another enhance the program, because every mathematics program can be improved in some way. As we mentioned at the outset of this chapter, the teaching profession *can* be a lonely endeavor, but it certainly doesn't have to be. When we open ourselves up to working with colleagues, a synergy is created—an enthusiasm and energy that is much greater than teachers can achieve on their own.

In some small school districts, a secondary or middle school mathematics teacher may be the only such teacher at that level. You might find yourself teaching in a small high school with three grade levels in which you teach all of the courses. So much for collegiality? No, not necessarily. As a mathematics teacher, you are one of hundreds of thousands of others around the country who are involved in the same activity. Teachers in very small school districts have an even greater need than those in larger districts to connect with mathematics teachers in other locales. Your willingness to share ideas, observe, and work with others around your county, state, or country will greatly enhance your own professional development as we discuss in the next section.

■ ONGOING PROFESSIONAL DEVELOPMENT

Making the Case for Long-Term Development

Throughout this book, we have discussed the importance of capturing teachable moments—those times when students ask just the right question at just the right time—and a teacher can capitalize on the query and turn it into a rich classroom discussion. However, the teaching profession is an art, and the process of making decisions in real time, as the class happens, is a skill that develops gradually. In Chapter 5, we described how a novice's lesson-planning procedure transforms into a lesson-imaging process for the expert teacher, and we emphasized the role of the teacher in directing classroom discourse in Chapter 6. Fennema and Franke (1992) describe a model for classroom teaching that shows how the teacher's beliefs and knowledge (of content, pedagogy, and learning psychology) interact during a class. Furthermore, Schoenfeld (1998) states that the actions of a teacher and the decisions made while that teacher is leading a lesson are the result of three interacting factors: the teacher's goals, beliefs, and knowledge as shown in Figure 10–1:

Figure 10–1 Interacting Factors That Drive a Teacher's Decisions in the Classroom

If you think about it, this model makes a great deal of sense. If a teacher firmly believes that mathematics is nothing more than a set of rules to be memorized and skills to be practiced, then a student who presents an alternative strategy for solving a problem is likely to be dismissed because of the *belief* that there is one best way to solve each type of problem—the presentation of another way to look at a problem gets in the way of the procedure the teacher feels is important to communicate to the class. In a similar way a lack of content knowledge can drive a teacher's response to a student question. Consider the following classroom situation:

Ms. Bronson's secondary mathematics students have been working on a unit on polynomials, and, without any previous instruction on quadratic equations, she asks them if they can figure out how to solve the equation $x^2 + 6 = 5x$.

> **Ms. Bronson:** Take a few minutes at your table and see if you can come up with a solution. (The students work for 10 minutes, and Sherry raises her hand.) Sherry, what did you and your partner come up with?
>
> **Sherry:** We got an answer of 2.
>
> **Matthew:** So did we. It was easy; you just use guess and check.
>
> **Ms. Bronson:** Is that how you solved it, Sherry?
>
> **Sherry:** No, I solved it like we did linear equations earlier this year. I can show you easier than I can tell you. (Sherry goes up to the board and writes.)
>
> $x^2 + 6 = 5x$, so I wrote it out like this:
>
> $x \cdot x + 6 = 5x$. Now, you just subtract two x's from both sides, so you get $6 = 3x$. If you divide both sides by 3, you get $x = 2$. That's all there is to it.

How would you handle this situation? What was the error in mathematical reasoning? Think about it for a minute and then read on. Let's suppose that Ms. Bronson's content knowledge is fairly weak. If so, she might respond to Sherry's solution by either accepting it as reasonable or, maybe even worse, *telling* Sherry that "you can't do that" and proceeding to show the class how to subtract $5x$ from both sides of the equation and factor. However, if Ms. Bronson is alert and has a solid mathematics background, she will immediately ask herself, "Why did Sherry's method work?" And, with a little thought, she would recognize that subtracting $x \cdot x$ from one side of the equation and $2x$ from the other side works only when $x = 0$ or $x = 2$ (because $0^2 = 2(0)$ and $2^2 = 2(2)$). In this case, by coincidence, $x \cdot x = 2x$ because $x = 2$, so her method worked. Thinking fast, Ms. Bronson could pose this follow-up equation to the class: $x^2 + 6 = 7x$. If Sherry used the same strategy as she had with the last problem, she would obtain an answer of $x = \frac{6}{5}$ (How?), which does not work. In this case, the actual solutions to the equation are $x = 1$ or $x = 6$, but $1^2 \neq 2(1)$, and $6^2 \neq 2(6)$. By discussing this second example, Sherry and the class recognize that her method does not work for *all* quadratic equations, and this will send the class in search of a third method.

Of course, Ms. Bronson's ability to recognize the error in Sherry's reasoning and to come up with an off-the-cuff counterexample is a result of her firm grasp of the lesson's mathematical content. Furthermore, if it were Ms. Bronson's *goal* to simply *show* the class how to factor to solve a quadratic equation, she never would have posed the problem without previous instruction in the first place. So, the point here is that if we analyze any teaching and learning situation, we will recognize the factors that influence the teacher's behaviors. In *Principles and Standards for School Mathematics* (1998), the NCTM authors stated that "in making decisions, teachers rely on their knowledge of mathematics, their understanding of students as learners, their experience in knowing what kinds of questions and misunderstandings students are likely to have, and on the mathematical learning goals they have identified for their students" (p. 31).

The point is that teaching is a very complex endeavor, and the power of experience and reflection must not be underestimated. When a teacher seeks out an inservice program, a graduate class, and so forth, those experiences may ultimately affect the teacher's goals, belief system, and knowledge level, thus changing the way the individual runs the classroom. On the contrary, if an undergraduate earns a degree and a teaching license but rarely, if ever, goes back for additional coursework, that person may hold the same goals, beliefs, and knowledge for many years. Consequently, that teacher may act almost exactly the same from class to class and from year to year over a long period of time until a program comes along that shakes the system. Professional development activities are designed to press educators into reflecting on what they believe about mathematics education and to provide them with additional content knowledge that may improve their classroom teaching practices.

Opportunities for Professional Development

A staff development specialist put on a workshop for secondary and middle school mathematics teachers in a local school district. As he was preparing his notes for the presentation, he overheard four comments as the teachers in the room spoke to one another:

- "I really don't want to be here!"
- "Do you know how many math classes I had in college? Just enough to jump through the hoops, and that was enough for me!"
- "I need this workshop like I need a hole in the head."
- "I teach sixth grade. Is there going to be anything in this for me?"

These types of comments are not unusual at professional development workshops, and they might be seen as a sad commentary about the teaching profession. As we analyze these statements closely, however, we realize that the root of this attitude is that teachers want and need something that is relevant to them. After all, students in school sometimes ask, "When are we ever going to have to use this?," so why shouldn't teachers ask the same question? As we discussed in Chapter 2, mathematics needs to be relevant to our students to capture their interest and attention, and adults are no different in this respect. Unfortunately, many teachers have taken classes or workshops that were simply not helpful. So, if you want workshops and courses to be meaningful, you have to be selective about organizations that you join and programs that you attend. And, above all, it is important to attend these types of inservice opportunities with an open mind and to assume that you will always pull at least one gem from an inservice presentation. There are many opportunities available to mathematics teachers who want to enhance their ongoing professional development.

First, it is important for mathematics teachers to interact with colleagues. For teachers new to the profession, this might involve a mentor teacher, under whom they apprentice as they gain the critical first years of experience. For more experienced teachers, this may be a peer with whom they can share their successes and challenges and with whom they can discuss pedagogical and content-related issues.

It is very difficult to grow as a professional without conversations with others, just as it is more difficult to learn mathematics without group interaction.

Teachers also need to take an active role in their own professional development by becoming members of local, state, or national organizations designed to assist their growth process. The National Council of Teachers of Mathematics, for example, has well over 100,000 members and publishes four professional journals throughout the academic year (for information, visit the NCTM on the Web at <http://www.nctm.org>). The NCTM also has an affiliate in each state, such as the Colorado Council of Teachers of Mathematics, and most states have affiliates at the local level, such as the Greater Toledo Council of Teachers of Mathematics. Each organization has its own newsletters and other publications and ordinarily offers in-service programs or meetings that provide teachers with an opportunity to connect with others in the profession. Teachers in small school districts can have discussions with professionals in other districts, and those who teach in large districts can get a sense of how other departments and districts function. Membership in professional organizations tends to be relatively inexpensive (a teacher, for example, can generally join the national, state, and local councils for a total of less than $100 a year) but pays major benefits by allowing you to stay connected with the evolving field of mathematics education.

Third, teachers can attend conferences organized by professional organizations. Each year, the NCTM has a national meeting and several regional conferences, and each state generally has one annual conference as do many of the local affiliates. At a conference, teachers can attend sessions relevant to their grade level and content interest and pick up a great deal of classroom-ready, practical teaching ideas. Between workshops or presentations, teachers also have plenty of time to stand in the hallway and talk to others or to browse displays of the latest texts and materials. Conferences are excellent opportunities to recharge the batteries.

Mathematics teachers can also benefit from regularly reading such publications as the many self-help and resource books available as well as journals such as *Mathematics Teacher* or *Mathematics Teaching in the Middle School,* which feature everything from philosophical essays to practical classroom teaching ideas. Just taking an hour a month to browse through a couple of books or journals can provide a practicing teacher with a number of ideas for lesson plans and ways to improve the teaching and learning process.

Similarly, the World Wide Web has become a popular means for finding lessons and ideas, as we discussed in Chapter 7. Sites on the Web can feature hundreds of lesson-plan ideas, hands-on activities, and theoretical pieces for reading and discussion. There is much more on the Web than one can deal with in a short period of time, so it is recommended that a teacher take even an hour or two each month just to surf the Web and look for new sites that may feature ideas for classroom implementation. Browsing on the Web can be an excellent growth tool as we explore what others are doing and try to rethink some of our own lessons in light of many readily-available suggestions. Appendix E contains a categorized listing of suggested websites to get you started using the Internet as a professional development tool.

Many universities offer evening, weekend, and summer workshops and graduate courses. It is important for practicing teachers to take part in these workshops and course offerings in order to stay up to date on local, state, and national education issues. One way that practicing teachers get in touch with new standards and trends is by enrolling in university offerings. As soon as one is enrolled and has paid for a class, it becomes a commitment that is difficult to neglect. A commitment such as browsing the Web for an hour a month can easily become a low-priority activity, but class assignments require a commitment of several hours, days, or weeks. In many states, graduate coursework is required to maintain certification or licensure, but these graduate programs may be offered free of charge to classroom teachers and are funded by federal or state grants. The best way to find out about the grant-funded programs is to be a member of the professional organizations, which generally advertise programs for professional development through their newsletters and informal networking systems.

Read any good books lately? Another way to improve your knowledge of the teaching profession is to select and read a book on mathematics education. The book might be a practical discussion of classroom projects or a more theoretical book on psychology or cooperative learning, but such a book can help teachers to identify their strengths and challenges and to set goals for the future. Finally, never underestimate the power of observing another teacher at work within your own school or in another community. We can learn a great deal about ourselves just by walking into another classroom and seeing how another person manages the students. For many, student teaching was the only time in their careers that they actually spent some time observing someone else's classroom. Yet, in the business world, people work with other departments, visit other plants and corporate offices, and explore alternate ways of doing business all the time. Some school districts not only *allow* but *require* teachers to visit other classrooms at least once a year—this can be a very powerful experience.

In the end, a teacher is simply not "made" in four years of undergraduate college preservice experiences. A teacher grows, develops, and becomes a professional over a period of many years. A college degree indicates that the person is ready to enter the profession, but the first five to ten years of teaching are the critical time during which most teachers experience a significant amount of growth. Of course, with the world changing as quickly as it does, much of our current knowledge will be outdated within five years, so it becomes important and necessary to explore avenues to continue our development over time and try to stay current. Selecting any one or a few of the suggestions discussed here can be helpful in making that first step to long-term growth.

The Professional Development Plan

Some districts and states are now requiring that teachers complete and implement an annual Professional Development Plan or PDP. The PDP is relatively simple; it is a written statement in which a teacher points out personal strengths and challenges as a professional and describes a plan for development in the coming academic year.

PROFESSIONAL DEVELOPMENT PLAN

Name: _____

School District/Building: _____

Date: _____

My greatest strength as a teacher is . . .

My greatest challenge as a teacher is . . .

To address this/these challenge(s) in the coming academic year, I plan to do the following:

Signed: _____

- -

Postconference

Administrator's Name: _____

Comments on the degree to which the plan was implemented:

The PDP is essentially a contract or agreement between the teacher and the school district, outlining an intended plan of personal growth for the year. For example, the teacher may decide that a major challenge for the year is to learn to use graphing calculators effectively in the classroom. So, the teacher's plan may include taking a course during the summer at the local university and implementing at least one new unit in the school year that makes effective use of graphing calculators. At the end of the school year, one of the items that the teacher adds to the professional portfolio is the PDP and a written statement about how it was implemented during the academic year. The administrator can sign off on the PDP form and make comments about whether the teacher met the objectives set for the year. The PDP might contain implementation strategies that include visiting other classrooms, joining a professional organization, attending a conference, conducting Internet research, and so on. And the PDP is just one more way of teachers reflecting on their practice and formalizing a plan to ensure long-term growth.

■ CONCLUSION ■

The world of teaching mathematics can be very exciting as we watch the minds of our students develop and change over time. But we, as teachers, must also be willing to grow as professionals, increasing our knowledge and skills and making each year of teaching better than the previous year. In this chapter, we have looked at the importance of developing a home-school connection, at the process of assessing and evaluating teachers, and at what it means to be a member of a department and to develop as a professional. In the *Professional Standards for Teaching Mathematics,* the authors state that "the current reform movement in mathematics education, and in education in general, has as a strong underlying theme the professionalism of teaching. This view recognizes the teacher as a part of a learning community that continually fosters growth in knowledge, stature, and responsibility" (NCTM, 1991, p. 6). Indeed, the teacher makes all the difference in the classroom—the difference between whether students get excited about mathematics and learn to become problem solvers or whether they develop a fear of and anxiety toward mathematics and are relatively unsuccessful in school.

It has been the intent of this textbook to encompass the background and underlying theoretical issues of the teaching profession. But, again, a teacher is not made in four years of college or even in five years of teaching after the initial licensure or certification. Instead, we develop and grow into a style that is all our own after many years of practice, reflection, and refinement. Just as a manuscript is transformed from a rough draft to a published work of art, so is a teacher developed from a naive "rookie" to a seasoned veteran who can eventually serve as a "buddy" to other novice teachers. One mathematics teacher was quoted as saying, "When I reach a point in my career where I feel I have 'arrived' and cannot improve upon what I did last year, I will know that it's time to retire and let someone else take over." The "good teacher" is always open to suggestions and willing to change for the sake of the students—after all, students are what teaching is all about.

■ DISCUSSION QUESTIONS ■

1. Make a list of ways to actively involve parents in the teaching and learning of mathematics in addition to the suggestions provided in this chapter. What do you expect of the parents of your students?
2. Review the eight Standards for teacher evaluation by the NCTM. If you were a principal and had to weigh the eight criteria, similar to the way that we discussed weighing test scores versus journals and homework in Chapter 9, what relative weight would you assign to each of the criteria?
3. Interview mathematics teachers from three different school districts on how their performance is assessed and evaluated. Compare the teacher evaluation practices of the three school

districts to one another and to the eight criteria set forth by the NCTM.

4. Interview principals from three different school districts and ask them, "In what ways do you support and encourage ongoing professional development of your mathematics teachers?" Compare the responses. What level of support and encouragement do you expect for ongoing development as a professional teacher?

5. The mathematics department chair often conducts peer evaluations of other mathematics teachers in the school. Discuss some of the advantages and disadvantages of being supervised or evaluated by another teacher as opposed to being supervised by an administrator.

6. Suppose that you are one of five members in the mathematics department at your school. Your department chair would like to adopt a new textbook series for courses that you teach and favors a different series than the one that you selected. How do you deal with the situation in a professional manner, respecting the role of the chair while trying to promote a collaborative decision?

7. Observe a mathematics class or watch a class on videotape. As you watch the teacher in action, make notes about the teacher's apparent goals in the lesson, beliefs about mathematics and the teacher's role in the classroom, and knowledge of the content area and teaching strategies or pedagogy. Compare your notes to those of a peer who observed the same class or video.

8. With a partner, share your philosophy (beliefs) of mathematics education. Specifically, why do you believe that mathematics is in the curriculum in the first place, and what do you view as the role of mathematics in the total education of a secondary or middle school student? How does this philosophy influence the way that you run your classroom?

9. Discuss which of the strategies for obtaining ongoing professional development were most appealing to you and why. Which professional experiences do you believe are most valuable for inservice teachers?

10. Comment on the advantages and possible drawbacks to preparing an annual Professional Development Plan that is reviewed and commented on by the principal as described in the chapter.

11. It has been said that "It takes 10 years to make a person into a teacher." What does this statement say to you? Do you agree or disagree with this and why?

■ BIBLIOGRAPHIC REFERENCES AND RESOURCES ■

Aichele, D. B. (Ed.). (1994). *1994 Yearbook of the NCTM: Professional development for teachers of mathematics.* Reston, VA: National Council of Teachers of Mathematics.

Ball, D. L. (1993). With an eye on the mathematical horizon: Dilemmas of teaching elementary school mathematics. *Elementary School Journal, 93* (4), 373–397.

Chambers, D. L. & Hankes, J. E. (1994). Using knowledge of children's thinking to change teaching. In D. B. Aichele (Ed.), *1994 Yearbook of the NCTM: Professional development for teachers of mathematics,* pp. 286–295. Reston, VA: National Council of Teachers of Mathematics.

Clark, J. (1996). Involving parents in the middle school. *Teaching PreK–8, 27* (3), 52–53.

Driscoll, M. & Lord, B. (1990). Professionals in a changing profession. In T. J. Cooney (Ed.), *1990 Yearbook of the NCTM: Teaching and learning mathematics in the 1990s,* pp. 237–245. Reston, VA: National Council of Teachers of Mathematics.

Eckmier, J. & Bunyan, R. (1995). Mentor teachers: Key to educational renewal. *Educational Horizons, 73* (3), 124–129.

Eisenhower National Clearinghouse. (1998). Family involvement in education. *ENC Focus, 5* (3).

Epstein, J. L. & Hollifield, J. H. (1996). Title I and school-family-community partnerships: Using research to realize the potential. *Journal of Education for Students Placed at Risk, 1* (3), 263–278.

Fennema, E. & Franke, M. L. (1992). Teachers' knowledge and its impact. In D. A. Grouws (Ed.), *Handbook of research on mathematics teaching and learning,* pp. 147–164. Reston, VA: National Council of Teachers of Mathematics.

Ganser, T. (1996). Mentor roles: Views of participants in a state-mandated program. *Midwestern Educational Research, 9* (2), 15–20.

Kanter, P. F. (1992). *Helping your child learn math.* Washington, DC: U.S. Department of Education (Office of Educational Research and Improvement).

Licklinder, B. L. et al. (1996). Cooperative learning: Staff development for teacher preparation. *Schools in the Middle, 6* (1), 33–36.

Lord, W. J. (1996). Professional preparation: Implications for teachers and principals. *Schools in the Middle, 6* (1), 37–39.

Lovitt, C., Stephens, M., Clarke, D., & Romberg, T. A. (1990). Mathematics teachers reconceptualizing their roles. In T. J. Cooney (Ed.), *1990 Yearbook of the NCTM: Teaching and learning mathematics in the 1990s*, pp. 229–236. Reston, VA: National Council of Teachers of Mathematics.

Miller, L. D. & Hunt, N. P. (1994). Professional development through action research. In D. B. Aichele (Ed.), *1994 Yearbook of the NCTM: Professional development for teachers of mathematics*, pp. 296–303. Reston, VA: National Council of Teachers of Mathematics.

Nassau, C. D. (1995). The seventh-year stretch. *American School Board Journal, 182* (11), 30–32.

National Council of Teachers of Mathematics. (1998). *Principles and standards for school mathematics* (working draft). Reston, VA: National Council of Teachers of Mathematics.

National Council of Teachers of Mathematics. (1995). *Assessment standards for school mathematics.* Reston, VA: National Council of Teachers of Mathematics.

National Council of Teachers of Mathematics. (1991). *Professional standards for teaching mathematics.* Reston, VA: National Council of Teachers of Mathematics.

National Council of Teachers of Mathematics. (1989). *Curriculum and evaluation standards for school mathematics.* Reston, VA: National Council of Teachers of Mathematics.

Nolder, R. & Johnson, D. (1995). Professional development. Bringing teachers to the centre of the stage. *Mathematics in School, 24* (1), 32–36.

Price, J. (1995). Selling and buying reform: If we build it, will they come? *Mathematics Teacher, 88* (6), 532–534.

Schoenfeld, A. H. (1998). On theory and models: The case of teaching-in-context. In S. Berenson, K. Dawkins, M. Blanton, W. Coulombe, J. Kolb, K. Norwood, & L. Stiff (Eds.), *Proceedings of the Twentieth Annual Meeting of the North American Chapter of the International Group for the Psychology of Mathematics Education*, pp. 27–38. Columbus, OH: ERIC Clearinghouse for Science, Mathematics, and Environmental Education.

Sherman, H. J. & Jaeger, T. (1995). Professional development: Teachers' communication and collaboration—keys to student achievement. *Mathematics Teaching in the Middle School, 1* (6), 454–458.

Silver, E. A. & Kilpatrick, J. (1994). E Pluribus Unum: Challenges of diversity in the future of mathematics education research. *Journal for Research in Mathematics Education, 25* (6), 734–754.

Stenmark, J. K., Thompson, V., & Cossey, R. (1986). *Family math.* Berkeley, CA: Lawrence Hall of Science.

Tanner, B., et al. (1995). Scheduling time to maximize staff development opportunities. *Journal of Staff Development, 16* (4), 14–19.

Taylor, R. (Ed.). (1986). *Professional development for teachers of mathematics: A handbook.* Reston, VA: National Council of Teachers of Mathematics: National Council of Supervisors of Mathematics.

Texley, J. (1996). Mentor roles: Views of participants in a state-mandated program. *Midwestern Educational Researcher, 9* (2), 15–20.

Curriculum

■ NCTM Curriculum Standard 2, Grades 6–8: Patterns, Functions, and Algebra

■ NCTM Curriculum Standard 3, Grades 9–12: Geometry and Spatial Sense

(Reprinted with permission from *Principles and Standards for School Mathematics*, copyright 1998 by National Council of Teachers of Mathematics. All rights reserved.)

■ Sample State Model Strand, Grades K–12: Data Analysis and Probability

(Reprinted from Ohio Department of Education [1990]. *Model competency-based mathematics program*. Columbus, OH: Ohio Department of Education. Reprinted with permission.)

■ STANDARD 2: PATTERNS, FUNCTIONS, AND ALGEBRA

Mathematics instructional programs should include attention to patterns, functions, symbols, and models so that all students—

- understand various types of patterns and functional relationships;
- use symbolic forms to represent and analyze mathematical situations and structures;
- use mathematical models and analyze change in both real and abstract contexts.

Elaboration: Grades 6–8

Algebra can be thought of in many ways—as patterns, functions, and relations; as language, representations, and structures based on generalized arithmetic; or as a tool for modeling mathematical ideas and problems. All of these views of algebra are found in the middle grades. Although they are discussed here separately, they would be interwoven in a quality school mathematics instructional program.

The study of algebra in the middle grades involves an intermingling of conceptual and procedural work. Students work more formally with representations and symbolism than they did in their earlier school experience, but their instruction should have as its primary emphasis the development of a sound conceptual foundation. It is essential that students become proficient in working with simple algebraic expressions, including generating equivalent expressions and using and evaluating simple formulas. By the end of the middle grades, students should be able to solve linear equations in several ways, with or without a calculator, as appropriate. But it is also critical that they develop a conceptual understanding of variables and equations, that they learn to distinguish linear relationships from nonlinear ones, and that they connect their experiences with linear functions to their understandings of ratio and proportion. Through their experiences in the middle grades, students should develop an understanding of, and competence in, working with linearity. ·

Focus Areas for Grades 6–8

■ *Understand various types of patterns and functional relationships*

In grades 6–8, all students should—

- analyze, create, and generalize numeric and visual patterns paying particular attention to patterns that have a recursive nature;
- use patterns to solve mathematical and applied problems;
- represent a variety of relations and functions with tables, graphs, verbal rules, and, when possible, symbolic rules.

■ *Use symbolic forms to represent and analyze mathematical situations and structures*

In grades 6–8, all students should—

- develop a sound conceptual understanding of equation and of variable;
- explore relationships between symbolic expressions and graphs, paying particular attention to the horizontal and vertical intercepts, points of intersection, and slope (for linear relations);
- become fluent in generating equivalent expressions for simple algebraic expressions and in solving linear equations and inequalities;
- use symbolic algebra to represent situations and to solve problems, especially those that involve linear relationships.

■ *Use mathematical models and analyze change in both real and abstract contexts*

In grades 6–8, all students should—

- model and solve contextualized problems using various representations, such as graphs and tables, to understand the purpose and utility of each representation;
- develop an initial understanding of rate of change, with emphasis on the connections among slope of a line, constant rate of change, and their meaning in context;
- explore different types of change occurring in discrete patterns, such as proportional and linear change.

Discussion

■ *Patterns and Functions*

A major goal in the middle grades is to develop students' facility with analyzing, modeling, representing, and solving mathematical and real-world problems using patterns. Recursive patterns, that is, patterns in which each number is found from the previous numbers by repeating some process (e.g., figurate numbers and Fibonacci numbers), are becoming increasingly useful in these situations. The following example shows how recursive patterns and the use of a variety of different representations can aid in understanding and solving a problem related to geometry. Note how each representation adds a different dimension to the understanding. Specifically observe how the table of values allows students to see patterns, and how the figures help students understand why the patterns occur. An important learning goal is for students to develop the disposition of looking for reasons why patterns occur.

Suppose students are studying the relationship between the number of sides of a polygon and the sum of the interior angles or the total number of diagonals that can be drawn. They might organize their information as in table 6–1.

Table 6–1 Angle Sums and Diagonals for Various Polygons

Number of sides	3	4	5	6
Sum of interior angles	180	360	540	720
Number of diagonals	0	2	5	9

If studying interior angles, some students might observe that as the number of sides increases by one, the sum of the interior angles increases by 180. If studying diagonals, they may observe that the differences of consecutive pairs of numbers in the sequence 0, 2, 5, 9 is 2, 3, and 4. They then might conjecture that the numbers of diagonals in seven- and eight-sided polygons are 9 + 5 = 14 and 14 + 6 = 20, respectively. Other students might observe that the number of diagonals increases by $n - 2$, where n is the number of sides, so the numbers of diagonals of a seven- and eight-sided polygon is 9 + (7 – 2) = 14 and 14 + (8 – 2) = 20, respectively. Other students may observe that the number of degrees in the sum (S) of the interior angles of any polygon with n sides seems to be given by the equation $S = 180(n - 2)$, which happens to be a linear function.

Middle grades students should be encouraged to support their conjectures not only by appealing to the patterns, but also by logical arguments that explain why the generalizations must be true. By exploring with drawings or geometry software, students could see that when the number of sides of a polygon is increased by one, the sum of the interior angles increases by 180 degrees because another triangle is added. This is seen in the left polygon of figure 6–1 in which a four-sided polygon is converted to a five-sided polygon. Students could justify the formula $S = 180(n - 2)$ by drawing all the diagonals from any single vertex to form precisely $n - 2$ triangles.

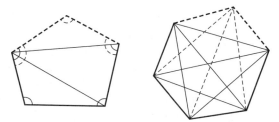

Figure 6–1 Diagonals of a Quadrilateral and a Pentagon

Students could justify that the number of diagonals increases by $n - 2$ by seeing that when another vertex is added, as in the right polygon of figure 6–1 (a five-sided polygon is converted to a six-sided polygon), $n - 3$ diagonals are added to the new vertex, and one side becomes a diagonal. If students have solved the well-known "handshake" problem, in which each person in a group shakes hands with each other person, they may be able to use similar logic to conclude that the total number of diagonals should satisfy $T = n(n - 3)/2$.

Recursive approaches, in which students reflect on how the numbers are changing, and closed-form solutions, such as $S = 180(n - 2)$, are legitimate methods for solving problems and both should be valued. When using a recursive approach, students should clearly write the relationship, such as "each number is 180 more than the previous number" or "next = 180 + previous." An even more powerful approach is to have students use spreadsheets to generate the numbers in the sequence. Because of technology, it is just as easy to generate almost any number needed using the recursive approach as it is using the formula. Because of this, recursive thinking is an important skill that will be built upon in high school.

■ Structure and Symbolic Notation

It is important to realize that developing students' understanding of variable is complicated, precisely because the concept of variable itself is multifaceted. A deep understanding of variable involves much more than simply recognizing that letters can be used to stand for unknown numbers in equations. Consider these expressions:

$$30 = 5x \qquad 1 = n\,(1/n) \qquad A = LW \qquad y = 3x.$$

In the first equation, x stands for a specific, nonvarying number that can be determined by solving the equation. The second equation generalizes an arithmetic pattern where n can take on a wide range of values (but not zero); it represents an identity. The third equation is usually considered a formula with A, L, and W standing for the quantities area, length, and width. These quantities actually feel more like knowns than unknowns. The last equation offers a more compelling example of "variability" than any of the others, since x takes on a variety of values, and the corresponding values for y can be computed. A graph could be used to represent the equation.

Middle grades students need a wide variety of experiences with equations of various sorts before they can be expected to develop a deep understanding of variable and equation. Although a complete understanding will probably not be solidified during the middle grades, by the end of grade 8 students should be able to solve equations like $30 = 5x$ for the unknown number, to recognize equations such as $1 = n(1/n)$ as identities (when n is not zero), to use formulas such as $A = LW$ in applied situations, and to recognize $y = 3x$ as a linear equation that holds true for many ordered pairs (x, y).

Students should become fluent with the graphical representation and solution of linear equations and simultaneous systems of linear equations. As with skill in other forms of symbolic manipulation, it is also important that this fluency be based on a sound conceptual foundation to ensure that these manipulations are meaningful and not merely rote exercises. In particular, middle grade students should understand and use the facts that 1) ordered pairs that satisfy two linear equations are precisely the set of points that lie simultaneously on the graphs of those equations; 2) the x- and y-intercepts of the graph of any function $y = f(x)$ correspond to places where y and x, respectively, are zero; and 3) for linear functions $y = mx + b$, the slope can be thought of as the steepness of the graph, how fast the function is rising or falling, or as a rate of change connected to a physical concept such as speed.

Learning to interpret and write symbolic expressions and to solve symbolic algebraic equations is important in the middle grades, but for most students extensive work with symbols should come only after they have become fluent with verbal, tabular, and graphical representations of relationships that symbols represent. Many teachers find it helpful to introduce algebraic expressions as models of quantities in contextual situations, such as the following. Suppose three friends attend a ball game and each purchases a hot dog and a soda. The total cost could be denoted $3(H + S)$, where H is the cost of a hot dog and S is the cost of a soda. But it is also possible to think separately about the cost of the hot dogs ($3H$) and the cost of the sodas ($3S$). In this case, the total cost would be denoted $3H + 3S$.

By working on problems like this, students can gain experience with symbolic algebraic representations of situations. Moreover, they can see that different symbolic expressions can be produced to represent the same situation. If these expressions are all valid, then the expressions should be equivalent. This can lead to an examination of algebraic equivalence. Also through such experiences, students learn that they can often examine the equivalence of expressions in many ways, such as by checking that the related graphs and tables are the same, or by using the distributive, associative, and commutative properties to transform expressions into equivalent forms. By the end of grade 8, most students should be able to use their understanding of equivalence and of the commutative, associative, and distributive properties to recognize the nonequivalence of expressions such as $\sqrt{36 + 9}$ and $\sqrt{36} + \sqrt{9}$, and the equivalence of expressions such as $2(x + 3)$ and $2x + 6$. Through such experiences, students can give meaning to work with algebraic expressions.

■ Modeling and Change

Students learn to think about algebra as a valuable tool for modeling when they create equations or graphs to represent contextualized situations. But the reverse is also important—that is, for students to be asked to interpret graphs or equations as models of situations. For example, students might be shown a piecewise linear graph of distance from home versus time, or total cost of tickets versus number of tickets bought, and asked to describe a situation that the graph might model. Teachers need to encourage students to provide clear, complete oral and written descriptions for such situation models. Asking interpretive questions can also help: When was the person at home? How much did the tickets cost? To answer these questions, students must be able to interpret intercepts and slope in a graph.

In the middle grades, students should have many experiences exploring problems using multiple representations, such as in investigating interior angles and diagonals of polygons, as discussed earlier. Through work with patterns, graphs, and symbols, middle grades students can consider change and co-variation—how changes in one variable affect another.

It is particularly important for middle grades students to gain a deep understanding of rate of change and how it relates to lines and slopes of lines. Students may have difficulty understanding rate of change, since it is often a derived object, such as velocity, and not a physical entity. Teachers can help overcome this problem by giving students experiences with problem situations in which change is occurring and by helping students reflect on the connections among the actual change, its visual representation on a graph, and the constant m in linear equations $y = mx + b$. Such experiences could relate to experiences with technology-based laboratories, computer simulations, or patterns such as $S = 180n - 360$, the relationship between the number of sides of a polygon and the sum of the interior angles. Students should also understand that any change must take place with respect to something: change in position over time, change in size over time, change in area with respect to change in sides, and—for patterns of numbers—change with respect to position in the sequence.

Middle grades students should also explore other functions, such as quadratics and exponentials. The derivation of the formula $T = n(n - 3)/2$ as the number of diagonals in an n-sided polygon, allows students to see quadratics arising naturally. By reflecting on the recursive approach to this problem, that is, that the *change* in the number of diagonals is increasing, 0, 2, 5, 9, students begin to understand the nature of the increasing and decreasing "slope" of quadratics. Exponential functions may also arise naturally in the middle grades when students consider situations such as this one: Put one grain of wheat on the first square of a chessboard, two grains on the second square, four grains on the third, and so on. In reflecting on the fact that the change is doubling, or is a ratio, students begin understanding the shape of exponential functions. Students should be able to recognize graphs of each type of relation, and they should be able to recognize the way in which these relations manifest themselves in tables of data. Another important goal is to assist students in building a solid understanding of the interplay among tables of data, graphs, and algebraic expressions as models of the relations and functions that arise from these problem situations. Beginning the development of an understanding of change is central to the study of functions and much of calculus in secondary school and beyond.

■ STANDARD 3: GEOMETRY AND SPATIAL SENSE

> Mathematics instructional programs should include attention to geometry and spatial sense so that all students—
>
> * analyze characteristics and properties of two- and three-dimensional geometric objects;
> * select and use different representational systems, including coordinate geometry and graph theory;
> * recognize the usefulness of transformations and symmetry in analyzing mathematical situations;
> * use visualization and spatial reasoning to solve problems both within and outside of mathematics.

Elaboration: Grades 9–12

Geometry teaching in grades 9–12 should build on student experiences from earlier grades to make more formal and complex levels of geometric knowledge accessible.

Students' previous geometric knowledge becomes deeper, they acquire important new tools that can be used in a wide range of applications, and they become proficient in proof.

The classes of objects that form the core of high school geometry (lines, angles, polygons, circles, and a variety of three-dimensional objects) are much the same as in previous grades. Geometry learning in grades 9–12 should be focused more on the relationships among these objects than on the objects themselves or their individual properties.

A critical element in the study of geometry for students in grades 9–12 is knowing how to judge, construct, and communicate proofs. Electronic technology enables students to explore geometric relationships dynamically, offers students visual feedback and measurement as they investigate geometric situations. Secondary school teachers face an important challenge in balancing this use of technology for exploring ideas and developing conjectures with the use of deductive reasoning and counter-example in establishing or refuting the validity of such conjectures. Students should be able to articulate for themselves why particular conclusions about geometric objects or relationships among objects are logically sound. It is not critical that students master any particular format for presenting proofs (such as the two-column format). What is critical, however, is that students see the power of proof in establishing general claims (theorems) and that they are able to communicate their proofs effectively in writing.

Students should understand a range of representations, including coordinates, trigonometric relationships, networks, transformations, vectors, and matrices, which they can flexibly apply in situations that are inherently geometric and where geometry is not the original setting. Not all of the geometric situations that students encounter lend themselves to analysis within a Euclidean system. Alternative systems, such as discrete graphs, spherical geometry, or fractals can provide avenues for exploring such situations. The study of geometry in high school provides a means of describing, analyzing, viewing, and understanding the physical world and seeing beauty in its structures.

Focus Areas for Grades 9–12

■ *Analyze characteristics and properties of two- and three-dimensional geometric objects*

In grades 9–12, all students should—

- explore relationships among, make and test conjectures about, and solve problems involving classes of two- and three-dimensional geometric objects;
- connect geometry to other strands of mathematics (e.g., measurement, algebra, trigonometry), relate it to other areas of interest (e.g., art, architecture), and use it to solve problems;
- recognize geometry as an example of a deductive system, built from undefined terms, axioms, definitions, and theorems; and use deduction to establish the validity of geometric conjectures and to prove theorems.

■ *Select and use different representational systems, including coordinate geometry and graph theory*

In grades 9–12, all students should—

- investigate and verify conjectures and solve problems involving two- and three-dimensional figures, represented with rectangular coordinates;
- explore other coordinate systems (e.g., navigational, polar, spherical) and their uses;
- explore discrete/finite geometry systems (networks) and their characteristics and applications;
- use trigonometric relationships to solve problems.

■ *Recognize the usefulness of transformations and symmetry in analyzing mathematical situations*

In grades 9–12, all students should—

- represent translations, reflections, rotations, and dilations/contractions of objects in the plane using sketches, coordinates, vectors, or matrices and use these representations to gain information about the transformation;
- extend transformations to three dimensions, to include reflectional and rotational symmetry of solids;
- understand transformations (under the operation of composition) as an algebraic system of functions.

■ *Use visualization and spatial reasoning to solve problems both within and outside of mathematics*

In grades 9–12, all students should—

- draw and interpret two- and three-dimensional objects including those involving overlapping figures/objects and those requiring auxiliary lines;
- analyze cross-sections, truncations, and compositions/decompositions of three-dimensional objects;
- visualize three-dimensional objects and spaces from different perspectives.

Discussion

■ *Shape and structure*

By high school, students should have command of a broad range of geometric objects and properties. They should have had experience making and justifying simple conjectures about the relationships among those objects. During grades 9–12 the complexity of the relationships, whether presented statically or dynamically, must be extended and deepened. Using dynamic geometry software or physical models, students can quickly explore a range of examples. They can analyze what seems to change and what seems to remain invariant, and they can create conjectures about a given geometric situation. For example, students may notice that the diagonals of a parallelogram appear to meet at their respective midpoints. Many students may be content to stop at this point, convinced that their observation must generalize because it works for so many examples. However, effective teachers must challenge such assumptions. They can take advantage of these opportunities to encourage students to develop deeper understandings by formulating verifiable conjectures, exploring possible explanations, and finally resolving them through counterexamples or proofs.

Dynamic geometry software offers opportunities for exploration and conjecture. For example, using such software students can draw a triangle and construct the midpoints of the sides. The midpoints of the three sides can then be joined and the ratio of the area of the midpoint triangle to the area of the original triangle can be computed (see figure 7–11A). As students drag one vertex to create many different triangles, the ratio appears to remain constant at 0.25. Whether this relationship always holds is a question; resolving the issue calls for logical argument and proof by the student. The proof might involve either a synthetic representation calling on properties of transversals of parallel lines or an analytic representation using algebra.

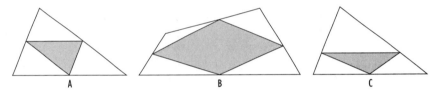

A   B   C

Figure 7–11 Exploring Midpoint Results

One natural extension is to look at whether any such constant ratio exists for convex quadrilaterals. After testing this conjecture, it appears that the ratio of areas is also constant (this time 0.5) in the quadrilateral case (see figure 7–11B). What about a convex pentagon? Students who are encouraged to explore this idea should discover that, when the midpoints of the sides of a general pentagon are joined, no constant area ratio emerges. A counterexample should then be the expected result of the investigation.

A second option for extension is to use the midpoint on one side of the triangle connected to a trisection point of each of the other two sides as shown in figure 7–11C. (And constructing the trisection point is a challenging problem in itself.) As other proportional divisions of the triangle are explored, patterns of the area ratio are interesting to analyze. In this type of exploratory environment, students can pose questions for extension and further exploration for themselves.

Students in grades 9–12 should be able to answer questions and prove theorems about geometric situations even when the diagrams that depict them are somewhat complex. Teachers might modify a task such as the one in figure 7–12 to assess students' inclinations to find relationships in a more open-ended way. For example, teachers might provide only the figure and ask students to find a pair of congruent triangles or a pair of similar triangles, or to list other relationships that hold for the figure. Students can then be asked to justify their claims on the basis of earlier theorems and facts.

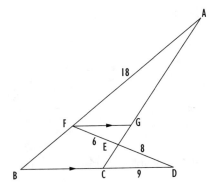

In the figure to the left, AF = BD, FG = FB, and FG is parallel to BD.

a) Name the triangle that is congruent to ΔAFG,

b) Prove that ΔAFE is similar to ΔDCE, and

c) Given that AF = 18 cm, FE = 6 cm, CD = 9 cm, and DE = 8 cm, calculate CE and EG

Figure 7–12 Complex Geometric Figure

(H. J. Beng (1995). *Secondary mathematics 5B* [2nd ed.]. Singapore: Curriculum Planning and Development Division, Ministry of Education, Pan Pacific Publications.)

Analogies between one-, two-, and three-dimensional situations offer opportunities for expanding student understanding. For instance, students could think about how the two points which are equidistant from a fixed point on a number line (one-dimensional situation) are analogous to a circle when the fixed point is located on the plane (two-dimensional situation) and a sphere when the point is located in space. Using the Pythagorean Theorem to compute the distance between two points in two dimensions (see figure 7–13A) has a three-dimensional counterpart, as in figure 7–13B. Applying the Pythagorean Theorem twice yields a generalized method for computing the distance.

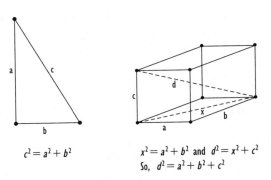

$$c^2 = a^2 + b^2$$

$$x^2 = a^2 + b^2 \text{ and } d^2 = x^2 + c^2$$
$$\text{So, } d^2 = a^2 + b^2 + c^2$$

Figure 7–13 The Pythagorean Theorem in Two and Three Dimensions

It still describes the distance between two points, but in space the points might be opposite corners of a rectangular box and would require three coordinates if described analytically.

Geometry provides methods for visualizing problems that come from non-geometric settings. For example, problems in probability can sometimes be made more accessible when viewed geometrically. The problem in figure 7–14 requires use of the triangle inequality.

A line segment, 18 inches long, is randomly divided into three lengths. What is the probability that the three lengths could be used as the sides of a triangle?

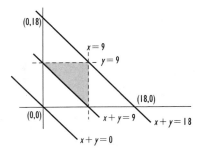

Figure 7–14 Probability of Making Triangles

Suppose x and y represent two of the three lengths. Since they are lengths, they must be nonnegative. Since the total of all three sides is 18, their sum must be less than 18. Thus all possible values for x and y must be contained in the region bounded by $x > 0$, $y > 0$, and $x + y < 18$—i.e., within the triangle with vertices (18,0), (0,0), and (0,18) shown in figure 7–14. To form a triangle, the Triangle Inequality implies that both x and y must be less than 9, but their sum must be greater than 9. Thus the shaded triangle in figure 7–14 contains all possible solutions for x and y so that a triangle is formed. Since the shaded triangle has 1/4 the area of the larger triangle, there is a 25% probability that a triangle will be formed.

Applications of geometry in practical situations abound. Designs of optimal packaging, machine tools and parts, art, and architecture all rely on geometric analysis for their creation. The natural physical world around us is more understandable when viewed through a geometric lens.

■ Coordinate geometry and other geometric models

Solving geometry problems often involves making a choice among a few possibilities for representation. Students in grades 9–12 need to develop enough facility in understanding various models so that they can benefit from alternative approaches to solving problems, alterative paths to understanding concepts, and the rich connections that such models afford.

Analytic geometry offers students a powerful way of linking algebraic and geometric concepts, thus enriching both. For example, when generalizing possible roots for quadratic equations, an examination of the graph of a parabola makes it clear that only three cases exist: two roots if the parabola crosses the x-axis, one if it is tangent, and none if it does not intersect the x-axis. On the other hand, the quadratic formula gives an algebraic interpretation of these cases. The quadratic formula may be stated as follows:

$$\text{If } ax^2 + bx + c = 0 \text{ and } a \neq 0, \text{ then } x = \frac{-b \pm \sqrt{b^2 - 4ac}}{2a}.$$

Students should see that this formula gives rise to two real roots, one real root, or two complex roots, depending on the value of the expression under the radical. Furthermore, these cases correspond exactly with the three geometric cases listed above. The expression $b^2 - 4ac$ is called the *discriminant* precisely because it discriminates among these possibilities.

High school students should also explore problems for which a polar, navigational, or spherical coordinate system might prove to be a more helpful representation. Right triangle trigonometry, including the Laws of Sines and Cosines, is useful in establishing a wide variety of area formulas. It also provides natural links to circular functions in algebra and to measurement topics and encourages yet another approach to solving problems. Students should be comfortable moving between any and all of these representational systems and making judgments about the advantages of each for a particular problem.

Two additional representation systems arise from more contemporary mathematics and should be part of the geometry that students encounter in high school. The first of these is finite graphs (structures of vertices and edges) together with their associated matrix representations. In problems where a finite number of objects or locations are to be linked by paths (networked), discrete graphs provide an effective model for answering questions about the number of possible routes, the lengths of those routes, and the optimal route under given conditions. Algorithmic thinking can be enhanced by considering methods for satisfying these conditions. An example follows.

There are seven small towns in Smith county that are connected to each other by dirt roads, as in the diagram to the right. (The diagram is not to scale.) The distances are in kilometers. The county, which has a limited budget, wants to pave some of the roads so that people can get from every town to every other town on paved roads, either directly or indirectly, but so that the total number of miles paved is minimized. Find a network of paved roads that will fulfill the county's requirements. Eliminate any non-paved roads from your drawing. (Adapted from A. F. Coxford, J. T. Fey, C. R. Hirsch, & H. L. Schoen [1996]. *Contemporary mathematics in context, course 2.* Chicago, IL: Janson Publications.)

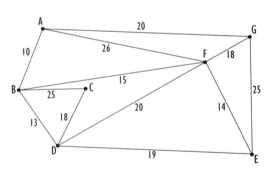

■ Transformations and symmetry

By high school, students should have experience with basic geometric transformations: translation, reflection, rotation, and dilation/contraction. High school students should be ready to engage with increasingly general ways of representing these transformations, including graphs, notation such as $R_{90°}$, and matrices. Matrix representation allows study of transformations as objects in their own right and illuminates natural and powerful connections to concepts found in number and algebra. Consider how the following extended example might help students understand matrices as representational tools, and also gain deeper understanding of geometric transformations. Students might be asked to read the following explanation and fill in details so that they can explain it adequately to themselves and their peers.

ΔABC with A(−5,1), B(−4,7) and C(−8,5) can be represented by the matrix

$$\begin{pmatrix} -5 & -4 & -8 \\ 1 & 7 & 5 \end{pmatrix}$$

TO THE STUDENT:
What do the rows and columns of this matrix represent?

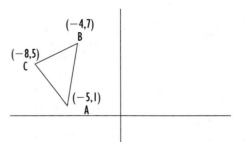

Reflection of ΔABC over the line $y = x$ can be represented by the following multiplication

$$\begin{pmatrix} 0 & 1 \\ 1 & 0 \end{pmatrix}\begin{pmatrix} -5 & -4 & -8 \\ 1 & 7 & 5 \end{pmatrix} = \begin{pmatrix} 1 & 7 & 5 \\ -5 & -4 & -8 \end{pmatrix}$$

so that the vertices of the image are A′(1,−5), B′(7,−4), and C′(5,−8).

TO THE STUDENT:
Why does multiplication by

$$\begin{pmatrix} 0 & 1 \\ 1 & 0 \end{pmatrix}$$ accomplish this reflection?

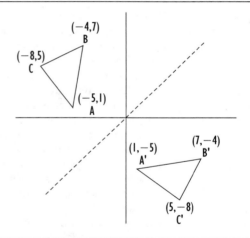

A subsequent rotation of the image 90° clockwise about the origin can be represented as follows:

$$\begin{pmatrix} 0 & -1 \\ 1 & 0 \end{pmatrix}\begin{pmatrix} 1 & 7 & 5 \\ -5 & -4 & -8 \end{pmatrix} = \begin{pmatrix} 5 & 4 & 8 \\ 1 & 7 & 5 \end{pmatrix}$$

so that the vertices of the second image are A″(5,1), B″(4,7), and C″(8,5).

TO THE STUDENT:
Why does multiplication by

$$\begin{pmatrix} 0 & -1 \\ 1 & 0 \end{pmatrix}$$ accomplish this rotation?

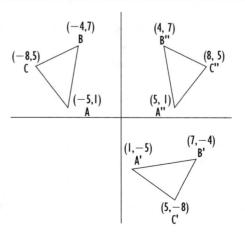

Note that the product of the two transformation matrices, as shown to the right, produces the matrix of another transformation. This matrix represents a reflection over the y-axis, the transformation mapping $\triangle ABC$ to $\triangle A''B''C''$.

$$\begin{pmatrix} 0 & -1 \\ 1 & 0 \end{pmatrix}\begin{pmatrix} 0 & 1 \\ 1 & 0 \end{pmatrix}=\begin{pmatrix} -1 & 0 \\ 0 & 1 \end{pmatrix}$$

TO THE STUDENT:
Use matrix multiplication to find the image of $\triangle ABC$ using the transformation represented by $\begin{pmatrix} -1 & 0 \\ 0 & 1 \end{pmatrix}$. Did the vertices of $\triangle A''B''C''$ result?

Matrices are a useful way to represent transformations, where their product represents a composition of transformations.

TO THE STUDENT:
Explain what this means, based on the discussion above.

Note that the order of operations is important. If the two factors are reversed, as shown to the right, a different transformation will be represented.

$$\begin{pmatrix} 0 & 1 \\ 1 & 0 \end{pmatrix}\begin{pmatrix} 0 & -1 \\ 1 & 0 \end{pmatrix}=\begin{pmatrix} 1 & 0 \\ 0 & -1 \end{pmatrix}$$

TO THE STUDENT:
What transformation does this matrix represent? How would you compose the two given transformations to produce this transformation? Draw the image of $\triangle ABC$ using this composition of transformations and verify your answer using matrix multiplication.

There are interesting extensions for this problem. Can transformation of a quadrilateral be represented using matrix multiplication? What other transformations can be represented by matrices? Are there conditions under which matrix multiplication is commutative?

Students in the upper grades should formalize symmetry in two- and three-dimensional objects, recognizing symmetries as reflections or rotational mappings of a figure onto itself. Sets of transformations and the operations defined on them can be studied as objects in their own right. Structural questions such as closure, existence of inverses, and commutativity can be investigated and applied when analyzing sets of transformations.

■ *Visualization and spatial reasoning*

Students must learn to pay attention to the details of a drawing or description of a physical object, and they should work to form a mental image of it if they are expected to analyze its relationship to other objects. A diagram such as the one in figure 7–12 is complex. It is difficult for a student to answer questions about it unless its key features can be identified and visually isolated. In figure 7–12, FG is parallel to BD. The line segments AB, FD, and AC all form transversals for this pair of parallel segments. Students need to be able to concentrate on the parallel segments and each of these transversals in order to identify pairs of congruent or supplementary angles and answer the questions posed. It is through a rich variety of experiences, first with simple figures and sets of directions, and later with more complex ones, that students can develop this visual ability.

While students should arrive in high school with experience creating three-dimensional objects from two-dimensional patterns (nets), finding volume, and computing surface area, additional concrete experience is necessary in grades 9–12 to help students extend their understandings of objects in space. Visualizing such things as the solid swept out when a plane figure is rotated about an axis, the shape of a cross-section formed when a plane slices through a cone (a conic section) or other solid object, or the shape of the two solids formed by such a slicing process, requires that students work with physical models as well as drawings. Visualization software can also be helpful in this endeavor.

Interesting geometry problems set in a context of perspective drawings can build visualization skill as well as geometry knowledge. Consider the following problem (adapted from ARISE [1998]. *Unit 16: The geometry of art* (pilot materials). Cincinnati, OH: Southwestern Educational Publishing.):

> *In the drawing below are two telephone poles drawn in perspective. We would like to draw another pole, EF, that appears to be the same distance from pole CD as pole CD is from pole AB.*

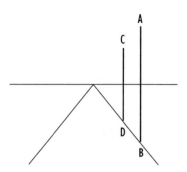

If students think about the situation in two dimensions, they may recognize that ABFE will be a rectangle, and that the diagonals of that rectangle will intersect at the midpoint of CD, as shown in figure 7–15A. Applying these relationships to the situation shown in perspective may clarify what can be done, as shown in figure 7–15B.

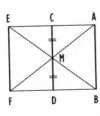
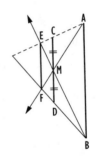

A B

Figure 7–15 Solutions to the Telephone Pole Problem

Thinking about and depicting three-dimensional objects is difficult for many students. Creating and analyzing perspective drawings, thinking about how lines or angles are formed on a spherical surface, and working to understand orientation and drawings in a three-dimensional rectangular coordinate system all contribute to students' abilities to think and reason spatially. These, along with two-dimensional experiences and a solid core of deductive reasoning should be key components of the high school geometry experience.

■ SAMPLE STATE MODEL STRAND, GRADES K–12: DATA ANALYSIS AND PROBABILITY

Understanding of the processes of data collection, representation, and interpretation is crucial in today's world. It is essential that students develop the ability to summarize and analyze data, to draw inferences, and to make accurate predictions and judgments based on that analysis.

Students should be given ample opportunities to examine real-world situations. This strand provides an excellent opportunity for students to become active participants in mathematics learning. The vast variety of potential topics for investigation provides the opportunity for considering a variety of interests and abilities, and thus makes the classroom a motivating and exciting place to be.

The study of data analysis should start in the early grades with the comparison, classification, and organization of objects, then proceed to the collection, organization, and representation of more abstract data through the use of tables, charts, graphs, and maps. Finally, students should learn to analyze the data, note trends, draw conclusions, and make predictions.

It is essential that students understand how statistics can be manipulated, and recognize the potential uses and misuses of statistical information.

The availability of computing technology presents today's students with the ability to perform statistical computations and comparisons which would have proved too unwieldy just a few short years ago.

Kindergarten

The student will be able to . . .

1. describe objects or pictures according to distinct attributes.
2. classify objects or pictures and use given categories or attributes in sorting.
3. create a floor/table graph by arranging actual objects in appropriate categories.

the development of verbal skills is important

use attribute blocks or any common objects

Grade One

The student will be able to . . .

1. use given categories in sorting information.
2. create a picture graph (each picture representing a single unit) by drawing a picture of a floor/table graph, as mentioned in the kindergarten objectives.
3. explore meanings of a picture graph by making identifications, comparisons, and predictions.
4. collect data and record by tallying.
5. identify events that are sure to happen, events that are sure not to happen, and those we cannot be sure about.

children may suggest categories, but some will need help

Grade Two

The student will be able to . . .

1. collect and organize data and represent with a picture or bar graph.
2. develop a variety of categories for sorting information.
3. explore picture and bar graphs (scaled by one) by making identifications, comparisons, and predictions.
4. identify information on a labeled picture map.

Grade Three

The student will be able to . . .

1. read and interpret pictographs in which pictures represent more than a single unit.
2. create, read, and interpret tables and charts.
3. explore bar graphs (scaled by one) by making identifications, comparisons, and predictions.
4. identify information on a labeled picture map using a picture-symbol key.
5. collect and record data on the frequency of events.

students need to develop independence in interpreting symbols from contextual clues

6. investigate, display, and record all possible arrangements of a given set of objects.
7. translate freely among pictographs, tables, charts, and bar graphs.

abstract data from all of them

Grade Four

The student will be able to . . .

1. collect data and create a picture or bar graph representing the data.
2. make predictions and modify them as additional data are collected.
3. read and interpret diagrams and time lines.
4. explore picture and bar graphs by making identifications, comparisons, and predictions, and use them to solve application problems.
5. investigate, display, and record all possible arrangements of a given set of events.
6. find simple experimental probabilities.

scaling of graphs becomes an important focus

use spinners, coin tossing, random selection, etc.

Grade Five

The student will be able to . . .

1. explore the effect of changing scales on bar graphs.
2. select a scale and create a line graph.
3. identify the ordered pair for a point on a labeled grid.
4. identify a direction, distance, and/or location using a political map containing a key, a scale, and a compass.
5. explore the concept of average and calculate the arithmetic mean of a given set of numbers.
6. determine experimental and theoretical probabilities.
7. make predictions based on experimental or theoretical probabilities.

geographical maps

Use fractions, ratios, and percents to describe the probability of a given event.

Grade Six

The student will be able to . . .

1. collect data and create a circle graph.
2. explore circle graphs and use them to solve application problems.
3. read, interpret, and use tables, charts, maps, and graphs to identify patterns, note trends, and draw conclusions.

make identifications, comparisons, predictions

4. explore the concept of average and calculate the arithmetic mean and the mode of a given set of numbers.
5. explore changes in the mean and the mode when some data are changed.
6. construct a tree diagram to list alternatives and procedures.
7. read and construct scale drawings.
8. investigate probabilities for the possible outcomes of a simple experiment.
9. make predictions of outcomes of experiments based on theoretical probabilities and explain actual outcomes.

Grade Seven

The student will be able to . . .

1. collect data and create the appropriate type of graph and use the appropriate scale.
2. create, read, and interpret tables, charts, diagrams, and maps.
3. identify the ordered pair for a point on a labeled coordinate plane.
4. calculate and explore relationships between the mean, median, mode, and range of a given set of numbers.
5. explore permutations and combinations and the relationships between them.
6. make logical inferences from statistical data.
7. detect misuses of statistical or numerical information.
8. develop and interpret frequency tables.
9. compute averages.

Grade Eight

The student will be able to . . .

1. collect data and create appropriate graphs to illustrate.
2. make identifications, comparisons, and predictions, and solve application problems using picture, bar, circle, and line graphs.
3. find the mean, mode, median, and range of a set of data and use them in application problems.

4. detect misuses of statistical or numerical information.
5. use elementary notions of probability.
6. explore the role of sampling and collecting data in making a statistical argument.

A spreadsheet can be used to create simulations to broaden students' experiences.

Grade Nine

The student will be able to . . .

1. organize data into tables, charts, and graphs.
2. understand and apply measures of central tendency, variability, and correlation.

data from real-world situations

and, in addition, college-intending students will be able to . . .

3. transform data to aid in data interpretation and prediction.

Grade Ten

The student will be able to . . .

1. use curve fitting to predict from data.
2. use experimental or theoretical probability, as appropriate, to represent and solve problems involving uncertainty.
3. use computer simulations and random number generators to estimate probabilities.

and, in addition, college-intending students will be able to . . .

4. test hypotheses using appropriate statistics.
5. read, interpret, and use tables, charts, and graphs to identify patterns, note trends, draw conclusions, and make predictions.
6. determine probabilities of events involving unbiased objects.

Grade Eleven

The student will be able to . . .

1. use sampling and recognize its role in statistical claims.
2. design a statistical experiment to study a problem, conduct the experiment, and interpret and communicate the outcomes.

and, in addition, the college-intending student will be able to . . .

   3. describe, in general terms, the normal curve and use its properties.

Grade Twelve

The student will be able to . . .

   1. create and interpret discrete probability distributions.
   2. understand the concept of random variable.

and, in addition, the college-intending student will be able to . . .

   3. apply the concept of a random variable to generate and interpret probability distributions, including binomial, uniform, normal, and chi square.

Teaching

- ■ NCTM Professional Teaching Standard I: Worthwhile Mathematical Tasks

  (Reprinted with permission from *Professional Standards for Teaching Mathematics*, copyright 1991 by National Council of Teachers of Mathematics. All rights reserved.)

- ■ NCTM Guiding Principle: The Equity Principle

  (Reprinted with permission from *Principles and Standards for School Mathematics*, copyright 1998 by National Council of Teachers of Mathematics. All rights reserved.)

■ STANDARD 1: WORTHWHILE MATHEMATICAL TASKS

The teacher of mathematics should pose tasks that are based on—

- sound and significant mathematics;
- knowledge of students' understandings, interests, and experiences;
- knowledge of the range of ways that diverse students learn mathematics;

and that

- engage students' intellect;
- develop students' mathematical understandings and skills;
- stimulate students to make connections and develop a coherent framework for mathematical ideas;
- call for problem formulation, problem solving, and mathematical reasoning;
- promote communication about mathematics;
- represent mathematics as an ongoing human activity;
- display sensitivity to, and draw on, students' diverse background experiences and dispositions;
- promote the development of all students' dispositions to do mathematics.

Elaboration

Teachers are responsible for the quality of the mathematical tasks in which students engage. A wide range of materials exists for teaching mathematics: problem booklets, computer software, practice sheets, puzzles, manipulative materials, calculators, textbooks, and so on. These materials contain tasks from which teachers can choose. Also, teachers often create their own tasks for students: projects, problems, worksheets, and the like. Some tasks grow out of students' conjectures or questions. Teachers should choose and develop tasks that are likely to promote the development of students' understandings of concepts and procedures in a way that also fosters their ability to solve problems and to reason and communicate mathematically. Good tasks are ones that do not separate mathematical thinking from mathematical concepts or skills, that capture students' curiosity, and that invite them to speculate and to pursue their hunches. Many such tasks can be approached in more than one interesting and legitimate way; some have more than one reasonable solution. These tasks, consequently, facilitate significant classroom discourse, for they require that students reason about different strategies and outcomes, weigh the pros and cons of alternatives, and pursue particular paths.

In selecting, adapting, or generating mathematical tasks, teachers must base their decisions on three areas of concern: the mathematical content, the students, and the ways in which students learn mathematics.

In considering the mathematical content of a task, teachers should consider how appropriately the task represents the concepts and procedures entailed. For example, if students are to gather, summarize, and interpret data, are the statistics they are expected to generate appropriate? Does it make sense to calculate a mean? If there is an explanation of a procedure, such as calculating a mean, does that explanation focus on the underlying concepts or is it merely mechanical? Teachers must also use a curricular perspective, considering the potential of a task to help students progress in their cumulative understanding of a particular domain and to make connections among ideas they have studied in the past and those they will encounter in the future.

A second content consideration is to assess what the task conveys about what is entailed in doing mathematics. Some tasks, although they deal nicely with the concepts and procedures, involve students in simply producing right answers. Others require students to speculate, to pursue alternatives, to face decisions about whether or not their approaches are valid. For example, one task might require students to find means, medians, and modes for given sets of data. Another might require them to decide whether to calculate means, medians, or modes as the best measures of central tendency, given particular sets of data and particular claims they would like to make about the data, then to calculate those statistics, and finally to explain and defend their decisions. Like the first task, the second would offer students the opportunity to practice finding means, medians, and modes. Only the second, however, conveys the important point that summarizing data involves decisions related to the data and the purposes for which the analysis is being used. Tasks should foster students' sense that mathematics is a changing and evolving domain, one in which ideas grow and develop over time and to which many cultural groups have contributed. Drawing on the history of mathematics can help teachers to portray this idea: exploring alternative numeration systems or investigating non-Euclidean geometries, for example. Fractions evolved out of the Egyptians' attempts to divide quantities—four things shared among ten people. This fact could provide the explicit basis for a teacher's approach to introducing fractions.

A third content consideration centers on the development of appropriate skill and automaticity. Teachers must assess the extent to which skills play a role in the context of particular mathematical topics. A goal is to create contexts that foster skill development even as students engage in problem solving and reasoning. For example, elementary school students should develop rapid facility with addition and multiplication combinations. Rolling pairs of dice as part of an investigation of probability can simultaneously provide students with practice with addition. Trying to figure out how many ways 36 desks can be arranged in equal-sized groups—and whether there are more or fewer possible groupings with 36, 37, 38, 39, or 40 desks—presses students to produce each number's factors quickly. As they work on this problem, students have concurrent opportunities to practice multiplication facts and to develop a sense of what factors are. Further, the problem may provoke interesting questions: How many factors does a number have? Do larger numbers necessarily have more factors? Is there a number that has more factors than 36? Even as students pursue such questions, they practice and use multiplication facts, for skill plays a role in problem solving at all levels. Teachers of algebra and geometry must similarly consider which skills are essential and why and seek ways to develop essential skills in the contexts in which they matter. What do students need to memorize? How can that be facilitated?

The content is unquestionably a crucial consideration in appraising the value of a particular task. Defensible reasoning about the mathematics of a task must be based on a thoughtful understanding of the topic at hand as well as of the goals and purposes of carrying out particular mathematical processes.

Teachers must also consider the students in deciding on the appropriateness of a given task. They must consider what they know about their particular students as well as what they know more generally about students from psychological, cultural, sociological, and political perspectives. For example, teachers should consider gender issues in selecting tasks, deliberating about ways in which the tasks may be an advantage either to boys or to girls—and a disadvantage to the others—in some systematic way.

In thinking about their particular students, teachers must weigh several factors. One centers on what their students already know and can do, what they need to work on, and how much they seem ready to stretch intellectually. Well-chosen tasks afford teachers opportunities to learn about their students' understandings even as the tasks also press the students forward. Another factor is their students' interests, dispositions, and experiences. Teachers should aim for tasks that are likely to engage their students' interests. Sometimes this means choosing familiar application contexts: for example, having students explore issues related to the finances of a school store or something in the students' community. Not always, however, should concern for "interest" limit the teacher to tasks that relate to the familiar everyday worlds of the students; theoretical or fanciful tasks that challenge students intellectually are also interesting: number theory problems, for instance. When teachers work with groups of students for whom the notion of "argument" is uncomfortable or at variance with community norms of interaction, teachers must consider carefully the ways in which they help students to engage in mathematical discourse. Defensible reasoning about students must be based on the assumption that all students can learn and do mathematics, that each one is worthy of being challenged intellectually. Sensitivity to the diversity of students' backgrounds and experiences is crucial in selecting worthwhile tasks.

Knowledge about ways in which students learn mathematics is a third basis for appraising tasks. The mode of activity, the kind of thinking required, and the way in which students are led to explore the particular content all contribute to the kind of learning opportunity afforded by the task. Knowing that students need opportunities to model concepts concretely and pictorially, for example, might lead a teacher to select a task that involves such representations. An awareness of common student confusions or misconceptions around a certain mathematical topic would help a teacher to select tasks that engage students in exploring critical ideas that often underlie those confusions. Understanding that writing about one's ideas helps to clarify and develop one's understandings would make a task that requires students to write explanations look attractive. Teachers' understandings about how students learn mathematics should be informed by research as well as their own experience. Just as teachers can learn more about students' understandings from the tasks they provide students, so, too, can they gain insights into how students learn mathematics. To capitalize on the opportunity, teachers should deliberately select tasks that provide them with windows on students' thinking.

Vignettes

1.1   Mrs. Jackson is thinking about how to help her students learn about perimeter and area. She realizes that learning about perimeter and area entails developing concepts, procedures, and skills. Students need to understand that the perimeter is the distance around a region and the area is the amount of space inside the region and that length and area are two fundamentally different kinds of measure. They need to realize that perimeter and area are not directly related—that, for instance, two figures can have the same perimeter but different areas. Students also need to be able to figure out the perimeter and the area of a given region. At the same time, they should relate these to other measures with which they are familiar, such as measures of volume or weight.

The teacher analyzes the content and how to approach it, and she considers how it connects with other mathematical ideas.

Mrs. Jackson examines two tasks designed to help upper elementary-grade students learn about perimeter and area. She wants to compare what each has to offer.

Task 1:

Find the area and perimeter of each rectangle:

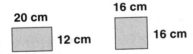

Task 1 requires little more than remembering what "perimeter" and "area" refer to and the formulas for calculating each. Nothing about this task requires students to ponder the relationship between perimeter and area. This task is not likely to engage students intellectually; it does not entail reasoning or problem solving.

Task 2:

Suppose you had 64 meters of fence with which you were going to build a pen for your large dog, Bones. What are some different pens you can make if you use all the fencing? What is the pen with the least play space? What is the biggest pen you can make—the one that allows Bones the most play space? Which would be best for running?

This task can engage students intellectually because it challenges them to search for something. Although accessible to even young students, the problem is not immediately solvable. Neither is it clear how best to approach it. A question that students confront as they work on the problem is how to determine that they have indeed found the largest or the smallest play space. Being able to justify an answer and to show that a problem is solved are critical components of mathematical reasoning and problem solving. The problem yields to a variety of tools—drawings on graph paper, constructions with rulers or compasses, tables, calculators—and lets students develop their understandings of the concept of area and its relationship to perimeter. They can investigate the patterns that emerge in the dimensions and the relationship between those dimensions and the area. This problem may also prompt the question of what "largest" or "smallest," "most" or "least," mean, setting the stage for making connections in other measurement contexts.

1.2   Ms. Pierce is a first-year teacher in a large middle school. She uses a mathematics textbook, published about ten years ago, that her department requires her to follow closely. In the middle of a unit on fractions with her seventh graders, Ms. Pierce is examining her textbook's treatment of division with fractions. She is trying to decide what its strengths and weaknesses are and whether and how she should use it to help her students understand division with fractions.

Many beginning and experienced teachers are in the same position as this teacher: having to follow a textbook quite closely. Appraising and deciding how to use textbook material is crucial.

She notices that the textbook's emphasis is on the mechanics of carrying out the procedure ("dividing by a number is the same as multiplying by its reciprocal"). The text tells students that they "can use reciprocals to help" them divide by fractions and gives them a few examples of the procedure.

The teacher wants her students to understand what it means to divide by a fraction, not just learn the mechanics of the procedure.

The picture at the top of one of the pages shows some beads of a necklace lined up next to a ruler—an attempt to represent, for example, that there are twenty-four $\frac{3}{4}$-inch beads and forty-eight $\frac{3}{8}$-inch beads in an eighteen-inch necklace. Ms. Pierce sees that this does represent what it means to divide by $\frac{3}{4}$ or by $\frac{3}{8}$—that the question is, "How many three-fourths or three-eighths are there in eighteen?" Still, when she considers what would help her students understand this, she does not think that this representation is adequate. She also suspects that students may not take this section seriously, for they tend to believe that mathematics means memorizing rules rather than understanding why the rules work.

> The teacher senses that the idea of "using the reciprocal" is introduced almost as a trick, lacking any real rationale or connection to the pictures of necklaces. Furthermore, division with fractions seems to be presented as a new topic, unconnected to anything the students might already know, such as division of whole numbers.

Ms. Pierce is concerned that these pages are likely to reinforce that impression. She doesn't see anything in the task that would emphasize the value of understanding why, nor that would promote mathematical discourse.

> The practice exercises involve dividing one fraction by another, and the "problems" at the end do not involve reasoning or problem solving.

Thinking about her students, Ms. Pierce judges that these two pages require computational skills that most of her students do have (i.e., being able to produce the reciprocal of a number, being able to multiply fractions) but that the exercises on the pages would not be interesting to them. Nothing here would engage their thinking.

> The teacher considers what she knows about her students—what they know and what is likely to interest them.

Looking at the pictures of the necklaces gives Ms. Pierce an idea. She decides that she can use this idea, so she copies the drawing only. She will include at least one picture with beads of some whole number length—2-inch beads, for example. She will ask students to examine the pictures and try to write some kind of number sentence that represents what they see. For example, this 7-inch bracelet has 14 half-inch beads:

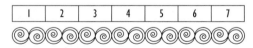

> The model used is a linear one rather than the pie or pizza diagrams most often used to represent fractions. The teacher sees the need for students to develop varied representations. Also, different representations make sense to different students. The teacher wants the task to help students make connections—in this example, between multiplication and division and between division of whole numbers and division of fractions.

This could be represented as $7 \div \frac{1}{2}$ or 7×2. She will try to help them to think about the reciprocal relationship between multiplication and division and the meaning of dividing something by a fraction or by a whole number. Then, she thinks, she could use some of the exercises on the second page but, instead of just having the students compute the answers, she will ask them, in pairs, to write stories for each of about five exercises.

> Writing stories to go with the division sentences may help students to focus on the meaning of the procedure.

She decides she will also provide a couple of other examples that involve whole number divisors: $28 \div 8$ and $80 \div 16$, for example.

Ms. Pierce feels encouraged from her experience with planning this lesson and thinks that revising other textbook lessons will be feasible. Despite the fact that she is supposed to be following the text closely, Ms. Pierce now thinks that she will be able to adapt the text in ways that will significantly improve what she can do with her students this year.

> The teacher keeps her eye on the bigger curricular picture as she selects and adapts tasks. Juxtaposing whole number and fraction division will help her students review division and make connections.

1.3 After recently completing a unit on multiplication and division, a fourth-grade class has just begun to learn about factors and multiples. Their teacher is using the calculator as a tool for this topic. This approach is new for her. The school has just purchased for the first time a set of calculators, which all the classrooms share. She and many of her colleagues attended a workshop recently on different uses of calculators.

Using the automatic constant feature of their calculators (that is, that pressing 5 + = = = . . . yields 5, 10, 15, 20, . . . on the display), the fourth graders have generated lists of the multiples of different numbers. They have also used the calculator to explore the factors of different numbers. To encourage the students to deepen their understanding of numbers, the teacher has urged them to look for patterns and to make conjectures. She asked them, "Do you see any patterns in the lists you are making? Can you make any guesses about any of those patterns?"

Two students have raised a question that has attracted the interest of the whole class: Are there more multiples of 3 or more multiples of 8?

The teacher encourages them to pursue the question, for she sees that this question can engage them in the concept of multiples as well as provide a fruitful context for making mathematical arguments. She realizes that the question holds rich mathematical potential and even brings up questions about infinity. "What do the rest of you think?" she asks. "How could you investigate this question? Go ahead and work on this a bit on your own or with a partner and then let's discuss what you come up with."

The children pursue the question excitedly. The calculators are useful once more as they generate lists of the multiples of 3 and the multiples of 8. Groups are forming around particular arguments. One group of children argues that there are more multiples of 3 because in the interval between 0 and 20 there are more multiples of 3 than multiples of 8. Another group is convinced that the multiples of 3 are "just as many as the multiples of 8 because they go on forever." A few children, thinking there should be more multiples of 8 because 8 is greater than 3, form a new conjecture about numbers—that the larger the number, the more *factors* it has.

The teacher is pleased with the ways in which opportunities for mathematical reasoning are growing out of the initial exploration. She likes the way in which they are making connections between multiples and factors. She also notes that students already seem quite fluent using the terms *multiple* and *factor*.

Although it is nearing the end of class, the teacher invites them to present to the rest of the class their conjecture that the larger the number, the more factors it has. She suggests that the students record it in their notebooks and discuss it in class tomorrow. Pausing for a

The teacher uses this exploratory task to spur students' mathematical thinking. She knows that the initial task is likely to generate further, more focused tasks based on the students' conjectures. The calculators help the students in looking for patterns.

All year, this teacher has encouraged her students to take intellectual risks by asking questions.

Judging that this question is a fruitful one, the teacher picks up on the students' idea and uses it to further the direction of the class's exploration, even bringing up questions about infinity.

The question promotes mathematical reasoning, eliciting at least three competing and, to fourth graders, compelling mathematical arguments. Students are actively engaged in trying to persuade other members of the class of the validity of their argument.

The task has stimulated students to formulate a new problem. The idea that lessons can raise questions for students to pursue is part of an emphasis on mathematical inquiry.

The teacher provides a context for dealing with students' conjectures. She is also able to formulate tasks out of the students' ideas and questions when it seems fruitful.

moment before she sends them out to recess, she decides to provoke their thinking a little and remarks, "That's an interesting conjecture. Let's just think about it for a sec. How many factors does, say, 3 have?"

"Two," call out several students.

"What are they?" she probes. "Yes, Deng?"

"1 and 3," replies Deng quickly.

"Let's try another one," continues the teacher. "What about 20?"

After a moment, several hands shoot up. She pauses to allow students to think and asks, "Natasha?"

"Six—1 and 20, 2 and 10, 4 and 5," answers Natasha with confidence.

The teacher throws out a couple more numbers—9 and 15. She is conscious of trying to use only numbers that fit the conjecture. With satisfaction, she notes that most of the students are quickly able to produce all the factors for the numbers she gives them. Some used paper and pencil, some used calculators, and some did a combination of both. As she looks up at the clock, one child asks, "But what about 17? It doesn't seem to work."

"That's *one* of the things that you could examine for tomorrow. I want all of you to see if you can find out if this conjecture always holds."

"I don't think it'll work for odd numbers," says one child.

"Check into it," smiles the teacher. "We'll discuss it tomorrow."

> The teacher provides practice in multiplication facts at the same time that she engages the students in considering their peers' conjecture.

> The teacher does not want to give them a key to challenging the conjecture, but she does want to get them into investigating it.
>
> She tries to spur them on to pursuing this idea on their own.

> The teacher deliberately leaves the question unanswered. She wants to encourage them to persevere and not expect her to give the answers.

Summary: Tasks

The teacher is responsible for shaping and directing students' activities so that they have opportunities to engage meaningfully in mathematics. Textbooks can be useful resources for teachers, but teachers must also be free to adapt or depart from texts if students' ideas and conjectures are to help shape teachers' navigation of the content. The tasks in which students engage must encourage them to reason about mathematical ideas, to make connections, and to formulate, grapple with, and solve problems. Students also need skills. Good tasks nest skill development in the context of problem solving. In practice, students' actual opportunities for learning depend on the kind of *discourse* that the teacher orchestrates, an issue we examine in the next section.

THE EQUITY PRINCIPLE

Mathematics instructional programs should promote the learning of mathematics by *all* students.

A commitment to equity was one of the hallmarks of the original NCTM *Standards,* and its importance is reaffirmed here. One of the most notable aspects of NCTM's

1989 *Curriculum and Evaluation Standards for School Mathematics* was the insistence that mathematics instructional programs address the learning of mathematics by *all* students.

An emphasis on "mathematics for all" is important because of the role that school mathematics has historically played in educational inequity. A student's mathematical proficiency is often used as a basis for decisions regarding further schooling and job opportunities. Furthermore, mathematics has been one of the school subjects frequently associated with "tracking," a practice in which students are sorted into different instructional sequences that often results in inequitable educational opportunities and outcomes for students.

An emphasis on "mathematics for all" is also important because it challenges a pervasive belief among some members of society that a great number of students are not capable of acquiring mathematical proficiency. This belief is quite different from the equally pervasive view that all students can learn to read and write in English. Verbal literacy has been expected of all students, and school programs that do not produce literate students are regarded as failures. It is striking that a contrary set of beliefs has traditionally been held regarding mathematical literacy and proficiency. The education system has been expected to succeed only with the "mathematically able."

To underscore the need for a high-quality mathematics instructional program for all students, the *Professional Teaching Standards for School Mathematics* explicitly stated as one of its undergirding assumptions that "all students can learn to think mathematically" (NCTM 1991, p. 21). By "all students," the authors meant—

- students who have been denied access in any way to educational opportunities as well as those who have not;
- students who are African American, Hispanic, American Indian, and other minorities as well as those who are considered to be part of the majority;
- students who are female as well as those who are male;
- students who have not been successful as well as those who have been successful in school and in mathematics. (ibid., pp. 21–22)

The importance of equity was also emphasized in NCTM's 1995 *Assessment Standards for School Mathematics*. One of the six mathematics assessment standards was the Equity Standard, "Assessment should promote equity" (p. 15).

Striving for Equity and Excellence

In a democratic society, a commitment to equity should be of central importance in mathematics education. Traditionally, school mathematics has been viewed as a sorting machine, in which many students are considered unlikely to study higher mathematics and in which a few students are identified as capable of succeeding in the discipline of mathematics or in mathematically related fields of study. Arguably, for a society in which the mathematical needs of most citizens are quite low, this form of mathematics education might be adequate, even if not equitable. In recent decades, however, more and more citizens—most of whom would not be identified as "mathematically talented"—need to comprehend and respond competently to quantitative information. Consider our current culture, in which banks have become increasingly "self-service" with ATM machines and on-line banking. Widely available consumer reports offer information on product safety and effectiveness. Employment opportunities in fields such as health care, auto manufacturing, news reporting, and fashion design require a more sophisticated knowledge of mathematics. As a consequence, a "sort and discard" form of school mathematics education is inadequate.

An alternative conception of school mathematics instructional programs assumes the primary purpose of ensuring that all citizens are quantitatively literate. That is, all students must become fluent and flexible in dealing with quantitative information. This view goes well beyond arithmetic computation and algebraic equation solving, which are often thought to be the hallmarks of mathematics education for all students. Moreover, a commitment to equity should support another central goal of mathematics education—namely, excellence. Achieving these two goals is a complex and interrelated task. Equity will be achieved when excellent mathematics instructional programs exist for every student in every school.

School mathematics instructional programs need to nurture the development of mathematical proficiency and quantitative literacy in students who are exceptionally talented and in those who will be productive, quantitatively competent citizens. If school mathematics instructional programs serve their purpose well, there will be no shortage of students well prepared to pursue further education and careers in mathematics, science, and engineering, and all citizens will have adequate quantitative skill.

Believing and Acting

Adopting the belief that all students can learn mathematics is critical. But it will take more than good intentions to enact equitable mathematics instructional programs. As stated above, one impediment is the widely held belief that only some students can succeed in mathematics. Low expectations are especially problematic because they are not randomly distributed across the entire population. Females, students who live in poverty, students who are not native speakers of English, and many non-white students have traditionally been far more likely than their demographic counterparts to be the victims of low expectations.

Lower expectations can manifest themselves in both obvious and subtle ways in the elementary school—in patterns of classroom instruction and interaction, in the grouping of students for instruction, and in differential assignments. In the secondary school, low expectations are communicated in these ways and also in the enrollment of students in low-level courses with minimal objectives and payoff and in advising these students away from more demanding elective courses or career objectives. It is essential that expectations be raised for all students, especially for students in demographic groups that have in the past been underserved by school mathematics education.

Inequity is pervasive, but it can be corrected in mathematics instructional programs. Consider the case of gender equity, which has been a concern in mathematics education for at least several decades. In the 1960s and 1970s, numerous studies and surveys indicated a substantial gap between males and females with respect to mathematics participation and performance. In the past two decades, great progress has been made in addressing this issue (Fennema and Leder, 1990; Leder, 1992). Although gender inequity still exists in some schools and mathematics classrooms, it is clear that the "gender gap" has been substantially reduced. For example, males and females now enroll in college preparatory mathematics courses and in elective, advanced courses at the secondary school level in about equal numbers, and their mathematics achievement on many measures is quite similar. Similar results have also been noted in the elementary and middle grades on most measures of mathematics achievement.

Improvements with respect to gender equity in school mathematics have resulted from a combination of higher expectations on the part of many persons—teachers, teacher educators, developers of curriculum and supplemental instructional materials, organizers of special programs, school administrators, researchers, parents, and community members—and the consistent and sustained efforts over a long period of time to address the sources and symptoms of inequity. Continued efforts in this regard are still needed, but substantial progress has been made. An increase in expectations, accompanied by a similarly robust and concentrated effort, is now needed to address inequities associated with factors such as ethnicity and poverty.

Schools in middle- and high-income communities are typically able to attract better qualified mathematics teachers than schools in low-income communities, and teachers in more affluent communities are more likely to have access to a variety of instructional materials and good professional development opportunities. Teachers and students in middle- and high-income communities often have ready access to role models who can demonstrate the value of schooling in general and mathematics education in particular. Students in these communities also often have easy access at home to academic support materials, such as calculators, computers, and supplemental books. Some research suggests that the cultural and family norms of families in middle- and high-income communities tend to be more closely aligned with school expectations for students and parents than is typically the case in low-income communities (Oakes 1990; Secada 1992; Singham 1998). All students, including those from poor communities, bring strengths from outside of school that should be recognized and rewarded. For example, many students who reside in poor communities and whose first language is not English find their understandings assessed in school only in English. This practice ensures that school assessments often underestimate the mathematical proficiency of non-native speakers of English. As was true for gender, many of the sources of inequity reside outside the control of schools. But there is much that can be done by teachers and other educators.

Research-based examples exist to demonstrate the validity of the view that all children, including those who have been traditionally underserved, can learn mathematics when they have access to quality mathematics instructional programs (Campbell, 1995; Griffin, Case, and Siegler, 1994; Knapp et al., 1995; Silver and Stein, 1996; Silver, 1998). Actions are needed to make these examples the norm rather than the exception in school mathematics education. Data that are disaggregated by ethnicity, language, gender, or social class can be very useful in examining the effects of district and school policies and teachers' classroom practices and in developing plans to address the problem. At the secondary school level, for example, such analyses could help to detect patterns of differential course offerings between and among schools; differential enrollment in elective courses within a school; or differential achievement within a classroom, school, district, state, or province. States, provinces, school districts, schools, and classroom teachers all should examine potential inequities associated with mathematics instructional programs and act on them.

Holding High Expectations and Providing Strong Support

Higher expectations alone are not sufficient to accomplish the goal of an equitable school mathematics education for all students. Along with higher expectations, many students will need greater support in their mathematics instructional program. All students need access to a coherent, challenging mathematics curriculum that is taught each year by a competent and well-supported mathematics teacher. Moreover, students' learning and achievement need to be assessed and reported in ways that attend to a reasonable range of important dimensions of mathematics and mathematical performance. The suggestions that are made in the following principles about mathematics curriculum, teaching, learning, assessment, and technology are applicable to all students.

In order to achieve educational equity, it is critical that students who need the most assistance in learning mathematics have access to an excellent mathematics instructional program that provides solid support for their learning and is responsive to their prior knowledge, intellectual strengths, and personal interests. Students who have been underserved by traditional mathematics instructional programs need this and more. Instructional programs that address both the challenges and strengths that students bring with them to the classroom are more likely to be successful. In addition to excellent teaching, some students also may need additional assistance with their mathematics work, such as peer or cross-age tutoring and after-school programs. Others may need social supports, such as role models who demonstrate the possibilities for success. Students who arrive at school speaking a language other than English may need special attention in order to ensure that they can participate fully in classrooms in which mathematical discourse is central. All students should be able to use their own language to develop mathematical ideas as they simultaneously develop proficiency in English.

Technology can be of assistance in achieving equity. For example, technology provides access to hardware and software tools and environments that afford opportunities for exploring complex problems and new mathematical ideas; give structured tutorials to students needing additional instruction and practice on skills; or link students in rural communities to instructional opportunities or intellectual resources not readily available in their locales. The most interesting new mathematical ideas that are suggested by developments in technology must be part of school mathematics programs for all students. Moreover, it is critical that all students have opportunities to use technology in appropriate ways in the mathematics classroom. Access to technology must not become yet another dimension of educational inequity associated with mathematics.

■ WORKS CITED ■

Campbell, P. (1995). *Project IMPACT: Increasing mathematics power for all children and teachers* (Phase I, final report). College Park, MD: Center for Mathematics Education, University of Maryland.

Fennema, E., & Leder, G. C. (1990). *Mathematics and gender.* New York, NY: Teachers College Press.

Griffin, S. A., Case, R., & Siegler, R. S. (1994). Rightstart: Providing the central conceptual prerequisites for first formal learning of arithmetic to students at risk for school failure. In K. McGilly (Ed.), *Classroom lessons: Integrating cognitive theory and classroom practice.* Cambridge, MA: MIT Press.

Knapp, M. S., Adelman, N. E., Marder, C., McCollum, H., Needels, M. C., Padilla, C., Shields, P. M., Turnbull, B. J., & Zucker, A. A. (1995). *Teaching for meaning in high-poverty schools.* New York, NY: Teachers College Press.

Leder, G. C. (1992). Mathematics and gender: Changing perspectives. In D. A. Grouws (Ed.), *Handbook of Research on Mathematics Education,* pp. 597–622. New York, NY: Macmillan Publishing Company.

National Council of Teachers of Mathematics. (1995). *Assessment standards for school mathematics.* Reston, VA: National Council of Teachers of Mathematics.

National Council of Teachers of Mathematics. (1991). *Professional standards for teaching mathematics.* Reston, VA: National Council of Teachers of Mathematics.

National Council of Teachers of Mathematics. (1989). *Curriculum and evaluation standards for school mathematics.* Reston, VA: National Council of Teachers of Mathematics.

Oakes, J. (1990). *Multiplying inequalities: The effects of race, social class, and tracking on opportunities to learn mathematics and science.* Santa Monica, CA: Rand Corporation.

Secada, W. G. (1992). Race, ethnicity, social class, language, and achievement in mathematics. In D. A. Grouws (Ed.), *Handbook of Research on Mathematics Education,* pp. 623–660. New York, NY: Macmillan Publishing Company.

Silver, E. A. (1998). *Improving mathematics in middle school: Lessons from TIMSS and related research.* Washington, DC: U.S. Department of Education.

Silver, E. A., & Stein, M. K. (1996). The QUASAR project: The revolution of the possible in mathematics instructional reform in urban middle schools. *Urban Education, 30,* pp. 476–521.

Singham, M. (1998). The canary in the mine: The achievement gap between black and white students. *Phi Delta Kappan, 80* (1), pp. 8–15.

Appendix C

Assessment

■ NCTM Assessment Standard: The Inferences Standard

■ THE INFERENCES STANDARD

Assessment should promote valid inferences about mathematics learning.

Assessment is a process of gathering evidence and of making inferences from that evidence for various purposes. The primary technical question involves defining procedures for making valid inferences from evidence of a student's learning. An inference about learning is a conclusion about a student's cognitive processes that cannot be observed directly. The conclusion has to be based instead on the student's performance. Many potential sources of performance are available. Mathematics assessment includes evidence from observations, interviews, open-ended tasks, extended problem situations, and portfolios as well as more traditional instruments such as multiple-choice and short-answer tests.

An inference about learning is a conclusion about a student's cognitive processes that cannot be observed directly. The conclusion has to be based instead on the student's performance.

A valid inference is based on evidence that is adequate and relevant. Valid inferences also depend on informed judgment on the part of whoever interprets and uses the evidence. Teachers make instructional decisions daily that are based on inferences they have made about students' learning. They use their professional judgment in examining relevant evidence. The validity of their inferences depends on their expertise and the quality of the assessment evidence they have gathered. Similarly, valid inferences from large-scale assessments require relevant evidence and are based on the best professional judgment.

A valid inference requires evidence that is adequate and relevant.

Using multiple sources of evidence can improve the validity of the inferences made about students' learning. The *Curriculum and Evaluation Standards* urges that decisions concerning students' learning be based on a convergence of evidence from a variety of sources. The use of multiple sources allows strengths in one source to compensate for weaknesses in others. It also helps teachers judge the consistency of students' mathematical work.

A threat to the validity of inferences comes from potential bias in the evidence. New forms of assessment, such as portfolios or extended projects, may create new sources of bias. Extended projects may allow students to complete some of the work at home, with the result that differences in home resources (including assistance from parents) may bias the results. To ensure the equality of resources, additional materials may have to be provided at school or in the community so that all students can do the projects to the best of their ability. Another source of potential bias lies in assessment activities that rely heavily on students' ability to use the English language to communicate mathematical knowledge. This bias can be addressed through additional activities that allow alternative forms of communication. A third source of bias may derive from the forms of scoring used in many assessment activities. Complex tasks require considerable judgment by the scorers. Bias in that judgment is addressed through suitable training and scoring procedures. Involving individuals with relevant expertise not only helps guard against biased scores but also contributes to equity and openness by offering diverse perspectives.

Inferences about mathematics learning have various consequences. Some inferences affect what students study tomorrow; others affect whether they graduate. Regardless of the consequences, the validity of each inference must be established. The amount and type of evidence that is needed, however, depends on the consequences of the inference. On the one hand, an informal interview of a student can provide a teacher with sufficient evidence of a student's progress to enable the teacher to determine what mathematical task is most appropriate for the student to engage in next. On the other hand, a large-scale, high-stakes assessment where results are used for certification or a culminating experience in school mathematics requires much more evidence and a more formal analysis of that evidence.

New forms of assessment require increased attention to the procedures for making valid inferences about the mathematics that students know and can do. Assessments that are based on a framework of important mathematics, draw on multiple sources of evidence, minimize bias, and support students' learning provide the evidence needed for such inferences. Technical considerations relating to validity, evidence, and inferences should be thought of not as barriers to the use of new and interesting assessments but rather as opportunities to enhance the instructional benefits of assessment.

To determine how well an assessment promotes valid inferences, ask questions such as the following:

- What evidence about learning does the assessment provide?
- How is professional judgment used in making inferences about learning?
- How sensitive is the assessor to the demands the assessment makes and to unexpected responses?
- How is bias minimized in making inferences about learning?
- What efforts are made to ensure that scoring is consistent across students, scorers, and activities?
- What multiple sources of evidence are used for making inferences, and how is the evidence used?
- What is the value of the evidence for each use?

Cases

■ CASE 1: THE MARBLE LINE

Part A

The Flood

"Oh my Gawd! There's too much water in the glass. It's going to spill!" Andie Lucas screamed. Maggie Cantor turned just in time to see the waif-like girl bringing a beaker full of water toward her mouth.

"Don't drink it, Andie!" Maggie yelled. "Just dump it back into the jug."

Andie quickly complied and poured the contents of the beaker back into the plastic milk container from which it had come. She exhaled an audible "Whew" when she had completed her task, looking as if she had just averted some great peril.

"Good job, Andie," Maggie proclaimed with a grin, "you saved us all! Do you think we should build an ark before going any further?"

Andie answered with her unique, purse-lipped "Oh come on Ms. Cantor."

The Raven

Maggie stopped the videotape at this point. (Maggie had enlisted an aide to videotape the lesson so that she could review her teaching and her students' performance.) She sank back and let the worn stuffed chair in her living room envelope her. The segment of Andie and the overflowing vessel, which she had affectionately termed the Biblical Flood Part II, was one of her favorite parts of a lesson recorded two days earlier. "The Raven," as the activity was called, was an algebra experiment intended to strengthen student understanding of linear functions. Essentially, the investigation involved starting with a clear cylindrical vessel, pouring in an arbitrary amount of water, depositing marbles of uniform size into the container, measuring the height of the water level, and plotting the height as a function of the number of marbles in the container. As published by Addison-Wesley, the activity includes worksheets for collecting data, determining the equation, and then interpreting the data.* The activity took its name from an old Native American legend in which a raven, dying of thirst, drops pebbles into a deep well until the water level is raised to the point where it may be reached by the bird's beak.

Investigations

Maggie had divided her Algebra I class into five groups. The video camera, because of the physical arrangement of the classroom, focused primarily on two student groups. One of these groups, composed of Andie and her partner Sam, received an ordinary glass jar of undetermined volume. The other group, comprising Becca, Veda, and Tom, was given a 100 ml. graduated cylinder, taller and with a smaller diameter than the glass jar.

Maggie had decided to try the activity on the advice of Bill Jacobs, a veteran colleague who, along with Maggie, taught all basic beginning algebra sections at Amoskeag Regional High School. This was Maggie's second year of teaching, both at Amoskeag. Although she felt that she had good rapport with her students, they had

---

*Carlson, R. J. & Winter M. J. (1993). The raven and the jug. *Algebra experiments I: Exploring linear functions*, pp. 37–41. Menlo Park, CA: Addison-Wesley.

complained occasionally that they were bored, especially in her two sections of Algebra I. Part of the problem, she believed, was the regional nature of Amoskeag. Its 1000 students came from five different towns. Consequently, the students arrived in Maggie's class with varying mathematical backgrounds. Many had taken a full year of algebra in eighth grade, but had not passed Amoskeag's test to allow placement into geometry. Some of these students had even used the same textbook as they now used at Amoskeag. Others had only completed pre-algebra. Maggie found it difficult to challenge the former and not lose the latter.

Bill had suggested that she try to include more activities in her teaching, rather than relying solely on the text. As a result, she had conducted one activity at the end of each chapter. She had completed eight chapters and was on target to complete the remaining four chapters of the book. The students seemed to enjoy the break from the routine, and the "investigations," as she called the activities she introduced at the end of each chapter, seemed to deepen student understanding and help her assess their learning.

Maggie fast forwarded the videotape in order to view the parts of the investigation which she felt required more scrutiny. She bypassed such topics as the amount of water to use, how many marbles to drop in each time, how to measure the water level, and the designation of independent vs. dependent variables. She felt there was little student confusion in these areas. Slope and y-intercept, however, were more problematic. Although the class had spent two days working with the $y = mx + b$ form of the line, the discussion seemed to indicate that the students still had some conceptual difficulties. Maggie resumed playing the tape.

b—All That It Can Be

"Do you want us to find the y-intercept?" inquired Becca.

"Sure. You've got to find that and the slope, right? How would you find the y-intercept?" asked Maggie.

Becca did not respond, suddenly retreating as Maggie waited uncomfortably for an answer.

"You could plug into $y = mx + b$, couldn't you?" volunteered Veda Penta uneasily, her face flushing with the realization that attention was now directed toward her.

"Okay, tell to me how you'd do it?" Maggie probed.

"Well," explained Veda, "from our chart, we could put in 2 for x and 11 for y."

"And could you then find b?" asked Maggie.

Veda looked puzzled.

"I think so, couldn't I?"

"Try it, Veda," suggested Maggie.

Veda looked at the group's tabulated data and performed the substitution.

x	y
0	10.5
2	11
4	11.5
6	12
8	12.5
10	12

$y = mx + b$

$11 = m(2) + b$

"No," Veda concluded, "Cause we still don't know m."

"Right," added Maggie, "you'd have two unknowns, the *y*-intercept and the slope. Would that happen with every pair of *x*, *y* values you selected from your chart?"

"I think so. You'd still have two things you didn't know," responded Veda.

"What do you think, Tom?" Maggie asked the group's silent member. Tom generally liked to sit alone in class, interacting with no one. At least part of the reason for his self-isolation may have been due to the fact that his family had moved to the United States from Poland just seven years ago. Although his English was fairly good, something seemed to prevent him from feeling a fully-vested member of his school group.

"I think Veda's right," he said quickly.

"Well, Tom, look at the first set of points, 0 for *x* and $10\frac{1}{2}$ for *y*. Try putting those values into the equation $y = mx + b$," urged Maggie.

Tom complied.

$$10\frac{1}{2} = m\,(0) + B$$

"I still don't know what *m* is," he replied after substitution.

"But what is zero times anything?" Maggie pressed.

"Zero."

"Then simplify your equation, Tom."

$$10\frac{1}{2} = 0 + B = B$$

"I get $10\frac{1}{2}$ equals *b*."

"So would you agree that *b* is 10 and one half centimeters?"

"Yeah, I think so," Tom responded quietly.

"Is there any other way we could have found *b*?" Maggie continued. "How about you, Becca?"

Still apparently in her silent mode, Becca shrugged and looked away.

"Veda, can you think of another way?"

"Not right now."

"How about graphing," suggested Maggie. "Go ahead, each of you quickly plot the points from your data table."

With several glances at each others' papers, the trio quickly constructed graphs. (Becca's graph is shown below.)

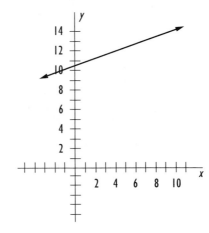

"Now, can you see what b is?" asked Maggie.

No one spoke.

"Come on, what is b called?" Maggie pleaded.

"The y-intercept" replied a suddenly animated Becca.

"Right. Now what is the y-intercept on the graph?"

"It's where the line hits the y-axis," Becca once again contributed.

"And what is the value of this on your graph?"

"$10\frac{1}{2}$ cm."

"Good, Becca," Maggie applauded with relief.

"Can you tell me what b means physically in this investigation?"

Again there was no response, only looks of bewilderment.

"Look at your table. What is y when x is zero? Tom?"

"Ten and a half."

"And that's b, right? Physically, what does it mean if y is $10\frac{1}{2}$ cm. when x is zero?"

Blank stares greeted the question.

"Okay, if there are zero, or no, marbles in the beaker, then the water height is $10\frac{1}{2}$ centimeters," Maggie added with obvious exasperation. "Since b is $10\frac{1}{2}$ centimeters in this experiment, how would you physically describe b in terms of the water height and the number of marbles?"

"b is the height of the water with no marbles in it," Veda finally added.

"Thank you, Veda," Maggie sighed with relief. "Now, why don't you three try to find the slope."

The Slippery Slope

Maggie moved to check in with the other groups. None seemed to have had the same difficulty finding and interpreting the y-intercept as Becca's group. She made her way back to the trio.

"How are you coming finding the slope?"

"Not so good," sulked Becca.

"What's the matter?"

"Tom and I say you gotta use the first and last points to find it. Veda says it doesn't matter which points we use. Who's right?"

"Well, why don't you try using different sets of points. Tom, why don't you use $(0, 10\frac{1}{2})$ and $(10, 13)$, Becca you use $(2, 11)$ and $(6, 12)$, and Veda you try $(4, 11\frac{1}{2})$ and $(8, 12\frac{1}{2})$. See what you come up with."

After a couple of minutes' calculation, Becca and Veda both computed values of $\frac{1}{4}$. Tom, on the other hand, found a slope of .35.

(Becca's work is below at left; Tom's is at right.)

$$\frac{y_1 - y_2}{x_1 - x_2} = \frac{11 - 12}{-2 + 6} = \frac{1}{4} \qquad\qquad \frac{13 - 10\frac{1}{2}}{10 - 0} = \frac{3\frac{1}{2}}{10} = \frac{3.5}{10} = .35$$

"See," said Becca. "$\frac{1}{4}$ is .25, not .35. We were right, you do hafta use the beginning and end points."

"Wait a minute, Becca," Maggie cautioned. "Let's check Tom's work. Tom, what is 13 minus $10\frac{1}{2}$?"

"$3\frac{1}{2}$."

"Is it? 13 minus 10 is 3. 13 minus 11 is 2. What's 13 minus $10\frac{1}{2}$?"

"$2\frac{1}{2}$," interjected Veda.

"Right, Veda. Tom, you forgot to borrow one from 13 and rewrite it as $12\frac{2}{2}$. Do you see that?"

"Yeah," he said barely audibly.

"Do it correctly now, Tom."

He obeyed.

$$\frac{10\frac{2}{2} - 10\frac{1}{2}}{10} = \frac{2\frac{1}{2}}{10} = \frac{2.5}{10} = .25$$

"So what's the slope for your points, Tom? What's $2\frac{1}{2}$ divided by 10?"

".25."

"Good, $\frac{1}{4}$, the same as Becca's and Veda's calculations. Now do you think it matters which pair of points you use to find the slope?"

"I guess not," answered Becca, "but I still don't see why not."

"Try thinking of it as walking up a ramp," explained Maggie. "It doesn't matter whether you're walking up the bottom of the ramp or walking up near the top, the slope is the same. As you walk up the ramp you get higher, but the steepness of the ramp doesn't change. Is that any clearer?"

"Yeah, Ms. Cantor, I'm kinda gettin it," said Becca with a certain resignation. "Let's just go on."

"So, you all agree that the slope is $\frac{1}{4}$, right?" Maggie inquired, trying to summarize.

Three heads nodded agreement.

"Now, what does that mean physically in this investigation?" asked Maggie.

Nothing.

"Remember, the slope has units. It isn't really $\frac{1}{4}$, it's 1 cm. per 4 marbles. Does that help?" Maggie said looking at the students' calculations.

"Yeah," Becca exclaimed, "one marble makes the water go up 4 spaces."

"Look at your table, Becca. How much water did you start with?"

"$10\frac{1}{2}$."

"Right, $10\frac{1}{2}$ cm. Now when you added two marbles, what was the water height?"

"11 cm."

"So if 2 marbles made the water rise $\frac{1}{2}$ cm., do you think 1 marble would make it rise 4 cm.?"

"No.

"If it takes 2 marbles to make the water rise $\frac{1}{2}$ cm., how many marbles would it take to make the water rise 1 whole centimeter?"

"4," Tom interrupted.

"You're sure?"

"Yeah."

"How about you, Becca and Veda?"

Both shook their heads in assent.

"So it takes 4 marbles to make the water rise 1 cm. Explain to me what the slope of $\frac{1}{4}$ means?"

"It means that it takes 4 marbles to make the water go up 1 cm.," Veda quickly responded.

"What do you think, Becca?"

"Yup, that's right."

"What if someone said that 1 marble made the water level rise $\frac{1}{4}$ cm. Would she be right?"

"Yeah," Tom replied. "They're the same thing . . . I mean, the ratio is the same."

"And do you agree, too, Becca?"

"I think so . . . I'm not sure."

"Think of it this way, Becca. You drop in 4 marbles and the water goes up 1 whole space. So if you drop in only 1 marble, or $\frac{1}{4}$ the amount, it goes up $\frac{1}{4}$ of a whole space. That means 1 space per 4 marbles is the same as $\frac{1}{4}$ space per 1 marble. Get it?"

"Yeah, I'm starting to see it. I still think I'll come after school and see you . . . just to be sure."

"Okay, I'll be here until 3:30 today."

Maggie shut off the VCR to take a break and to reflect on what she had seen. Overall she was happy with the way the lesson had gone. Still, there was something about the students' understanding of slope and intercept that had made her a bit uneasy, something she couldn't quite put her finger on. . . .

CASE 1, PART A QUESTIONS

1. By the end of the lesson, how well do you think Becca understood slope/intercept?
2. What are the advantages and disadvantages of using physical models in math classrooms?
3. Comment on Maggie's questioning techniques. Did they help her to learn about her students' thinking? Were they helpful in developing student understanding?

■ CASE 1: THE MARBLE LINE

Part B

Refreshed from her break and a glass of iced tea, Maggie returned to the VCR. Still not sure about what bothered her about the first segment, she decided to go on with the viewing. She hit the play button and was immediately transported back to the classroom, where Andie Lucas and her partner Sam Foster had constructed a graph of their data.

The Domain—an Integral Part

"Andie, why did you connect your points?" inquired Maggie, glancing at Andie's paper.

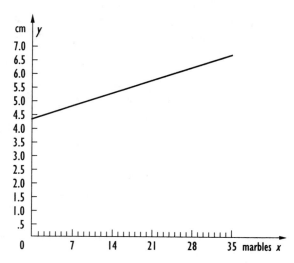

Marbles	H₂O
x	y
0	4.4
7	4.85
14	5.3
21	5.75
28	6.2
35	6.65

"You always connect 'em when ya graph," she responded, her brown eyes sparkling with confidence as she wrote with one hand and twirled her ever-present blonde pony tail with the other.

"Always, Andie?"

"Yeah."

"Can you tell me why?"

"Nope. I just know ya can do it." She unconsciously snapped her gum as if to add emphasis.

"Just think a minute." Maggie took her pencil and indicated a point on the line that Andie had just drawn. "What's the water level at this point?"

Andie squinted and drew her finger horizontally across the graph to the vertical axis.

"I dunno, a little more than 4.4?" she answered questioningly.

"That's right, just over 4.4 centimeters," Maggie replied. "Now how many marbles are in the jar when the water is at this level, Sam?"

Sam put his finger on the same point as Andie had, but instead of sliding his finger across the paper, he drew it straight down to the horizontal axis. "About one and a half," he responded.

"Does this answer make sense?" Maggie inquired.

"I guess so," replied Sam to a surprised Maggie.

"What do you mean?"

"It's on the graph."

"But what does the $1\frac{1}{2}$ stand for? $1\frac{1}{2}$ what?"

"One and a half marbles," said Sam matter-of-factly.

"Well, can you have $1\frac{1}{2}$ marbles?"

"Sure," Sam responded with a half grin.

"Show me."

Sam grabbed the bag of marbles and counted,

"One, one and a half."

To Maggie's complete surprise Sam had somehow found a fraction of a marble in the bag. "Okay, Sam, you got me on that one," Maggie laughed sheepishly.

Sam and Andie could scarcely contain their merriment at seeing Ms. Cantor so completely fooled. Maggie suspected that Andie was at the bottom of the caper. Still, Sam could not be completely discounted. Sam was often the target of Andie's humor for his credulity and propensity for turning crimson with embarrassment. Maggie enjoyed having Sam in class for, although he was a bit of an underachiever, he was usually attentive and contributive.

"Seriously, Sam," Maggie continued after he had had his time in the limelight, "assuming normal whole marbles, what's wrong with a line that contains the point for 1 and $\frac{1}{2}$ marbles, or $5\frac{2}{3}$ marbles, or any whole number plus any fraction of a marble?"

"It doesn't really make sense," Sam responded to Maggie's query.

"Would points representing 1 marble, 2 marbles, 3 marbles and so on make sense?"

"Sure."

"So if you made dots on the graph at these points, you're representing a real situation, is that right?"

"Yeah."

"What are you doing if you connect these dots? Aren't you really putting points in between them, points that really don't exist, like 1 and some fraction of a marble?"

"Yeah, I get all that stuff."

"How about you, Andie?"

"Uh huh, I get that," she replied nodding her head. "But what do we do? I mean, how do we make it a line?"

"What do your points look like when you plot them?" Maggie answered with a question.

"They're just a bunch of dots in a row," Andie responded.

"But they're in a line, they're collinear, aren't they?" commented Maggie.

"Yeah, but what's the point?" Andie interjected, her confidence suddenly shaken.

"The point is," clarified Maggie, "that a series of points in a line that are not connected represents the real situation of your experiment, doesn't it? If you connect the points, aren't you adding points that were not part of your experiment, such as $6\frac{1}{4}$ marbles, for example?"

"Yeah, I get all that," added Andie, shaking her head in knowing agreement. "I just didn't think you could leave dots like that without connecting 'em."

"In real life you do that a lot," said Maggie. "It all depends on what values are allowed for your x and y variables."

Homing in on the Range

"What'd you get for your equation of the line?" Maggie asked Sam and Andie as she checked their work.

$$\begin{array}{c} 4.85 \\ \underline{-4.40} \\ .45 \end{array} \qquad \begin{array}{c} 7 \\ \underline{-0} \\ 7 \end{array} \qquad m = \frac{.45}{7}$$

$$y = mx + b \qquad 4.4 = \frac{.45}{7}(0) + b \qquad b = 4.4$$

$$y = \frac{.45}{7}x + 4.4$$

$$y = \frac{.45}{7}x + 4\tfrac{2}{5} \qquad y = .064x + 4.4$$

"We got $y = \frac{.45}{7}x + 4\tfrac{2}{5}$ for the rational form and $y = .064x + 4.4$ for the decimal," Sam replied.

"Good. What do x and y represent?"

"x is how many marbles you put in," answered Sam.

"And what is y, Andie?"

"How much the water goes up when you put the marbles in."

"Are you sure?"

"I think so."

"How much did the water rise when you added 7 marbles?"

"4.85 cm."

"Did it? How much did it rise when you added zero marbles?"

"Uh 4.4 cm. . . . No, wait a minute, that doesn't make sense."

"Why?"

"'Cause if we don't put in any marbles, why should the water go up?"

"Good thinking, Andie. So if y doesn't stand for how much the water rises, what do you think y stands for?"

"How high it is?"

"Are you sure?" asked Maggie for confirmation.

"No," replied Andie honestly, "but I think so. It's not how much it goes up. I don't see what else it can be."

"Well, you are right," Maggie conceded. "x is the number of marbles and y is the height of the column of water. Are there any values x and y can't be? Sam?"

"x can't be fractions."

"Can it be zero?"

"Yeah.

"Can it be negative?"

"No, you can't put in less than no marbles."

"Very good. What about y, Andie? Is there anything y can't be?"

Andie looked puzzled.

"Andie, remember that y is the height of the water. Can it be a fraction?"

"I don't see why not."

"Good. Can it be zero?"

"Yeah, if there wasn't any water in the glass."

"Right. Can y be negative?" Maggie continued.

"No, zero means there's none. You can't have less water than that."

"Very good. Now we know the domain and the range."

The Shape of Things to Come

"Let's look at your equation. You've got $y = \frac{.45}{7}x + 4\frac{2}{5}$ for the rational form. What would be the water level if you put 14 marbles into the water?"

"5.3 cm.," answered Sam after a few seconds of calculations.

"How'd you get that?"

"I just put 14 in for x in the equation."

"Okay, adding 14 marbles makes the water level 5.3 cm. How much does adding 14 marbles increase the water level? What do you think, Andie?"

"It's the same, 5.3 cm."

"Is it? How much did the water rise every time you added 7 marbles. Look at your table."

Andie scribbled.

$$\begin{array}{r} 4.85 \\ -4.40 \\ \hline .45 \end{array}$$

".45?"

"Right. If you put in another 7 how much would it rise again?"

More calculations produced the same result.

$$\begin{array}{r} {}^{4}5.\overset{2}{\cancel{3}}0 \\ -4.85 \\ \hline .45 \end{array}$$

".45?"

"Sure. Then if you put in both groups of 7 at once, or 14 marbles at a time, how much would the water level increase?"

".45 twice."

"Suppose you started with a different amount of water in the beaker. How high would the water be if you put in 14 marbles?"

".90, no, I don't know," Andie shook her head.

"What do you think, Sam?"

"I don't think you can tell, can you?"

"Why?"

"Because you have to know how much you put in at first."

"Do you agree, Andie?"

She shook her head up and down tentatively.

"What determines how much the water level rises each time you drop in a certain number of marbles, Andie?"

"How thin the glass is?"

"What determines how high the water level is?"

"How much water you put in," said Andie.

"Good, and what else?"

"How many marbles you put in," Sam interjected.

"Suppose you have two graphs" (Maggie drew them as she talked). "Graph A starts at 5 cm. on the *y* axis, while Graph B starts at 3 cm. What can you tell about cylinder A and cylinder B used in the experiments?"

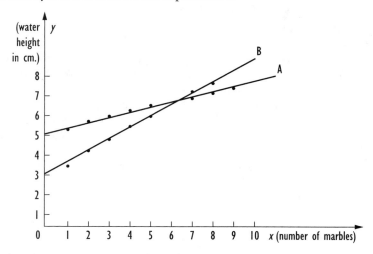

"A had more water in it?" Andie volunteered.

"What do you think, Sam?"

"It might've, but if B was really wide, it could've had more water. All you know is that the water is higher in A when you start."

"Excellent. In general you're right, Sam. But how about in this case? Remember the slope of graph B is greater than that of graph A. Try drawing pictures of the cylinders which represent the situation."

Sam took a couple of minutes and drew possible representations.

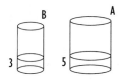

"Andie's right," he exclaimed in apparent surprise. "A's fatter and higher so it does have more water."

"Nice thinking. How high was the water level in each container at the beginning, Andie?"

"5 in A and 3 in B?"

"Good, 5 cm. in cylinder A and 3 cm. in cylinder B. What else do you know about the two cylinders, Andie?"

Andie started to speak, but hesitated.

"What about their shapes, Andie?"

"B is skinnier."

"Why?"

"'Cause the water goes up faster when you put in marbles."

"Good thinking, Andie."

Maggie shut off the VCR. It was time to prepare dinner. Cutting vegetables would give her time to mull over how to proceed with the class.

CASE 1, PART B QUESTIONS

1. What concepts involving linear functions was Maggie Cantor trying to assess and re-inforce?
2. How effective was the activity in accomplishing Maggie's objectives? Do you think that the end of a unit was an appropriate place for the activity?
3. How well do you think the students understood the difference between the rate of change and the absolute change of the water level?
4. Maggie uses questions to develop student understanding. How well do you think this works?

PRE-CASE DISCUSSION WORKSHEET

1. Suppose for a particular version of the Raven experiment, one marble gives a height of 12.3 cm and five marbles give a height of 15.3 cm.

   a) What is the height of the water in a cylinder with no marbles?
   b) How much does the depth of the water rise when one marble is added?
   c) Write an equation relating the depth of the water, d, to the number of marbles, n.

2. Sketch graphs of the following equations with x and y both integers.

   a) $y = 2x + 1$ b) $2x + 3y = 24$

3.

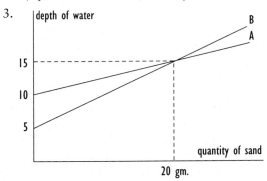

Suppose sand is poured into a cylindrical beaker containing some water. The depth of the water depends on the quantity of sand which has been poured in. The graph shows the results for two different beakers, A and B.

   a) What is the depth of the water in each cylinder with no sand in it?
   b) How much does the water rise in each cylinder when 1 gram of sand is put in it?
   c) Which cylinder has a smaller diameter?

■ CASE 2: CHANCES ARE

"What did you think of today's activity?" Mrs. Wexler asked Brendan as he headed out the door.

"Well," he squinted at the tiled floor, "it was fun and it really made me think. I guess I really don't know this stuff." He shrugged his shoulders. "I thought I did." Brendan wiped the sweat from his brow as the muggy June air blew through the open windows. "Our group thought we had figured it out—I mean we all agreed. But when we talked about it just now in the big group, I guess we had that sample size thing all wrong."

Mrs. Wexler smiled. "Well, tomorrow we'll go over it again. See if you can get it straight in your own mind so you can help the others in your group, okay?" She patted him on the back as he nodded and turned to leave.

Mrs. Wexler sat down at her desk and started to sort through the papers her students had just deposited there. She thought back to the class. Not all the groups in her Algebra II/Trig class seemed to have as many difficulties as Brendan's group, which was quite vocal in disagreement. In her mathematics classroom, Mrs. Wexler concentrated on fostering her students' ability to clearly explain their mathematical reasoning to others. She felt today's exercise was a great way to encourage this, and was thrilled to see her students so engaged and wrestling with the many tricky notions of probability. But, as usual, with so many students and so little time, she wasn't sure how well it all really went. Were others confused? Did they make any sense of the problems?

With her desk now organized, Mrs. Wexler headed for the teachers' room to make a cup of tea and have a moment for reflection.

The Class

After ten minutes of homework review, Mrs. Wexler quieted down the boisterous afternoon group of thirty 11th grade students and explained the activity. They had spent the last few days studying probability and sample size. Mrs. Wexler decided to use an activity from a conference she had recently attended. It was produced by teachers in a Woodrow Wilson summer project that targeted the main ideas she wanted her students to understand in probability. Knowing that the activity contained difficult questions which were designed to root out misconceptions in probability, Mrs. Wexler only gave the students the first of the four questions on the sheet that day. First, the students were asked to take five minutes to individually answer the question. Then, according to a number written at the top of their sheet, the students would gather in random groups of 5 students to discuss, explain, and reach consensus about it.

Wasting little time, the students completed the individual work. Then, without further direction, they formed groups throughout the room. They were accustomed to doing group work. Group 4 gathered in a corner by an open window. In that circle sat Maggie, Dawn, Laura, Andy and Brendan.

Small Group 4

Andy, a lanky basketball player, began, "Okay, let's get this going." His spirit and friendliness outshone his low test and homework scores. Mrs. Wexler often used notes to remind him about missed quizzes he needed to make up. He apologized, but rarely came in during his study halls to make them up. He began to read the problem out loud.

A town has two hospitals. On the average, there are 45 babies delivered each day in the larger hospital. The smaller hospital has about 15 births each day. Fifty percent of all babies born in the town are boys. In one year each hospital recorded those days in which the number of boys born was 60% or more of the total deliveries for that day in that hospital.

Do you think that it's more likely that the larger hospital recorded more such days, that the smaller hospital did, or that the two recorded roughly the same number of such days?

Laura glanced up from her paper and looked at Dawn and Maggie. "It won't matter how many people are in the hospital. It is just asking us for how many people there is overall when it comes out to 60%. There is no difference between the 15 group and the 45."

Maggie backed her up, "Yeah, it does not matter the size of the group when you are looking for percentages." Maggie was one of Mrs. Wexler's favorite students. She had a very gentle manner and made better mathematical connections than any of her other students. On her midyear evaluation, Mrs. Wexler wrote, "You really know how to think for yourself—not just memorize formulas." Frequently, when they got stuck on a problem in class, she came in the next day with a solution all worked out. With her high grades and activity in the student government, most teachers thought that she would get into the college of her choice.

Andy looked at Brendan, who was silently drawing some numbers on his paper.

"But won't the smaller group make a difference?" Dawn whispered to Laura. Dawn did average work in class; she and Laura were best friends. Mrs. Wexler didn't mind that they were in the same group. In the past, when working in groups with others she did not know, Dawn would either not participate or protest to Mrs. Wexler after class.

"Yeah, Dawn, you're right," garbled Andy while chewing his pen.

"See," Dawn spoke up. "Andy knows what I am talking about."

Andy turned his baseball cap backwards. "It's all about the damn sample size, man. Like, if it is smaller, then you are more likely to have more boys than girls."

No one in the group responded. Andy leaned back and continued to chew his pen.

"Dawn, why would it?" Laura pressed. "Just 'cause you're in a smaller hospital you're gonna have more boys? That makes no sense." Andy and Maggie listened as Brendan continued to write numbers on a piece of scrap paper.

Mrs. Wexler approached the group and peered over Brendan's shoulder.

"N-not just more boys," Dawn stuttered as she looked at her paper, "but you could have more girls. If it is a larger amount it would be closer to 50/50. But if you have 3 babies, then 2 of the 3 may be girls or boys. It could go either way."

Laura laughed and touched Dawn's shoulder. "Now that makes no sense. That's 66%! It has to be 50/50. It says so right here." She pointed to the question.

"Well," Mrs. Wexler encouraged, "it sounds like a good discussion. These may help you straighten out the differences." She produced a small box of 150 pennies. Smiling, she set the pennies on Brendan's desk and walked over to another group.

Brendan

Mrs. Wexler regarded Brendan as one of the more capable students in her class, although he did not always apply himself. He had spent the previous year in the 9th-grade advanced course but was unable to keep up with the work. After consultation with his parents, both he and his teacher decided it would be best for him to move to a less demanding course for the following year. Because students in AP math were a year ahead of their peers, Brendan was moved to a standard 11th-grade math class. He was one of only three 10th-graders there. Brendan's lack of organization and focus continued to plague him, however. His parents desperately tried to help, and eventually had him start therapy so that he could work with a professional on his inability to focus on his schoolwork. He seemed eager to do well, but he continued to struggle.

"Look," said Brendan as he discarded his work, "why don't we try it using these pennies, instead of arguing about it?"

"Why, what did you put?" Laura asked.

"Well," he scratched his head, "originally, I put that they would be the same, it won't make any difference. But look, Mrs. Wexler gave us all these pennies for a reason. Let's try it. Some of us take 45, others only take 15. We'll let heads be boys, tails be girls. We'll flip 'em ten times and then we'll see if it comes out to be the same."

"Yeah," Andy nodded. "Let's all do that. Otherwise, we'll be here all day."

The students grabbed pennies and began flipping and recording their results.

After collecting the results of ten trials, Laura turned to Dawn. "I don't get why we're doing this. I mean, the problem is when there are 45 babies born in a hospital and there are 15 in another hospital, then what are the percentage of days that will be 60% boys born, right? You and Andy think that it will be in the smaller hospital. I think that it will be the same. Now we flipped these coins. But what did they tell me? I mean to me it is just common sense that they will be the same."

Brendan insisted, "How else will we find out? We have to use the pennies. I mean, Mrs. Wexler gave them to us."

"I guess," Laura said, scanning her data. "But it doesn't make sense."

Mrs. Wexler appeared over Brendan's shoulder. "So, is your group in consensus over this?"

They all shook their heads, saying that they weren't in agreement.

"Where's the split?" Mrs. Wexler probed, leaning forward into the group.

"Between the same and the smaller hospital," said Maggie.

"Yeah," Andy sat up. "I think the size matters, and Dawn agrees. A smaller hospital has a better chance. Because, c'mon, the more trials you do, like 45 every day, the closer the average will come out to 50%."

"So who speaks for the side of same?" Mrs. Wexler glanced around the group.

"I do," began Maggie again. "See, the amount of trials is going to be the same—365 days in a year. Plus, you don't know if you will have more girls or more boys. So it doesn't matter how many babies are being born in each hospital. Because *they* didn't know how many babies were being born in each hospital. They just knew that x were born in one hospital, and y in another hospital. They did 365 days to figure out how many days more boys were born—60% or more on how many days. They would have to pick one still, but we don't know if x is bigger or y is bigger." Maggie pointed to Laura and Brendan. "And they said that they thought that it would be the same, too."

"Well," began Mrs. Wexler, "it is one or the other. You have to figure it out."

"Look," Brendan said, resting his elbows on his desk, "the hospitals are never more likely to have more girls than more boys. Yes, there will be days when they have more boys, and there will be days when they have more girls. But those days will also be 50/50."

"It's no use. Just tell us the answer." Andy folded his hands in back of his head.

"When do we get to find out the answer?" Laura demanded. Laura was a marginal student more well known for her cheer leading skills. She generally avoided competition. Often Mrs. Wexler had to remind Laura to pay attention, or to stop talking with her friends. She frequently left questions blank on her homework and waited for the answer to be given in class.

"Well, eventually," Mrs. Wexler encouraged. "But how can you figure this out? If the simulation didn't work well, how else?"

The group sat in silence.

Finally Maggie spoke. "Well, we have been trying to figure it out by arguing. But we just keep going back and forth and no one is changing."

Brendan took a deep breath. "But can we agree that neither hospital is likely to have 60% more boys? They are equally likely."

"Yes, I understand that," agreed Maggie. "But the thing is, is that the smaller hospital might also have more girls."

"But it is also not like we are talking about any one day!" Brendan tapped his desk emphatically. "It is as if we take a huge number of days and put them together and ask if the small hospital has 60% or more that are boys."

"No," Dawn raised her palm in the air, "what you're saying makes sense. But I just think that the smaller hospital will have more."

Mrs. Wexler nodded and left the group.

"So let me understand this," Laura turned to Dawn. "After 365 days, do you think that the smaller hospital will have more boys than the larger hospital?"

"Look," Maggie interrupted, "we agree that the percentages are skewed because you have less babies. But you don't know in what direction it will go."

"Right, you don't know." Dawn quietly cleared her throat. "Like if you have 15 babies you don't know. But if you have 45 babies, there are more babies, so it is more likely to be closer to 50%."

Brendan turned to Dawn. "But the question is not will it be more likely to be 50%. The question is will you have more than 60% on any given day."

Laura interjected. "Saying that the smaller hospital has a higher chance is like saying that they will put some chemical in the water so the women there have more of a chance to have a boy." The group laughed.

"No, I am just saying that in the smaller hospital it only takes a few boys to make it up to 60%, but in the larger hospital it takes a lot more boys to get it up to 60%." Dawn leaned back in her chair and chewed on her finger.

"It is more boys," Laura nodded, "but you have more mothers giving birth. I mean if you have 15 mothers and one produces a boy, 1/15 is the same as 3/45 in the larger hospital. You have more chances for boys to be born in the bigger hospital. So, if anything, maybe the bigger one has a better chance!"

Brendan waved his arms in the air, "Look, all we have proven by doing this exercise is that it is completely random! It could be anything. That proves that on any given day, neither hospital is more likely to have 60% boys."

"I still think that it is the small one," Dawn said to herself

Mrs. Wexler shouted across the class, "Okay, you want to be finishing up soon. Make sure your groups have reached consensus."

Andy stretched his arms. "Look, let's just agree, I'll switch sides."

Dawn leaned towards Brendan "I still think that it is the smaller hospital because of what we did with the pennies."

Brendan threw up his arms in desperation and cried, "You can't prove it with the pennies because you would have to do it so many times! There is no way to prove it! No way! You don't know what you're talking about! All it is saying is that if you have 15 births, you are more likely to have a skewed number than the big hospital. The hospital is not more likely to have more boys, it is more likely to have a skewed number. Which is not the question! The question specifically asks for boys."

"All right, all right." Dawn sat back in her chair. "I'll switch."

"Yeah, okay," Laura agreed. "I guess it makes sense that they are both equally likely."

"So we're all in agreement? Both are equally likely! Good!"

At that moment Mrs. Wexler interrupted the class. "Okay, we only have a few more minutes. So let's put our chairs back into rows and come back as a large group to talk about your results."

The groups disbanded and reassembled as a class in rows.

Whole Class Wrap-Up

"Okay," Mrs. Wexler waved the din down with her arms, "let's talk a moment about what happened today. Who would like to begin?" A boy in the back of the room raised his hand. "Josh?"

"Okay, we said that the smaller hospital had a better chance at having the 60% because it had a smaller sampling. It affected the total number less than the large one. Because 60% boys being born of 45 and 60% of 15 each comes out to the same ratio—60%. So if they are each coming out to the same each time, the smaller sampling has a better chance of having a bad outcome. . . ."

"Is that right?" Mrs. Wexler asked as the class murmured. "Can someone else explain it?" A girl in the front row with red hair raised her hand. "Go ahead Betsy."

"Well it is because of the smaller sample. One number in that sample is a larger percent. So in the smaller group, the 15 has a better chance."

"Yeah," Josh echoed, "like it is more likely that if you flip 10 coins you will get 6 heads and 4 tails, than if you flip 100 coins and get 60 heads and 40 tails."

"Well, what do the rest of you think?" Mrs. Wexler paused, waiting for a response. She glanced toward the clock and noticed the time. "Oops, we're just about at the end of class." The bell interrupted her. "I'm not convinced everyone's clear about these questions, so we'll pick up here tomorrow, okay?"

Brendan lingered for a moment while he shuffled through his back-pack looking for his homework so he could hand it in before he left. Producing the paper, he slowly packed up his notebook and headed toward the door.

CASE 2 QUESTIONS

1. What concepts was Mrs. Wexler trying to teach? How did the activity fulfill her goals? Did her students engage these concepts? What were some of the ways they tried to understand these mathematical ideas?
2. If you were the teacher, what would you do the next day? Why?
3. How effective were Mrs. Wexler's questioning techniques? Do you think she gained a good understanding of the students' understanding? What might you do differently? Why?
4. Mrs. Wexler used coins as a manipulative. What purpose did they serve? What else could she have used?
5. Mrs. Wexler grouped her students randomly in rather large groups of 5. How did that work? How might you group students to do an activity like this?

PRE-CASE DISCUSSION WORKSHEET 1

The following problem is the main focus of the case, *Chances Are*. Provide a solution to the problem. Make a list of the assumptions you are making while solving the problem.

PROBLEM

A town has two hospitals. On the average, there are 45 babies delivered each day in the larger hospital. The smaller hospital has about 15 births each day. Fifty percent of all babies born in the town are boys. In one year each hospital recorded those days in which the number of boys born was 60% or more of the total deliveries for that day in that hospital.

Do you think that it's more likely that the larger hospital recorded more such days, that the smaller hospital did, or that the two recorded roughly the same number of such days?

PRE-CASE DISCUSSION WORKSHEET 2

How would group 4 fare using the following techniques of assessing group work:

Small group evaluation of group work:

Answer these questions as you think Small Group 4 would have responded.

1) Did your group achieve at least one solution to the problem or task?
2) Did everybody understand the solution?
3) Did individuals ask questions when they did not understand?
4) Did everyone have a chance to contribute ideas?

5) Did people listen to one another?
6) Did any one person dominate the group?
7) Was there enough time for exploration?
8) List things that your group did that **helped** your team work together.
9) List things your group did that **did not help** your team work together.
10) Write a statement to describe how you felt your group performed in this project.

Individual peer evaluation of group work:

Choose one of the members of Small Group 4 and complete the following form from his or her perspective.

Group Evaluation Form					
1 = Yes 2 = Most of the Time 3 = Frequently 4 = Rarely 5 = Never					
	Your Name	Member 2	Member 3	Member 4	Member 5
Had a positive attitude					
Helped come up with ideas					
Participated in making decisions					
Was helpful organizing work					
Followed through on promises					
Helped figure out what to do next					
Stayed on task					
Stayed with group					
Made sure that all group members participated					

Teacher observation and evaluation of group work:

How would you assess group 4 on each of the following attributes:

___ dividing the task among the members of the group;

___ agreeing on a plan for tackling each problem;

___ taking time to ensure that all members understand the task;

___ using the time in a productive way;

___ considering seriously and using the suggestions and ideas of others.

Suggested Websites

Professional Organizations

AAAS—American Association for the Advancement of Science
  <http://aaas.org>
  The AAAS on-line includes membership information, news stories, benchmarks for mathematics and science literacy, and a great deal of other information and updates on the state of mathematics and science education.

AMS—American Mathematical Society
  <http://www.ams.org/>
  e-MATH, the website of the AMS, includes a vast array of information about the society and updates, along with links to mathematics publications and research tools, what's new in mathematics, meetings and conferences, and more.

COMAP—The Consortium for Mathematics and Its Applications
  <http://www.COMAP.com/ac.htm>
  COMAP is an award-winning nonprofit organization whose mission is to improve mathematics education for students of all ages. COMAP's purpose is to create learning environments in which mathematics is used to investigate and model real issues in our world.

IEA—International Association for the Evaluation of Educational Achievement
  <http://uttou2.edte.utwente.nl/>
  The IEA is the organization responsible for conducting the Third International Mathematics and Science Study (TIMSS) research. Their website includes the results of several studies, on-line publications, and descriptions of current projects.

MAA—Mathematical Association of America
  <http://www.maa.org/>
  The MAA on-line includes information on membership, books, columns, news and features, and many links to other math-related material.

NCTM—National Council of Teachers of Mathematics
  <http://www.nctm.org/>
  NCTM is the largest professional organization for improving the teaching of mathematics at the Pre-K–12 grade levels. This website includes membership information, an on-line catalog of materials, and feature articles.

NSTA—National Science Teachers Association
  <http://www.NSTA.org/>
  National Science Teachers Association is committed to promoting excellence and innovation in science teaching and learning for all. This site includes membership information, awards and competitions, and resources such as science and math links.

RCML—Research Council on Mathematics Learning
<http://www.unlv.edu/RCML/>
RCML reviews and conducts research on how children learn mathematics and what teachers can do to promote mathematical understanding for all. The site contains information about the organization, annual conference information, and reprints of articles from RCML's quarterly newsletter, *Intersection Points.*

SSMA—School Science and Mathematics Association
<http://www.ssma.org/>
SSMA is an organization committed to improving mathematics and science education in grades K–12. The site features information about SSMA and its professional journal, access to the SSMA Newsletter, grant opportunities, special publications, and more.

TERC Homepage
<http://www.terc.edu/>
TERC is a nonprofit research and development organization committed to improving mathematics and science learning and teaching. Through this site one can access information on TERC's projects, educational materials, publications, workshops, and more.

Activities and Lesson Plan Ideas

Appetizers and Lessons for Math and Reason
<http://www.cam.org/~aselby/lesson.html>
A fun and intriguing site that is guaranteed to engage your brain.

ASPECT—Assessment Project for Erie County Teachers
ASPEN—Assessment Project Extended to the Northwest
ASPIRE—Assessment Project Involving Regional Educators
<http://www.bgsu.edu/colleges/edhd/programs/ASPECT>
<http://www.bgsu.edu/colleges/edhd/programs/ASPEN>
<http://www.bgsu.edu/colleges/edhd/programs/ASPIRE>
These sites include descriptions of each component for the first three years of a project on mathematics assessment for teachers of grades Pre-K–12. Hundreds of assessment activities are provided and are grouped according to grade levels. The sites also provide additional mathematics website links.

Brain Teasers
<http://www.eduplace.com/math/brain/>
Weekly brain teasers provided by Houghton Mifflin for students in grades 4–8.

Clever Games for Clever People
<http://www.cs.uidaho.edu/~casey931/conway/games.html>
Adapted from John Conway's book *On Numbers and Games,* this site features classroom logic games for secondary and middle school students.

CEC—Columbia Education Center
<http://www.col-ed.org/>
CEC offers over 600 lesson plans created by teachers for use in their own classrooms.

COOLMATH.COM
<http://www.coolmath.com>
Designed "for the pure enjoyment of math," this site contains mathematics lesson plans and links, organized by subject area (algebra, geometry, trigonometry, calculus, and so on). It features fractals, puzzles, problems, and career information.

DO MATH
<http://www.domath.org/>
Do math . . . and you can do anything! This site, provided as a service by NCTM, is designed to be a resource to parents of school children and community members.

Eisenhower National Clearinghouse
<http://www.enc.org/>
K–12 mathematics and science lesson plans, activities, resource finder, reviews of software, on-line help desk for students, and much more.

The Explorer
<http://unite.ukans.edu/>
A collection of educational resources (instructional software, lab activities, lesson plans, student-created materials . . .) for K–12 mathematics and science education.

Fractals
<http://spanky.triumf.ca/>
Gives information about what is new in fractal geometry. There is a collection of interactive software, fractal programs, and images. It is a good site to explore what fractals can really do.

Frank Potter's Science Gems: Mathematics
<http://www-sci.lib.uci.edu/SEP/math.html>
An exhaustive collection of K–12 lesson plans and activities organized in 23 categories.

Fun With Numbers
<http://newdream.net/~sage/old/numbers/>
"Pointless" fun with numbers such as π expanded, the first 28,915 odd primes, and many more oddities.

Gallery of Interactive Geometry
<http://www.geom.umn.edu/apps/gallery.html>
Practice and play with interactive software for building rainbows, projective conics, and many more.

The Geometry Center
<http://www.geom.umn.edu/>
The Center has a unified mathematics computing environment supporting math and computer science research, mathematical visualization, software development, application development, video animation production, and K–16 math education. A good place to start to find other links, ideas, and resources!

Gopher Menu
<gopher://bvsd.k12.co.us:70/11/Educational_Resources/Lesson_Plans/>
Dozens of on-line lesson plans on a variety of mathematical topics.

The Hub
<http://ra.terc.edu/alliance/HubHome.html>
Coordinated by TERC and funded by the U.S. Department of Education, the Regional Alliance provides professional development opportunities, technical assistance, and resources to schools seeking to improve their math, science, and technology programs.

The Internet Mathematics Library
<http://forum.swarthmore.edu/~steve/>
Direct link to quick and power searches for specific math concepts. Also, one may browse by resource type, topic, and grade level.

MasterWeb
<http://imagiware.com/masterweb/>
An on-line version of the game Mastermind.

Math Archives
<http://archives.math.utk.edu/>
Many materials available such as topics in mathematics, software, teaching materials, other links, and more.

Math Comics and Cartoons
<http://www.csun.edu/~hcmth014/comics.html>
A collection of humorous math-related comics and cartoons suitable for grades 6–12.

MathCounts
<http://mathcounts.org>
MathCounts is a seventh and eighth grade mathematics competition, and this site includes information about the competition, a popular Problem of the Week, and a link to other websites that feature mathematics activities, games, competitions, and teacher resources.

MathDEN: Mathematics Resource for the Home and Classroom
<http://www.actden.com>
This is the home of the Digital Education Network, and MathDEN can be accessed from this site by clicking on the MathDEN icon and typing "guest" in both the Name and Password boxes. MathDEN provides the user with tips on learning mathematics, multiple choice mathematical problems at various difficulty levels, and links to other math websites including math puzzles, educational resources, and math software.

Math Gems
<http://www-sci.lib.uci.edu/SEP/math.html>
Mathematics content areas are listed by name, and the site is updated regularly with new information. This is a place to visit if you are looking for a particular branch of math.

Math Magic
<http://forum.swarthmore.edu/mathmagic/>
Challenges in math for different grade levels.

Math Online
<http://www.kqed.org/cell/school/math/mathonline/index.html>
This site includes lesson plans, resources, and other mathematics news.

Math Pages
<http://www.seanet.com/~ksbrown/>
This site contains over 300 articles on a variety of mathematical topics, including number theory, combinations, geometry, algebra, calculus, differential equations, probability, statistics, physics, and the history of mathematics.

Math Problem Solving Task Centres
<http://www.srl.rmit.edu.au/mav/PSTC/index.html>
Offers monthly mathematics problems for students in grades 4–12.

Math Resources
<http://www-personal.umd.umich.edu/~jobrown/math.html>
Mathematics site for information and resources for grades 5–8.

Mathematics Education Directory—Yahoo!
<http://dir.yahoo.com/Science/Mathematics/Education/>
Links to math websites that feature lesson plans, tutoring, research, etc.

Mathematics Hotlist
<http://sln.fi.edu/tfi/hotlists/math.html>
Links to many websites dealing with general mathematics and computing.

The Mathematics of Cartography
<http://math.rice.edu/~lanius/pres/map/>
Cynthia Lanius' Web page discusses how maps are used and gives examples of different kinds of maps. It covers history of maps and math topics related to cartography, including lines, points, areas, coordinates, etc.

Mathematics Strategies Lesson Plans
<http://www.dpi.state.nc.us/Curriculum/Mathematics/MathMatrix.html>
Lesson plans, provided by the North Carolina Department of Public Instruction, provide math teaching strategies in mathematics for grades K–12.

Mathematics WWW Virtual Library
<http://euclid.math.fsu.edu/Science/math.html>
Collection of mathematics-related resources maintained by the Florida State University Department of Mathematics.

Megamathematics
<http://www.c3.lanl.gov/mega-math/menu.html>
Each smaller section contains activities, vocabulary, background information, big ideas and key concepts, evaluation, for further study, prep and materials, and NCTM (relation to Standards).

The Most Colorful Math of All
<http://www.cs.uidaho.edu/~casey931/mega-math/workbk/map/map.html>
This site focuses on the mathematics topic of coloring, complete with activities.

Pi Home Page
<http://www.ncsa.uiuc.edu/edu/RSE/RSEorange/buttons.html>
Pi Home Page contains various resources for teaching students about π. It includes lesson plans, activities, projects, etc.

Problem of the Week
<http://forum.swarthmore.edu/pow/>
This site provides ideas for a Problem of the Week for classroom teachers at all grade levels. It is updated each week.

Sphinx
<http://stud1.tuwien.ac.at/~e9226344/Themes/Puzzles/sphinx.html>
This site offers a variety of logic/math puzzles that are sorted by category and level of difficulty for Grades 8–12.

Sprott's Fractal Gallery
<http://sprott.physics.wisc.edu/fractals.htm>
A new fractal is generated each day by the author, Julien C. Sprott. The site also contains an archive of previous fractals and links to other resources.

Susan Boone's Lesson Plans
<http://www.crpc.rice.edu/CRPC/GT/sboone/Lessons/lptitle.html>
This site features internet-based math lessons and activities for grades 6–12.

Topology Games—Jeff Weeks
<http://www.northnet.org/weeks/>
Enjoy some well-known games such as tic-tac-toe and chess in a different format. Give them a try!

21st Century Problem Solving
<http://www2.hawaii.edu/suremath/home.shtml>
This site promotes problem-solving skills through algebra, chemistry, and physics.

World of Escher
<http://www.WorldOfEscher.com/>
M. C. Escher was successful in combining math and art. This site provides information on Escher himself, puzzles based on his work, and essays.

General Mathematics Education Sites

Alan Selby's Math Appetizers
<http://www.cam.org/~aselby/lesson.html#math>
This Web page offers lessons for mathematics, featuring pattern-based reasoning, algebra, slopes, curriculum, and elements of reason.

AskERIC
<http://ericir.syr.edu/>
The variety of education information at this site ranges from a virtual library to research and development.

COMPASS—Curricular Options in Mathematics Programs for All Secondary Schools
<http://www.ithaca.edu/compass/frames.htm>
This site assists schools, teachers, administrators, parent groups, and other community members and constituencies interested in improving secondary school mathematics opportunities and experiences for their students.

The Cornell Theory Center Math and Science Gateway
<http://www.tc.cornell.edu/Edu/MathSciGateway/>
Intended for secondary school students and educators, this site provides an easy starting point for locating science and mathematics resources on the web. It is tailored to the needs of students in grades 9–12, with links to resources in subject areas such as astronomy, biology, chemistry, computing, the environment, health, mathematics, and physics.

Federal Resources for Educational Excellence—Mathematics
<http://www.ed.gov/free/s-math.html>
Organized by the U.S. Department of Education, this site provides a lengthy list of links to free resources that support mathematics education and are available to teachers and students.

Key Issues for the Math Community
<http://forum.swarthmore.edu/social/index.html>
Key Issues: Key questions, key problems and opportunities, equity and access, minorities and mathematics, women and mathematics, the job market and new teachers, mathematics and the public policy, public understanding of mathematics and ethical guidelines of the American Mathematical Society.

The Math Forum
<http://forum.swarthmore.edu/>
Check it out. From this homepage you can access what seems an endless amount of information on mathematics. Some of the links include the teachers' place, student center, research division, parents and citizens, and Ask Dr. Math, where students can seek advice on problem solving. One may also search by subject resources, math education, key issues in math, and forum features.

The Math Learning Center
<http://www.mlc.pdx.edu/>
The Math Learning Center site gives teachers access to information about this nonprofit organization's curriculum materials, programs, and workshops that exemplify the NCTM standards.

NAEP—The Nation's Report Card
<http://nces.ed.gov/nationsreportcard>
The home of the National Assessment of Educational Progress, this site features the results and analyses of past NAEP tests at the fourth, eighth, and twelfth grade levels, as well as sample items, news articles, and links to other mathematics education websites.

NASA Lewis Learning Technologies K–12 Classroom Activities and Projects
<http://www.lerc.nasa.gov/Other_Groups/K–12/classproject.html>
Assorted resource center activities can be accessed through this site, along with NASA's computer workshop teacher projects.

NCTM Standards
<http://www.enc.org/reform/journals/ENC2280/nf_280dtoc1.htm>
All of 1989 NCTM curriculum Standards are available on-line at this site.

The Numeroscope—Paul Burchard
<http://www.woodrow.org/teachers/math/numeroscope/>
The Numeroscope is a multimedia, interactive laboratory for exploring number systems that form the basis for mathematical cryptography.

PBS MATHLINE
<http://www.pbs.org/teachersource/math/about.html>
PBS Mathline is a teacher-resource service of public television utilizing the power of telecommunications to provide quality resources and services to teachers of mathematics, grades K–12.

SAMI Math curriculum
<http://www.learner.org/sami/>
This site is designed to be a road map to many other mathematics education sites.

Show-Me Center
<http://showmecenter.missouri.edu/>
The Show-Me Center, in partnership with five NSF-sponsored middle grades curriculum development satellites and their publishers, provides information and resources needed to support selection and implementation of standards-based middle grades mathematics curricula.

Standards for Teaching Mathematics (Instruct Homepage)
<http://instruct.cms.uncwil.edu/standard.html>
This site is intended to introduce the reader to the NCTM Standards for teaching mathematics as found in the *Professional Standards for Teaching Mathematics* (1991).

TIMSS—Third International Mathematics and Science Study
<http://nces.ed.gov/timss/> or <http://ustimss.msu.edu>
The goal of these sites is to allow you to view the results of a comparative study of mathematics and science education from nearly 50 countries. The TIMSS study was designed to provide a comparative assessment of international educational achievement. The TIMSS sites also report student outcomes for various countries, sample items, instructional practices, cultural contexts, press releases, overhead transparency masters, and links to other sites.

The Well Connected Educator

<http://www.techlearning.com/>

A publishing center and forum at which teachers, administrators, parents, and others write about educational technology, join in conversations, and learn from one another.

Mathematics History and Miscellaneous

Biographies of Women Mathematicians

<http://www.agnesscott.edu/lriddle/women/women.htm>

This project illustrates the numerous achievements of women in the field of mathematics.

B. J. Pinchbeck's Homework Helper Website

<http://tristate.pgh.net/~pinch13/>

A student, B. J. Pinchbeck, and his dad provide a great collection of over 340 sites on the Internet designed to help students with their homework.

Calculus and Mathematica Homepage

<http://www-cm.math.uiuc.edu/>

If you are using or want to use Mathematica, this will help you get started by providing new ideas, lessons, and resources.

Cybermath

<http://www.cybermath.com/>

Waterloo Maple's Cybermath offers an interactive way of exploring and exchanging mathematical ideas.

Dictionary of Computing

<http://wombat.doc.ic.ac.uk/foldoc/index.html>

A searchable dictionary with over 10,000 definitions for acronyms, jargon, programming language, tools, architectures, operating systems, networking, theory, and more.

Dictionary of Computing Mathematical Topics

<http://wombat.doc.ic.ac.uk/foldoc/contents/mathematics.html>

This is an on-line dictionary filled with mathematical terms.

Dr. Math

<http://forum.swarthmore.edu/dr.math/dr-math.html>

Ask questions and have them answered across all levels of education. You choose the level and the subject to see the questions that have been asked and answered.

Earliest Uses of Various Mathematical Symbols

<http://members.aol.com/jeff570/mathsym.html>

This page presents the names of the individuals who first used various common mathematical symbols as well as the dates the symbols first appeared.

History of Mathematics

<http://aleph0.clarku.edu/~djoyce/mathhist/mathhist.html>

Includes timelines, chronologies, and links to history-oriented sites.

History Topics Index

<http://www-groups.dcs.st-and.ac.uk:80/~history/HistoryTopics.html>

Mathematics history may be explored by topic or one may choose to search by mathematician, year, or location.

Kids Hotlist

<http://sln.fi.edu/tfi/hotlists/kids.html>

Materials developed solely by kids. It is interesting and covers more than just mathematics information.

The MacTutor History of Mathematics Archive
<http://www-groups.dcs.st-and.ac.uk:80/~history/>
Contains biographies of thousands of mathematicians along with other added features.

Teachers Helping Teachers
<http://www.pacificnet.net/~mandel/>
The site contains weekly updated material in many subject areas and is divided up into content areas, classroom management, and a topic of the week. There is also a list of other websites, a poem of the week, and a stress reduction moment of the week. You can also contribute lessons and enter any questions or problems if you wish.

A Visual Dictionary of Special Plane Curves—Xah Lee
<http://www.best.com/~xah/SpecialPlaneCurves_dir/specialPlaneCurves.html>
Come to this site to explore the many properties of plane curves.

What to Expect Your First Year of Teaching
<http://www.ed.gov/pubs/FirstYear/>
Every first-year teacher has questions and concerns, and this site assists one with these topics by providing the results of a research study conducted with novice teachers.

Web66: A K12 World Wide Web Project
<http://web66.coled.umn.edu/>
The Web66 project is designed to facilitate the introduction of Internet technology into K–12 classes. It provides a global perspective as well as hours of fun searches. Web66 will also walk you through the Internet and describe how to find resources.

Web66-Math
<http://web66.coled.umn.edu/Schools/Lists/Math.html>
This page provides links to multiple schools that have math home pages and to state-level home pages devoted to mathematics.

On-line Catalogs of Mathematics Education Materials and Supplies

The Annenberg/CPB Projects Learner Online
<http://learner.org/>

Broderbund Software, Inc. (computer software)
<http://www.broderbund.com/>

Cuisenaire/Dale Seymour Publications
<http://www.cuisenaire-dsp.com/>

Delta Education
<http://www.delta-ed.com/>

Didax Educational Resources
<http://www.didaxinc.com/>

ETA—A Universe of Learning
<http://www.etauniverse.com/>

The Geometer's Sketchpad
<http://www.keypress.com/product_info/sketchpad3.html>

Key Curriculum Press
<http://www.keypress.com/>

The Math Learning Center
  <http://www.mlc.pdx.edu/>

National Council of Teachers of Mathematics
  <http://www.nctm.org/>

Sunburst Online (computer software)
  <http://www.sunburst.com/>

Sample Search Engines for the Internet

AltaVista
  <http://www.altavista.com/>

Excite
  <http://www.excite.com/>

HotBot
  <http://main.hotbot.com/>

Infoseek
  <http://infoseek.go.com/>

Lycos
  <http://www.lycos.com/>

WebCrawler
  <http://webcrawler.com/>

Yahoo!
  <http://www.yahoo.com/>

Sample Lessons and Activities

▪ ALGEBRA—SAMPLE LESSON PLAN

I. **Goal(s)**
   - To develop the concept of writing and graphing linear and two-dimensional inequalities

II. **Objective(s)**
   - The student will represent a real-life situation by writing an inequality.
   - The student will graph a two-dimensional inequality by hand and with a graphing calculator.
   - The student will interpret numerical data in a table.
   - The student will draw a scatterplot of tabular data.

III. **Materials** (for each student)
   - a copy of the "How Well Do You Know Yourself?" data sheet
   - graph paper and a straightedge
   - graphing calculator (an overhead graphing calculator is also needed)

IV. **Motivation**
   1. On the way to school today, I saw a sign that said, "Speed Limit 55." What does that mean? How fast or slowly am I allowed to drive? (Students should note that any speed is possible as long as it does not exceed 55 miles per hour.)
   2. Ask the class to write a mathematical statement that represents a speed, s, that may not exceed 55 mph. ($s \leq 55$). (We may get into a discussion about whether this is reasonable because a car has to be moving faster than 0 mph. Therefore, it may be more accurate to say $0 < s \leq 55$.)
   3. On another stretch of road, the sign also reads, "Minimum 45." What does that mean? How can we express the acceptable speed at which you can drive on that road? (Students may need to review the notion of a compound inequality and the meaning of $<$ versus $\leq$. They should find the inequality: $45 \leq s \leq 55$).

   Transition: Explain to the students that the focus of today's lesson is on writing and graphing two-dimensional inequalities. They will learn to do this by hand and on a graphing calculator.

V. Lesson Procedure

4. Remind the class that when they took a 50-point quiz last week, I had them predict their scores. After grading the quizzes, I typed a sheet entitled "How Well Do You Know Yourself?" The sheet contains a random list of student scores with a prediction in one column and an actual score in another.

5. Distribute a copy of the sheet to each student. Ask the class to take a minute to look over the data. Have one person explain what the table is telling us. (Someone should be able to describe, for example, that Student 3 predicted a 40 on the quiz but actually scored a 35 out of 50.) Then, ask the students what they notice about the data in the table. (They should notice that most students predicted slightly higher than their actual scores, but the actual average for the class was almost identical to the predicted average.)

   Transition: "Let's see if we can construct and analyze a graph of the data."

6. Ask the students to take out a piece of graph paper and a straightedge and to draw a scatterplot of the data, where the x-value is the predicted score, and the y-value is the actual score. (Walk around the room to informally assess their skill in constructing a scatterplot.)

   Transition: "Now, we will use your scatterplots of the data to answer some questions."

7. Raise the question, "What if everyone in our class had predicted exactly the same score that they earned? What would the scatterplot look like?" (Students should realize that the points would lie on a diagonal line containing (50, 50), (49, 49), etc.) What would be the equation of the line if the predictions had been perfect? (Students should realize that if the actual equals the predicted, then the equation must be the line $y = x$.)

8. Discuss the fact that, unfortunately, our predictions were not perfect. Some people earned an actual score that was lower than the predicted score. Can you show me where those people's data points are located? (Students should point out that these points lie "beneath" the line $y = x$.) What do the points that lie beneath the diagonal line have in common? (In each case, the y-value is less than the x-value.) How might we represent that set of points, all of which lie underneath the line $y = x$? (Students should recognize that these points satisfy the inequality $y < x$.) How about the points that lie above the line (where the actual score was higher than the predicted score)?

9. Have one student from each table come up and get enough graphing calculators for each person at their table. Using the overhead graphing calculator, demonstrate how to graph $y < x$ with the technology. As it shades one side of the line, explain to the class that when we do these by hand, we will use a colored pencil or marker to shade the appropriate area. Ask a student to explain why it is shading and what this means. (Try to reiterate that these are points that have y-coordinates that are less than the x-coordinates.)

10. Tell the students to turn off their graphing calculators and set them aside. Ask them to draw on graph paper a graph of each of the following:

$$y > 2x + 5$$

$$y \geq 2x + 5$$
$$y \leq -\tfrac{2}{3}x - 4$$

(As students work, encourage them to talk to one another about their solutions, and walk around the room to assist and observe how they are thinking about the problems.)

11. Once everyone has finished, ask the students to talk about the differences and similarities between the first two problems. (When they recognize that the only difference is whether the boundary line is included in the graph, introduce them to the notation of using a dotted versus a solid line in the graph.) Have a student come to the chalkboard and draw a quick sketch of the third inequality.

12. Have students turn their graphing calculators back on and graph the inequalities. They will notice that the first two look the same, and we will discuss how the "calculator doesn't tell you everything" and how we need to know how to handle the borderlines ourselves.

VI. **Closure**

13. We have been working with inequalities today, both by hand and on the graphing calculator. On a sheet of paper, ask the students to write down a set of instructions for how to graph a two-dimensional inequality and share the instructions at the table. Before class ends, ask one or two students to share their instructions with the whole group.

14. Ask one person from each table to return the graphing calculators back to the front table and assign the homework problems (textbook, p. 237, #1, 5, 9, 14, 20, 22–24).

VII. **Extension**

If time allows, prior to the closure, ask the students to draw a sketch of $y > 7$ and $x \leq -3$ on graph paper. Discuss the meaning of these two inequality graphs in two dimensions and how they compare to the graphs of inequalities that we constructed on number lines earlier this year. (This question comes up again on the homework assignment, but if there is time to address it in class, that would be helpful.)

VIII. **Reflections**

■ ALGEBRA—ACTIVITIES SAMPLER

1. **Fist Size and Height:** Provide students with tapemeasures or yardsticks (metersticks) and ask them to carefully measure (a) the distance across their knuckles when making a fist and (b) their height in inches (or centimeters). Each student should write the measurements on a Post-it note and place it on the chalkboard. Read the measurements to the class and have each student make a scatterplot of the data for everyone in the class. The points should be roughly linear, and this will lead to a discussion of selecting two of the plotted points to use for finding a line of best fit. By counting off the slope between the two selected points, students can find the slope, and by extending the line until it intersects the y-axis, they can

find the *y*-intercept and determine an equation for the line of best fit. Similar explorations can be carried out to compare height with shoe size, length of the forearm with diameter of the head, and so forth. This activity gives students practice with collecting and representing data while they think about equations that describe lines in real settings.

2. **Numbers from Dates:** Give students the digits that form the current month and day, and have them use those digits, together with the four operations, square roots, exponents, and grouping symbols to generate a list of expressions that simplify to answers from 1 to 20. For example, suppose that it is March 15. The date would be 3/15, so students would be allowed to use 3, 1, and 5 in their calculations. Here are some examples of possible answers: $5 - (1 + 3) = 1$, $(5 - 3)^1 = 2$, $5 - \sqrt{(3 + 1)} = 3$, $5 - 1^3 = 4$, and so forth. Students can determine (a) whether it is possible to write an expression for every number from 1 to 20 and (b) how many possible solutions they can find for each of the numbers. This experience can be repeated on a regular basis (e.g., once per month) to help students practice order of operations and to develop general problem-solving skills.

3. **Bending Aluminum:** Give students a piece of paper that measures 8 × 10 in. Explain that the paper represents a piece of aluminum, out of which a rain gutter for a house will be formed. They need to fold up the 8-in. width on both sides so that the cross-section is a rectangle (with no top, just like a gutter). The task is to fold it so that the cross-sectional area is maximized. So, for example, if they fold it up 1 in on each side, the gutter will measure 1 × 6, so the area will be 6 sq in. If they fold it up 1.5 in., the gutter would measure 1.5 × 5, so the area would be 7.5 sq in. As they continue the investigation, they will notice a pattern—that the area goes up until it peaks at 8 square inches when the gutter is folded at 2 in. on each end—and are likely to see that the numbers fall back down at the same rate that they increased. By extending the problem to its algebraic representation, *Area* = $x(8 - 2x)$, students can view the graph as a parabola and begin to see how quadratic functions are graphed and can be used to find maximum and minimum values.

4. **Twelve Days of Christmas:** A traditional Christmas song—"The Twelve Days of Christmas"—describes receiving one gift the first day (a partridge in a pear tree), three gifts the second day (two turtle doves *and* a partridge in a pear tree), six gifts on the third day (three French hens, two turtle doves, and a partridge in a pear tree) and so forth. Have students review (and sing?) the words to this song. The task, then, is to determine how many gifts a person receives on each of the twelve days and how many gifts they receive altogether over this timespan. Students will discover a number of patterns, shortcuts, and formulas for finding the answers and may be surprised to discover that a person would receive 78 gifts on the twelfth day and 364 gifts altogether! As an extension, have students estimate the cost of each gift and determine how much it would cost to actually give someone that many gifts over twelve days. A similar problem can be solved by placing it in the context of the eight days of Hanukah.

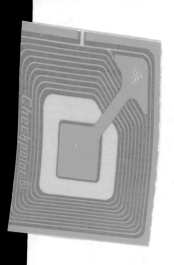

5. **Functions Stations:** As a group project, have students visit several stations over the course of two days, at which they collect some type of data and estimate a line of best fit. Stations might include the following: (1) Provide a tape measure and several circular objects and have students graph and find a list of best fit comparing the diameter (x) to the circumference (y). (2) Provide a small birthday candle, a stopwatch, and a ruler and have students burn the candle, comparing in a table and on a graph the amount of time (x) compared to the height (y). [Of course, there is a safety issue here, so make sure they are well supervised and that proper precautions for using a flame have been taken.] (3) Set up a water jug containing a tap, a yardstick, and a bucket under the tap. Students should turn on the tap, empty the water into the bucket, and compare the amount of time (x) that the tap has been opened to the height of the water level (y) in the jug. (4) On the Internet, find another set of statistical data, such as a comparison of the number of people in a country who smoke (x) to the incidence of coronary heart disease (y). In each of these cases, students collect data, draw scatterplots by hand or on a graphing calculator, and determine a line of best fit.

6. **Real-Life Systems:** As an individual project, have students identify and solve a real-life problem that involves a system of linear equations. For example, they might compare the cost of two long-distance carriers, and by writing equations or drawing graphs of the payment plans, determine how many minutes a person would have to call long distance in a month for one plan to be better than the other. Students can use the same process to compare Internet service providers (ISPs) or the value of free compact discs by mail, when the shipping charges and the cost of making a required purchase may be more than simply going to the store and buying the products off the shelf. Then, students can generate a written paper and make a presentation to the class on their results.

7. **Bicycle-Rotation Trick:** Here is a mathematical trick called the bicycle-rotation problem that students may find interesting: Start with two numbers, such as 3 and 5. Then, follow this sequence of steps: (a) Take the greater number (5), add 1, and divide by the lesser number ($\frac{5 + 1}{3} = 2$). (b) Take the result (2) and add 1 again, this time dividing by the previous number that was added to 1, which was 5 ($\frac{2 + 1}{5} = 0.6$). (c) Take the new result, 0.6, add it to 1, and divide by the previous number added to 1, which was 2 ($\frac{0.6 + 1}{2} = 0.8$). Continuing this process, the next two steps would be (d) $\frac{0.8 + 1}{0.6} = 3$ and (e) $\frac{3 + 1}{0.8} = 5$. Notice that the last two numbers that were generated were the original two numbers with which you started. Choose any two integers, and follow this process; you will find that the fourth and fifth steps will regenerate the original numbers. Of course, the algebra appears when the students attempt—using specific numbers at first, then x and y later—to show why this process always works. Many students find the exercise interesting, and it provides plenty of practice in simplifying rational expressions.

8. **Infinite Series:** Students often have difficulty understanding why the infinite series $\frac{1}{2} + \frac{1}{4} + \frac{1}{8} + \frac{1}{16} + \ldots = 1$. Here is a way that they can see what is happening. Provide each student with a square piece of paper and a pair of scissors. Ask them to fold the square in half and cut it into two congruent rectangles. Because the original square was 1, they could model $\frac{1}{2} + \frac{1}{2} = 1$ by putting the two rectangles back together. Tell them to set one rectangle aside and cut the other one in half. Each of these halves represents one fourth of the original square. Putting all of the pieces together, students can model $\frac{1}{2} + \frac{1}{4} + \frac{1}{4} = 1$. Now, ask them to take the one fourth piece and cut it in half so that the two new pieces each represent one eighth. Putting the pieces together again, students can see that $\frac{1}{2} + \frac{1}{4} + \frac{1}{8} + \frac{1}{8} = 1$. Finally, the class takes the leap of assuming that if they were to keep cutting the remaining pieces in half infinitely, the sequence would continue, but there would still always be the original square of paper with which they started. Therefore, the sum of all of the pieces would still equal 1.

9. **Pendulums:** Students can make a connection to physics and the use of formulas by exploring a pendulum. Materials required include a 50-cm string with a weight (such as a nut from a bolt) tied to the end and marked every 5 cm and a stopwatch. The *period* of the pendulum is the amount of time it takes for the pendulum to swing from a given position back to its starting place. Holding the pendulum at the 5-cm mark, a student lets the pendulum swing for 30 seconds while another student counts and records the number of swings. Dividing 30 by the number of swings allows them to calculate the period (length of time for one swing). Then, students should repeat the process with the pendulum held at 10 cm, 15 cm, 20 cm, and so forth, to 50 cm. Students can then put the collected data into a graphing calculator, where x = the length of the pendulum (L) and y = the period (T). They will notice that the data points are not linear and can discuss how much more sensitive a pendulum is when it is shorter in length (i.e., a change from 5 cm to 15 cm makes a greater difference in the period than a change from 40 cm to 50 cm). Also, students can attempt to fit a curve to the data by doing a Power Regression on the calculator, and they may recognize it as a square root function. If they are given the information that the function can be generalized as $T = k\sqrt{L}$, they can substitute their T and L values for each pendulum length and approximate the value of k. In physics, the actual equation for

period (T) is: $T = 2\pi\sqrt{\dfrac{L}{980}} \approx 0.2\sqrt{L}$. By using collected data, students should be

able to approximate this formula and will gain an appreciation for the usefulness of the square root function. Finally, they may also want to try using different weights on the pendulum and will discover that the period has nothing to do with the weight on the end—only with the length of the pendulum.

10. **Tagging Fish:** Biologists often face the problem of determining how many of a particular variety of fish live in a body of water or how many species of animal live in a particular woods or mountain range. They may be interested in knowing how many trout live in a lake. Of course, it is impossible to count them all, so they catch a sample of fish and tag them on the gills. Then, they throw the fish

back into the water and allow them to mix with the other fish. Taking another net, they catch a second group of fish and compare the number of tagged trout to the total number of trout caught. Using a simple proportion, they can estimate how many trout are in the lake (i.e., $\dfrac{TT}{N} = \dfrac{tt}{n}$, where TT is the number of tagged trout released into the water; N represents the total number of trout in the lake; tt is the number of tagged fish that were recaptured, and n represents the total number of trout that were caught on the second try). Give each pair of students a paper bag containing an unknown number of "fish" (you can use goldfish crackers, colored tiles, colored cubes, etc.). Students should reach into the bag, pull out a handful, count them, "tag" them (i.e., exchange a goldfish with a pretzelfish or a blue cube with a red one), and put them back in the bag. After shaking up the bag, students should reach in and pull out another handful. By counting the total number of fish in the handful and noting how many of them are tagged, they can set up and solve a proportion to estimate the number of fish in the bag. If every pair of students has the same (unknown) number of fish, it can generate an interesting class discussion about the different answers that students produced after their sampling process and then a conversation about how this method is moderately effective but only generates estimates, some of which may not be very accurate.

■ GEOMETRY—SAMPLE LESSON PLAN

I. **Goal(s)**
- To analyze the characteristics of two-dimensional geometric objects

II. **Objective(s)**
- The student will accurately measure an angle with a protractor.
- The student will use proper polygon terminology (e.g., sides, vertices, angles, quadrilateral, pentagon, hexagon, etc.).
- The student will collect, organize, and interpret data.
- The student will generalize and apply a formula for determining the sum of angle measures in a polygon.

III. **Materials** (for each student)
- sheet of white paper
- straightedge
- protractor
- TI-92 handheld computer (1 for each pair of students)

IV. **Motivation**
1. When you write a number such as 23, what does the "2" represent? Why do we group things together by 10s? (More than likely, it was because we have 10 fingers, so it made 10s convenient.)
2. People have not always grouped things by 10s, however. In ancient times (over 2,000 years ago), the Babylonians viewed 60 as the perfect number and grouped things by 60s. So, their number 23 would have stood for 2 groups of 60 and 3 leftover—our 123! Can you think of any modern-day examples

of how we still think like the Babylonians? (Students should recognize 60 minutes in one hour and 60 minutes in a degree as a carryover from ancient times.)

3. How many degrees, altogether, are there in a triangle? (180°) It is easy to remember that there are 180° in a triangle when we think of an equilateral triangle as having three 60° angles—the ideal triangle in the days of the ancient Babylonians.

4. Draw an irregular quadrilateral on the board. How many degrees are there, altogether, in this figure? (Most students probably realize that a rectangle contains 360° but don't know that this applies to all quadrilaterals.) What if the figure had 10 sides? 20?

Transition: Explain to the students that today our class will focus on determining the total number of degrees in a polygon. We already know the answer for a triangle, but what about the rest?

V. **Lesson Procedure**

5. Since the desks are arranged in pairs, have one person from each pair (the person with the latest birthdate in the year) come up and pick up 2 blank sheets of paper, 2 protractors, 2 straightedges, and 1 TI-92 handheld computer. Remind the students that they may not use the computers until instructed to do so.

6. Using the straightedge and blank paper, each student should draw three polygons on the paper. Tables 1, 2, 3, and 4 should all draw pentagons. Tables 5, 6, 7, and 8 should all draw hexagons, and Tables 9, 10, 11, and 12 should all draw heptagons. After they have drawn their figures, each student should use the protractor, measure, and sum all of the angles in each of the three diagrams.

7. When the students have completed the drawing, measuring, and adding, make a chart on the board such as this:

Polygon	No. of Angles	Angle Sum
Table 1		
Table 2		
Table 3		
and so forth		

Ask each pair of students to find the mean (average) of their measured sums and to report them to the class. As they read their answers, record them on the table on the board. What do you notice about the numbers on the board? How do the answers from different students compare? (The answers are likely to be different, due to measurement errors, but it will at least get students thinking about how increasing the number of sides increases the angle measures.)

Transition: On the board, we have measured estimates, but, of course, they are only as accurate as our protractors and students who use them. To get a more precise set of data, we will turn to our handheld computers.

8. Ask the students to open and turn on their TI-92 handheld computers. Pressing the APPS button will get them to a menu from which they can open the Geometry software. Using the Polygon, Angle, and Calculate tools, students can draw polygons, measure their interior angles, sum the angles, and interact with the polygon so that vertices are dragged around. They should make observations and take notes about what they see. Beginning with a quadrilateral, students should test each polygon up to a decagon and record any patterns or trends that they notice.

9. After students have explored the different polygons, ask them to turn off their calculators and set them aside. Have one person from each pair (the person with the earliest birthdate in the year) bring the protractors, straight-edges, and TI-92 back to the front table. Set up the following table on the chalkboard and have students volunteer answers to complete the Angle Sum column (they should have noticed that each polygon has a fixed angle sum, regardless of how it was oriented, dragged, or stretched on the screen):

Polygon	No. of Angles	Angle Sum
Triangle	3	180°
Quadrilateral	4	360°
Pentagon	5	540°
Hexagon	6	720°
Heptagon	7	900°
Octagon	8	1080°
Nonagon	9	1260°
Decagon	10	1440°

10. Ask the students to describe patterns that they see. (They should notice that each time another side is added to the polygon, another angle and 180° are also added.) Without drawing or measuring a dodecagon (12 sides), can you tell me the interior angle sum? How do you know? (Students should see the interior angle sum as increasing by two more sets of 180°.)

   Transition: "Let's see if we can generalize the formula for any polygon."

11. What if the polygon had n sides? How could we find the number of angles and the sum? (Students should recognize that if it has n sides, it must also have n angles. The sum is found by taking $(n - 2) \times 180°$, and this becomes the rule for finding an interior angle sum.)

VI. **Closure**

12. You have just developed a very useful and important formula for the study of geometry. With your partner, try each of the following:

   (a) Find the sum of the interior angles for an 18-gon.
   (b) How many sides does a polygon have if the sum of its interior angles is 4500°?

13. Observe students working on the two problems to assess their understanding of the formula. Invite two students to come to the chalkboard and explain how they found their answers.

14. Assign the homework problems (textbook, p. 145, #2, 4, 6, 12, 15, 18, 26).

VII. **Extension**

If time allows, prior to the closure, ask the students to figure out why this formula makes sense (i.e., why 180° per side?) by drawing some polygons and analyzing them. Students should recognize that a diagonal drawn in a quadrilateral divides it into two triangles, each of which contains 180°. A pentagon can, likewise, be divided into three triangles, and so forth. If we do not get to it today, it might make a nice place to begin tomorrow's lesson.

VIII. **Reflections**

■ GEOMETRY—ACTIVITIES SAMPLER

1. **Rectangle Folding:** Provide each student with a rectangular strip of paper (2 in × 8 in works well). Ask the students how many rectangles they see. Of course, there is one rectangle, so have them fold it in half and ask the same question. They should now be able to identify three rectangles—the original rectangle plus two smaller ones that were formed when the paper was folded. Now, take half of the strip (one of the smaller rectangles) and fold it in half again. At this point, they should see six rectangles. Continue this process several times, and have students generate a table of values (i.e., 0 folds = 1 rectangle, 1 fold = 3 rectangles, 2 folds = 6 rectangles, 3 folds = 10 rectangles, etc.). Engage the students in a discussion of how they do the counting and how they can be sure that they have counted *all* of the rectangles. Then, ask the students to generalize the number of rectangles for n folds. The resulting sequence is the set of triangular numbers, generalized by the formula $\frac{(n + 2)(n + 1)}{2}$, where n represents the number of folds. This activity allows students to develop spatial reasoning skills in identifying rectangles while analyzing a recursive pattern and generalizing a formula.

2. **Perimeter and Area:** Provide the students with a set of colored tiles (or some other square tiles or cubes). Ask them to arrange a set of tiles on the table so that the perimeter of the shape is 24 units and to record its dimensions (length and width) and its area, where each tile has an area of 1 square unit. Then, they should rearrange tiles to find another rectangle with a perimeter of 24. Students should continue this process until they have identified and recorded the dimensions and area of all of the possible rectangles. They will discover that the area is changed each time, and the perimeter remains constant. Which dimensions generate the greatest area? (They will find that the dimensions can be 1 × 11, 2 × 10, 3 × 9, 4 × 8, 5 × 7, or 6 × 6, and the greatest area is formed when the figure is a square.) To extend the problem, use x to stand for one of the dimensions. Since $2x$ added to twice the other dimension will sum to 24 units, then the other dimension must be $(12 - x)$. Therefore, the equation $y = x(12 - x)$ describes the possible areas, and students can generate the parabola on a graphing calculator, noting that the maximum is at (6, 36). This problem allows students to connect the concepts of perimeter, area, and quadratic functions.

3. **Straw Triangles:** Provide each pair of students with a bag containing five straws cut to the following lengths: 1 in, 2 in, 3 in, 4 in, and 5 in. Begin by asking the students to reach in the bag, randomly pull out any three straws, and try to put them together to form a triangle. Then, place the straws back into the bag and repeat the process. One person should serve as the recorder and keep track of how many times a triangle could be formed and how many times it could not, while the other person is in charge of pulling out the three straws each time. After 20 trials, students should calculate and compare experimental probabilities. Then, ask students to make a list of all of the possible combinations of straw lengths that could be pulled out three at a time and make an organized list. They should try to make a triangle out of each combination and note when this is possible and when it is not. (Students should discover that there are 10 possible combinations and that only three of them—2-3-4, 2-4-5, and 3-4-5—actually form triangles.) Students can determine that the theoretical probability of drawing a triangle from the bag is 0.3 and compare this to the experimental probability from the beginning of the investigation. Finally, students should discuss any patterns that they noticed regarding the relative lengths of sides when it is possible and not possible to form triangles. They will, more than likely, discover the triangle inequality that states that the sum of the lengths of any two sides in a triangle must be greater than the length of the third side. Students can, then, use this generalization to determine whether, for example, a 5-7-9 triangle can be formed without actually trying to make one. This problem helps students to develop an important triangle relationship, while they are dealing with key concepts in the study of probability.

4. **Matrices, Trigonometry, and Transformations:** The coordinates of the vertices of a triangle can be written in a 2 × 3 matrix format, where each column contains a vertex's coordinates (x is the first row, and y is the second row). Multiplying a 2 × 2 such as $\begin{bmatrix} 0 & -1 \\ 1 & 0 \end{bmatrix}$ by the 2 × 3 triangle matrix has the effect of generating three new triangle vertices that represent a 90° clockwise rotation or turn of the original triangle. Using a graphing calculator that can handle matrix multiplication, a piece of graph paper, and a protractor, have students try to find a transformation matrix that would rotate the original triangle 90° *counterclockwise* or one that would rotate it by 180°. If students have a background in trigonometry, they can determine that sin(90°) = 0, and cos(90°) = 1. Then, they can try to use this information, along with the original transformation matrix, to figure out how one might use sin(60°) and cos(60°) to find a matrix that rotates a triangle by 60° clockwise. This matrix is:

$$\begin{bmatrix} \cos(60°) & -\sin(60°) \\ \sin(60°) & \cos(60°) \end{bmatrix} = \begin{bmatrix} 0.5 & -.87 \\ .87 & 0.5 \end{bmatrix}$$

Using sine and cosine values, students can generalize the process to find a transformation matrix that will rotate a triangle for any given number of degrees. This exploration involves several connected mathematical topics, such as geometric transformations, matrix algebra, and right triangle trigonometry.

5. **The Scarecrow:** In the movie *The Wizard of Oz,* when the scarecrow receives his brain, he holds a diploma in his hands and announces that "the sum of the square roots of any two sides of an isosceles triangle is equal to the square root of the remaining side." Obtain a copy of the video and show this brief segment to the class. Then, have students analyze the statement to determine whether it is true. At first glance, it appears to be a pronouncement of the Pythagorean Theorem, but it deals with the *square roots* of the lengths of the sides, not the squares. Students will need to consider two cases: (1) The case in which the sides being added are the legs of the isosceles triangle and (2) the case in which the sides being added are a leg and the base. If the lengths of the sides are x, x, and y, then for the first case to be true, $\sqrt{x} + \sqrt{x} = \sqrt{y}$. However, for this statement to be true, $4x = y$, so $y = \frac{1}{4}x$. However, if $y = \frac{1}{4}x$, the triangle inequality would not be true because the sum of the lengths of the legs would be less than the length of the base, so the construction of this triangle is impossible. For the second case to be true, $\sqrt{x} + \sqrt{y} = \sqrt{x}$, but this is only true when $y = 0$, which is not possible either. Therefore, the Scarecrow's statement is false—maybe he hadn't received a brain after all. This activity leads to a rich discussion of isosceles triangles, the use of proper geometric terminology, and the generation of a deductive proof.

6. **How Many Diagonals?:** A triangle has no diagonals. If a quadrilateral is drawn on a piece of paper, it will contain two possible diagonals. If a pentagon is drawn, five diagonals can be formed. Students should continue to draw polygons with an increasing number of sides to look for patterns in the number of diagonals that are possible. Students should discover that, in any polygon containing n sides, there are n choices for the endpoint of a given diagonal. Then, the other endpoint can be any other point in the polygon, other than the point itself or the two points adjacent to the selected point. Therefore, there are $(n-3)$ possible endpoints for the diagonal. Consequently, if we multiply $n(n-3)$, this product will tell us how many diagonals can be formed *except* it assumes that, for example, the diagonals $\overline{AC}$ and $\overline{CA}$ are distinct, which they are not. Therefore, we must divide the product by 2, and the formula that students can derive for the number of diagonals in a polygon is: $\frac{n(n-3)}{2}$. The process of deriving this formula involves sketching and analyzing polygons and their diagonals, collecting data to identify patterns, and using a variable to generalize the pattern.

7. **Pattern Block Angles:** A fairly simple but rich activity can be conducted by giving each student (or pair of students) one of each of the six standard pattern blocks—a hexagon, trapezoid, rhombus, smaller rhombus, square, and triangle. The task is for the students to find the angle measures for every angle of every pattern block without using a measuring device such as a protractor. Students might decide, for example, that the square has four right angles and that the equilateral triangle has three 60° angles, and use those angles to measure the others. If they know that the angles of a quadrilateral sum to 360° and that the blue rhombus contains two 60° angles, they can determine the remaining two angles by performing the calculation: $\frac{360 - 2(60)}{2} = 120°$. Have students go to the overhead and dem-

onstrate a variety of methods of determining each angle measure—there are *many* different ways to find the angles. This problem involves an exploration of angle measure but can quickly develop into a discussion of anything from the properties of polygons to angles formed by the intersection of parallel lines.

8. **Greatest Volume:** Provide each student with a 3 in × 5 in index card and pose the following problem: We would like to fold the card into a rectangular prism. One way to fold it is by making it tall and skinny, and the other way is make it short and wide. Which of these designs would result in a container with the greater volume? Or would the volumes be the same? Distribute tape, a paper plate, and a cup of rice to each group of students and have them fold and tape their cards and fill them with rice to compare the volumes. Then, ask whether a "short and wide" container would have the greatest volume if made into a triangular prism, a rectangular prism, or a cylinder. Again, allow the students to build the shapes and compare their volumes with rice. Many students will begin the investigation by assuming that any two containers made out of the exact same size card will have the same volume, and they will quickly be surprised to find that this is not the case. By studying the relative volume of the containers, students can generalize that the more sides the prism has, the greater the volume, and a circular base will maximize the volume. This investigation can lead to a discussion of why soup and soda cans are cylindrical; after all, their manufacturers make efficient use of a sheet of aluminum to maximize profits. The activity is primarily an exploration of volume but also involves the construction and discussion of three-dimensional objects and the application of estimation and problem-solving skills.

9. **Euler's Formula:** Begin by having students construct a number of three-dimensional solids with materials such as straws. (Students can use a bendable straw, cut a slit in the short end, and insert it into another straw to build polygons that can be taped together to form solids.) After students have constructed solids such as cubes, tetrahedra, and square-base pyramids, collect classroom data on the number of base edges, the total number of edges, the total number of faces, and the number of vertices for each solid. Students should then analyze the data and look for patterns. They will rediscover Euler's formula, which states that the sum of the total number of faces added to the total number of vertices is always two more than the total number of edges in a right prism or pyramid (or, $f + v = e + 2$). Students can also cover the solids with newspaper and fill them up with materials such as rice or candy to explore the relative surface areas and volumes of the solids. This investigation allows students to explore the properties of three-dimensional solids and to use proper terminology, such as "face," "vertex," and so on. At the same time, students are collecting and analyzing data, generalizing patterns using algebraic expressions, and exploring concepts of measurement such as surface area and volume.

10. **Squares on a Geoboard:** Give each student a 25-peg geoboard, a recording sheet with pictures of geoboards on it, and several geobands (rubber bands). The task is to find all of the possible squares that can be formed on the geoboard. Each square must be a different size (i.e., a student cannot count a 1 × 1 square 16

times by simply sliding (translating) it around the geoboard). This task is not as simple as it sounds. Most students will find the first four squares (1 × 1, 2 × 2, 3 × 3, and 4 × 4) rather quickly because they are oriented the same way as the board itself; however, students generally have a more difficult time locating the rest of the squares, which are offset from the horizontal. In all they should find eight different squares. Then, students can be challenged to determine the area of each square. The four less-obvious squares will require either a thought process involving moving pieces of the square to visualize the area or using the Pythagorean Theorem to determine the lengths of the sides. The possible areas of the eight squares are: 1, 2, 4, 5, 8, 9, 10, and 16 square units. Finally, students can look at each square and record the number of pegs located inside and outside of the square. Noting these peg numbers for each of the eight squares, they should notice patterns such as the number of inside pegs progressing as a list of squares from 1 to 4 to 9. This activity emphasizes problem solving and visualization while pushing students to identify squares, determine areas, use the Pythagorean Theorem, and identify and generalize patterns.

■ STATISTICS AND PROBABILITY—SAMPLE LESSON PLAN

I. **Goal(s)**
- To develop skills of collecting and analyzing data
- To determine and use probabilities in problem solving

II. **Objective(s)**
- The student will determine the probability of an event.
- The student will apply the fundamental counting principle.
- The student will use the problem-solving strategies of generating a table, listing all possibilities, and extending a pattern.

III. **Materials** (for each student)
- sheet of paper and pencil
- TI-83 graphing calculator (including an overhead model for the class)

IV. **Motivation**
1. Begin the class by asking students to clear their desks and take out a sheet of paper for a quiz. Ask them to number their papers from 1 to 5 for a five-question True-False quiz.
2. Once students are organized and ready to begin the quiz, look at the lesson plan book as if confused, and admit to the class that the quiz questions are at home. Tell the students that they will have to guess at the five answers because, luckily, there is an answer key in the plan book.
3. When students have finished the "quiz," ask them to exchange their papers with a partner and grade them. Read the answers as F, F, T, T, F. Have students write the number correct at the top of the page and hand the papers back to their owners.

Transition: "You might have guessed that I'm not planning to count this quiz today. Actually, I was just making up the part about forgetting to bring the questions, and I would like for us to take some time today to analyze this quiz and the results."

V. **Lesson Procedure**

4. Ask for a show of hands to determine how many people in the class got all 5 correct, then 4, 3, 2, 1, and 0. Record the results on the board. Is this the number of people that you would have *expected* to get those scores? Why or why not? (The answers to this question will depend on the results of the quiz and whether the class is surprised by them.)

5. On the overhead, display the following three questions, and tell the students to discuss them at their tables for about ten minutes. Be ready to share your answers and reasoning at the end of that time.

   (a) How many possible answer keys are there to this quiz?
   (b) What is the probability that you will score 100% when guessing?
   (c) How does the theoretical probability compare with the experimental probability for our class?

   (As students work, walk around with a Group Observation Checksheet and be sure to take careful notes about Groups 2 and 3 today, because the other teams received formal feedback earlier in the week.)

6. After about ten minutes, ask for a volunteer to provide an answer for (a) and someone to write the possible answer keys on the chalkboard. (It is possible that someone will come up with $2 \times 2 \times 2 \times 2 \times 2 = 32$ because of experience with counting techniques.) Engage the class in a discussion, comparing the answers on the board to their group's solutions and discussing (b) and (c). (Students should have found 32 answer keys, so the probability of scoring 100% is $\frac{1}{32} \approx 0.03$. Thus, we would expect no more than one or two students in a class to score 100%.)

Transition: "Let's take a slightly different approach to determining the probability of getting a perfect score by randomly writing down answers."

7. On the chalkboard, make a table like this one:

No. of Questions	No. of Keys
1	1
2	4
3	8
4	16
5	32

Have students determine the number of answer keys, given the number of questions. After completing the first five entries in the table, ask the students the following: What patterns do you see? How could we find out the number of answer keys for a 10-question quiz? Why does the number of keys double each time? (Students should be able to figure out that adding an extra question takes all of the previous keys and adds one new key ending in True and another that ends in False, so there would be twice as many keys.) What if there were x questions on the test?

8. When students determine that for x questions there are 2^x keys, ask them to take out their graphing calculators. How can we use the graphing calculator to help us explore this problem? (Students should recognize that they can key in $Y_1 = 2^x$ and go to TABLE mode and view the x-column as the number of questions and the y-column as the number of answer keys.)

Transition: "Let's take this example one step further. . . ."

VI. **Closure**

9. How can we use the technology to determine the probability of scoring 100% on a quiz with ten multiple choice items, where each question has four choices—a, b, c, and d? (Give students a couple of minutes to work at their tables and circulate around the room to check for understanding.) Ask a student to come up to the overhead TI-83 and demonstrate the solution for the class.

10. For a homework assignment, answer the following questions:

   (a) Suppose that 60% or higher is passing. What is the probability of passing a five-question True-False quiz by randomly guessing answers?

   (b) If 60% or higher is passing, what is the probability of passing a ten-question multiple choice quiz by randomly guessing answers?

VII. **Extension**

If time allows, an important discussion on sample size can be inserted into step 6. In a class of only 20 students, we may or may not even have a 100% score on the quiz. To gain a more accurate experimental probability, we would need to pool our class's data with several other classes. We could also model additional trials by rolling a number cube (1–3 would be a True for the item, and 4–6 would be a False), which would make a possible extension for today or another exploration for tomorrow's class.

VIII. **Reflections**

■ STATISTICS AND PROBABILITY—ACTIVITIES SAMPLER

1. **Which Letter?:** Which letters are the most commonly used in the English language? Provide the students with a newspaper and have each person randomly select a paragraph anywhere in the paper. Have students count the number of times that each letter of the alphabet occurs in the paragraph and keep a tally of the totals. Then, compile the whole class's data and construct a bar graph showing the relative frequencies of the occurrence of each letter. Students can consult a library resource book and check whether the most frequently occurring letters in the newspaper sample are the same letters that are reported to occur most fre-

quently in the English language in general. How does this information influence the way that contestants play "Wheel of Fortune" or friends play "Hangman" by guessing letters? An extension to this data collection and analysis activity is to sample a paragraph from a book, magazine, or newspaper printed in another language and conduct a similar count. Are the same letters the most common in another language such as Spanish, or does the language affect the frequency of letter usage? Finally, students learning to use a computer can copy a passage from the Internet to the clipboard, paste it into a word processing document, and run a "Search" or "Find" on each letter to count the frequency. Then, they can use a spreadsheet program to generate the bar graph of the frequencies for discussion. This is an activity that will engage students in collecting, representing, and analyzing data, as they learn about the nature of the English (or another) language at the same time.

2. **Carnival Guessing Game:** A common game played at carnivals and amusement parks is "Guess My Birth Month." Generally, the game is played by asking the contestant to pay a certain amount of money and to write down the month in which the person was born. Then, someone has to guess the month of the person's birthday within one month. Model the game by having students pair up: When one person randomly chooses a month, the other person tries to guess it within one month. To keep the months truly random, students might put the names of the twelve months on cards and draw them from a bag each time. Collect enough class data to determine how often the contestant wins and how often the "guesser" wins. Ask students to determine the theoretical probability that the contestant will win. (When the guesser chooses a particular month, there are actually 9 months that will cause the contestant to win, so the contestant has a $\frac{9}{12} = 0.75$ probability of winning.) How does the theoretical compare to the experimental probability for the class? Suppose that the "guesser" charges \$2.00 to play the game. What is the maximum value of each prize that can be given away so that the "guesser" at least breaks even on the game? (On the average, the "guesser" will lose 3 out of every 4 games, so for the \$8.00 collected, three prizes will be given out. Therefore, each prize should have a value less than or equal to \$2.67. However, in the real world, the "guesser" also gets paid a few dollars per hour, so the prizes must also cover the cost of the person's salary and turn a profit for the carnival. The need to make a profit can lead to a rich classroom discussion about the nature of this game.) Finally, challenge students to think of what the "guesser" might do to increase the chances of winning the game. This activity is a real-life exploration of how probability is used by businesspeople for setting up a situation that turns a profit. Students will enjoy the familiar context of the problem and engage in determining experimental and theoretical probabilities while developing problem-solving skills along the way.

3. **A Probabilistic Approximation of π:** Assume that a circle has a radius of 1 and is inscribed in a square that measures 2 × 2. If the center of the circle is located at the origin, (0, 0), then Quadrant I contains a sector with an area of $\frac{\pi}{4}$ and a square with an area of 1. Suppose that the square that makes up Quadrant I was

a dartboard. If you were to throw a dart at it, what is the probability of the dart hitting within the boundaries of the sector?

$$\frac{P(\text{hitting the sector})}{P(\text{hitting the square})} = \frac{\text{Area of the sector}}{\text{Area of the square}} = \frac{\frac{\pi}{4}}{1} = \frac{\pi}{4}$$

So, if we could find an experimental value for the probability, then multiplying this result by 4 would give us an approximation for π. Using a random number generator on a spreadsheet or graphing calculator, students can generate coordinates of points that lie within a square having vertices at $(0, 0)$, $(1, 0)$, $(1, 1)$, and $(0, 1)$. Using the two random coordinates for x and y, students can determine $x^2 + y^2$. If $x^2 + y^2 \leq 1$ (i.e., it is located within the sector), then the point is a hit, and if not, it is a miss. After testing several random points, determine the ratio of hits to total points tried. This result, multiplied by 4, will result in an approximation for the value of π. This activity is a rich investigation that engages students in an exploration involving probability, while developing the geometric concepts of π, area, and the proper use of Cartesian coordinates.

4. **Misleading Graphs:** A common advertising trick is to take a set of data and attempt to mislead the public by graphing it using a scale that makes the information appear more impressive than it really is. Students can see a simple example of the effects of changing scales by graphing the line $y = x$ on a graphing calculator with the window at a standard setting of -10 to $+10$ in the x- and y-directions. Changing the window to a Ymin at -100 and a Ymax at $+100$ will show a graph dramatically different from the first. Yet, both lines have the same equation. On a graphing calculator, students can enter a variety of function equations and explore how changes in the window size can affect the look of the graph. Then, students can be challenged to try to find newspaper or magazine advertisements that contain misleading graphs. For example, a company recently published an advertisement about how their product was 98% effective, and those of their competitors were 97%, 96.5%, and 95.5% effective. But by drawing a bar graph of the four brands with the origin at $(0, 95)$ and the y-axis extended to $(0, 99)$, the bars looked dramatically different. As an extension, students can also be given a set of data and asked to represent it as some type of graph that is deliberately misleading to emphasize some feature of the data. This exploration involves the representation and analysis of data in a very real setting to which students can relate. The graphing calculator is an excellent aid in helping students to view the effects of scale changes on a graph.

5. **The Birthday Problem:** One of the most famous probability problems is often referred to as the birthday problem: Suppose that N people are gathered together in a room. What is the probability that at least two of the N people were born on the same day of the year (i.e., share the same birthday)? Most students find this problem interesting because it defies intuition. If there are, for example, twenty people in a room, then the probability that at least two of them will have the same birthday is about 0.411, and by the time the group size is up to 41 people, there is over a 90% chance that at least two of them will have the same birth-

day. Students should begin exploring this problem by collecting data from classes in the school. In each class is a collection of N students, and they can find out birthdays and determine how the N-size relates to the number of birthday matches. Then, students can explore the theoretical probability. Suppose that there are ten people in the room. The probability that at least two people have the same birthday can be found by taking "1 – (the probability that there are no matches)." The probability would, then, be calculated as follows:

$$P(\text{at least one match}) = 1 - \left(\frac{365 \times 364 \times \cdots 356}{365^{10}}\right) \approx 0.117.$$

So, there is about a 12% chance of at least one match of birthdays in a room with ten people. Extending the formula to a room with N individuals, the general probability would be:

$$P(\text{at least one match}) = 1 - \left(\frac{365 \times 364 \times \cdots (365 - N + 1)}{365^{N}}\right).$$

If a class contains 28 students, this formula shows that the probability of having at least one birthday match is 0.654. At a party with at least 68 people, the probability is 0.999. This problem is motivating because of the curiosity evoked when the expected answer does not match the actual solution, and it is rich in that it gives students experience with thinking about probabilities and generalizing a process into a general algebraic formula.

6. **What Is Average?:** The word "average" is often misused because a central tendency can be expressed as a mode, a median, or a mean, and the term "average" can be used with any of these measures. As a result, data can be misleading unless the public is clear about how the "average" was determined. For example, in 1996, the mean income in the United States was $25,466—a figure that represents the quotient of the total of all incomes in the country divided by the number of people who earned the money. However, the median income in the same year was $17,587, meaning that half of the people in the country earned less than this figure. The problem, of course, is that a few extremely wealthy people can boost a national "average" if the measure used is the mean; whereas, individuals who earn a high income have little effect on the median. Students should generate sets of data in which (a) the mean provides an accurate picture of the data, but the median may be misleading; (b) the median provides the accurate picture, and the mean is misleading, and (c) the mean and the median are both fairly accurate measures of the data. The presentation of these sets of data should, then, result in a discussion of when it is most appropriate to use median versus mean. (Generally, when there are extremely high or extremely low outlier data points, the median will become the most accurate measure.) Finally, students can search the Internet for data on populations, salaries, etc., to locate an interesting set of data and properly use a measure of central tendency to generalize the data. Although the skills of finding a mean and a median are fairly simple and taught in the middle grades, the selection of the most appropriate measure is not as easy as it sounds. This activity will help students to think

about situations in which one would chose mean over median or vice versa when describing a data set.

7. **Winning the Lottery:** Most states have a lottery that is designed to make a profit for the state treasury. In many cases, up to six numbers are selected at random, and a match on all six numbers can make one a million dollars or more in prize money. However, the lottery has been dubbed by mathematicians as "a tax on the innumerate" because most people have no idea how unlikely it is to actually win a significant amount of money. Have students research the lottery process in your state or region and determine the probabilities of winning the grand prize. They can, then, put the probability into more understandable terms. For example, suppose that the chances of winning the lottery were "one in a million." If you place one million dollar bills end to end and walk along them, trying to pick up the "right one," the string of bills would extend nearly 95 miles—imagine walking 95 miles and hoping to stop at precisely the right time and pick up that *one* bill that is marked. Students can also explore other games of chance, such as the Powerball lottery that involves several states working together. This problem gets students actively involved in researching a situation in which the state uses probability to make money to fund such endeavors as education.

8. **Grades and Marbles:** Pose the following problem to the students: In order to determine grades this quarter, we will let your understanding of probability be our guide. Each person will be given two jars, ten red marbles, and ten white marbles. You can distribute the marbles into the two jars in any way that you wish, but you must use all twenty marbles. I will come to your desk and randomly select one of the jars and then randomly draw one marble from that jar. If I draw out a red marble, you get an A, and if I draw out a white marble, you fail. The question is: How should you distribute the marbles in the jars to maximize your chances of earning an A? Students typically begin to explore this problem by thinking about placing all ten red marbles in one jar and all ten white marbles in the other, thus making the probability of getting an A equal to 0.50. However, with some additional thought, they should also recognize that placing five red and five white in each of the jars or even one red and nine whites in one jar and nine red and one white marble in the other will always result in a probability of 0.50. After additional exploration and discussion, students will probably realize that they were in a mind set about having ten marbles in each jar—by placing one red marble alone in one jar and nine reds and ten whites in the other jar, the probability increases to almost 0.74 (calculated by taking $\frac{1}{2} + \frac{1}{2}\left(\frac{9}{19}\right) \approx 0.74$). Interestingly, if there were 20 marbles of each color, and the same procedure were followed, the probability of drawing a red marble would still be about 0.74 ($\frac{1}{2} + \frac{1}{2}\left(\frac{19}{39}\right) \approx 0.74$). As a final step, students can generalize the marble problem by writing an equation that expresses the maximum probability of drawing a red marble (y) as a function of the number of marbles (x): $y = \frac{1}{2}\left(1 + \frac{x-1}{2x-1}\right)$. Graphing this function on a graphing calculator or computer can give students a visual image of how the probability approaches 0.75 as $x \to \infty$. An investigation that begins as a simple probability question becomes an exploration of patterns and the gen-

eralization of a pattern into a function that can be graphed and analyzed to determine its limit.

9. **Spaghetti and Probability:** Suppose that you randomly placed two points on a line segment so that it is divided into three smaller segments. Determine the probability that these three segments will form a triangle. Distribute several strands of thin spaghetti to each pair of students and ask them to randomly break the noodles into three pieces. Then, instruct the students to try to put the pieces together to form a triangle. As a class, tally the number of times that triangles could be formed and determine an experimental probability. In order to gather additional data, a graphing calculator can randomly assign two break distances for a segment that is one unit long. Then, using the triangle inequalities, a decision can be made as to whether the triangle can be formed with these random lengths. Finally, students can analyze the problem from a more theoretical perspective. Suppose that a line segment has endpoints labeled as 0 and 1 and contains two breaks at X and Y. The three segments would have lengths of X, $Y - X$, and $1 - Y$. Therefore, three triangle inequalities must be true if the new segments can form a triangle: $X + (Y - X) > 1 - Y$, $(Y - X) + (1 - Y) > X$, and $X + (Y - X) > 1 - Y$. Solving these inequalities simultaneously, by graphing boundary lines and shading, can approximate the probability. Students should recognize, however, that it is possible for X to be greater than Y, and this results in three additional inequalities that must be graphed on the same set of axes. By finding the area of the shaded regions, the mathematical probability can be determined. Students should compare their answers from the physical breaking of spaghetti to the random number generated on the calculator and the theoretical value found from calculating the areas of the triangles. This problem connects the concepts of collecting and analyzing data to the calculation of probabilities, the application of triangle inequalities, and the graphing and interpretation of two-dimensional inequalities.

10. **World Series:** The World Series baseball championship requires that the "best" team win four out of a maximum of seven games. Suppose that two teams are evenly matched, in that the probability of either team winning a given game is 0.5. If they play one another in the World Series, what is the probability that the series will be completed in four games? Five? Six? Seven? Students can model this problem by tossing a fair coin. Working in pairs, one student tosses a coin while another student records the data. The two teams playing against one another are the Heads and the Tails. Each pair of students should play several series so that the class can combine all of the data to determine the frequency with which the series ended in four, five, six, or seven games. Then, move the students toward a more theoretical approach to the problem. Suppose that the Heads and the Tails want to finish the series in four games. The probability of the Heads winning four times in a row is $(\frac{1}{2})^4 = \frac{1}{16}$, and the Tails have the same probability of winning four games in a row, so the chances of the series ending in four games is $(\frac{1}{2})^4 + (\frac{1}{2})^4 = \frac{1}{8}$. If we want the Heads to win the series in five games, then the Tails must win one of the first four games. There are four possibilities for which of the first

four games the Tails can win, so the probability of the Heads winning in five games is: $4 \times (\frac{1}{2})^5 = \frac{1}{8}$, and because the Tails could also win four of five games, the probability of the series going exactly five games is $\frac{1}{8} + \frac{1}{8} = \frac{1}{4}$. Using similar logic, students can determine that the chances of having either a six- or seven-game series is $\frac{5}{16}$. Therefore, if the teams are evenly matched, we can expect the series to generally go six or seven games, but there is only a 1 in 8 chance that one team would win the first four games in a row. Students can compare their experimental and theoretical probabilities and discuss the similarities and differences. This activity is very real to young adolescents and can be very motivating because of their interest in professional athletics. The problem can be extended by having students determine what might happen if the teams were not evenly matched (e.g., Team A has a 0.6 chance of winning each game). The activity involves the collection and analysis of data, use of counting rules, and determination of experimental and theoretical probabilities.

■ DISCRETE MATHEMATICS—SAMPLE LESSON PLAN

I. **Goal(s)**
   - To develop recursive thinking skills and apply recursive thinking to mathematical problem solving

II. **Objective(s)**
   - The student will provide an example and a description of the process of recursion.
   - The student will use recursion to solve problems, including modeling recursion on a graphing calculator.
   - The student will calculate compound interest, given the interest rate and the investment period.

III. **Materials**
   - glass pitcher filled with iced tea (or lemonade made from concentrate)
   - pitcher filled with water
   - drinking glass
   - two-problem activity sheet for each student
   - graphing calculator for each student

IV. **Motivation**
   1. As class begins, show the students a pitcher filled with iced tea. Describe a situation in which I made a pitcher of tea and intended to use it for dinner when guests arrived last Friday, but I got thirsty at lunchtime and drank a glass of the tea. Then, invite a student to the front of the room to model the problem. Pour a small glass of tea and have the student drink it. Explain how I was upset that the pitcher wasn't filled anymore, so I just filled it with water (after all, tea starts out as water). Later in the afternoon, I got thirsty again, so I drank another glass, but I filled the pitcher up again. Have the student drink another small glass of the tea and fill the pitcher again. Continue this process about five times and ask the student to sit down.

2. At 7 P.M., the guests arrived, and I served the drink in the pitcher. Is it still iced tea? What if I continued to refill the pitcher throughout the evening, every time that someone drank another glassful. Would we ever reach a point at which the tea becomes pure water? Why or why not? (Students will struggle with this because the intuitive notion is that the tea will become so diluted that it will cease to be "tea," yet if there is some tea in the pitcher, there will always be some tea in the next mixture.)

Transition: "The process that we just illustrated is called *recursion* because it featured a repeated set of steps (i.e., pour out a glass, then fill up the pitcher). Today, we will explore several examples and applications of recursion as an introduction to the topic."

V. Lesson Procedure

3. Distribute a copy of a two-problem activity sheet. Explain to the students that they are to work with their partners and take about ten minutes to solve both problems. The problems on the sheet are as follows:

   (a) Suppose that the teacher started at the front desk and walked halfway to the door and stopped. Then, the teacher walked halfway to the door once again and stopped, continuing this process over and over. How long would it take the teacher to walk out the door?

   (b) A scientist put one bacterium into a jar at 11 A.M. She knew that bacteria divided into two cells (doubled) every minute. If the jar was completely filled with bacteria at 12:00 noon, at what time was the jar half filled with bacteria? Thinking fast, the scientist realized that the jar was going to be filled by noon, so she added three new jars for the bacteria to spill into. At what time were all four of her jars completely filled?

   As students work on the problems, walk around the room and individually interview at least three pairs of students to get a sense of how they are viewing and attempting to solve the problems.

4. Once it appears that all of the students have explored both problems, ask each pair of students to join another pair and take two minutes to share their thoughts on the two problems. Then, conduct a full-class discussion to process the results. (Students should realize that in (a) the teacher will never reach the doorway because "half of something" still leaves "something." In (b), the students should recognize that the jar was only half filled at 11:59 A.M. but full at noon. If the scientist added three new jars, they would be filled at 12:02 P.M.) Ask the students to explain how both of these problems involve the process of recursion. (In each case, there is some process—halving or doubling—that is applied to the situation and repeated over and over.)

   Transition: "Let's take a look at how recursion can be modeled in a numerical way by using a graphing calculator."

5. Ask students to take out their graphing calculators and clear the screen. Suppose that the teacher's desk was 20 ft from the door. How far would the teacher walk on the first move? (10 ft) How far on the second move?

(5 ft) The third? (2.5 ft) The calculator has a function built in that allows us to quickly apply a recursive rule. Key in 20 and ENTER. Then, key in ANS * 0.5 and press ENTER (actually, if they simply press * 0.5, the calculator will automatically display ANS * 0.5). The calculator automatically takes half of the previous answer (ANS). Press ENTER again, and the calculator will take half of the displayed answer once again. Each time that you press ENTER, it will continue to take half of the previous answer. Press ENTER 50 times. What do you see? (Students will discover that the answer is an extremely small distance but not equal to 0; therefore, the teacher has still not reached the doorway.)

6. In the second problem, we started with one bacterium, and the population doubled every minute. How can we model the doubling process on the graphing calculator? How many bacterium are there after thirty minutes? (Students should ENTER 1 and then use ANS * 2 to find subsequent populations. In thirty minutes, the population exceeds 1 billion bacteria cells.)

Transition: "Now, let's apply this process to something with which you are more familiar—earning interest on money invested in the bank."

7. Raise your hand if you have some type of savings account that earns interest on your investment. How does it work? (Students should be led to explain how the interest earns interest over time, and we will define this as compound interest.) Compound interest is a recursive process because, each year, the previous amount of money earns interest and is added to the principle.

8. Suppose that you had $10,000 and wanted to invest it at 6% interest per year. How can we model the compounding process on the graphing calculator? Take a few minutes to discuss this with your partner. (There are a couple of ways the students can do this, but it will be acceptable if they come up with pressing ENTER 10,000 and then use ANS + ANS * .06 for the recursive formula. They might even come up with 1.06 * ANS for the formula, which is probably better but not necessary at this point.) Have students share their thinking and then look at how much money would be accumulated after a 10-year, 6% investment of $10,000. (about $17,909)

Transition: "I would like for you to use what you know about recursion, together with your graphing calculator, to explore a final problem today."

VI. Closure

9. I am going to give you three possible ways to earn interest, and you need to choose the offer that would give you the most money:

(1) I could give you $150 per year for the next 15 years with no interest being paid at all.

(2) I could lend you $2,500 to invest at 6% interest for 10 years, and you could keep the interest at the end of that period and return the $2,500 to me.

(3) I could lend you $2,500 to invest at 3.5% interest for 20 years, and you could keep the interest at the end of that period and return the $2,500 to me.

Work the problem alone for a few minutes and then discuss your solutions at your tables. (Students should discover that, despite the low interest rate, the last choice yields the highest interest because of the time factor— $2,474.) Discuss the solutions and the effects of interest rates and time.

10. For homework, assign page 114, #4, 7, 11, 15, 20 in the textbook.

VII. **Extension**

If time allows, the class could explore the graphs and tables that result from applying a recursive process. Specifically, after Step 6, students could determine that the function can be represented by the equation $y = 2^x$, and they could use the graphing calculator to sketch its graph, describe the effects of compounding, and use the TABLE function to view the numerical data. Similarly, after Step 8, students could explore the function $Y_1 = 10,000(1.06)^x$ to generate a discussion about the benefits of long-term investments. By entering $Y_2 = 10,000(1.07)^x$, and viewing Y_1 and Y_2 simultaneously, students can use the TABLE function to readily compare the growth of an investment at 6% versus 7% interest over time.

VIII. **Reflections**

■ DISCRETE MATHEMATICS—ACTIVITIES SAMPLER

1. **Possible Burgers:** On a national television advertisement, a fast-food chain promoted their restaurant by saying that "there are 512 ways to have a burger" at their establishment. Have students investigate the underlying mathematics of this claim by attempting to explain how the fast-food restaurant did their calculation. More than likely, the restaurant chain had nine different ingredients available for putting on their hamburgers (e.g., ketchup, mustard, mayonnaise, onion, relish, cheese, etc.). Since a customer can choose either to include the ingredient or not to include it, the number of possibilities can be calculated by taking $2^9 = 512$. Interestingly, if there are eight possible ingredients, then there are 256 different burgers that can be made, and if there are ten ingredients, the number of possible burgers increases to 1,024. Students should recognize that the number of possible burgers doubles each time another ingredient is added and be able to explain why this happens. (Imagine the list of 512 possible burgers with "no olives" added to the end and another 512 with "include olives" added to the end, so the total number of burgers when olives are added as an option increases to 1,024.) Students should, then, be challenged to watch the media for similar advertisements as they are typical for pizza restaurants and salad bars who make claims about how many different meals are possible. This problem engages students in a real-life situation that involves combinatorics, a major concept in the study of discrete mathematics.

2. **Traveling Salesperson:** One of the classic discrete mathematics problems is the Traveling-Salesperson problem (TSP). Here is an example: A businessperson lives in Miami, Florida, and has to visit four other cities—San Francisco, CA, Denver, CO, Minneapolis, MN, and Boston, MA—must end up at home, and may not visit the same place twice. There is a certain cost associated with travel between any two of these cities, primarily airfare charges. By contacting a travel agent or accessing airline information on the Internet, students can determine the cost to travel between all possible pairs of these cities. Then, they should attempt to determine the least expensive way to make the business trip. Ironically, they will discover that distance does not always dictate airfares, and they will also determine that there is no algorithm or procedure available for solving this problem other than exploring all of the possible routes. Since there are five different cities (the home city, plus four places to be visited), there are $C_2^5 = 10$ routes for which the students have to collect airfare information. They should be able to determine which combination of costs is the lowest. This problem is not terribly difficult if the person is only visiting four or five cities, but suppose the individual is going to travel to ten cities before returning home—forty-five airfares would have to be investigated before even attempting to list all of the possible routes. The Traveling-Salesperson problem is an example of an unsolved problem in mathematics in that there is no procedure yet available that will allow a person to solve it in any way other than trying all of the combinations of paths. The Traveling-Salesperson problem emphasizes the use of diagrams and the listing of all possibilities when doing problem solving, involves graph theory as students attempt to trace possible business trips, and makes use of combinatorial principles to investigate the choices.

3. **Handshakes:** Another classic discrete mathematics problem is often referred to as the handshake problem. Suppose that all of the students in a classroom were to get up and shake the hand of every other person in the room. How many handshakes would take place altogether? The problem is sometimes framed in a different context, such as: If a tennis tournament involves each participant playing every other person for one match, how many matches will need to be played? Or, on Valentine's Day, if everyone in a class exchanges a Valentine card with every other student, how many cards are exchanged during the day? All of these problems are rooted in the same "handshake" principle. When students are initially posed the problem, they should be asked to make a conjecture about the answer and write it down. In a class of 25 students, a typical initial response is to multiply 25×25, but some will recognize that they can't shake their own hands and attempt to multiply 25×24, which is more accurate but still incorrect. Students should take their notebooks and walk around the room, having every other student sign their pages. Discussing this process, students generally realize that when "Dan signed Anne's notebook" and "Anne signed Dan's notebook," it only actually took one "meeting" or handshake. Therefore, the total number of handshakes can be determined by taking $\dfrac{25 \times 24}{2} = 300$. Some students may

also discover that they can find the same solution by adding $24 + 23 + 22 + \ldots 1 = 300$, and this can lead to a discussion of Gauss's method for quickly adding this string of numbers. By systematically exploring what happens when two, three, or four people are in the room, students can also generate a pattern in a table and generalize the handshake problem solution to $\frac{n(n-1)}{2}$, where n represents the number of people in the room (tournament, Valentine exchange, etc.). This problem is very rich because it involves the problem-solving skills of solving a simpler problem, organizing information into a table, and looking for patterns, while it emphasizes counting methods and can involve generalizing a pattern into an algebraic expression.

4. **The Game of Sprouts:** Students can explore the nature of graph theory by playing a popular discrete mathematics game called "Sprouts." The rules are simple, but winning requires a great deal of careful planning and strategy. The game is intended to be played with two people. Sprouts begins with one person making three dots on a piece of paper; all of the moves for the rest of the game will "sprout" from these three points. Opponents take turns, following these rules: Each will draw an arc (edge) that either connects two of the points (vertices) or loops around to connect a vertex to itself. After drawing the new edge, the player must draw another vertex somewhere on it. Players are never allowed to intersect an existing edge, and a vertex may not have any more than three edges "sprouting" from it. Whoever draws the last sprout, leaving the opponent without a play, wins the game. Sprouts is an enjoyable way for students to think about graph theory, to develop their reasoning and problem solving skills, and to gain experience in using the proper graph theory terminology of vertices and edges.

5. **Write an Algorithm:** An important part of the study of discrete mathematics is the development of algorithmic thinking—the ability to spell out a process in a clear, step-by-step, procedural manner. Mathematics teachers can include this skill in the context of almost any topic studied through the secondary or middle grades. For example, suppose that a class has learned how to solve quadratic equations by factoring. Students may be asked to write an algorithm for solving quadratics, such as (1) add or subtract terms from the equation to arrange it in descending order and equal to 0; (2) factor the polynomial; (3) if the polynomial does not factor, discontinue this method; (4) if the polynomial *does* factor, then set each of the factors equal to 0; (5) solve the new equations to find the two solutions to the equation; (6) if the solutions are the same, then the equation has a double root. Students can write similar algorithms for many other mathematical processes, such as simplifying fractions, finding the missing side of a right triangle, or determining the limit of a function. It is not the intent of this activity to have students be given or simply memorize algorithms but, rather, to make them reflect on a mathematical process that they have learned and to try to put it into words in a systematic, step-by-step manner.

6. **Double the Money:** Ask the students to consider making this proposal to their parents: For my allowance this month, I would like 1¢ today, 2¢ tomorrow, 4¢ the next day, then 8¢, 16¢, and so forth. Or, I will settle for $100 in cash at the beginning of the month. Before doing some of the mathematics, it appears that $100 is rather expensive; after all, the parents will only have to pay a few cents a day during the first week. However, what effect does the doubling have throughout the rest of the month? This problem lends itself to exploration on a computer with a spreadsheet as a student can put 0.01 in the first cell, then *2 in the second cell, and have it fill down to show 30 days. Similarly, the ANS button on a graphing calculator can be used to do the recursion for 30 days of allowance-collecting. On the tenth day of the month, the student would receive $5.12, which is still minimal compared to the $100 "up front" alternative. However, by the 20th day of the month, the daily allowance climbs to over $5,000, and the 30th day represents an allowance of over $5 million. Students can use this problem to think about the effect of investing money over a long period of time and the rate at which the investment can grow. They can consider the cost of paying interest on a loan and the long-term effects of carrying a credit card balance or paying interest on a 30-year mortgage for a home. The activity serves as an interesting motivator for the discussion of recursion and interest rates, while making use of technology to generate the relevant numbers for discussion.

7. **Three Coins:** An interesting problem surfaced on the Internet that students will enjoy trying to solve. Suppose that you are given three coins that have the numbers 6, 7, and 8 displayed on them. You are told that the flip side of each coin contains a digit between 1 and 9 and that no digit may be repeated. The sum of the three coins, when tossed, will always be a number between and including 15 and 22 (i.e., $15 \leq sum \leq 22$). Each sum from 15 to 22 must be possible. The task is to find which digit is on the reverse of each of the coins. Students generally begin the problem by realizing that if 6–7–8 is displayed, the sum is 21, so they can eliminate those three digits and one of the sums. In addition, the only way to get a sum as high as 22 without repeating a digit is to have the combination 6–7–9, so a 9 must be on the back of the 8. This means that the back of the 6 and the 7 must contain two of the digits 1, 2, 3, 4, or 5. There are two possible solutions to this problem, one of which is 6–2, 7–5, and 8–9. You and your students should be able to find the other solution. This problem is rich in that it tends to capture students' curiosity and is accessible because it involves reasoning skills but not a great deal of heavy mathematical background. It involves the discrete mathematics skill of counting all of the possible combinations and checking them to see which work. The problem can also be used as a motivator for a topic such as exploration of the Traveling-Salesperson problem or factoring a polynomial, both of which rely heavily on guess-and-check methods to find workable solutions.

8. **You Have My Vote:** One of the content areas within the field of discrete mathematics is social choice, which includes the study of the mathematical fairness of various voting methods. At an organizational meeting of a professional group,

nominations were taken from the floor for president. Three people were nominated and about to be voted on by the group of about seventy people in attendance. Just before the vote was taken, one of the candidates stood up and announced, "I want to withdraw my name. I think both of the other people are as well qualified as anyone, so there's no point in voting for me since I don't want the job anyway." Consequently, the election was held with only the two remaining candidates. The question for students to consider is: What effect, if any, does a third-party candidate have in this type of an election? Is it likely, or even possible, that this person's last-minute withdrawal changed the outcome of the election? Students can, then, explore presidential elections in the United States to determine the effect that Independent Party candidates have had on elections. For example, would Bill Clinton have defeated George Bush in 1992 if Ross Perot had not drawn away a significant share of the Republican votes? Should the United States have a policy whereby a run-off election takes place prior to the presidential election so that only two candidates remain? Students should be able to generate various voting scenarios that demonstrate cases in which the Independent Party or third-party candidate does or does not have a significant effect on the outcome of the election. This activity is also a natural for working with the social studies instructor to initiate an integrated social studies/mathematics unit.

9. **Reading Bar Codes:** Perhaps you have looked at an envelope and noticed the bar code at the bottom that represents your Zip code. Students will enjoy breaking the code and determining which sets of bars represent which Zip code digits. The codes are made up of a series of long and short bars; a string of five bars translates into one digit. Obtain some copies of postcards or envelopes containing Zip codes and their related bar codes and provide students with the copies. Explain to the class that their task is to figure out which five-bar sequence represents each digit. It will be helpful to know that a bar code for a five-digit Zip code always contains 32 bars (or 52 bars if it is a 5 + 4 Zip code)—the first and the last are long bars that tell the reader that the code is about to begin and that it has finished. In the middle are 30 bars that represent six digits—the first 25 bars (5 digits) are the Zip code. The last five bars represent an error-correction number. The error-correction digit is the number that, when added to the sum of the nine digits comprising a 5 + 4 Zip code, adds up to a multiple of 10. So, if the Zip code is 48161-9978, then the error correction number would be 7 because 4 + 8 + 1 + 6 + 1 + 9 + 9 + 7 + 8 = 53, and 7 has to be added to 53 to get a multiple of 10. With this information, students can figure out which set of bars stands for which number. They should also be encouraged to look for patterns when they study the sequence of bars and might notice that every digit is made up of two long bars and three short ones. This makes sense because the two long bars can be placed in 10 different possible positions in a sequence of five bars ($C_2^5 = \dfrac{5 \times 4}{2} = 10$), and

10 different patterns are needed to represent the digits 0 through 9. Cracking a code makes for an interesting discrete mathematics activity that gives the students

experience with counting rules, patterns, and making generalizations. Students might also be fascinated with the way that UPC labels on items in grocery stores or secret messages sent during wartimes are coded and decoded.

10. **Meeting Schedules:** A student's ability to organize a schedule or sequence of events is a discrete mathematics skill associated with graph theory. Here is an actual meeting-schedule problem that was given to a manager of a business by the boss who was attempting to plan a day for employees in the business to connect with one another: The business has twelve full-time employees and five secretaries. The boss wants the twelve full-time workers to meet with one another for twenty-minute meetings until everyone has met with everyone else. In addition, the five secretaries each need to meet with one another for twenty minutes, but they do not need to meet with the other twelve employees. A meeting day to accomplish this task needs to be planned. If the meeting day is to begin at 9:00 A.M., then (a) How many twenty-minute meetings will have to take place altogether? (b) What is the earliest time that all of these meetings could be completed? (c) What is the latest time that the secretaries need to arrive so that they finish at the same time as the other twelve? (d) Design an actual master schedule that shows who meets with whom during each of the twenty-minute time slots. Students should work in small groups to complete this task, put their answers in writing, and be prepared to share their thinking and solutions with the rest of the class. (They should be able to determine, for example, that the twelve employees will need $C_2^{12} = 66$ meetings for all of the pairs to get together, and because six meetings can take place simultaneously, eleven twenty-minute time slots—three hours, forty minutes—will be required.) A worthwhile extension to the activity is for students to contact a local business, such as a pizza place, and interview the manager of the store about how work schedules are determined and the factors that need to be taken into account when planning a master work schedule for a week or more. The meeting-schedule problem engages students in thinking about how many combinations (of meetings) are possible and necessary and how to organize the sequence of meetings so that all three of the conditions are met.

Index

Photo Credits

pp. 17, 69, 119, 235: Will Hart; pp. 93, 177: Will Faller.

Text Credits